PADS 2001

Proceedings

15th Workshop on Parallel and Distributed Simulation

15-18 May 2001

Lake Arrowhead, California

Sponsored by

IEEE Computer Society Technical Committee on Simulation (TCSIM)
ACM Special Interest Group on Simulation (SIGSIM)
Society for Computer Simulation (SCS)

IEEE COMPUTER SOCIETY

Los Alamitos, California

Washington Brussels Tokyo

IEEE Computer Society Order Number PR01104
ACM Order Number 577010
ISBN 0-7695-1104-X
ISBN 0-7695-1105-8 (case)
ISBN 0-7695-1106-6 (microfiche)
ISSN 1087-4097

Additional copies may be ordered from:

IEEE Computer Society
Customer Service Center
10662 Los Vaqueros Circle
P.O. Box 3014
Los Alamitos, CA 90720-1314
Tel: + 1 714 821 8380
Fax: + 1 714 821 4641
http://computer.org/
csbooks@computer.org

IEEE Service Center
445 Hoes Lane
P.O. Box 1331
Piscataway, NJ 08855-1331
Tel: + 1 732 981 0060
Fax: + 1 732 981 9667
http://shop.ieee.org/store/
customer-service@ieee.org

IEEE Computer Society
Asia/Pacific Office
Watanabe Bldg., 1-4-2
Minami-Aoyama
Minato-ku, Tokyo 107-0062
JAPAN
Tel: + 81 3 3408 3118
Fax: + 81 3 3408 3553
tokyo.ofc@computer.org

ACM Order Department
P.O. Box 11405
New York, N.Y. 10286-1405
Tel: + 1 800 342 6626 (USA and Canada)
Tel: + 1 212 626 0500 (All other countries)
Fax: + 1 212 944 1318
acmhelp@acm.org

Editorial production by Danielle C. Young

Cover art design by Marcus Thiebaux

Cover art production by Joe Daigle/Studio Productions

Printed in the United States of America by The Printing House

IEEE
COMPUTER
SOCIETY

Table of Contents

15th Workshop on Parallel and Distributed Simulation (PADS 2001)

Session 4: HLA

Session 5: Applications

Session 6: Panel: Large Scale Network Modeling

Session 7: Optimistic Simulation II

Message from the General Chairs

Welcome to the 15th meeting of the Workshop on Parallel and Distributed Simulation jointly sponsored by ACM, IEEE and the Society for Computer Simulation. The first meeting of this conference in the new millennium is being held in the Conference Facilities of UCLA located in the picturesque town of Lake Arrowhead. It is our pleasure to welcome all the authors, attendees, and invited speakers.

We would like to thank Phil Wilsey and the Program Committee for their time and energy in putting together our technical program.

We are pleased to have Dr. Sri Kumar of the DARPA Information Technology Office (ITO) as our keynote speaker. Given the dramatic growth in the use of simulation and analysis for analyzing next generation technology in diverse areas ranging from computer networks, telecommunication networks, advanced computer architectures, and the emerging field of bio-computation, parallel simulation has an increasingly critical role in advancing our understanding of these disciplines.

It is our pleasure to acknowledge the help of the Lake Arrowhead Conference Facilities Staff in preparing for this meeting. We would like to thank Janice Martin of the UCLA Computer Science Department for her continuous help in making all the arrangements to ensure a smooth and productive meeting. Lastly, I would like to acknowledge the contributions of the student and staff members of the Parallel Computing Laboratory at UCLA.

We hope you will enjoy the technical discussions at the meeting, renew and establish new collaborations and friendships, and participate in the various recreational activities afforded by our location.

Rajive Bagrodia

Ewa Deelman

PADS 2001 General Chairs

Message from the Program Chair

Welcome to the Fifteenth ACM/IEEE/SCS Workshop on Parallel and Distributed Simulation. This year we are pleased to have Sri Kumar of DARPA for our keynote speaker. In addition to the keynote address, the conference has 7 sessions of technical papers, one panel discussion, and the work-in-progress session.

This year there were 31 papers submitted to PADS and we continued the tradition of double blind reviewing. Each paper was sent to five reviewers for comments, at least two of whom were program committee members. A program committee meeting was held in Orlando, FL in December and after much debate, 21 manuscripts were eventually accepted for publication and presentation at the conference.

Following the program committee meeting, a best paper selection committee was formed. The program committee members were contacted for best paper nominations from which the following manuscripts were selected for consideration:

"Improving Lookahead in PDES of Large-Scale Applications Using Compiler Analysis"
E. Deelman, R. Bagrodia, R. Sakellariou, and V. Adve

"A Causality Based Time Management Mechanism for Federated Simulation"
B.-S. Lee, W. Cai, and J. Zhou

"The Dependence List in Time Warp"
J. Zhang and C. Tropper

Following tradition, the winner of the best paper will be kept in suspense until the awards ceremony at the conference. The best paper will be reported in next year's proceedings. Speaking of which, on behalf of last year's Program Chair (David Bruce) I am delighted to confirm that the PADS'00 best paper award went to:

"Grain Sensitive Event Scheduling in Time Warp Parallel Discrete Event Simulation"
F. Quaglia and V. Cortellessa

Congratulations!!

I would like to thank all who have helped make PADS 2001 a success. I would especially like to thank the program committee and reviewers for their hard work and commitment to a very tight reviewing schedule. I also want to thank the paper shepherds who helped work with some authors in the preparations of their final manuscripts. I also want to thank David Nicol for his wonderful WIMPE system. Without it I would have never been able to track the manuscripts.

I would also like to thank those individuals who reached out to help. I would especially like to note the assistance of David Bruce, David Nicol, Alois Ferscha, Richard Fujimoto, and Steve Turner. Thanks, you have all been great!! Paul Fishwick also did an excellent job locating (on short notice) a meeting room for the program committee meeting. As always, the IEEE, particularly Danielle Young, has been a pleasure to work with.

Finally, thanks to the steering committee for their support and to Rajive Bagrodia and Ewa Deelman, who as Co-General Chairs have always been available with advice and suggestions. I am looking forward to enjoying PADS 2001, and I hope that you do too!

Philip A. Wilsey

PADS 2001 Program Chair

Committees

General Chair

Rajive L. Bagrodia, *University of California at Los Angeles, USA*

Ewa Deelman, *Information Sciences Institute/USC, USA*

Program Chair

Philip A. Wilsey, *University of Cincinnati, USA*

Steering Committee

R. L. Bagrodia, *University of California at Los Angeles, USA*
D. I. Bruce, *Defense Evaluation and Research Agency, UK*
A. S. Elmaghraby, *University of Louisville, USA*
R. M. Fujimoto, *Georgia Institute of Technology, USA*
B. W. Unger, *University of Calgary, Canada*
F. P. Wieland, *The MITRE Corporation, USA*
P. A. Wilsey, *University of Cincinnati, USA*

Program Committee

A. Boukerche, *University of North Texas, USA*
D. I. Bruce, *Defense Evaluation and Research Agency, UK*
W. Cai, *Nanyang Technical University, Singapore*
C. D. Carothers, *Rensselaer Polytechnic, USA*
J. G. Clearly, *University of Waikato, New Zealand*
S. R. Das, *University of Cincinnati, USA*
A. Ferscha, *University of Vienna, Austria*
P. A. Fishwick, *University of Florida, USA*
R. M. Fujimoto, *Georgia Institute of Technology, USA*
D. M. Nicol, *Dartmouth College, USA*
C. D. Pham, *University of Lyons, France*
F. Quaglia, *University of Rome, Italy*
B. R. Ronngren, *Royal Institute of Technology, Sweden*
M. Takai, *University of California at Los Angeles, USA*
C. Tropper, *McGill University, Canada*
S. J. Turner, *University of Exeter, UK*
B. W. Unver, *University of Calgary, Canada*
F. P. Wieland, *The MITRE Corporation, USA*

Publicity Chair

Sushil K. Prasad, *Georgia State University, USA*

Reviewers

Rajive Bagrodia
Azzedine Boukerche
David Bruce
Wentong Cai
Christopher Carothers
Roger Chamberlain
Malolan Chetlur
Samir Das
Ewa Deelman
Adel Elmaghraby
Lois Ferscha
Steve Franks
Richard Fujimoto
Boon Ping Gan
Maria Hybinette
Jandhyala Gowri Krishna
Tom Lake
Michael Liljenstam
Brian Logan
Margaret Loper
Wayne Loucks
Johannes Luethi
Thom McLean
Richard Meyer
Katherine Morse
Anand Natrajan
David Nicol
Brad Noble
James Nutaro
Benno Overeinder
Luiz Perrone
Kalyan Perumalla
CongDuc Pham
Anna Poplawski
Francesco Quaglia
Radharamanan Radhakrishnan
Dhananjai Rao
Peter Reiher
George Riley
Robert Rönngren
Rob Simmonds
Roger Smith
Ha Yoon Song
Boleslaw Szymanski
Mineo Takai
Gary Tan
Georgios Theodoropoulos
Carl Tropper
Steve Turner
Brian Unger
Frederick Wieland
Philip Wilsey
Paul Wonnacott
Christopher Young
Jingyue Zang
Jonnhy Zulca

PADS Past Chairs

PADS 2000

May 1-4, Bologna, Italy
General Co-Chairs: Stephen J. Turner and L. Donatiello
Program Chair: David I. Bruce

PADS'99 (part of FCRC'99)

May 1-4, Atlanta, USA
General Chair: Richard M. Fujimoto
Program Chair: Stephen J. Turner

PADS'98

May 26-29, Banff, Canada
General Chair: Brian Unger
Program Chair: Alois Ferscha

PADS'97

June 10-13, Lockenhaus, Austria
General Chair: Alois Ferscha
Program Co-Chairs: Rassul Ayani and Carl Tropper

PADS'96 (part of FCRC'96)

May 22-24, Philadelphia, Pennsylvania
General Chair: Mary Bailey
Program Co-Chairs: Wayne Loucks and Bruno Preiss

PADS'95

June 14-16, Lake Placid, New York
General Chair: Jason Yi-Bing Lin
Program Chair: Mary Bailey

PADS'94

July 6-8, Edinburgh, Scotland
General Chair: Rajive L. Bagrodia
Program Co-Chairs: Damal Arvind and Jason Yi-Bing Lin

PADS'93 (part of FCRC'93)

May 16-19, San Diego, California
General Co-Chairs: Richard Fujimoto and Brian Unger
Program Co-Chairs: Rajive L. Bagrodia and David Jefferson

PADS'92

January 20-22, Newport Beach, California
General Chair: Paul Reynolds
Program Chair: Marc Abrams

PADS'91

January 23-25, Anaheim, California
General Chair: David Nicol
Program Chair: Vijay Madisetti

PADS'90 (Distributed Simulation)

January 17-19, San Diego, California
General Chair and Program Chair: David Nicol

PADS'89 (Distributed Simulation)

March 28-31, Tampa, Florida
General Chair: Brian Unger
Program Chair: Richard Fujimoto

PADS'88 (Distributed Simulation)

February 3-5, San Diego, California
General Chair: Brian Unger
Program Chair: David Jefferson

PADS'85 (Distributed Simulation)

January 24-26, San Diego, California
General Co-Chairs: Bernard Zeigler and Sallie Sheppard
Program Co-Chairs: Paul Reynolds and Horst Wedde

Session 1

Keynote Address

Session 2

Conservative Simulation

Improving Lookahead in Parallel Discrete Event Simulations of Large-Scale Applications using Compiler Analysis

Ewa Deelman[†]
ISI/USC
deelman@isi.edu

Rajive Bagrodia
UCLA
rajive@cs.ucla.edu

Rizos Sakellariou
Manchester University
rizos@cs.man.ac.uk

Vikram Adve
UIUC
vadve@cs.uiuc.edu

Abstract

This paper addresses the issue of efficient and accurate performance prediction of large-scale message-passing applications on high performance architectures using simulation. Such simulators are often based on parallel discrete event simulation, typically using the conservative protocol to synchronize the simulation threads. The paper considers how a compiler can be used to automatically extract information about the lookahead *present in the application, and how this can be used to improve the performance of the null protocol used for synchronization. These techniques are implemented in the MPI-Sim simulator and dHPF compiler, which had previously been extended to work together for optimizing the simulation of local computational components of an application. The results show that the availability of lookahead information improves the runtime of the simulator by factors ranging from 9% up to two orders of magnitude, with 30-60% improvements being typical for the real-world codes. The experiments also show that these improvements are directly correlated with reductions in the number of null messages required by the simulations.*

1 Introduction

Direct-execution simulators make use of available system resources to execute directly portions of the application code and simulate architectural features that are of specific interest, or are unavailable. For instance, direct execution simulators can be used to study various architectural components such as the memory subsystem or the interconnection network. The benefits of this direct-execution simulation are obvious: first, one can estimate the value of the new hardware without the expense of manufacturing or purchasing it; second, one can do the simulation fast: there is no need to simulate the workstation's behavior (for example down to the level of memory references) since that part of the hardware is readily available. However, the constraint of direct execution requires the simulator to use at least as much memory as the target application and constrains the simulator to run at least as long as the application.

To alleviate the cost of direct execution while still maintaining accuracy, in recent work we used compiler support to optimize the simulation of local code [3]. Compiler analysis identifies portions of local code whose *results* do not affect program performance. These sections of the local code are replaced by estimates of their execution time using an analytical model of their performance built by the compiler. Data used only in such computations can also be eliminated. As a result, we observed dramatic savings both in the simulator's runtime as well as its memory requirements [3].

In this paper, we examine how compiler analysis can be used to improve *lookahead* in parallel simulation, and hence further reduce simulation time. When a simulation thread (Logical Process (LP)) knows that before sending the next message, it will process a local code block whose execution time can be predicted, the LP can communicate that information (increased lookahead) to other LPs in the system, possibly allowing those LPs to process events that might not be otherwise processed.

This paper makes three main contributions to parallel simulation of parallel applications:

1. It demonstrates how compiler analysis of a target application program can be used to extract lookahead information useful to a parallel simulation algorithm.
2. It augments an existing compiler-supported simulation system (the MPI-Sim simulator and the Rice dHPF parallelizing compiler) to incorporate this technique in parallel simulation, and
3. It presents a preliminary experimental evaluation demonstrating the potential benefits of this technique.

We present preliminary results evaluating the potential improvements that could be obtained by exploiting lookahead information when using the null message protocol [11] for LP synchronization. Using two synthetic codes and two standard applications (an ASCI benchmark, Sweep3D, and the NAS benchmark, SP), we compare how the simulator performs when it has no lookahead information versus when it can use the compiler-generated lookahead. The synthetic codes allow us to vary the granularity of computation between communications, which has a direct impact on the benefit of lookahead information. The two real codes have deterministic

[†] This work was performed while at UCLA.

communication patterns for which MPI-Sim would not require a synchronization protocol, but by forcing the null protocol we can examine how much similar applications would potentially benefit from the information about lookahead. Our results show that the simulations of the two real codes are 9% to 60% faster when using the lookahead information, and the improvements are higher when the granularity of local computations is higher. The synthetic applications show improvements by up to two orders of magnitude, as the granularity of computations is varied. In all the benchmarks, the improvements in simulation time are directly caused by reductions in the number of null messages required for the simulations. Although these results are preliminary and need to be confirmed by studies with additional applications, they illustrate the large potential benefits that could be achieved via compiler analysis of lookahead in target applications.

2 Related Work

Many of the early program simulators were designed for sequential execution [8, 12, 13]. However, even with the use of direct execution, sequential program simulators tended to be slow with slowdown factors ranging from 2 to 35 for each process in the simulated program [8]. Several efforts have been exploring the use of parallel execution [10, 14, 17, 19, 22] to reduce the model execution times, with varying degrees of success. Many such simulators use sequential or parallel implementations of the quantum protocol. In order to support multiple simulation processes (possibly executing on multiple processors) and maintain accuracy, parallel simulation protocols are used to synchronize the processes. The Quantum protocol lets the processes compute for a given quantum before synchronizing them. In general, synchronous simulators that use the quantum protocol must trade-off simulation accuracy with speed; frequent synchronizations slowdown the simulation, but synchronizing less frequently introduces errors, by possibly executing statements out-of-order [24].

Parallel simulators include MPI-Sim [6, 21], described in the next section, the Wisconsin Wind Tunnel (WWT) [18, 22], a shared memory architecture simulation engine and SimOS [24], a complete system simulator (multiple programs plus operating system). SimOS, which simulates the MIPS architecture, takes into account system details such as cache and CPU models as well as device drivers. It is possible to use the emulation mode, which in part uses direct execution to characterize the program execution. In the emulation mode, the simulation is still ten times slower than real time. The main drawback of SimOS is that it does not use any synchronization protocol when running multiple simulation processes on a parallel platform [23], thus reducing the accuracy of the simulations.

Although MPI-SIM is the only simulator that identifies communication patterns and directly exploits them for the purposes of synchronization, other simulators have used techniques to reduce the synchronization overhead. Among them are LAPSE [14] and Parallel Proteus [17]. Both LAPSE and Parallel Proteus use some form of program analysis to increase the simulation window beyond a fixed quantum, without sacrificing accuracy. LAPSE uses a quantum protocol called WHOA (Window-based Halting On Appointments) and runtime analysis to determine the size of the simulation quantum. An appointment is the earliest time the message can be placed in the network. Adding the latency of the network to the appointment time gives the earliest possible arrival for the message. Processes use the minimum of their appointment times (incoming) to determine whether a message can be processed or not. Parallel Proteus reduces the synchronization overhead caused by frequent barriers of the quantum protocol by using *predictive barriers* and *local barriers*. The predictive barriers method uses runtime and compile time analysis to determine, at the beginning of a simulation quantum, the earliest simulation time at which any process will send a message to any other process.

In previous work [21], we designed a novel approach to synchronization in which the blocking time at the *receive* statement is reduced by analyzing the communication patterns in the program. Specifically, each simulation process uses this analysis to locally identify whether an incoming application message is safe to process right away or whether synchronizations with other processes are necessary. In some cases, the optimization resulted in simulations where no synchronization was necessary.

3 Background

3.1 Simulation of Large-Scale Applications with MPI-Sim

The starting point for our work is MPI-Sim [6, 21], a direct-execution *parallel* simulator for performance prediction of MPI programs. MPI-Sim simulates an MPI application running on a parallel system (referred to as the *target program* and *system* respectively). The machine on which the simulator is executed (the *host machine*) may be either a sequential or a parallel machine. In general, the number of processors in the host machine will be less than the number of processors in the target architecture being simulated, so the simulator must support multi-threading. The simulation kernel on each processor schedules the threads and ensures that events on host processors are executed in their correct timestamp order. A target thread is simulated as follows. The local code is simulated by directly executing it on the host processor. In the compiler-enhanced version of MPI-Sim, portions of the local code are modeled by an analytical performance model, while the remaining local code is directly executed. Communication commands are trapped by the simulator, which uses an appropriate model to predict the execution time for the corresponding communication activity on the target architecture.

MPI-Sim supports most of the commonly used MPI communication routines, such as point-to-point and collective communications. In the simulator, all collective communication functions are implemented in terms of point-to-point communication functions, and all point-to-point communication functions are implemented using a set of core non-blocking MPI functions. The simulator has been validated against several MPI implementations including those on the IBM SP and SGI Origin 2000 [6].

The simulation kernel provides support for sequential and parallel execution of the simulator. Parallel execution is supported via a set of conservative parallel simulation protocols [20], which typically work as follows: Each application process in the simulation is modeled by a Logical Process (LP). Each LP can execute independently, without synchronizing with other LPs, until it executes a *wait* operation (such as an MPI-Recv, MPI-Barrier, etc); a synchronization protocol is used to decide when such an LP can proceed. We briefly describe the default protocol used by MPI-Sim. Each LP in the model computes local quantities called Earliest Output Time (EOT) and Earliest Input Time (EIT) [5]. The EOT represents the earliest future time at which the LP will send a message to any other LP in the model; similarly the EIT represents a lower bound on the receive timestamp of future messages that the LP may receive. Upon executing a wait statement, an LP can safely select a matching message (if any) from its input buffer, that has a receive timestamp less than its EIT. Different asynchronous protocols differ only in their method for computing EIT. However, in this paper, we concentrate on the Null Message protocol [11], where the EOT is communicated between the LPs via *null messages*. In our model, when an LP is blocked at a receive statement and cannot find a matching message, the LP requests null messages from all LPs in the system (or a subset of LPs with which it communicates) and recomputes its EIT whenever a null message arrives. An LP can get a null message request at any time, at which point it returns its EOT. Later, we show how we use the compiler derived analytical models to extract the lookahead present in the application and thus improve an LP's estimate of its EOT.

3.2 Compiler Analysis

In previous work [3], we implemented and evaluated compiler techniques to improve the performance of parallel simulation of very large message-passing parallel programs. The key idea underlying this work was to apply compiler analysis to locate fragments of local computation whose resulting values do not affect performance, and to avoid simulating those fragments in detail by replacing them with (symbolic) analytical performance estimates. For example, computations of values that determine loop bounds, branches, message patterns, and message sizes all have a direct impact on performance. In contrast, the results of other computations do not affect performance, and only their execution times are required for performance prediction. The latter, which we term as '*redundant*', do not need to be simulated in detail and can be abstracted away and replaced by an analytic performance estimate of their execution time, while simulating the rest of the program in detail. During simulation, the simulator can use the analytical estimate to advance the clock accordingly. As a corollary, it is also possible to avoid performing data transfers[1] for many messages whose values do not affect performance, while simulating the *performance* of the messages in detail.

The compiler analysis for accomplishing the above has three major aspects: (1) identifying the values in the program that do not affect performance (a *value* is a pair <*variable, statement*> representing the data stored in that variable at that statement); (2) identifying computations that only affect these values and therefore can be abstracted away; and (3) generating symbolic estimates for the execution time of these computations.

For the first step, we use a compiler-synthesized *static task graph* model [2, 4], an abstract program representation that identifies the sequential computations (tasks), the parallel structure of the program (task precedences, explicit communication), and the control-flow that determines the parallel structure. The symbolic expressions in the task graph for control flow conditions, communication patterns and volumes, and scaling expressions for sequential task execution times capture all these program variables that have a direct impact on program performance.

For the second step, we use a compiler technique called *program slicing* [16] to identify those portions of the computation that determine the values of those variables; these are exactly the computations that must be retained. (Given a particular value in a program as defined above, program slicing uses data and control dependence information to identify those portions of the computations that may directly or indirectly affect that value in some execution of the program. This analysis must be performed interprocedurally, and can be performed for an entire set of values at once.) The compiler then generates *simplified MPI code* that contains those computations plus the communication. The remaining code fragments are replaced by a call to a function that will be interpreted by the simulator as a command to advance its clock by a specified value; this value should correspond to the execution time of the abstracted computation.

---

[1] This saves simulation time because performing the data transfer may require significant overhead, e.g., if the source and destination threads of the message are mapped to different host processors in the simulation.

Finally, in order to estimate the execution time of the abstracted code, the compiler generates simple symbolic expressions parameterized by direct measurement.

The above techniques have been implemented in the Rice dHPF compiler [1]. In [3], we evaluated the above techniques for three benchmarks: Sweep3D [25], a key ASCI benchmark; NAS SP from the NAS benchmark suite [7] and Tomcatv, a SPEC92 benchmark. Over a wide range of problem sizes and numbers of processors (on the distributed memory IBM SP), the errors in the predicted execution times, compared with direct measurement, were at most 17% in all cases we studied, and often were substantially less (the direct execution MPI-Sim had errors of about 7%). Moreover, in each application, the compiler techniques led to a significant reduction in simulator memory usage (up to 2000 times) and simulation time (up to 10 times), thus allowing us to simulate problem sizes *up to 100 times larger* than what was possible with state-of-the-art simulation tools before.

This paper extends the preceding work in two directions. First, we assume that the receive statements are not deterministic and an LP must use some synchronization algorithm to identify safe messages (we use a conservative null message algorithm for this). Second, we use the compiler-derived representation to extract the lookahead present in the application to improve performance of the null message protocol.

4 Lookahead Extraction

Lookahead plays an important role in improving the performance of conservative simulation protocols. In the context of the application, we focus on portions of the code where the simulation thread is blocked (such as in blocking receives and sends). When a logical process (LP) executes a receive statement, it checks if its input message queue contains any *safe* messages, i.e., any message with a timestamp less than the EIT of the LP. If so, the safe message(s) can be processed; otherwise the LP is blocked until its EIT is advanced using the underlying null message based protocol.

In general, for program simulations using direct execution, the lower bound on the EOT of an LP is its current simulation time (T) plus L, the minimum latency of any message that can be sent. However, if the LP can compute an accurate lower bound on the execution time of a local code block that precedes any message transmissions, perhaps via compiler analysis, it can compute a more accurate EOT. At some point in its execution, let T_{LC} represent the execution time of a code block of an LP, then its EOT becomes $T+L+T_{LC}$, and thus enables the blocked LPs to have a better estimate of the EIT. In previous work, researchers have estimated this execution time using pre-simulation [15]. In this paper, we show how this can be computed using compiler analysis, and used to improve the efficiency of the resulting model.

Example 1:

```
MPI_Recv(......)
for (j=1; j<N; j++) {
        mdiag[j] = mdiag[j-1];
        ndiag = ndiag + mdiag[j];   }
MPI_Recv(&a, ... ...);
for (k=0; k<ndiag; k++ )
        a[k] = a[k-1] + ...
MPI_Send(&a, ... ...);                          (a)
```

```
for (j=1; j<N; j++) {
        mdiag[j] = mdiag[j-1];
        ndiag = ndiag + mdiag[j]; }
MPI_Recv(&a, ... ...);
advance_clock(ndiag * w_3);
MPI_Send(&a, ... ...);                          (b)
```

```
for (j=1; j<N; j++) {
        mdiag[j] = mdiag[j-1];
        ndiag = ndiag + mdiag[j]; }
set_lookahead(ndiag* w_3);
MPI_Recv(&a, ... ...);
reset_lookahead();
advance_clock(ndiag*w_3);
MPI_Send(&a, ... ...);                          (c)
```

Example 1a shows a portion of a code where boundary conditions of a loop are calculated, a receive statement is posted[2], values of an array "a" are calculated, and finally the computed data is sent to the next processor. Such a code structure is common in many scientific applications, including applications discussed in this paper. The compiler can estimate that the amount of time the second loop is executed is the number of times the second loop is executed (`ndiag`) times the average duration of a single iteration of the loop (w_3)[3]. The compiler also determines, based on the task graph analysis described in the previous section, that in order to predict the performance of the code, the actual values computed in array a are not necessary. Hence, it replaces that portion of the code with a call to advance the simulation clock by the estimated execution time of the loop (Example 1b) (For details about how the compiler calculates the analytic estimates, please see [3].) The first loop cannot be abstracted away since the value of `ndiag` computed by the loop body is needed to estimate the performance of the second loop. The compiler can also notice that a communication primitive precedes

[2] In real applications, the receive would be posted before the loop boundary calculation. We use this code here only to illustrate better the example.

[3] This is clearly a simplistic estimate, but it can be improved using existing compiler-driven modeling techniques for sequential code (e.g., [9]). The specific choice of this model is orthogonal to the optimizations we have proposed.

the second loop, and assumes that simulation process synchronization might occur during the communication call. The compiler then provides the simulator with lookahead information before the communication call is made (`set_lookahead(ndiag*w_3)`) and then resets the lookahead to 0 after the communication call. Note that this use of lookahead information introduces no *additional* approximations in the simulation, beyond the compiler-enhanced simulation described in our previous work.

Example 2:

```
for (j=1; j<N; j++) {
        mdiag[j] = mdiag[j-1];
        ndiag = ndiag + mdiag[j];}
MPI_Recv(&a, … …);
for (k=0; k<ndiag; k++ ) {
        a[k] = a[k-1] + …}
MPI_Send(&a, … …);                    (a)
```

```
Set_lookahead(N*w_2);
MPI_Recv(… …)
reset_lookahead();
for (j=1; j<N; j++) {
        mdiag[j] = mdiag[j-1];
        ndiag = ndiag + mdiag[j]; }
set_lookahead(ndiag*w_3);
MPI_Recv(&a, … …);
reset_lookahead();
advance_clock(ndiag*w_3)
MPI_Send(&a, … …);                    (b)
```

Even though we used analytic performance estimates only for code blocks that were abstracted away, for the purpose of lookahead we can also use compiler-generated performance estimates for portions of the code that need to be directly executed (such as loop boundary calculations). The key requirement is that these estimates must be lower-bounds for the actual execution time, so that the simulator does not violate causality. Consider Example 2. In 2a, there is a receive before the loop boundary calculation. Although we need to calculate the value of `ndiag` in the loop body, the compiler can let the simulator know that, when it is blocked in communications, it will not send a message with a timestamp smaller than the current simulation time plus the minimum message latency (L) plus the lookahead (`N*w_2`) (Example 2b). After the communication call is completed, the lookahead is reset to 0. This extension is not included in this paper because developing lower-bound performance estimates via compiler analysis requires substantial new research and is a subject for future work.

5 Results

MPI-Sim and the compiler optimized MPI-Sim have been previously validated [3, 6, 21] on a variety of applications such as NAS, ASCI and SPEC92 benchmarks on two hardware platforms: the IBM SP and the SGI Origin 2000. The original MPI-Sim predicted the performance of the applications within 7% of the measured system. The compiler-enhanced simulator, which used analytical models for portions of the computation, validated to within 17% of the measured system. The use of lookahead information in this work does not introduce any additional approximations over the latter. Therefore, we focus here on the improvement in performance of the null message protocol achieved by using the compiler-extracted lookahead information. All the following experiments were run on the IBM SP-2 at Lawrence Livermore, and used up to 128 processors on the machine.

5.1 Benchmarks

We use two synthetic benchmarks and two real world applications in our experiments. In the first synthetic code, the processes of the application are logically arranged in a ring topology. The processes execute several computation and communication iterations. First, the even processors perform a given amount of computation and then decide whether to send the results to the "right" or to the "left". The odd processes then enter the computation and communication phase. In each iteration, the receiving process does not know where the next message is coming from and therefore may need to request null messages from other simulation processes (assuming that a demand driven null message algorithm is used) to decide whether a given message is safe to process. The second application increases the dimension of the process topology to two. Again the processes are divided into two communicating groups. The first group computes its values and decides whether to send the values first horizontally and then vertically, or the other way around. Once again, the receiver needs to use null messages to identify safe messages. In both applications, the computation is abstracted away by the compiler and replaced with compiler generated analytical models. We will refer to the two synthetic benchmarks as 1D and 2D, respectively.

We also use two standard benchmarks, the ASCI Sweep3D code [25], a key benchmark used in the DOE ASCI program, and NAS SP, a fluid dynamics code from the NAS benchmark suite [7]. The compiler abstracted away most of the computation present in the codes. The most aggressive version of MPI-Sim [21] detects from the parameters to MPI calls that the null message protocol is not necessary for these two codes. We force the simulator to use the null message protocol in order to characterize the value of the lookahead in these codes and examine the potential benefits of the optimization. Many other applications such as NAS LU (which solves the same problem as NAS SP using a different algorithm) do require the null protocol, but are currently not supported by our dHPF compiler extensions for simulation.

In the following experiments, we compare the absolute performance improvement between MPI-Sim using no lookahead information (NOL) and MPI-Sim using the lookaheads calculated by the compiler (LO). In both versions, the previous compiler optimization of abstracting away redundant computations is included so that we use a sophisticated and efficient simulation system as a baseline, and so that the two versions have identical accuracy.

5.2 Impact of Lookahead for Synthetic Benchmarks

The amount of computation in the 1D synthetic benchmark is related to the minimum message latency in the system (L=54μsec). The amount of computation (which is abstracted away) is taken from a normal distribution with three different means. Experiments are conducted for means of L/4, L/8 and L/20 and a standard deviation of 10% of the mean. In the first experiments, the number of host processors is the same as the number of target processors.

Table 1 shows the results for the 1D benchmark with the 3 different means. The rows are divided into three groups, representing the three means 2.7μsec, 6.75μsec and 13.5μsec. The number of target processors is varied from 4 to 100. The shaded areas represent a simulator's runtime greater than 2hrs (7,200sec), the maximum readily available machine time. Clearly, the simulator's ability to extract lookahead results in better performance. As the amount of lookahead increases (when the mean of the distribution for the abstracted computation is increased), the performance difference between NOL and LO also increases.

Mean = L/20= 2.7μsec	**Runtime in seconds**	
Procs	**NOL**	**LO**
4	862.428	26.9109
16	4262.14	127.972
64	>7200	500.037
100	>7200	853.927
Mean = L/8= 6.75μsec		
4	2565.98	63.2986
16	>7200	325.567
64	>7200	1344.2
100	>7200	2413.35
Mean = L/4= 13.5μsec		
4	5901.44	149.262
16	>7200	859.935
64	>7200	4873.38
100	>7200	>7200

Table 1: Runtime for MPI-Sim with and without lookahead, 1D benchmark with various means.

Mean = L/20= 2.7μsec	**Number of Protocol Messages**	
Procs	**NOL**	**LO**
4	4,445,148	111,258
16	22,226,220	556,800
64		2,351,223
100		3,713,391
Mean = L/8= 6.75μsec		
4	13,333,479	333,483
16		1,673,325
64		7,017,570
100		11,065,032
Mean = L/4= 13.5μsec		
4	30,613,356	740,817
16		4,558,590
64		24,971,247
100		

Table 2 Null message performance for the 1D synthetic benchmark.

The great differences in the runtimes of the simulators are directly related to the number of protocol messages needed to perform the simulation, as can be seen from Table 2.

Similarly, for the 2D benchmark (with a fixed amount of lookahead), MPI-Sim is able to use the lookahead to improve the simulator's performance by as much as two orders of magnitude for up to 49 target processors (host processors = target processors), as seen in Figure 1. For more than 49 processors, the simulator which had no lookahead information did not complete the simulation in the available time (7,200sec). The improvement in performance is directly related to the reduction in the number of necessary null messages, as shown in Figure 2.

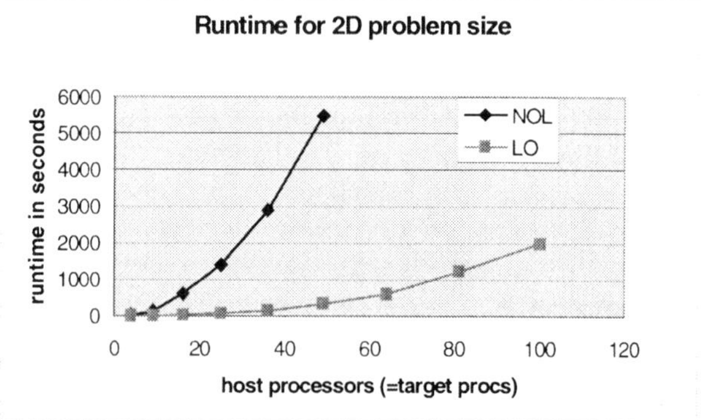

Figure 1: 2D Synthetic Problem, the number of host processors equals the number of target processors.

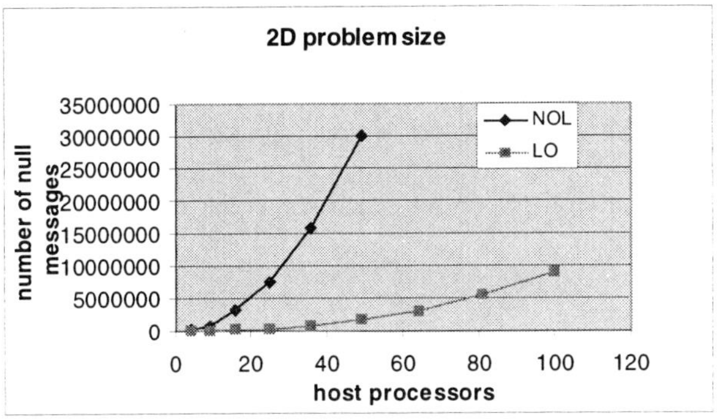

Figure 2: Null message performance for the 2D synthetic benchmark.

5.3 Impact of Lookahead for Sweep3D and SP

The previous results characterized the simulator's performance when the number of available host processors was equal to the number of simulated (target) processors. However, it is more often the case that the number of host processors is smaller than the number of target processors. Table 3 shows how the simulator performs when four host processors are used to simulate a system of 4, 16, 64 and 100 processors. The benchmark is the 1D code and the results are shown for normal distributions with means of 2.7μsec, 6.75μsec and 13.5μsec. The shaded areas represent again a simulator's runtime greater than 7,200sec. The NOL version is on the average 36 times slower than the LO version.

Mean	Target procs	NOL	LO
2.7μsec	4	850.096	24.3271
	16	891.166	27.26
	64	1123.99	29.1321
	100	1494.79	38.8056
6.75μsec	4	2577.2	66.2126
	16	2704.15	67.6685
	64	3363.05	84.3307
	100	4476.27	114.975
13.3μsec	4	5952.25	145.72
	16	6148.76	260.634
	64	>7200	457.22
	100	>7200	489.049

Table 3: Simulator's runtime for the 1D problem running on 4 host processors.

Although MPI-Sim with lookahead performed well for synthetic benchmarks, it is important to evaluate its performance on standard codes. We first look at the NAS SP benchmark, size A (the smallest size in the suite). Figure 3 shows the runtime of both NOL and LO when simulating NAS SP. In this case, the number of host processors is equal to the number of target processors. For the NAS SP benchmark, the lookahead we were able to extract allowed MPI-Sim to execute on the average 58.4% faster then the original simulator. Again, the improvement in performance is consistent with the decreased number of messages. The simulator without lookahead needs on average 72.5% more protocol messages (Figure 4).

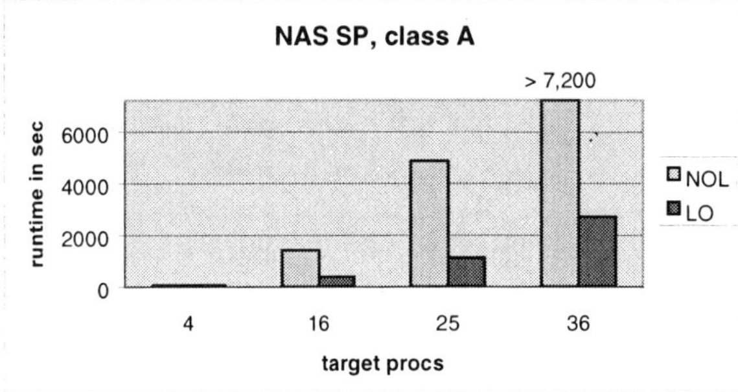

Figure 3: Runtime of MPI-Sim when simulating NAS SP class A.

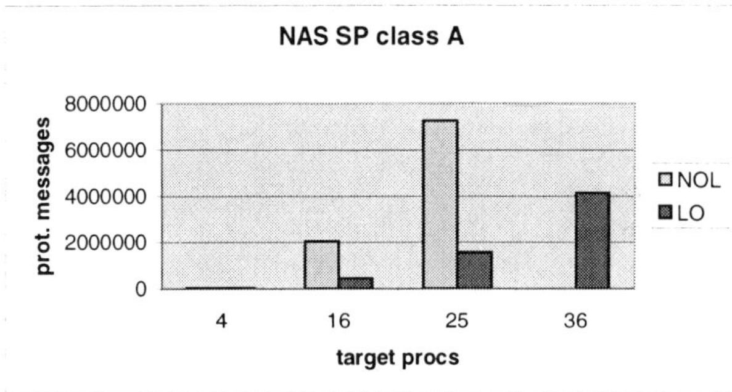

Figure 4: The number of protocol messages needed for synchronization in NAS SP.

The last set of experiments is for the Sweep3D benchmark. Figures 5 and 6 show the performance of MPI-Sim with a per processor fixed problem size of 4×4×255. The host system uses 16 processors to simulate up to 64 target processors. For this configuration, LO runs on the average 29.83% faster than the version without lookahead (Figure 5), which corresponds to the 25% reduction in the number of null messages (Figure 6).

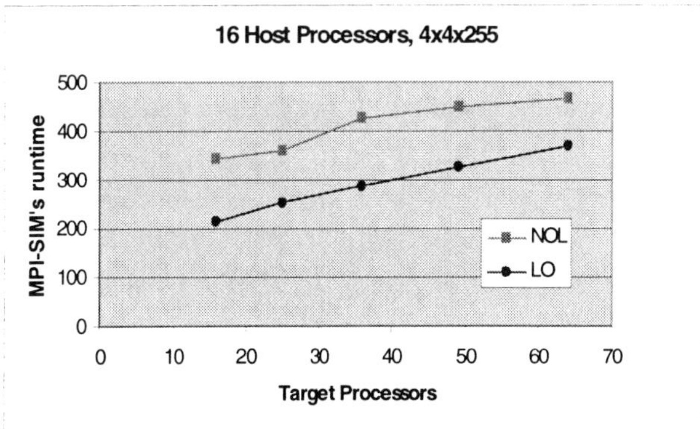

Figure 5: Runtime of MPI-Sim simulating Sweep3D, 4×4×255 per processor size, using 16 processors.

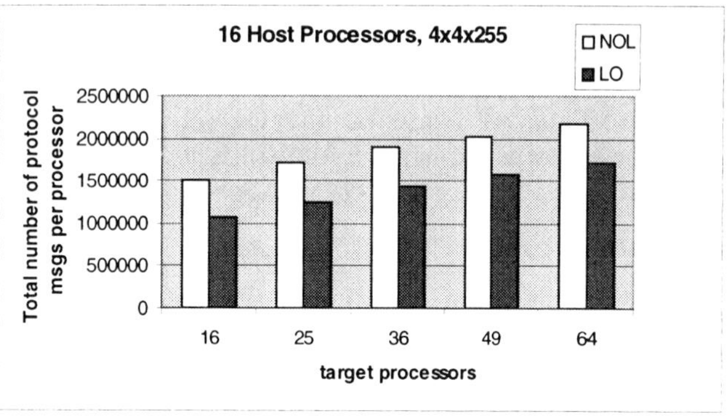

Figure 6: Number of null messages used by MPI-Sim simulating Sweep3D, 4×4×255 per processor problem size.

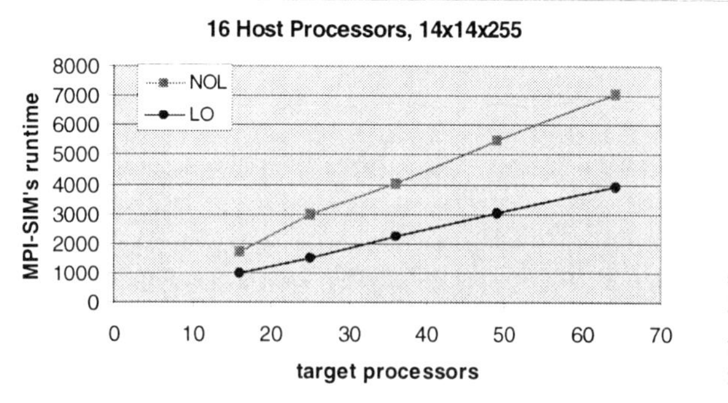

Figure 7: Runtime of MPI-Sim simulating Sweep3D, 14×14×255 per processor size, using 16 processors.

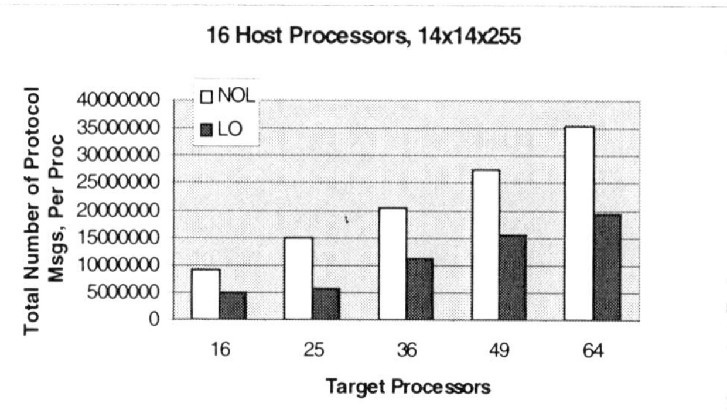

Figure 8: Number of null messages used by MPI-Sim simulating Sweep3D, 14×14×255 per processor size.

When the per-processor problem size is larger (14×14×255 per processor size), the granularity of the computation is greater (the lookahead is greater) and thus the benefit from lookahead is increased. Figure 7 shows the runtime of NOL and LO when using 16 host processors and simulating target systems from 16 to 64 processors. The performance improvement in the LO version is on the average 45% faster and the decrease of null messages is on the average 48%.

Our final two figures study the impact of lookahead information on the speedup of the simulator. We simulate Sweep3D for a fixed total problem size of 100^3 cells running on a fixed target system of 128 processors, and vary the number of host processors. The LO version of MPI-Sim performs on the average only 9.2% better than the NOL version, mainly because the granularity of computation per target processor is quite low for this case (Figure 9).

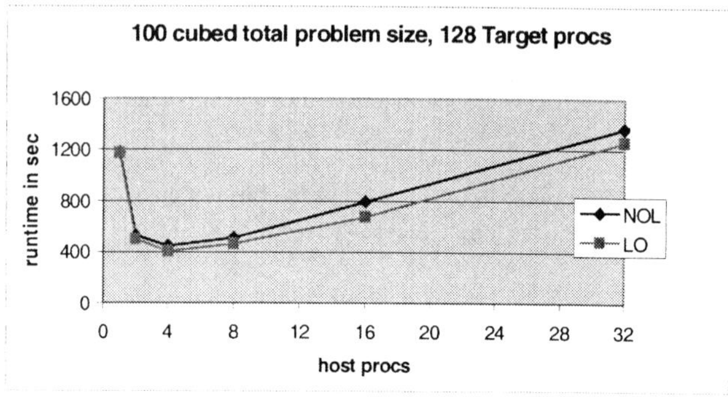

Figure 9: Runtime of MPI-Sim predicting the performance of 100^3 total problem size and a 128 processor target system.

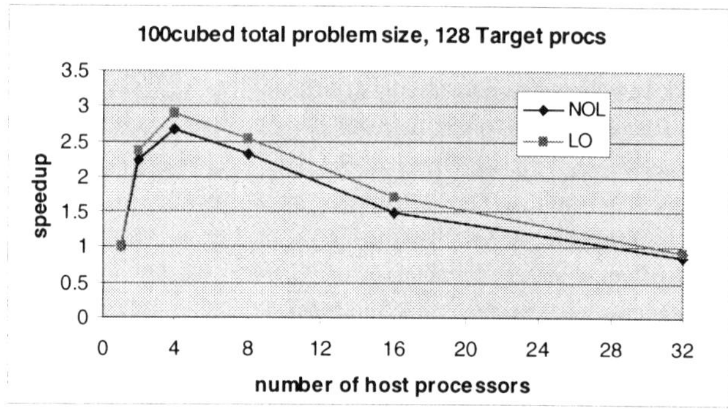

Figure 10: Speedup of MPI-Sim predicting the performance of 100^3 total problem size and a 128 processor target system.

Figure 10 shows that both versions achieve a maximum speedup of about 3 when using 4 host processors, and their speedup degrades beyond that point because the computation granularity *per host processor* is decreasing, thus decreasing the available lookahead. Since only a relatively small lookahead is available, the efficiency of the parallel simulation is relatively poor and the difference in performance of the LO and NOL versions is not as great as in the cases where computation granularity is greater.

6 Conclusions

In this paper, we have considered how compiler analysis can extract lookahead information to improve the performance of parallel simulation of message-passing parallel applications. Our prior system used compiler analysis to abstract away portions of the computational code and replace them with analytical performance estimates, yielding large benefits in simulator efficiency (those benefits are obtained for either sequential or parallel simulation). In this paper, we showed that the compiler estimates can be used to provide lookahead information to the simulator, which can reduce the synchronization messages required for the synchronization protocol used in parallel simulation. We presented preliminary experiments using two synthetic applications and two widely used real world codes, which showed that using lookahead information may potentially lead to large reductions in the running time of the simulator.

We identify two key issues for future work. First, we must examine additional applications to evaluate to what extent these applications benefit from techniques to improve lookahead in parallel simulation. Second, and perhaps most exciting, we aim to explore how lookahead estimation techniques could be used for arbitrary computations, not just those whose results do not affect performance. This is important because such a technique could lead to significant additional improvements for a broad range of codes, especially irregular codes. The key challenge in this work would be to develop compiler techniques for reliable lower-bound performance estimates for computational fragments.

7 Acknowledgments

This work was supported by DARPA/ITO under Contract N66001-97-C-8533, by the NSF Next Generation Software program under contract number EIA-9975024, and by the NSF Operating Systems and Compilers program under grant number CCR-9988482. Thanks to Lawrence Livermore Laboratory for providing extensive computer time on the IBM SP/2.

References

[1] V. S. Adve and J. Mellor-Crummey, "Using Integer Sets for Data-Parallel Program Analysis and Optimization," *ACM SIGPLAN PLDI'98*, 1998.

[2] V. S. Adve and R. Sakellariou, "Compiler Synthesis of Task Graphs for Parallel Program Performance Prediction," *LCPC'00*, Springer-Verlag LNCS, vol. 2017, 2001.

[3] V. S. Adve, R. Bagrodia, E. Deelman, and R. Sakellariou, "Compiler-supported simulation of highly scalable parallel applications," *Journal of Parallel and Distributed Computing, Special Issue on Parallel Simulation (to appear)*. A preliminary version appeared at *ACM/IEEE SC99*, 1999.

[4] V. S. Adve and R. Sakellariou, "Application Representations for a Multi-Paradigm Performance Modeling Environment for Parallel Systems," *International Journal of High-Performance Computing Applications*, vol. 14, pp. 304-316, 2000.

[5] R. Bagrodia, R. Meyer, M. Takai, C. Yu-An, Z. Xiang, J. Martin, and S. Ha Yoon, "Parsec: a parallel simulation environment for complex systems," *Computer*, vol. 31, 1998.

[6] R. Bagrodia, E. Deelman, S. Docy, and T. Phan, "Performance Prediction of Large Parallel Applications using Parallel Simulations," *ACM SIGPLAN PPoPP*, 1999.

[7] D. Bailey, T. Harris, W. Shaphir, R. v. d. Wijngaart, A. Woo, and M. Yarrow, "The NAS Parallel Benchmarks 2.0," NASA Ames Research Center NAS-95-090, 1995.

[8] E. A. Brewer, A. Colbrook, C. N. Dellarocas, and W. E. Weihl, "PROTEUS: a high-performance parallel-architecture simulator," *ACM Sigmetrics*, 1992.

[9] C. Cascaval, L. DeRose, D. Padua, and D. Reed, "Compile-Time Based Performance Prediction," *LCPC'99*, Springer-Verlag LNCS, vol. 1863, 2000.

[10] S. Chandrasekaran and M. D. Hill, "Optimistic simulation of parallel architectures using program executables," *PADS*, 1996.

[11] K. M. Chandy and J. Misra, "Distributed simulation: a case study in design and verification of distributed programs," *IEEE TSE*, vol. 5, pp. 440-52, 1979.

[12] R. C. Covington, S. Madala, V. Mehta, J. R. Jump, and J. B. Sinclair, "The Rice parallel processing testbed," *ACM Sigmetrics*, 1988.

[13] H. Davis, S. R. Goldschmidt, and J. Hennessy, "Multiprocessor Simulation and Tracing using Tango," *Proceedings of ICPP'91*, pp. 99-107, 1991.

[14] P. Dickens, P. Heidelberger, and D. Nicol, "A Distributed Memory LAPSE: Parallel Simulation of Message-Passing Programs," *PADS*, 1994.

[15] P. M. Dickens, P. Heidelberger, and D. M. Nicol, "Parallelized direct execution simulation of message-passing parallel programs," *IEEE TPDS*, vol. 7, pp. 1090-1105, 1996.

[16] S. Horwitz, T. Reps, and D. Binkley, "Interprocedural slicing using dependence graphs," *ACM TOPLAS*, vol. 12, pp. 26-60, 1990.

[17] U. Legedza and W. E. Weihl, "Reducing Synchronization Overhead in Parallel Simulation," *PADS'96*, pp. 86-95, 1996.

[18] S. S. Mukherjee, S. K. Reinhardt, B. Falsafi, M. Litzkow, S. Huss-Lederman, M. D. Hill, J. R. Larus, and D. A. Wood, "Wisconsin Wind Tunnel II: A Fast and Portable Parallel Architecture Simulator," *Workhop on Performance Analysis and its Impact on Design (PAID)*, 1997.

[19] S. Prakash and R. Bagrodia, "An adaptive synchronization method for unpredictable communication patterns in data parallel programs," *IPPS*, 1995.

[20] S. Prakash and R. L. Bagrodia, "MPI-SIM: using parallel simulation to evaluate MPI programs," *IEEE WSC*, 1998.

[21] S. Prakash, E. Deelman, and R. Bagrodia, "Asynchronous Parallel Simulation of Parallel Programs," *IEEE TSE*, vol. 26, 2000.

[22] S. K. Reinhardt, M. D. Hill, J. R. Larus, A. R. Lebeck, J. C. Lewis, and D. A. Wood, "The Wisconsin Wind Tunnel: Virtual Prototyping of Parallel Computers," *ACM Sigmetrics*, 1993.

[23] M. Rosenblum, S. A. Herrod, E. Witchel, and A. Gupta, "Complete Computer System Simulation: The SimOS Approach," *IEEE Parallel and Distributed Technology*, vol. 3, pp. 34-43, 1995.

[24] M. Rosenblum, E. Begnion, S. Devine, and S. A. Herrod, "Using the SimOS Machine Simulator to Study Complex Computer Systems," *ACM TOMACS*, vol. 7, pp. 78-103, 1997

[25] "The ASCI Sweep3D Benchmark Code". http://www.llnl.gov/asci_benchmarks/asci/limited/sweep3d/asci_sweep3d.html

Looking Ahead of Real Time in Hybrid Component Networks

Kaixin Xu, Mineo Takai, Jay Martin, Rajive Bagrodia
University of California, Los Angeles
Computer Science Department
Los Angeles, California
{xkx, mineo, jmartin, rajive}@cs.ucla.edu

Abstract

While network simulation is a widely used technique for developing, testing and evaluating network protocols and applications, it is difficult and time-consuming to develop detailed models of the entire protocol stack and the application that is being evaluated. Hybrid component networks combine simulation models of protocols and applications with physical implementations of other protocols and/or applications, which can alleviate modeling complexity and build accurate models. However, hybrid component networks require that the simulated components execute faster than real time. Parallel simulation techniques can greatly improve the performance of hybrid component networks and facilitate evaluation of larger networks than would be feasible only with sequential execution. In parallel simulation, one of the most important properties to be exploited from the simulation is "lookahead," but none of the previous studies has exploited the lookahead from the physical implementation of protocols or applications. We have developed Virtual Socket Interface (VSI), which exploits real time lookahead from the interactions between operational applications and simulated networks in GloMoSim [1], a parallel discrete event network simulator. This paper presents the implementation of VSI with the notion of real time lookahead and evaluates VSI for typical wireless ad hoc network scenarios. The results of the study demonstrate that the parallel simulation with the real time lookahead greatly enhances the capability of hybrid component networks.

1. Introduction

The growing availability of infrastructure to support mobile wireless communication and computing has led to significant growth of applications that can exploit such infrastructure. It is a truism that such systems are complex to design, and new techniques are needed to predict their performance in an efficient manner. Existing performance studies of such systems have typically emphasized either the application or the network such that one of the two components is modeled in detail, and the other is represented by an abstract model. Thus, networking-oriented performance studies tend to develop a detailed model of the network including protocols and communication media, while representing the application simply as stochastic, or possibly trace-based traffic streams. On the other hand, application-centric studies tend to develop detailed models of the application, while using an abstract model to represent the network. However, in contexts where there are closed loop interactions among the application and the network, or where changes in network connectivity dynamically affect the traffic generated by the application in a statically unpredictable manner and vice versa, such models are inadequate. The ability to incorporate detailed application behavior in a performance prediction environment for mobile wireless networks thus appears to have significant value. More generally, composition of physical implementations of some network layers with simulated models of other layers appears to offer substantial benefits.

A major impediment to widespread use of simulation for wireless network is their execution inefficiency. Due to the broadcast nature of wireless transmission medium, the simulation of mobile wireless networks requires significantly higher computational cost than that of wired networks. This problem has previously been addressed by using abstract models and parallel execution model. Abstract models may be inadequate for the mobile wireless systems discussed in this paper, as an abstract model of the network, for instance, will not be able to account for the impact of different MAC layer protocols on application behavior. Parallel execution has been shown to yield substantial improvements in the execution time of detailed wireless network simulations, but still suffers from two problems: detailed models can be expensive to design, debug, and validate, and the detailed system specifications that are needed for such models may be unavailable to the analyst. This is often true for

0-7695-1104-X/01 $10.00

wireless radio devices, where implementation details like timer settings, buffer sizes, and other performance-critical protocol parameters may not be released by the manufacturer. In such situations, an alternative to modeling the network is to directly incorporate the wireless radio network in the model. Such methodologies have been referred to variously as hybrid component networks or network emulation [5][6][7][8][9][10]. A key requirement of these hybrid component networks is that the simulated components execute sufficiently fast, at least faster than the real time, thus effective support for parallel execution of the simulated components can substantially enhance their applicability.

The performance of parallel simulation is often restricted by "lookahead," which indicates how far in time the simulator can foresee the occurrence of future events. Exploiting lookahead from the simulation models is critical to achieve good parallel simulation performance. This is also true in the hybrid component networks with parallel execution of simulated components. While most techniques proposed in the literature to improve lookahead are applicable to these hybrid component networks, the simulated components that may receive messages directly from the physical components are regarded to have no lookahead, as they can hardly predict when they receives messages from the physical components. This can be a serious problem if physical components send burst traffic to simulated components.

This paper presents a technique to exploit *real time lookahead*, which is defined as the ability of simulated components to foresee the interactions with physical components, and shows the impact of the real time lookahead on the performance of hybrid component networks with parallel execution of simulated components. We have developed a socket-based interface called Virtual Socket Interface (VSI) to construct hybrid component networks, with an existing parallel network simulation library called GloMoSim [1]. VSI can exploit real time lookahead from interactions between operational TCP applications and simulated TCP protocol models for the parallel simulation. As VSI is implemented at the application layer of GloMoSim, it is very portable and supports most of the TCP applications that support proxy servers without modifying applications themselves. This paper describes the implementation details of VSI and its use in performance prediction of TCP-based applications in hybrid component networks for mobile wireless environments.

The remainder of the paper is organized as follows: Section 2 describes our implementation of hybrid component networks and how it can exploit real time lookahead. Section 3 validates the hybrid component networks against real wireless networks, and Section 4 evaluates the effects of parallel simulation and real time lookahead on the performance of hybrid component networks. Section 5 describes the related work and Section 6 concludes the paper.

2. Hybrid Component Networks

The hybrid component network is composed of three primary types of components: the simulated components, the physical components and the hybrid interface. The simulated component is part of the network, which does not really exist, but is provided by simulation. The physical component is operational and is a part of the actual network. In this study, they are operational TCP applications like http, telnet or ftp. The simulated components interact with the physical components via the hybrid interface. The simulated and physical components must be able to exchange data in a semantically correct manner. First, the simulated components must not receive any packets with timestamps in the past unless the simulation have a rollback capability. Second, it is crucial that the packets sent from the simulated components to the physical components are received by the hybrid interface before the corresponding wall clock time. The packets should then be buffered at the interface until the wall clock advances to their timestamps, at which point they are given to the physical component. If the packet is sent after the corresponding wall clock time, the best the hybrid interface can do is to send the packet to the physical component immediately. However, this may introduce inaccuracies in the model. The hybrid interface is implemented to ensure that these two requirements are met.

2.1. GloMoSim simulation library

In this study, we used GloMoSim [1] as an underlying network simulator. GloMoSim (Global Mobile Information Systems Simulator) is a network simulation library with a rich set of detailed protocol models, particularly for mobile wireless networks. Such networks require significantly higher computational cost compared to wired networks due to the broadcast nature of wireless transmission medium, and the parallel simulation techniques are essential to yield the simulation results in a reasonable amount of execution time. Its simulation kernel has been built on top of PARSEC [4], a portable parallel simulation environment that allows GloMoSim to run on various multiprocessor machines including the SGI Origin 2000 and the Sun Enterprise. GloMoSim adopts the OSI seven-layer architecture in its APIs between layers such that operational applications and protocols can be integrated into the simulation environment without much modification. For instance, the TCP Lite model in GloMoSim was taken out of the FreeBSD operating system whose protocol behaviors have already been validated in real networks. This technique significantly reduces the development, testing, and validation costs of detailed protocol models. However, this is feasible only when the source code of the protocol is available, and the use of hybrid component networks is essential to integrate devices, protocols and applications whose source codes are not available or unable to modify for the integration.

All protocol and device models of GloMoSim used in this study have been validated against the real network as demonstrated in Section 3. Live traffic generated by the physical components goes through the GloMoSim models as if it does in the real wireless network, and a variety of network statistics can be collected for the analysis of protocols or specific scenarios.

2.2. Implementation of Virtual Socket Interface (VSI)

The Virtual Socket Interface (VSI) is implemented as a hybrid interface at the application layer of GloMoSim such that it is not necessary to modify either the operating system or the operational applications to retrieve live traffic data. It emulates the socket interface supported by the operating system and listens on several ports to send (receive) data streams to (from) the operational applications. Its functionality is very similar to proxy servers, and thus it can support most of the TCP applications. An alternative to this implementation is to build the hybrid interface at a lower layer and use PCAP packet capture libraries, but it has to response to the ARP requests to trap packets, which is complex and may cause portability problems. The socket emulation is simple and enough for most applications commonly used in real life.

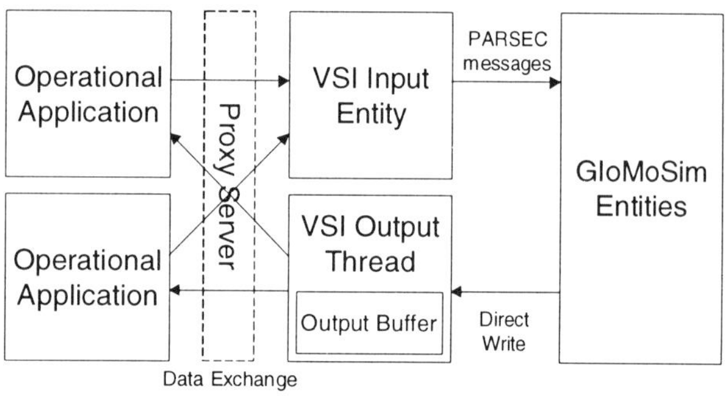

Figure 1: Virtual Socket Interface

The implementation of VSI together with GloMoSim is depicted in Figure 1. In order for VSI to be operated separately from both GloMoSim entities (simulated components) and operational applications (physical components), it is comprised of one PARSEC entity (VSI physical input entity) and one non-PARSEC thread (VSI physical output thread). The VSI input entity receives data streams from the operational applications, and sends PARSEC messages timestamped with the current wall clock time to GloMoSim. The VSI output thread monitors its output buffer and gives the operational applications any data in messages from GloMoSim whose timestamps are equal to the current wall clock time. Note that GloMoSim writes messages on the output buffer directly without using the PARSEC mechanism, as the VSI output thread would not otherwise see messages until its simulation clock becomes greater than or equal to their timestamps. The VSI output thread does not rely on a simulation clock and delivers messages to the operational applications by comparing the current wall clock time and timestamps of messages. If a message whose timestamp is in the past is written on the buffer, the VSI output thread regards that GloMoSim missed the deadline for the message. It calculates the miss rate as the number of messages that missed their deadlines divided by the number of total messages written on its output buffer.

2.3. Synchronization protocol for the parallel execution of simulated components

A simple synchronous protocol [25], which is referred to as the synchronous protocol henceforth, is used for all the experiments that employ parallel execution of simulated components in this paper. It uses barriers to compute T_W, a lower bound on the timestamp of messages sent by any entity to another in future. T_W is calculated as the minimum of T_{WI} $(I = 1, \ldots, N)$ for all the entities in the simulation, and T_{WI} is computed as the earliest timestamp of messages in the Ith entity plus its *lookahead*. *Lookahead* of an entity is defined as the duration for which it will not send any messages to its outgoing links, and its value can greatly affect the parallel simulation performance. After T_W is calculated, each entity processes all the events with timestamps earlier than T_W without any further synchronization because no messages with timestamps earlier than T_W will be sent out. The protocol repeats this operation to proceed the simulation, and its execution is very synchronous because it requires a barrier for each operation. As this synchronous protocol does not utilize the topological information of entities, its performance is not affected by the connectivity of LPs, which is very suited for mobile wireless network simulations.

In the context of hybrid component networks, the lookahead values of the operational applications are 0 for most cases because they may unpredictably generate data at any time. The VSI input entity can have lookahead whose value represents the data processing time at the simulated mobile node, but such lookahead is not enough to keep up with the real time as the detailed simulation requires the same amount of data processing (real) time in the real system. We discuss how the VSI input entity can further improve its lookahead in the next subsection. GloMoSim needs to exploit enough lookahead from the simulated network to meet the deadlines of its outgoing messages to the VSI output thread.

2.4. Exploiting lookahead from VSI

Assuming that the VSI input entity has little lookahead, its simulation clock is bounded by the wall clock time, as the operational applications may generate data at any time. This may result in little tolerance of simulation performance against burst traffic from the operational applications, as such traffic creates numerous events within a small time window during which the simulation may not keep up with the real time. However, as the maximum throughput of each traffic flow is limited by the link capacity, such burst traffic given by the application can not go out of the mobile node immediately, and need to stay in its data buffer. In other words, even if the VSI input entity artificially delays the delivery of application data to GloMoSim, the data stream transmitted to the air by the mobile node will not change as long as its data buffer does not become empty. This allows the VSI input entity to have extra lookahead and go ahead of the real time without changing the simulation results. Figure 2 shows an example of such cases. In the figure, arrows indicate the communication between the VSI input entity and GloMoSim. Since the VSI input entity sends GloMoSim messages with timestamps equal to the current wall clock time, GloMoSim needs to run a little behind of the VSI input entity. However, if GloMoSim receives enough data from the VSI physical input entity to keep its data buffer not empty until simulation clock of T_2, it tells VSI that timestamps attached to the messages will not change the simulation until T_2. VSI can then simply advance its simulation clock by $(T_2 - T_1)$, and send subsequent messages to GloMoSim with timestamps of T_2, which is greater than the wall clock time. Consequently, GloMoSim can also run ahead of the real time if its execution is fast enough, creating a simulation time cushion for the impact of burst traffic. Figure 3 depicts the interface between the VSI physical input entity and GloMoSim in more detail. We call this lookahead *real time lookahead* to distinguish with lookahead exploited among the simulated components, and show its impact on the performance of hybrid component networks in Section 4.

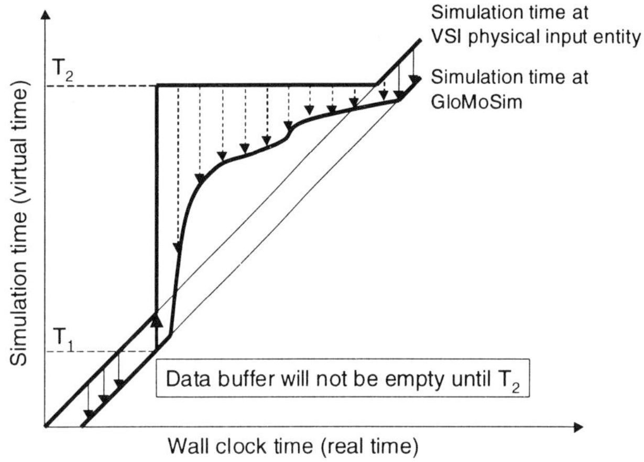

Figure 2: Simulation going ahead of the real time

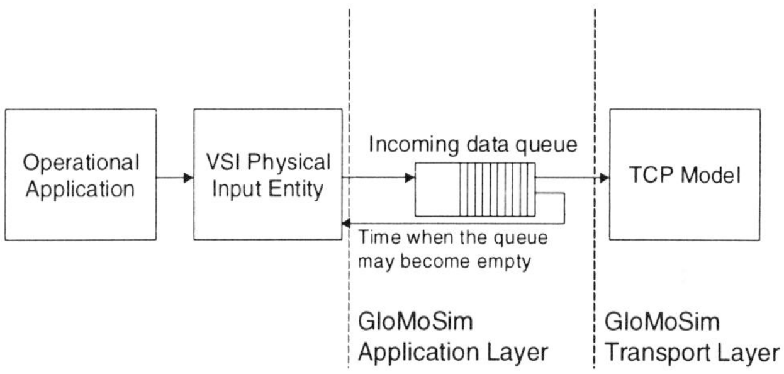

Figure 3: Control flows between VSI and GloMoSim

3. Validation of hybrid component networks

This section validates our hybrid component networks against real wireless networks. We used FTP as the operational application in this study for its traffic consistency, and both hybrid component networks and real wireless networks use the identical FTP servers (War FTP daemon) and FTP clients (Cute FTP). The real wireless networks are configured with up to 4 laptops (128MB memory, 500MHz Intel Celeron running Windows NT) with a Lucent WaveLAN card [24], which runs the IEEE 802.11 DCF (Distribution Coordination Function) MAC (Medium Access Control) protocol with the IEEE 802.11b DSSS (Direct Sequence Spread Spectrum) PHY (physical layer). In hybrid component networks, GloMoSim models are configured based on the real wireless networks except that its TCP model is taken from the FreeBSD operating system, although both FreeBSD and Windows NT TCP protocols stem from the same flavor of TCP.

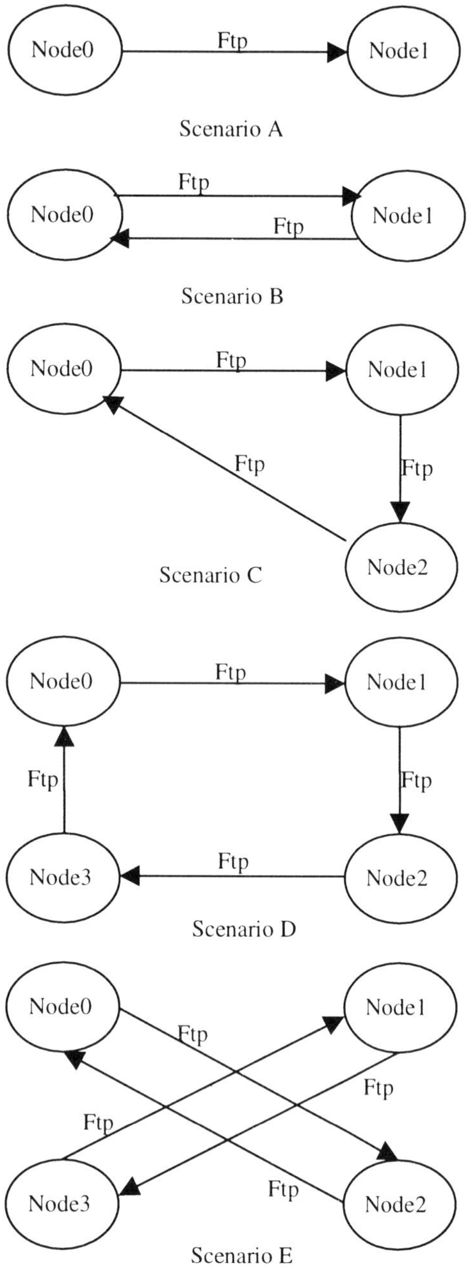

Figure 4: TCP traffic flows among network nodes in each scenario

Figure 4 depicts the FTP sessions given to each of five scenarios used in this section. The number of nodes and the complexity of the traffic patterns increase from Scenario A to Scenario E. All FTP sessions begin at the same time and continue until each session finishes transferring a 10Mbyte file. We use the average throughput of all the TCP sessions as the primary metric for the comparison.

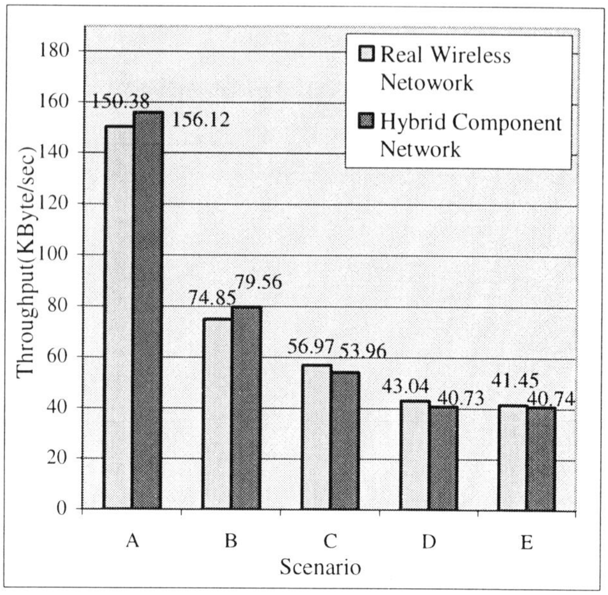

Figure 5: Average TCP throughput measured from real and hybrid networks

Figure 5 shows the average throughput yielded by the real wireless network and the hybrid component network for each scenario. In the hybrid component networks, we run GloMoSim sequentially for all the scenarios, as their network sizes are relatively small. Please note, however, that the hybrid component network utilizes three processors of the Sun Enterprise 6500 for the sequential execution of GloMoSim, VSI physical input entity and VSI physical output thread. This eliminates any inaccuracies incurred by the scheduling overheads of multiple processes (or threads) on a single processor, which other sequential emulation tools cannot avoid. As shown in the figure, both hybrid component and real networks yielded almost the same throughput for each scenario, indicating that the wireless networks simulated by GloMoSim generate the same output as the real wireless networks for the same input. We also made sure that other metrics including packet loss rates in the real wireless network and the hybrid component network are the same for each scenario, and miss rates discussed in detail in the next section are less than 4% for all the scenarios in this section.

4. The effects of parallel simulation and lookahead

In this section, we evaluate the effects of parallel simulation as well as real time lookahead on the performance of hybrid component networks using a typical scenario for ad hoc wireless networks. Seventy nodes are spread over a 2000 × 1750 m flat terrain whose path loss characteristic is defined as the two-ray model [23]. Each node moves based on the random waypoint mobility model [22], in which each node chooses a random location on the terrain and heads towards there directly with a constant moving speed chosen between 0 and 20 m/s. Once the node arrives at the destination, it stays there for 10s and starts moving towards a new destination. All the nodes run the same protocol models, e.g., the IEEE 802.11 DSSS PHY, DCF MAC, IP, AODV [16][17][22] and FreeBSD TCP models. AODV (Ad-hoc On-Demand Distance Vector) routing protocol is a reactive protocol whose route discovery process is initiated on demand. Two nodes are selected prior to the simulation as a CBR (Constant Bit Rate) server and a CBR client, both of which are the operational applications and communicate with each other via VSI. The CBR server generates 1024 byte data packets to its client with a time interval specified in the scenario. We change the traffic rate of the CBR session from 1 pps (packet per second) up to 200 pps to control the amount of traffic given to the simulated network. Please note that the maximum data throughput for the IEEE 802.11 radio card (2 Mbps) with the RTS / CTS option is less than 200k bytes per second, thus the buffer of the CBR server never becomes empty when the traffic rate is 200 pps. Each case is run for five minutes and the miss rates are measured as the primary metric to evaluate the accuracy of the hybrid component networks. The miss rate is the total number of packets that missed the deadlines divided by the total number of packets output to the operational applications as defined in Section 2.2, and we assume that the execution with a miss rate of less than 10% can yield reasonably accurate results in this study.

Figure 6 shows the miss rates measured by the VSI output thread with varied CBR traffic flow given to the sequential execution of GloMoSim. Two lines in the chart show the miss rates of executions with and without real time lookahead respectively. Note that the real time lookahead is the ability of VSI to advance its simulation clock ahead of the real time, thus even the sequential execution of GloMoSim should be able to benefit from the real time lookahead for cases with heavy traffic. However, as shown in the figure, the miss rates are too high to yield the accurate results for all the cases regardless of the use of real time lookahead, while all the cases took only a little more than the real time (300 to 305 seconds). Therefore, GloMoSim did not miss the deadlines by much, but it ran a little too behind of real time to schedule outgoing messages to the operational application at right wall clock times. We found that the miss rate of GloMoSim with 1 pps of CBR traffic is less than 4.0% if there is no mobility in the scenario, and the high miss rates in Figure 6 are mostly due to a number of events to simulate the link breaks caused by the mobility and the route discovery processes of AODV followed to those breaks. Once GloMoSim runs behind of real time due to such events incurred by the mobility and the route discovery, it needs to run faster than the real time to keep up with the real time, which turned out to be very hard in this scenario.

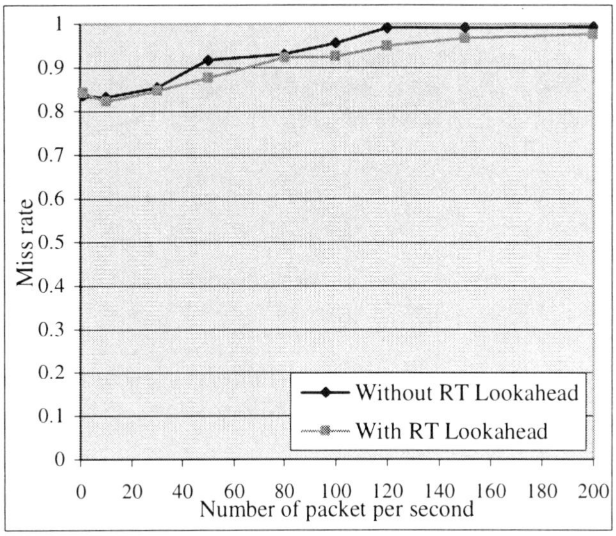

Figure 6: Miss rates measured by the VSI output thread with the sequential executions of GloMoSim

Figure 7 demonstrates how these high miss rates are reduced by the parallel execution of GloMoSim. The CBR traffic given to the network is set to 100 pps in this experiment. As shown in the figure, GloMoSim can greatly reduce the miss rates with more processors, from 96% to 24% with 8 processors for executions without real time lookahead, and from 92% to 8% with 8 processors with the real time lookahead. Figure 8 shows the miss rates measured by the VSI output thread for the same configurations as shown in Figure 6, except that GloMoSim utilizes 8 processors in its execution. In the figure, although the parallel executions of GloMoSim could not keep the miss rates low enough for cases with more than 100 pps, its miss rates are significantly lower compared to those in Figure 6. Moreover, the effects of real time lookahead are also larger when 8 processors are used, reducing the miss rates by 15 to 20% for cases with 50 to 120 pps. When its effects are evaluated at the 10% miss rate line, GloMoSim is capable of executing 100 pps CBR traffic, up from 30 pps without the real time lookahead. These results demonstrate the significance of both parallel execution of simulated components and use of real time lookahead for the hybrid component networks.

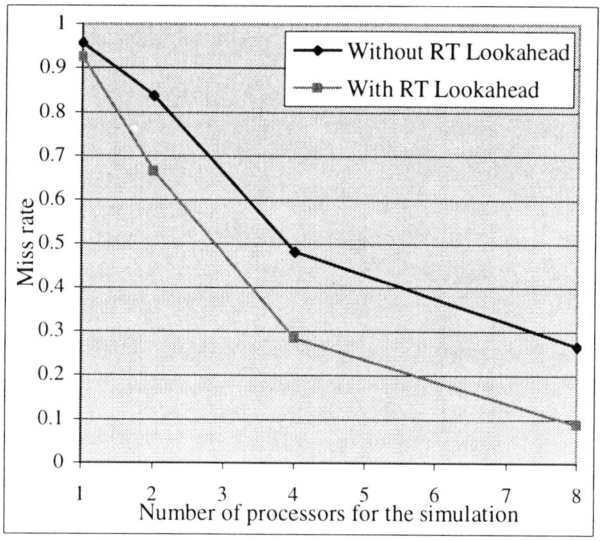

Figure 7: Reduction of miss rates with multiple processors for the GloMoSim execution

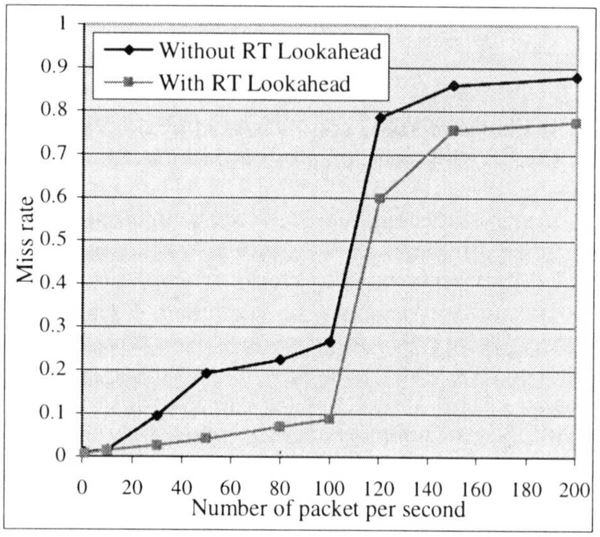

Figure 8: Miss rates measured by the VSI output thread with the parallel executions of GloMoSim (8 processors)

The last figure (Figure 9) shows how long VSI could benefit from the real time lookahead in this study. Its y-axis indicates the duration for which VSI ran ahead of the real time in their five-minute executions. Clearly, VSI could run ahead of the real time longer for heavier CBR traffic, but this does not necessarily mean that GloMoSim can yield lower miss rates for its outgoing messages for heavy traffic cases. Since GloMoSim needs to process more number of events for heavier traffic, it may not be able to run faster than the real time even if VSI eliminate the upper bound on the simulation clock for a long time. For instance, VSI ran ahead of the real time for about 40 % of the entire execution time for GloMoSim with 8 processors for cases with 80 to 200 pps, but miss rates of GloMoSim for the CBR traffic of more than 100 pps are very high as shown in Figure 8.

In all these experiments, we disregard how much GloMoSim missed the deadlines. However, the metric of miss rate seems too sensitive as even an outgoing message with a slight delay is counted as one miss. For more detailed evaluation of hybrid component networks, we need to measure how much each outgoing message is missed its deadline, which is one of our future work.

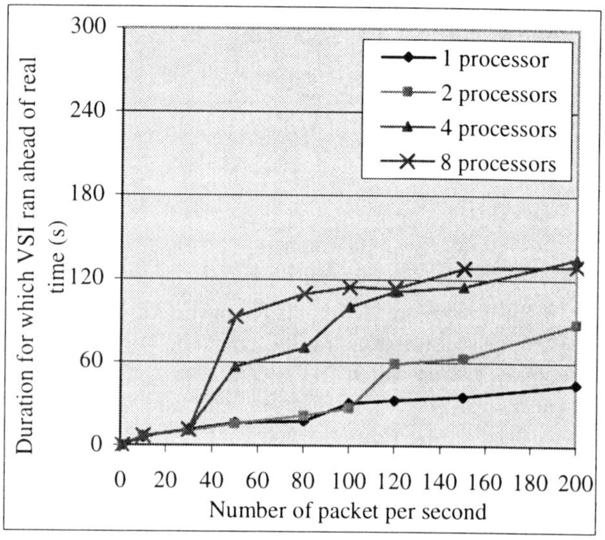

Figure 9: Duration for which VSI ran ahead of real time

5. Related work

In the networking community, hybrid component networks have been used often with sequential simulation, and it is primarily referred to as network emulation. Major emulation tools found in the past include Hitbox [5], NistNet [6], DelayLine [7], Trace-based network emulation [8], ns-2 emulator [2], and IP-TNE [9]. IP-TNE is the only network emulator that uses parallel simulation techniques, and it emulates interactions between real IP packets generated by external sources and IP packets generated within the parallel network simulator. It uses a channel based conservative (implicit null message) synchronization protocol in its simulation kernel with a task scheduler to meet the deadlines for messages going out of the simulator. Since the study in [9] only provides preliminary results, the effectiveness of parallel simulation techniques implemented with IP-TNE is not very clear. The module that interfaces physical and simulated components is implemented at the IP network layer, which may limit the portability of this work. Both IP-TNE and our work use the conservative approach for the synchronization of multiple simulated components, and the primary difference between the two can be found in the exploitation of lookahead.

6. Conclusions

In this paper, we have presented the performance of hybrid component networks with operational TCP applications and GloMoSim. The VSI has been implemented as the hybrid interface between the operational TCP applications and GloMoSim. We introduce the notion of "real time lookahead," which allows the simulation clock of GloMoSim to advance ahead of the real time without deteriorating the results yielded by the hybrid component networks. The experimental results have shown that both parallel simulation and real time lookahead can enhance the capability of the hybrid component networks. Future work related to the topics of this paper include the further evaluation of the hybrid component networks with parallel simulation techniques using more elaborated evaluation metrics, and the practical use of hybrid component networks for the development of mobile wireless network protocols.

7. Acknowledgements

This research was partially supported by the US Department of Defense / DARPA under Contract N66001-00-1-8937 "Maya: Next Generation Performance Prediction Tools for Global Networks." We would like to thank Dr. Daniel J. Valentino and Maroon Tabbal for their assistance and the use of the Advanced Research Computing (ARC) Facility in the UCLA School of Medicine.

References

[1] L. Bajaj, M. Takai, R. Ahuja, K. Tang, R. Bagrodia, and M. Gerla, "GloMoSim: A Scalable Network Simulation Environment", Technical Report, UCLA Computer Science Department-990027.

[2] S. McCanne and S. Floyd, UCB/LBNL/VINT Network Simulator – NS (version 2), http://www-mash.cs.berkeley.edu/ns/.

[3] H. Akhtar, "An Overview of Some Network Modeling, Simulation, and Performance Analysis Tools, " Proceedings of 2nd IEEE Symposium on Computers and Communications, 1997.

[4] R. Bagrodia, R. Meyer et al., "PARSEC: A Parallel Simulation Environment for Complex Systems". IEEE Computer, October 1998.

[5] J. S. Ahn, P. B. Danzig, Z. Liu, and L. Yan, "Evaluation of TCP Vegas: Emulation and Experiment", Proceedings of ACM SIGCOMM'95, BOSTON 1995.

[6] NIST Advanced Network Technologies Division. NIST Net home page, 1999. http://www.antd.nist.gov/itg/nistnet/.

[7] D. B. Ingham, and G. D Parrington, "Delayline: A Wide-Area Network Emulation Tool", Computing Systems, vol. 7, no. 3, 1994.

[8] B. D. Noble, M. Satyanarayanan, G. T. Nguyen,, R. H. Katz, "Trace-Based Mobile Network Emulation," Proceedings of ACM SIGCOMM'97, Cannes, France, September , 1997.

[9] R. Simmonds, R. Bradford and B. Unger, "Applying Parallel Discrete Event Simulation to Network Emulation", Proceedings of the 14th workshop on Parallel and Distributed Simulation (PADS), Bologna, Italy, May 2000.

[10] N. Davies, G. S. Blair, K. Cheverst, and A. Friday, "A Network Emulator to Support the Development of adaptive applications", In Proceedings of the 2nd USENIX Symposium on Mobile and Location Independent Computing, April 10-11, 1995.

[11] B. Tuch, "Development of WaveLAN, and ISM band wireless LAN.", AT&T Technical Journal, vol. 72, no. 4, 7-8 1993.

[12] R. M. Fujimoto, "Parallel Discrete Event Simulation", ACM Communications, Volume 33, Issue 10, p30-35, 1990.

[13] J. Broch, D. A. Maltz, D. B. Johnson, Y.-C. Hu, and J. Jetcheva, "A Performance Comparison of Multi-Hop Wireless Ad Hoc Nework Routing Protocols," In Proceedings of ACM/IEEE MOBICOM'98, Dallas, TX, Oct 1998.

[14] D. B. Johnson, and D. A.Maltz, "Dynamic Source routing in Ad Hoc Wireless Networks", In Mobile Computing, edited by Tomasz Imielinski and Hank Korth, Chapter 5, pages 153-181, Kluwer Academic Publishers, 1996.

[15] J. Broch, D. B. Johnson, D. A. Maltz, "The Dynamic Source Routing Protocol for Mobile Ad Hoc Networks", Internet-Draft, draft-ietf-manet-dsr-03.txt, Oct. 1999.

[16] C. E. Perkins and E. M. Royer, "Ad-hoc On-Demand Distance Vector Routing", In WMSCA'99, New Orleans, Louisiana.

[17] C. E. Perkins, S. R. Das, "Ad Hoc On-Demand Distance Vector (AODV) Routing", Internet-Draft, draft-ietf-manet-aodv-05.txt, March 2000.

[18] A. Iwata, C.-C Chiang, G. Pei, M. Gerla, and T.-W. Chen, "Scalable Routing Strategies for Ad hoc Wireless Networks", IEEE Journal on Selected Areas in Communications, Special Issue on Ad-Hoc Networks, Aug. 1999.

[19] WinDump: tcpdump for Windows, http://netgroup-serv.polito.it/windump/.

[20] Tcptrace. http://jarok.cs.ohiou.edu/software/tcptrace/tcptrace.html/.

[21] G. R. Wright, and W. R. Stevens, "TCP/IP Illustrated, Volume 2: The Implementation.", Addison-Wesley, Reading, Massachusetts, 1995

[22] J. Broch, D.A. Maltz, D.B. Johnson, Y. Hu and J. Jetcheva, "A Performance Comparison of Multi-Hop Wireless Ad Hoc Network Routing Protocols," MobiCom'98, Oct.25-30, 1998.

[23] T. Rappaport, "Wireless Communications: Principles & Practice," Prentice Hall, 1996.

[24] A. Kamerman and L. Monteban, "WaveLAN-II: a High-Performance Wireless LAN for the Unlicensed Band," Bell Labs Technical Journal, pp. 118 – 133, Summer 1997.

[25] R. Fujimoto, "Parallel and Distributed Simulation Systems," Wiley-Interscience, December 1999.

Lock-free Scheduling of Logical Processes in Parallel Simulation *

Jason Liu, David M. Nicol, and King Tan
Department of Computer Science
Dartmouth College
Hanover, New Hampshire 03755
{jasonliu,nicol,kytan}@cs.dartmouth.edu

Abstract

With fixed lookahead information in a simulation model, the overhead of asynchronous conservative parallel simulation lies in the mechanism used for propagating time updates in order for logical processes to safely advance their local simulation clocks. Studies have shown that a good scheduling algorithm should preferentially schedule processes containing events on the critical path. This paper introduces a lock-free algorithm for scheduling logical processes in conservative parallel discrete-event simulation on shared-memory multiprocessor machines. The algorithm uses fetch&add operations that help avoid inefficiencies associated with using locks. The lock-free algorithm is robust. Experiments show that, compared with the scheduling algorithm using locks, the lock-free algorithm exhibits better performance when the number of logical processes assigned to each processor is small or when the workload becomes significant. In models with large number of logical processes, our algorithm shows only modest increase in execution time due to the overhead in the algorithm for extra bookkeeping.

1. Introduction

Parallel discrete-event simulation [2] has been proven to be a viable approach for simulations of a broad range of real-world applications. It is especially suitable for large-scale simulations that both require long execution time and consume vast memory space. However, the success didn't bring widespread acceptance of parallel simulation due to inherent complications. The difficulty of parallelizing discrete-event simulation is to preserve causality constraints among events. An event with smallest timestamp has the potential to change the state of the simulation and therefore affect events that happen later in simulation time. This restrictive cause-and-effect relationship can be partially relaxed by partitioning the application into logical processes (LPs), where events on one LP can only be allowed to affect the state of that LP. State modification of other LPs can only be achieved by delivering events (sometimes called messages) to those LPs. Partitioning application into logical processes effectively separates the global event-list in a sequential simulation into multiple event-lists, one for each LP. The problem of parallelizing the simulation boils down to maintaining local causality constraints on each LP. That is, an LP only needs to decide whether to process the smallest event on its local event-list without introducing causality errors. Facing with the potential threat that other LPs would ship events with smaller timestamps to an LP, two major approaches separate parallel discrete-event simulation research: conservative and optimistic schemes. Conservative simulation [1] strictly prohibits out-of-order execution of events. The smallest local event cannot be processed unless it is guaranteed that there is absolutely no possibility having another event with smaller timestamp to arrive later at this LP. Optimistic simulation [5] allows events to be processed out of order. Once a causality error is detected, that is, when a "straggler" event with smaller timestamp later arrives at the LP, the simulation is rolled back to correct and recover from such error.

Our research focuses on simulation of large-scale communication networks. Since the memory utilization is considered essential in our application, we favor conservative simulation as it usually requires smaller memory footprint than most of its optimistic counterparts. It is well-known that lookahead in the simulation model is essential to the performance of conservative simulation. Lookahead is the ability to predict what will happen or will not happen in the simulated future. In loose terms, lookahead implies inherent asynchrony in the simulation model. With positive lookahead, an LP can process events and advance its local simulation clock well ahead of its neighbors. Extensive

*This work is supported in part by DARPA Contract N66001-96-C-8530, NSF Grant ANI-98 08964, NSF Grant EIA-98-02068, and Dept. Of Justice Contract 2000-CX-K001

0-7695-1104-X/01 $10.00 © 2001 IEEE

studies have been undertaken to illustrate the importance in extrapolating lookahead from the simulation model. In [11], Nicol gave a classification of lookahead based on different levels of knowledge extracted from simulation models. The use of different dimensions of lookahead underscores conservative synchronization protocols being developed so far. However, given that the lookahead is fixed in a simulation model, the overhead lies in the mechanism used for propagating the lookahead information in order for LPs to safely advance their local simulation clocks.

In this paper, we focuses on scheduling problems where many logical processes may be assigned to a processor. Our asynchronous algorithm extends the CMB algorithm [1] and applies to shared-memory multiprocessor machines, where, instead of sending NULL messages, each processor has an LP scheduler in charge of choosing the next LP ready for execution. It is well understood that the execution time of a conservative simulation is constrained by its critical path [4]. The optimal scheduling policy would choose the LP containing the event on the critical path. As pointed out by [12], it is however impractical to dynamically identify the event or logical process on the critical path. Yet several heuristics can be used to preferentially schedule LPs more likely on the critical path [14, 9]. In [12], the authors investigated the impact of various scheduling policies on the performance of conservative simulation.

To determine the safe time of an LP and ensure that an LP is scheduled as soon as it's ready, the scheduler needs to access variables potentially shared by different processors. A natural approach would be to use locks for mutual exclusion. In this traditional approach, shared objects are handled within critical sections to protect from simultaneous access by multiple processes. Mutual exclusion, however, has its disadvantage. A slow process holding a lock may deter the access of fast processes and, therefore, form a bottleneck that degrades the performance of the entire system. Moreover, the cost associated with gaining access to locks may impose a considerable overhead to applications that are sensitive to low-level synchronizations. Inter-processor locks are expensive on shared memory multiprocessor machines. As in most cases, locks are implemented as busy-waiting. Not only it means a waste of CPU cycles, but also it becomes taxing on system traffic because of cache invalidations. Locks can also give rise to problems like priority inversion and deadlock. In fault tolerance studies, the use of locks is well-known to cause problems when a process in a critical section fails to relinquish the lock.

To avoid some of these problems, we use a lock-free asynchronous conservative parallel synchronization algorithm that is based on the *fetch&add* primitive to schedule logical processes. The algorithm is designed to avoid locks when calculating the safe time of an LP. The concept of lock-freedom, along with the concept of wait-freedom, comes from research in fault tolerant distributed computing. Informally, lock-free synchronization refers to the property that some operations on the shared object must complete in a finite number of steps. That is, no process can block the system of further operations to the shared object. It is still possible that starvation may happen, where some process fails to access the shared object, as it is constantly preempted by other faster processes. A stronger criterion called wait-free synchronization dictates that every process is guaranteed to complete operations in a finite number of steps [3]. As we are more concerned with the efficiency of synchronization algorithms, wait-freedom is often too expensive to implement for synchronization. On the other hand, lock-free algorithms with careful implementation can be quite efficient [13]. In [8], the authors described an algorithm for constructing busy-wait synchronization that aims to reduce lock contentions.

Particularly, in our model of conservative parallel simulation, since the scheduler needs a snapshot of all incoming channels of an LP to calculate its safe time, the granularity of locks is larger than necessary and therefore may deter concurrency. Such problems become obvious when the number of logical processes per processor is small. Our lock-free algorithm avoids the problem and experiments show the algorithm has definitively better performance compared to the algorithm using locks. Moreover, since an LP may be waiting for more than one predecessor LP to advance its simulation clock, to determine which of the predecessor LPs is really responsible for scheduling the LP, a naive approach would involve unnecessary context switches by allowing all those predecessor LPs to take turns scheduling the LP. The lock-free algorithm can effectively avoid unnecessary context switches when dealing with critical channels.

The lock-free algorithm does not address all problems that come with using locks. We note that the use of *fetch&add* primitive still relies on mutual exclusion, albeit supported by hardware. On some shared memory machines, *fetch&add* primitive is not supported by the machine instruction set and, instead, it can only be emulated using other primitives. It should be noted, however, that it uses locks in a much smaller granularity. The lock-free algorithm in this case involves critical sections that are only used to enforce the atomic actions specified by the primitive. On the other hand, other algorithms with locks may have critical sections as large as the entire event processing session.

The structure of the paper is as follows. Section 2 defines the parallel discrete-event simulation model and some of the basic terms we will use to describe the algorithm. Section 3 presents related work and underlines the contribution of our approach. The lock-free scheduling algorithm is described in detail in section 4 and its correctness proof is given in section 5. Experiments and results are shown in section 6.

Finally, section 7 gives our conclusions.

2. Model

The parallel discrete event simulation model is composed of a set of logical processes (i.e. LPs) connected by unidirectional channels through which messages are sent from sender LPs to receiver LPs. We assume that the topology of the graph does not change during simulation. Such a model can be represented as a directed graph, where the nodes in the graph represent the LPs and the edges represent channels that connect the corresponding LPs. Let t_i be the local simulation clock of LP_i. Define $\delta_{i,j} \geq 0$ to be the delay associated with the channel from LP_i to LP_j. Note that $\delta_{i,j}$ is a simple form of lookahead. The event sent from LP_i to LP_j at time τ will show up at time $\tau + \delta_{i,j}$ in LP_j's event-list. To avoid deadlock, we assume that the sum of the delays of edges along any cycle in the graph is strictly larger than zero. For LP_i, let $PRED(i)$ be the set of predecessor LPs of LP_i and let $SUCC(i)$ be the set of successor LPs of LP_i.

Let $T_{i,j}$ be the *channel time* from LP_i to LP_j. The channel time may be constantly updated by the source LP of the channel (i.e. LP_i) whenever the local simulation clock of LP_i is updated: $T_{i,j} = t_i + \delta_{i,j}$. It is understood that channel times may not be updated instantaneously. Therefore, at any time during simulation, we are only sure that $T_{i,j} \leq t_i + \delta_{i,j}$. Let H_i be the *safe time* of LP_i, defined as the latest simulation time up to which events in LP_i can be safely processed without introducing the risk of causality errors. It is guaranteed that no events with timestamp smaller than H_i will later arrive at LP_i. Theoretically, the safe time of LP_i can be derived at any time from a global snapshot of the simulation: $H_i = \min_{j \in PRED(i)}\{t_j + \delta_{j,i}\}$, where t_j is the current simulation time of LP_j at the snapshot. In our algorithm, LP_i only looks at the times of its incoming channels. We define $H'_i = \min_{j \in PRED(i)}\{T_{j,i}\}$ and say that LP_i is *ready* if and only if $t_i < H'_i$. In practice, it is unnecessary and too expensive to obtain a snapshot in order to compute the safe time. Instead, the algorithm only needs a lower bound of the true safe time, which we call *event execution horizon* and is denoted as h_i. It is obtained by traversing the incoming channels of LP_i and storing the minimum of current channel time $T_{j,i}$ in h_i. It is understood that the predecessor LP_j may not update $T_{j,i}$ promptly. However, this will only cause a smaller h_i to be calculated, since we are sure that $T_{j,i}$ is non-decreasing.

An LP scheduling algorithm is described informally as follows. When a ready LP_i is dispatched for execution, the h_i that it computes is sure to be greater than its local simulation clock t_i. All events within LP_i with timestamps smaller than h_i are then processed in timestamp order. During the process, new events may be generated. Events local to LP_i are inserted directly into the LP's event-list. External events are queued up in the output channels and will be later withdrawn by the destination LPs. Once all safe events in LP_i have been executed, LP_i must be suspended from execution. It is obvious that the safe time of LP_i is determined by the predecessor LP with the smallest channel time. The safe time of LP_i will not increase unless the predecessor LP with smallest channel time advances its local simulation clock. Borrowing terms from the literature, we call that LP with smallest channel time the *critical parent* of LP_i. The channel between LP_i and its critical parent is called *critical channel*. Note that there could be more than one critical parent of an LP at the same time; they all possess the smallest channel time. To advance the safe time of an LP, all its critical parents must advance their simulation clocks. When an LP is suspended from further execution, the dispatcher should be able to dispatch another ready LP for execution. We call such transition a *context switch*. The execution of an LP between two consecutive context switches is called an *execution session* or a *session* in short. The simulation ends when the timestamps of all LPs reach the predefined simulation end time $\mathcal{H}_T > 0$ or some other termination condition is satisfied.

3. Related Work

It is well-known that conservative parallel simulation cannot beat the critical path [4]. To make things worse, it is considered as impractical to identify and therefore schedule events on the critical path as it unfolds dynamically. However, many conservative scheduling algorithms take advantage of the notion and strive to schedule events that are more likely to be on the critical path.

Stepping up at a higher level, scheduling critical events can be approximated as scheduling critical LPs[1]. When a ready LP is scheduled for execution, the session continues until the local simulation clock reaches its safe time. The LP cannot continue until its critical parents advance the channel times. The problem then translates into an LP scheduling policy that can preferentially schedule LPs that contain critical events. Naroska and Schwiegelshohn's scheduling algorithm [9] gives priorities to logical processes that directly influence computations on other processors. The communication latency among processors with distributed memory is more likely to put events sent between them on the critical path. An empirical performance study of alternative LP

[1] The notion of execution session of an LP does not necessarily mean a session should always run to completion, that is, until the local simulation clock reaches its safe time. The next critical event might not be on the same LP. Here, the approximation suggests that LP context switches in most cases are more costly and therefore should be avoided whenever possible. Of course, critical path may not be determined dynamically in an obvious way.

scheduling policies is presented in [12]. The paper examined a number of heuristics that can be used to predict LPs on the critical path. They include scheduling LPs on the basis of LP's next event timestamp, safe time, or local simulation clock. While the paper showed that some heuristic is better than others, the authors pointed out that the benefit of the scheduling algorithms is sensitive to overheads, e.g. sorting cost.

In [14], the authors introduced a multi-level scheduling algorithm, called Critical Channel Traversing (CCT), that achieves efficiency in simulation with low granularity events. At highest level of scheduling, tasks (i.e. LP groups) are scheduled as a single entity from a central priority queue where tasks are placed in increasing timestamp order. Within a task, the scheduling algorithm preferentially chooses LPs with the largest number of events that are ready to process. The algorithm uses spin-locks to synchronize logical processes when accessing shared variables in channels. In order to show comparison to our algorithm, the pseudo-code of the CCT algorithm that deals with LP scheduling is listed as follows for easy reference later. Note that the algorithm uses spin-lock at line 15. Later in the experiment section, we will compare performance of the CCT algorithm with our lock-free algorithm.

CCT LP SCHEDULING ALGORITHM

1: $WT_i := \infty$
2: **foreach** incoming channel (j, i)
3:    $busy_{j,i} := 1$
4:    $critical_{j,i} := 0$
5:    **if** $T_{j,i} < WT_i$ **then**
6:       $WT_i := T_{j,i}$
7:       $Keep\_c\_id_i :=$ i
8: Process safe events in order
9: $t_i := WT_i$
10: $critical_{Keep\_c\_id_i, i} := 1$
11: **foreach** incoming channel (j, i)
12:    $busy_{j,i} := 0$
13: **foreach** outgoing channel (i, j)
14:    $T_{i,j} := t_i + \delta_{i,j}$
15:    **repeat until** $busy_{i,j} = 0$
16:    **if** $critical_{i,j}$ **then** unblock LP_j

It is worthwhile to point out that LP scheduling with execution session running as long as possible inherently admits that the overhead caused by context switching is non-trivial. Depending on the application, longer execution session (i.e. fewer context switches) does not necessarily mean more savings in synchronization of parallel simulation. However, from scheduling point of view, fewer context switches not only translates to better memory locality and higher cache utilization, but also it means less cost for sorting LPs in the ready queue. On the other hand, the real time delay associated with updating subsequent channel times may give rise to artificial blocking,where the successor LP is waiting for the channel time to be updated while the predecessor LP has advanced its local simulation clock. There is a tradeoff for the length of an execution session before the outgoing channel times should be updated. It hinges on the scheduling overhead. Our algorithm aims to reduce the overhead when scheduling logical processes without the use of mutual exclusive locks. As a design decision, the number of context switches can be also reduced by averting unnecessary context switches caused by the existence of multiple critical parents. The algorithm uses *fetch&add* primitive, which is explained next.

4. The Algorithm

4.1. Intuition

Our scheduling algorithm uses the *fetch&add* primitive. A *fetch&add* operation, *fetch&add*(loc, k) where loc is a memory location and k is an integer, is defined as follows: Let m be the value of loc immediately before the *fetch&add* operation. Then m is the value returned by the operation and $m + k$ is the new value of loc. While some shared-memory machines directly provide *fetch&add* primitive as a well-defined machine instruction, the operation can be easily implemented using other intrinsics. For example, the operation can be implemented using a sequence of load-linked and store-conditional instructions in a loop.

We now describe the intuition behind our algorithm. To achieve lock-free synchronization, we use tokens as a means of communication among LPs. When LP_i detects that its predecessor LP_k is a critical parent, LP_i *issues* a token for LP_k. When LP_k next advances the channel time $T_{k,i}$ (thus ensuring that LP_k is no longer a critical parent of LP_i), LP_k will *retrieve* the token. LP_k must then *return* the token to LP_i, thereby notifying LP_i that LP_k is no longer a critical parent. Since LP_i may have $u (u \geq 1)$ critical parents, LP_i is ready (i.e. $t_i < H_i'$) if and only if all u tokens issued by LP_i are returned. A counter CNT_i records the number of unreturned tokens issued by LP_i. When $CNT_i = 0$, then LP_i is ready, and should be unblocked and made available for dispatch. The description above is intentionally imprecise; the behavior of the algorithm is considerably more complex. We provide rigorous claims about our algorithm in the lemmas and theorems to follow.

We now describe the implementation of the tokens and CNT_i. When LP_i issues a token for LP_k, LP_i writes 0 to $TOK_{k,i}$. Both LP_k and LP_i may attempt to retrieve a token previously issued by LP_i. An LP attempts to retrieve a token from $TOK_{k,i}$ by executing *fetch&add*($TOK_{k,i}$, 1). If the value returned by this operation is 0, then the token is retrieved. Otherwise, no token has been retrieved. After a token has been issued and before the next token is issued, the first attempt to retrieve a token will succeed, and all subsequent attempts will fail. CNT_i is implemented as follows: LP_i periodically adds the number of recently issued tokens that LP_i expects to be returned, say x, to CNT_i by executing *fetch&add*(CNT_i, x). A predecessor of LP_i returns a token to LP_i by executing *fetch&add*(CNT_i, -1). If the new value of CNT_i after executing any of these *fetch&add* operations is 0, then all tokens issued by LP_i have been returned.

4.2. Description of the algorithm

<u>LOCK-FREE SCHEDULING ALGORITHM</u>

1: $N := 0$
2: Compute $h_i := \min_{k \in PRED(i)}\{T_{k,i}\}$
3: **if** $t_i = h_i$ **then goto** 12
4: Execute safe events in order
5: $t_i := h_i$
6: **foreach** $LP_k \in SUCC(i)$
7:    $T_{i,k} := t_i + \delta_{i,k}$
8:    x := *fetch&add*($TOK_{i,k}$, 1)
9:    **if** x = 0 **then**
10:       y := *fetch&add*(CNT_k, -1)
11:       **if** y = 1 **then** unblock LP_k
12: $m := 0$
13: **foreach** $LP_k \in PRED(i)$
14:    **if** $T_{k,i} = h_i$ **then**
15:       $TOK_{k,i} := 0$
16:       **if** $T_{k,i} = h_i$ **then**
17:          N++
18:          m++
19:       **else**
20:          x := *fetch&add*($TOK_{k,i}$, 1)
21:          **if** x $\neq$ 0 **then** N++
22: **if** $m = 0$ **then goto** 2
23: **else**
24:    x := *fetch&add*(CNT_i, N)
25:    **if** x = -N **then goto** 1

Our algorithm is executed by any LP_i when it is dispatched to start a new session. It makes no assumption about how the dispatcher selects an LP for execution from the pool of unblocked LPs. During the initialization of the simulation, each channel time $T_{i,j}$ is set to $\delta_{i,j}$. For each LP_i, the local simulation clock t_i is set to zero and the safe time is computed as $H_i = \min_{j \in PRED(i)}\{\delta_{j,i}\}$. If $H_i > 0$, then LP_i is entered into the pool of unblocked LPs available for dispatch. If $H_i = 0$, then LP_i is blocked. For all $j \in PRED(i)$, $TOK_{j,i}$ is set to zero if $\delta_{j,i} = 0$. Otherwise, it is set to one. CNT_i is set to the number of zero-delay predecessor channels.

We now describe our algorithm as executed by LP_i. N is used to temporarily store the number of tokens issued by LP_i before it is added to CNT_i. At the beginning of a session, N is initialized to 0. LP_i then computes h_i, the event execution horizon (line 2). During a session, line 2 may be executed more than once. Each execution of line 2 initiates a new *round*. Rounds are numbered consecutively $1, 2, \cdots$, regardless of whether a new session has started. A round in which $t_i = h_i$ at line 3 is called *futile at time* t_i. Otherwise it is called *non-futile*. If $t_i = h_i$ at line 3, then there are no safe events to be executed in the current round, and no updates to LP_i's successor channel times are necessary. Therefore, LP_i bypasses lines 4-11 that process events and updates the successor channel times. If $h_i > t_i$, safe events are executed in order, and t_i is advanced (lines 4,5). For each of its successor channels, LP_i updates the channel time $T_{i,k}$ (line 7) and attempts to retrieve a token (line 8). If a token is indeed retrieved (this event is called *token retrieval at channel time* $T_{i,k}$), it is returned to the token issuer LP_k by decrementing CNT_k by one (line 10). If the execution of line 10 by LP_i results in $CNT_k = 0$, LP_i signals the unblocking of the next available blocked LP_k. The execution of line 10 that results in $CNT_k = 0$ is called an *unblock* event. LP_i next scans its predecessor channel times to see if any such channel time $T_{k,i}$ equals h_i. If $T_{k,i} = h_i$ at both lines 14 and 16, then LP_k is a *critical parent* of LP_i. Otherwise LP_k is *non-critical*. If $T_{k,i} = h_i$ at line 14, LP_i issues a token for LP_k (line 15). LP_i then reads $T_{k,i}$ again. If $T_{k,i} = h_i$ at line 16, then the token issued at line 15 is considered *delivered* (to a critical parent) and N, an interim counter of the number of delivered tokens, is incremented accordingly. m is also incremented. A positive m reflects the presence of a critical parent. However, if $T_{k,i} = h_i$ at line 14 and $T_{k,i} > h_i$ at line 16 (LP_K is non-critical), then LP_i attempts to retrieve the token that it issued at line 15. If LP_i successfully retrieves the token, then the token is not delivered. Otherwise it is considered *delivered* (to a non-critical parent). N is incremented (line 21) to reflect token delivery to a non-critical parent. We observe that a token delivered to a non-critical parent LP_k is known to have been retrieved by LP_k and will eventually be returned (i.e. CNT_i will eventually be decremented by LP_k).

At line 22, $m \neq 0$ if and only if there is a critical parent. If $m = 0$ at line 22, we call the current round *green*. When the current round is green, LP_i proceeds to the next round, starting at line 2 (hence not changing N). t_i is certain to advance in a round following a green round. If $m > 0$ at line 22, we call the current round *red*. In this case, LP_i adds N to CNT_i. If the resulting $CNT_i = 0$, then LP_i proceeds to the next round, starting at line 1 (thus setting N to 0). Such a red round is called *red-go*. If the resulting $CNT_i \neq 0$, then LP_i becomes blocked. Such a red round is called *red-stop*. The execution of line 24 is called a *boost* event. A boost event occurs only during a red round. A boost event is called *red-go* (*red-stop*) if it occurs during a red-go (red-stop) round. A blocked LP becomes unblocked (available to be dispatched to execute a new session) whenever there is an unexpended unblock signal (generated by an unblock event). (An unblock signal is expended if it has been used to unblock an LP.)

4.3. Empirical Considerations

As we mentioned earlier, the real time delay associated with updating subsequent channel times may give rise to artificial blocking. The tradeoff between reducing the number of context switches and increasing channel updates is balanced on the total overhead and is beyond the scope of this paper. In Section 4.2, for the sake of easy exposition, we showed that the algorithm processes all safe events up to the measured event horizon (at line 4) before updating subsequent channel times and then unblocking successor LPs (from line 6 to 11). In practice, the two steps can be interwoven.

Source LPs have no incoming channels and their event horizon will be infinite. Without proper flow control mechanism, they will run to completion in a single session. Sometimes this will create problems as generated events could exhaust memory. In our implementation, two sets of flow control mechanisms are used. The user can define a time period in which source LPs must reschedule themselves. Or, the user can set a memory threshold value for each execution session. When the generated events cause the memory usage above the threshold, LPs must reschedule themselves. A combination of both schemes can be also used. Flow control is extremely important especially when memory is tight for large-scale simulations. By no means our schemes reached total satisfaction. It warrants further study.

A problem with real-world *fetch&add* primitive is that it may wrap around since *fetch&add* operates on integer values. This is not a major concern in practice. Nonetheless, the problem can be detrimental if it happens in extreme cases. Here we present a simple solution for our algorithm. To obtain token (at line 8 and 20), we can instead use atomic swap to exchange values between TOK and one. Atomic swap is either provided as an machine instruction or can be easily implemented using other primitives. The range of values for CNT_i is dictated by the variable N. An additional condition can be added to line 22 so that when N is greater than certain threshold, the control will branch to line 24 and bring CNT_i back to normal range.

It should be noted that access to channel time $T_{i,j}$ must be sequentially consistent. This could be a problem if the simulator chooses to use larger or complicated data types whose read and write are not guaranteed sequentially consistent [10]. A vast literature exists for constructing atomic registers in distributed computing. Note that even sequential consistency is too strong on some of the shared memory machines. In that case, special care must be taken to read and write operations. Memory barrier instructions ought to be used to guarantee sequential consistency.

The algorithm does not specify how those newly generated events in the execution session are delivered to their destinations. It is simple to insert local events directly into the local event-list. For remote events, they can be queued up in the channels, from which they will be withdrawn when the destination LPs reach their execution sessions. Synchronization of the access is needed. Also, the algorithm does not specify the mechanism to unblock subsequent LPs. The unblocked LP could get into the ready list of the current processor. In our implementation, we prefer making the LP stay at its original processor for the sake of locality. In that case, further synchronization is needed.

5. Correctness Proof

In this section, we outline a proof of correctness of the algorithm. A more detailed proof is given in [7]. Since the algorithm does not deviate from existing LP scheduling algorithms, we omit the proof that events are processed in timestamp order in LPs (i.e. local causality constraint). However, we need to show that the algorithm does terminate. Consider that the simulation starts at time zero and terminates when all LPs have reached a predefined simulation end time $\mathcal{H}_T > 0$. We need to prove that all LPs will reach time $\mathcal{H}_T$. We make two standard assumptions in the following proofs:

A1: The sum of the channel delays along any cycle is positive.

A2: The events of an LP within a finite time interval can be executed in finite time.

Lemma 1 *After a boost event (the execution of line 24) in round r, and before the beginning of round r + 1, CNT_i = (number of tokens delivered by LP_i)− (number of returned tokens) ≥ 0 and its value is non-increasing during the interval in question.*

Proof: N cumulates the number of delivered tokens (lines 17,21) until a boost event (in round s, say) when N is added to CNT_i. N is then reset to 0 at the beginning of round $s+1$. (s and $s+1$ may or may not belong to the same session.) Hence, during the interval in question (after the boost event in round r, and before the beginning of round $r+1$), the number of tokens delivered by LP_i (in all rounds through r) has been added to CNT_i. Further, each returned token has been accompanied by an execution of line 10 that decrements CNT_i by one. Therefore, CNT_i = (number of tokens delivered by LP_i)− (number of returned tokens) during the interval in question. Since each returned token has been previously delivered, $CNT_i \geq 0$. During the interval in question, CNT_i may only be changed by an execution of line 10, and not by a boost event, hence its value is non-increasing.

Lemma 2 *Let r be a red round of LP_i. At the beginning of round $r+1$, $CNT_i = 0$ and all tokens delivered by LP_i have been returned.*

Proof: If r is a red-go round, the proof follows from Lemma 1, since a red-go boost leaves $CNT_i = 0$. Now suppose r is a red-stop round. We observe that the value of CNT_i is increased by boost events (line 24). Red-stop boost leaves $CNT_i > 0$. Red-go boost leaves $CNT_i = 0$. The value of CNT_i may decrease or remain unchanged, but not increase, between two boost events. Recall that an unblock event is an execution of line 10 by a predecessor of LP_i that results in $CNT_i = 0$. Therefore there is at most one unblock event between a red-stop boost and the next boost. Also, there is no unblock event between a red-go boost and the next boost. Thus, at any time, (number of red-stop boosts) $\geq$ (number of unblock events).

At the beginning of round $r+1$, each of the past red-stop rounds of LP_i can be paired with an unblock signal (generated by an unblock event) that was expended on its behalf (since there is a next round that follows each of these red-stop rounds). Hence, (number of red-stop boosts) $\leq$ (number of unblock events). Therefore, (number of red-stop boosts) = (number of unblock events). This means that there is an unblock event that follows the red-stop boost in round r. By Lemma 1, this implies that at the beginning of round $r+1$, $CNT_i = 0$, and all tokens delivered by LP_i have been returned.

Theorem 5.1 *Let LP_i be ready and blocked, with $t_i \leq \mathcal{H}_{\mathcal{T}}$. Then LP_i is eventually unblocked.*

Proof: Let the last round LP_i executed before LP_i became blocked be round s. (Round s is therefore a red-stop round.) Let $r(r < s)$ be such that round r is red, rounds $r+1, r+2, \cdots, s-1$ are green. By Lemma 2, at the beginning of round $r+1$, all tokens delivered by LP_i in rounds $1, 2, \cdots, r$ have been returned. Therefore, after the red-stop boost in round s, CNT_i = (number of unreturned tokens delivered in rounds $r+1, r+2, \cdots, s$). We observe that: (1) All tokens delivered in a green round (hence, in rounds $r+1, r+2, \cdots, s-1$) are delivered to non-critical parents. (2) Any token delivered to a non-critical parent has already been retrieved by the parent (by the time LP_i executes line 20), and will eventually be returned. These observations imply that if all tokens delivered to critical parents in round s are eventually returned, then eventually $CNT_i = 0$.

By assumption, LP_i is ready. Thus, each critical parent LP_k has already updated channel time $T_{k,i}$ to some value $\tau_{k,i}(\tau_{k,i} > t_i)$. The attempt by LP_k to retrieve a token at channel time $\tau_{k,i}$ happens after LP_i issues a token for LP_k (at line 15) in round s. If the token has not been previously retrieved by LP_k, it certainly will be retrieved by the attempt of LP_k at channel time $\tau_{k,i}$. Therefore all tokens delivered to critical parents in round s are eventually returned. This means that eventually $CNT_i = 0$ and that there is an unblock event that causes LP_i to be unblocked.

Lemma 3 *There is some $\Delta > 0$ such that, for all LP_i, the value of t_i increases by at least Δ in every non-futile round.*

We omit the proof as the Lemma simply restates the boundedness property proven in [1].

Lemma 4 *For any time τ, there is at most one round of LP_i that is futile at τ.*

Proof: Let round r of LP_i be futile at τ. Round $r-1$ must be red. There must be a predecessor of LP_i, say LP_k, that is critical with channel time $T_{k,i} = \tau$ in both rounds $r-1, r$. We claim that event (E1) precedes (E2), which in turn precedes (E3), where:

E1: LP_i executes line 14 in round $r-1$, reading $T_{k,i} = \tau$.

E2: LP_k retrieves the token delivered in round $r-1$ by LP_i.

E3: LP_i executes line 2 in round r, reading $T_{k,i} = \tau$.

(E1) precedes (E2) because (E1) precedes LP_i issuing the token for LP_k at line 15 of round $r-1$, which in turn precedes (E2). (E2) precedes (E3) because, by Lemma 2, the token delivered for LP_k in round $r-1$ has been returned at the beginning of round r.

Let α be such that event (E2) is LP_k's retrieval of token at channel time $T_{k,i} = \alpha$. If $\alpha < \tau$, then at (E1), LP_i must read $T_{k,i} < \tau$ (because (E1) precedes (E2)). If $\alpha > \tau$, then at (E3), LP_i must read $T_{k,i} > \tau$ (because (E3) follows (E2)). Therefore, $\alpha = \tau$. We have shown that if round r is futile at τ, then there is a critical parent LP_k that retrieves a token delivered by LP_i (in round $r-1$) at channel time τ.

Suppose there are more than one futile rounds at τ. Without loss of generality, let rounds $r, r+1$ be futile at τ. By the same argument, there is a critical parent LP_k who retrieves at channel time $T_{k,i} = \tau$ both the token delivered in round $r-1$ and the token delivered in round r. However, from line 3, there is at most one token retrieval by LP_k at channel time τ. This contradiction proves that there is at most one round of LP_i that is futile at τ.

Lemma 5 *Any unblocked LP eventually gets dispatched and executes a new session.*

This can be derived from Lemma 3, Lemma 4, and Assumption (A2).

Theorem 5.2 *Eventually all* $t_i > \mathcal{H}_T$.

We omit the proof as it's a consequence of Lemma 5 and Theorem 5.1.

6. Experiments

We implemented both the critical channel scheduling part of the CCT algorithm and the lock-free algorithm. The algorithms are embedded as part of Dartmouth Scalable Simulation Framework (DaSSF) kernel [6]. **SSF** is a process-oriented, conservatively synchronized parallel simulator, designed for but not exclusively for simulating large scale multi-protocol communication networks. As part of the synchronization mechanism, the scheduling algorithms work with process dispatching unit in the simulator where ready LPs are queued for execution according to the timestamps of the earliest events.

All our experiments were conducted on a Sun Enterprise 6500 that has 14 400MHz UltraSPARC-II processors with a total of 7 GB memory. Each processor is equipped with 8 MB secondary external cache. The system chassis consists of 7 CPU/Memory boards interconnected by Gigaplane system bus that can deliver up to 2.88 GB/sec peak rate data transfer. The machine is running Solaris 7 operating system. Every data collected in the experiments is an average value from five simulation runs. Also, almost all samples, the 95% confidence interval is less than 5% around the sample mean[2].

The benchmark model for our experiments contains an array of interconnected logical processes (called *entities* in **SSF**). The simple model is chosen because we only want to exercise synchronization overhead. Also, we do not allow messages to be sent between LPs and we do not want more than one event in the local event-list. Delivering external events or queueing more than one event will exercise other parts of the simulator that we are not interested in this study.

Several parameters control the instantiation and deployment of the model onto the multiprocessor machine. The parameter N specifies the number of LPs in the model. These LPs are logically arranged as a ring. The connectivity of the LPs is specified by the parameter R, which is called *connection radius*. Each LP connects to its neighbors within a radius of R. That is, every LP connects to R LPs ahead of it and R LPs behind it in the ring structure, effectively making all connections bidirectional. Each channel has a constant delay of one unit simulation time. These N LPs will be deployed evenly among P processors upon execution: LP_i will be statically assigned to processor (i *mod* P). Each LP will have at most one local event in its event-list. Upon processing the event, another local event will be scheduled with an exponentially distributed increment into the future. The length of the interval is controlled by the parameter D, called *event density*. An event density of D means there is an average of D events to be processed per unit simulation time by the LP. Note that if D is zero, no event is processed, which means that there is no workload and the simulation engine only relies on the synchronization mechanism to schedule LPs in order to advance their local simulation clocks.

In the first experiment, we set the number of LPs in the model to be the same as the number of processors used to run the bench mark application; each processor has only one LP assigned to it. In all cases, the LP graphs in the model are fully connected, that is, $R = \lfloor N/2 \rfloor$. We varied the number of processors and the event density. Figure 1 shows the ratio of the execution time of our lock-free algorithm to that of the CCT algorithm. This experiment demonstrates relative synchronization effect of the two scheduling algorithms. It is clear from the figure that, as event density increases, the lock-free algorithm performs much better than CCT. The result is expected, since, in the CCT algorithm, every LP in the model tends to block all other LPs during its execution session. This justifies our concern about algorithms using locks in which the delay of a single process in a critical section forms a bottleneck of the entire system. With moderate to heavy workload in the model, this experiment actually represents the worst case scenario for the CCT algorithm, since all LPs are fully connected, that maximizes the blocking effect, and there is only one LP per processor, that effectively avoids the benefit of latency hiding that can be achieved by assigning multiple LPs to each processor. As the result, we observed savings in execution time by the lock-free algorithm as much as 48%. However, it must be pointed out that, in the case of no workload (i.e. D=0), the lock-free algorithm also experiences slowdown, especially when the number of processors is small. We conjecture that this is due to the extra complexity in the lock-free algorithm for manipulating variables used for bookkeeping.

Figure 2 shows the ratio of the number of context switches of the lock-free algorithm to that of the CCT algorithm. As expected, the lock-free algorithm reduces the number of context switches. The saving becomes more noticeable as the event density increases, that is, when the workload becomes significant. Close inspection on the raw data showed that, varying event density, the lock-free algorithm has roughly constant number of context switches, while the number increases for the CCT algorithm. We noticed that as the workload increases, the difference between

[2]Only a few data points have larger variations that required more than five runs.

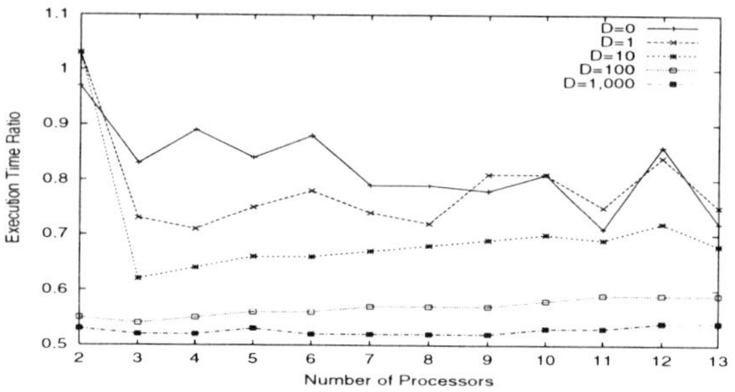

Figure 1. The ratio of execution time in the worst-case scenario of CCT.

fast and slow processors becomes obvious. Since it is more likely that LPs are each running at a different pace, there is a smaller chance of an LP having its critical channels updated when there are more than one critical parents present. These unnecessary context switches are less likely to be avoided by CCT and therefore result in smaller context switch ratios for the lock-free counterpart.

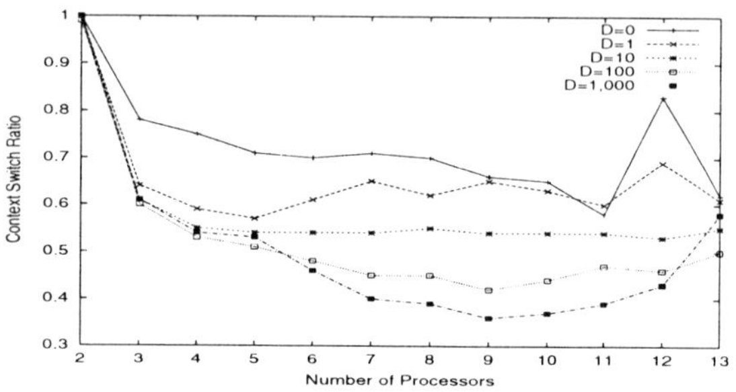

Figure 2. The ratio of the number of context switches in the worst-case scenario of CCT.

In the second experiment, we increased the number of logical processes assigned to each processor. As more LPs are ready for execution, blocking is less of a system bottleneck. In this experiment, we fixed the number of processors at 12 and increased the number of LPs assigned to each of the processors. The experiment was conducted in three settings with different event densities (0, 100, and 10,000) to represent different levels of workload. In each setting, we also changed the connection radius: one with connection radius being one, one with the radius being six, and one with fully connected LP graphs (denoted by infinite radius). The result is shown in Figure 3. The curves represent changing execution time ratio of our algorithm to the CCT algorithm. Note that the x-axes are in logarithmic scale.

In general, we see that the lock-free algorithm performs much better than CCT as the number of LPs per processor is small. As the number increases, the blocking effect in CCT is alleviated and the overhead of the lock-free algorithm due to extra complexity in bookkeeping begins to show. The overall performance caused by the overhead ranges from about 10% in light workload to less than 4% in moderate to relatively heavy workload when the number of LPs per processor is large. There are two important messages from the result. First, as the connectivity of the LP graph increases, the difference between the two algorithms increases. With small number of LPs per processor, the lock-free algorithm increases its performance advantage as the connectivity increases. This is because under higher connectivity, the slow process in the CCT algorithm is able to block more of its neighbors and further slow down the system. On the other hand, with large number of LPs per processor, the opposite seems to be true where the lock-free algorithm gets slower for large number of connections in the LP graph. This is the result of increasing overhead of our algorithm. Our algorithm requires access to many variables (both shared and private) to help avoid unnecessary

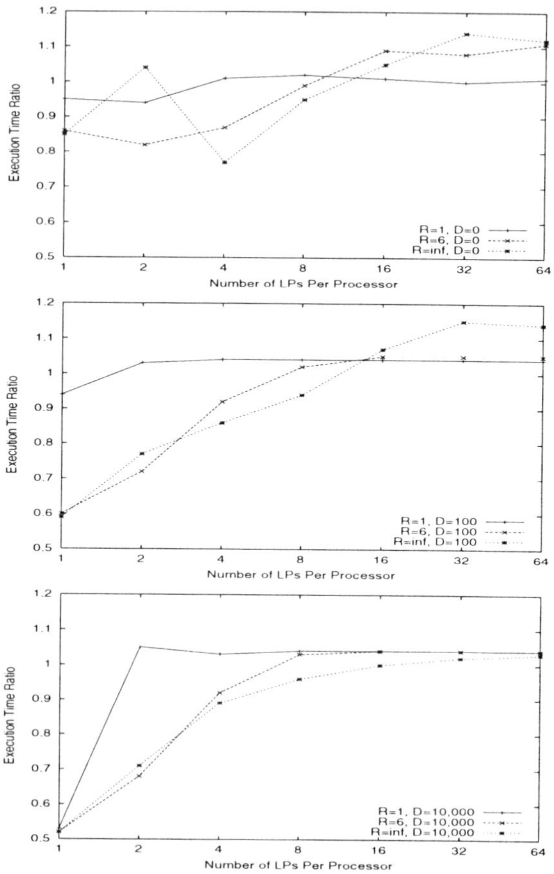

Figure 3. The ratio of the execution time with increasing number of logical processes per processor.

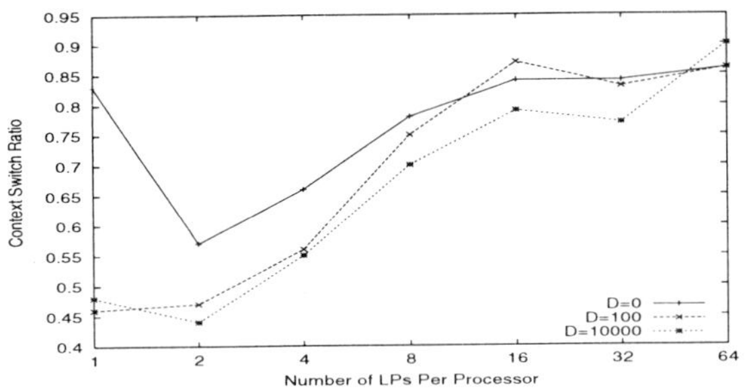

Figure 4. The ratio of the number of context switches with increasing number of logical processes per processor.

context switches. The overhead is proportional to the number of connections. Also, note that the crossing point shifts towards more LPs as the connectivity increases. Second, with increasing workload, the lock-free algorithm outperforms its counterpart in greater scale when the number of LPs is small. This is reflected by steeper curves as the event density is larger.

Figure 4 shows the ratios of context switches as we fixed the connection radius at 6. The curves coincide with the execution time ratios and show larger savings for the lock-free algorithm when the number of LPs is low. Also, it appears that the larger the event density, the smaller the number of context switches for the lock-free algorithm compared to CCT. As the savings in context switches for the lock-free algorithm decreases as we increase LP population, the overhead from the complexity of extra bookkeeping to avoid unnecessary context switches in the lock-free algorithm cannot be fully compensated any more. With more LPs ready for execution at any time on a processor, there will be a prolonged queueing time for all LPs on average. This makes it more likely that the remaining critical channels will be updated and therefore the unnecessary context switch will be avoided. That is, even though CCT does not try to avoid unnecessary context switches, multiprogramming certainly helps it avoid the issue with increasing number of processes. This further justifies the claim of CCT's authors to support simulation of low-granularity network models, which usually consist of large number of logical processes.

7. Conclusion

In this paper, we described a novel lock-free algorithm for scheduling logical processes in conservative parallel discrete-event simulation. We consider our algorithm as robust when compared with the algorithm using locks. In models with the number of LPs comparative to available processors, the algorithm shows much better performance and does not suffer from the defect of those algorithms using locks, where slow process may block other processes and form a bottleneck that degrades the performance of the entire system. The benefit, though, comes with a cost. The added complexity of the lock-free algorithm introduced some overhead from manipulating variables used for bookkeeping. The overhead, though, has only modest effect on the overall performance of the algorithm especially when the workload becomes non-trivial.

References

[1] K. M. Chandy and J. Misra. Distributed simulation: a case study in design and verification of distributed programs. *IEEE Transactions on Software Engineering*, SE-5(5):440–52, 1979.

[2] R. M. Fujimoto. Parallel discrete event simulation. *Communications of the ACM*, 33(10):30–53, 1990.

[3] M. Herlihy. Wait-free synchronization. *ACM Transactions on Programming Languages and Systems*, 13(1):124–149, 1991.

[4] D. Jefferson and P. Reiher. Supercritical speedup (discrete event simulation). *Proceedings of the 24th Annual Simulation Symposium*, pages 159–68, 1991.

[5] D. R. Jefferson. Virtual time. *ACM Transactions on Programming Languages and Systems*, 7(3):404–25, 1985.

[6] J. Liu, D. Nicol, B. Premore, and A. Poplawski. Performance prediction of a parallel simulator. *Proceedings of the 13th Workshop on Parallel and Distributed Simulation*, pages 156–64, 1999.

[7] X. Liu, D. M. Nicol, and K. Tan. Lock-free scheduling of logical processes in parallel simulation. *Technical Report TR2001-385, Computer Science Department, Dartmouth College*, 2001.

[8] J. Mellor-Crummey and M. Scott. Algorithms for scalable synchronization on shared-memory multiprocessors. *ACM Transactions on Computer Systems*, 9(1):21–65, 1991.

[9] E. Naroska and U. Schwiegelshohn. A new scheduling method for parallel discrete-event simulation. *Proceedings of European Conference on Parallel Processing EURO-PAR '96*, pages 582–93 vol.2, 1996.

[10] D. Nicol, J. Liu, and J. Cowie. Safe timestamps and large-scale modeling. *Proceedings 14th Workshop on Parallel and Distributed Simulation (PADS 2000)*, pages 71–8, 2000.

[11] D. M. Nicol. Principles of conservative parallel simulation. *Proceedings of 1996 Winter Simulation Conference Proceedings*, pages 128–35, 1996.

[12] H. Y. Song, R. A. Meyer, and R. Bagrodia. An empirical study of conservative scheduling. *Proceedings 14th Workshop on Parallel and Distributed Simulation (PADS 2000)*, pages 165–72, 2000.

[13] J. Valois. Lock-free data structures. *Ph.D Thesis, Rensselaer Polytechnic Institute*, May 1995.

[14] Z. Xiao, B. Unger, R. Simmonds, and J. Cleary. Scheduling critical channels in conservative parallel discrete event simulation. *Proceedings of the 13th Workshop on Parallel and Distributed Simulation*, pages 20–8, 1999.

Session 3

Optimistic Simulation I

The Dependence List in Time Warp

Jing Lei Zhang and Carl Tropper
School of Computer Science
McGill University, Montreal

February 28, 2001

Abstract

Time Warp is known for its ability to maximize the exploitation of the parallelism inherent in a simulation. However, this potential has been undermined by the cost of processing causality violations. Minimizing this cost has been one of the most challenging issues facing Time Warp.

In this paper, we present *dependence list cancellation*, a direct cancellation technique for Time Warp which is intended for use in a distributed memory environment such as a network of workstations. This approach provides for the swift cancellation of erroneous events, thereby preventing the propagation of their (erroneous) descendants. The dependence list also provides an event filtering function which detects erroneous future events, and also reduces the number of anti-messages used in the simulation. Our experimental work indicates that dependence list cancellation results in a dramatic reduction in the time required to process causality violations in Time Warp.

1 Introduction

In the optimistic approach to distributed simulation [Jeff 85] (a.k.a. Time Warp) processors are allowed to proceed even though there is a possibility of a causality violation. In this way it is easy to fully exploit the parallelism which is naturally present in a simulation model. The implicit tradeoff is that when a violation does occur, the system must be able to recover from this violation. There can be a large processing overhead associated with this correction, which may sometimes be unbounded. This has been a major obstacle to the efficiency of the Time Warp, and also to its stability. Therefore, reducing this associated cost has been, and remains, a challenging issue for Time Warp scheme.

We focus, in this paper, on reducing the processing time required for this correction. In doing so, we make use of the inherent dependence relationship between the events in a discrete event simulation. By this we mean the parent-child relationship between events; the child event is brought into the world as a result of processing the parent event.

We present algorithms for the swift cancellation of the children of erroneously processed events. These algorithms are oriented towards a distributed environment, e.g. a network of workstations. In the following, we describe the algorithms and the manner in which they serve to efficiently cancel events (sections 2 and 3) as well as experimental work intended to evaluate their efficiency (section 4). Our concluding remarks are contained in section 5.

2 The Notion of the Dependence List

The use of a distributed memory environment to host a distributed simulation poses a significant barrier towards the implementation of a cancellation system based on event dependence information. In a distributed network, events are sent between processors inside of messages. These communications are generally slow compared to the memory access time of a processor. In order to maintain network-wide dependence information for all of the events in a simulation, a large number of control messages would be needed, which could significantly burden communication channels. In addition, the cancellation of events in other processors poses a problem because the time a control message takes to arrive at a processor is limited by the latency of the communication channels. Furthermore, since an optimistic distributed simulation system runs asynchronously, it is almost

0-7695-1104-X/01 $10.00 © 2001 IEEE

impossible to have knowledge of an events' complete dependence information at any given time.

In order to avoid those difficulties, our dependence list only contains the dependence relationship between events within a single processor. The list includes those events which were sent from other processors but which are descendents of events originating in the given processor. The dependence list is maintained in the form of a linked list.

Certain applications such as VLSI simulation are convenient to simulate by making use of logical clusters of LPs. [Avril 95] contains a description of Clustered Time Warp and its application to VLSI simulation. A dependence list may be established either at the processor level or at the cluster level. If it is at the processor level, events can be linked or cancelled directly via dependence lists across different clusters, as long as their place of origin and their destination are within the same processor. If, on the other hand, the dependence list is at cluster level, events may be linked or cancelled directly within a cluster. Internal events are scheduled within a cluster, while external events are sent to different clusters. Our algorithmic descriptions are for clusters; to facilitate these descriptions, we assume one cluster per processor. Because one or more children may be produced by processing a parent, the dependence lists are tree structures.

There is, however, a limitation to the use of a dependence list – simulation of events within a single processor environment must be sequential in nature.

Figure 1 illustrates a dependence list.

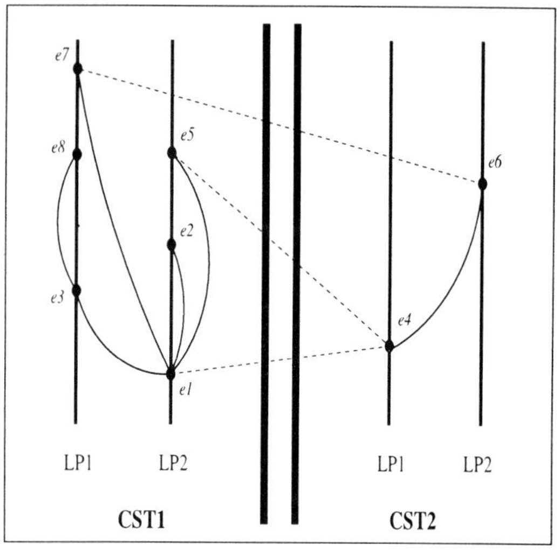

Figure 1: The Dependence List

- e_2, e_3, and e_4 are children of e_1. e_2 and e_3 are internal events. They are directly linked to e_1 in the dependence list. Like wise, e_8 is an internal child of e_3; e_6 is an internal child of e_4. So e_8 is directly linked to e_3, and e_6 is directly linked to e_4 to form their dependence links.
- e_4 is an external child of e_1. There is no link connecting between e_1 and e_4 , as dependence links do not extend across clusters. *When the descendents of the external child come back to the same cluster, dependence links are formed by linking these external descendents and their original ancestors within the same cluster.* In this example, both e_5 and e_7 are connected to e_1 in the dependence list.

From the above example, it can be seen that internal children are directly linked to their parents, while external descendents are directly linked to their ancestors. If we define the *length* of a dependence list between ancestor and descendent as being the number of generations separating them, then it can be easily concluded that a direct link to an internal child has a length of 1; and a direct link to an external descendent has a length of at least 2. In this example, the link between e_1 and e_7 has length of 3, and the link between e_1 and e_5 has length of 2. All other links are length 1.

2.1 The Construction of the Dependence List

Before describing the algorithm which establishes the dependence list, we first present some implementation details.

Since the number of descendents connected to a parent varies, we implement our dependence list connections from a parent to its descendents as being a pointer from the parent pointing to the head of a linked list of the descendents. So in our implementation a dependence list is associated with each event. There are three types of pointers:

ancestor: A pointer to an ancestor;

descendents: A pointer to the list of its descendents;

descendents_to_next: A pointer that links the descendents to form a linked list;

Besides those dependence list pointers, a **branch_ID**, an integer, is also added to each event. It is used to relate a branch of the dependence list connecting the parent to the child. (The details of how a branch_ID value is assigned to a branch of dependence list will be described in the next section. With this branch_ID, individual branches of the dependence list are identified. The cancellation of events can therefore be targeted only to branches containing erroneous events.)

In order to establish a link between an external descendent and its ancestor, we attach another data structure, a *vector table*, to each event. When an external descendent arrives from another cluster, the processor which contains the cluster will be able to discover the events' original ancestor by looking at the vector table of the incoming event.

The vector table contains M elements, where M is the number of processors or clusters in the system. Because the number of processors in an actual system is limited and usually is not very big, the size of this attached vector table is bounded.

Each element in a vector table contains: the *cluster ID*, which is used to indicate the cluster the element belongs to; the memory location of the ancestor that the event originated from; the dependence list *branch_ID*, which is used to provide branch_ID information when the links of an external descendent are established, and other information. To minimize the size of a vector table, the position of an element in the vector table can be used to implicitly indicate the ID value of the cluster that element belongs to, provided that these ID values are consecutive and they begin with 0 or 1. The cluster ID in the vector table can be eliminated in this case. In our implementation, we employ this implicit cluster ID technique. Hence, each element of the vector table contains the following fields: the memory location of the ancestor, the branch_ID, and the timestamp of the ancestor, which is used to minimize the sending of anti-messages. (described later)

The algorithm for establishing the dependence list is as follows:

- In the beginning of the simulation, the memory locations of ancestors in all vector tables of initial events are reset to $\vec{0}$.

- When an internal child is generated, before it is scheduled to the event heap a link is created between the parent and the child. The ancestor pointer from the child points to the parent, the child is put at the head of descendents list for the parent, and is pointed to by the parent's descendents pointer. At the same time, the content of the parent's vector table is copied to the child's vector table. In other words, this information is directly passed onto the child.

- When an external child is generated, before it is sent to another cluster, its vector table has to be updated. First, the content of the parent's vector table is copied to the child's. Then, in the element that represents the current cluster in the vector table, the memory location is updated to be the location of the parent; the branch ID variable is also updated to the value appropriate for the child (see the next section); the timestamp variable is set to the timestamp of the parent.

- When an external descendent arrives at a cluster, the processor containing the cluster looks at the element in the descendent's vector table which belongs to the current cluster. Based on the element's memory location information, a link is established between the descendent and its ancestor in this cluster. In our implementation, the ancestor pointer from the descendent is set to the ancestor and the descendent is placed at the head of descendents list for the ancestor. It is pointed to by ancestor's descendents pointer.

The following example illustrated in Figure 2 depicts how the dependence list is constructed:

Assume there are only two clusters in the system, CST_1 and CST_2. The attached vector contains only two elements. The simulation begins with e_1:

- The vector of e_1 is $< \vec{0}, \vec{0} >$. (Only the memory location of the ancestor is indicated.)

- e_2 and e_7 are internal children. They are directly linked to e_1. Their vectors are same as e_1's: $< \vec{0}, \vec{0} >$.

- e_3 is an external child of e_2. When it leaves CST_1, its vector is updated to $< \vec{e_2}, \vec{0} >$.

- e_4 is an external child of e_3. When it leaves CST_2, its vector has become $< \vec{e_2}, \vec{e_3} >$. When e_4 arrives at CST_1, the processor finds its original ancestor by looking at the first element

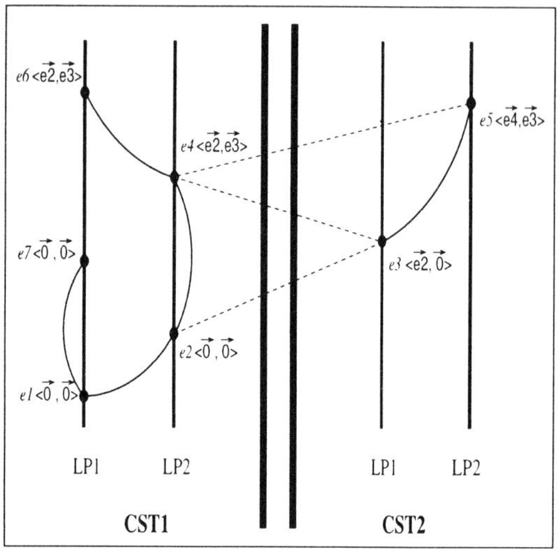

Figure 2: The Construction of Dependence List

(which corresponds to CST_1) in its vector table, the location for e_2. Hence e_4 is connected to e_2.

- e_6 is an internal child of e_4. e_6 and e_4 are directly linked. e_6's vector is same as e_4's: $< \vec{e_2}, \vec{e_3} >$.

- e_5 is an external child of e_4. When it leaves CST_1, its vector has updated to $< \vec{e_4}, \vec{e_3} >$. When e_5 arrives at CST_2, in the same way as for e_4, the processor in CST_2 looks at the second element in e_5's vector table, the location for e_3, and e_3 and e_5 are connected together.

As illustrated by this example, a vector table of size M (see definition earlier in this section) is sufficient to create the dependence list.

A dependence list may be traversed towards its *bottom* (or *root*) via the ancestor pointers, and may be traversed towards the *top* (or *leaf*) via the descendent's pointers. The bottom of a list is an event whose ancestor pointer is NULL. The top of a list is an event whose descendents list is also NULL.

When the timestamp of an ancestor is older than the GVT, the corresponding element in an event's attached table should be reset to $\vec{0}$, because the ancestor's information may no longer be valid. Any ancestor older than GVT is subject to fossil collection.

The dependence list is based on the intuition that if an event was created erroneously, all of its descendents are erroneous too, and all of them are to be removed from the system. As we shall see, the technique is quite fast compared to the traditional use of anti-messages.

3 The Application of the Dependence List

3.1 Related Work

Previous work has employed "direct cancellation" techniques.

[Das 94][Fuji 89] employ direct cancellation techniques in *Georgia Tech Time Warp* (*GTW*) in a *shared memory multiprocessor environment.* Pointers are used to link the children and the parents prior to scheduling the children, thereby eliminating the need for anti-messages. This approach relies on the use of a shared memory environment in which a processor may directly access another processor's memory. In a distributed network environment, however, anti-messages are indispensable as a means of communication between LPs in different processors.

[Deel 97] utilizes pointer links in a multiprocessor environment for the simulation of the spread of Lyme disease. Unlike our dependence list, the authors maintain dependence information on objects created only within a processor; i.e. no link is formed for an external event coming from outside the processor. Their cancellation is not much faster than the traditional approaches.

3.2 The Simulation System Using the Dependence List

To utilize the dependence list, the basic simulation system is modified. The output event queue for the cluster level or LP level is no longer used. (See [Avril 95] for a description of the output event queue at the cluster level). Instead, each parent carries a copy of its children in its *output event list.* Placing the output event list in an individual parent facilitates the removal of erroneously created children, as they are connected to their cancelled parent. Other uses are for the sending of anti-messages to other processors and to support lazy cancellation.

In our implementation, we add two pointers to each event, which constitutes the output event list:

output_event_list A pointer from a parent, pointing to the head of a linked list made up of its children;

output_to_next Pointers between children, so that the linked list is formed.

In addition, we also add another integer, **hasRun**, to each event which is used to indicate whether or not the event has been previously processed. In dependence list cancellation the rolled back events are reprocessed in order to determine if they have generated erroneous events. We describe how this is accomplished later.

In the dependence list, the output event list of a parent is used to identify a particular branch of a dependence list. Initially, there is no particular order necessary in which to place copies of the children in the output event list. Once the list has been generated, the order of each member in the list becomes important: the position of a child in the list becomes the branch_ID value of the dependence list.

The algorithm for producing the output event list and assigning the branch_ID values is as follows:

- When an event is processed, a counter containing the number of children in the output event list is set up and is created and initialized to 0.
- Whenever an internal child is generated, the counter is increased by 1.The child is linked to the parent via the dependence list; the branch_ID of the child is set to the value of the counter; then the child is scheduled to the event heap. In addition, a copy of the child is placed at the head of the parent's output event list.
- Whenever an external child is generated, the counter is increased by 1. The child's vector table is updated. The branch_ID variable of the element is set to the value of the counter and other fields are also renewed. Then, a copy of the child is placed at the head of the parent's output event list.
- When an external descendent arrives at its destination, it is linked to its ancestor via the dependence list. The branch_ID of this descendent is set to the value of the branch_ID variable in the element representing the destination cluster from the descendent's vector table.

Figure 3 shows an example of the relationship between the position of members in the output event list and their corresponding branches of the dependence list:

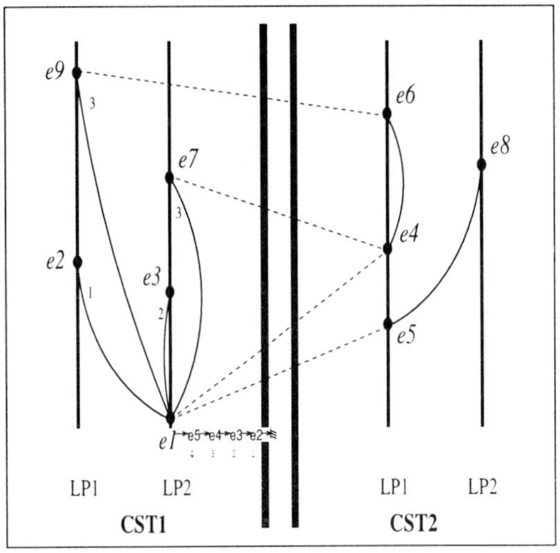

Figure 3: The Output Event List and the Branches of Dependence List

e_1 has four children: e_2, e_3, e_4, and e_5. The copies of these events in the output event list have the positions 1, 2, 3, and 4. Based on that, e_2's branch ID is 1, and e_3's branch ID is 2. e_7 and e_9 are the descendents of e_4, which has the position of 3, so the branch IDs of e_7 and e_9 are 3. This branch ID information is available since it is carried in the attached vector table of e_4.

We refer to the members in an output event list as *leads*. When there is at least one branch of a dependence list belonging to a lead, we say the lead is *connected*. Otherwise the lead is *open*. In our example, leads e_2, e_3, and e_4 in e_1 are connected, while lead e_5 is open. It can be easily seen that the leads of internal children are always connected. The leads of external children may either be connected, or be open. The significance of this is that when a lead is connected, the cluster is able to know that the corresponding external child has arrived at its destination, and has been processed by the other cluster; on the other hand, when the lead is open, no assumption can be drawn about either the arrival of the child, or its processing by the other cluster. A lead's being open or connected may serve as a kind of acknowledgement for external children. In this example, the arrival and the processing of e_4 is confirmed, while e_5's arrival is unknown by CST_1.

In summary, an event has following fields related to the dependence list mechanism:

e <*sender, receiver, send_time, receive_time, ancestor, descendents, descendents_to_next, branch_ID, output_event_list, output_to_next, hasRun, vector_table*>

3.3 Direct Cancellation

The main objective of the dependence list is to provide early detection and cancellation of erroneous events, while leaving "good" events intact. In the dependence list, the phase of rollback and the phase of cancellation are separated. The cancellation is delayed until erroneous events are actually identified. Thus it is "lazy", as in traditional lazy cancellation.

When a straggler arrives, the *LVT* of the corresponding *LP* is rolled back to the timestamp of the straggler. Events in the input queue whose timestamps are larger than that of the straggler, are rescheduled to the event heap for reprocessing. The *LP* state is recovered by the state stack (Coasting forward may be necessary if the checkpoint interval is larger than 1). After the rollback, the simulation is resumed immediately. When an unprocessed event is to be simulated, normal processing is performed. New internal children are scheduled to the processor heap and are linked to their parents by the dependence list; new external children are sent to their destination. A copy of these children is saved in the output event list.

When an already-processed event is to be simulated, the event is reprocessed. A copy of the new children is generated. This new copy is compared against the copy of the previously generated children. If they are identical, no cancellation is required. The simulation continues to the next event.

If, however, there is a difference between the new and old copy, this means the previous event is erroneous. The children of the previous event should be removed and be replaced by the new ones. Cancellation of the old children is then initiated; both the children and their descendents need to be cancelled. The cancellation starts from the previous event, traveling along the dependence list to all of their descendents. At the same time, all of the copies of external events are changed into anti-messages and sent to other clusters to cancel their original positive counterparts. After the rollback, the simulation resumes immediately.

When an anti-message arrives at an *LP*, the positive counterpart is cancelled. The *LP* is rolled back if the simulation has passed the timestamp of the cancelled event.

3.4 The Advantage of Dependence List Cancellation

Traditional aggressive cancellation is fast, as it is initiated as soon as a rollback occurs, but it is expensive. A tremendous overhead is incurred as a result of this correction; a large number of anti-messages are sent due to the indiscriminate nature of aggressive cancellation. This burdens the communication channels; further rollback and cancellations may also result (*cascading rollbacks*).

As to lazy cancellation, since erroneous events are not cancelled quickly, the number of erroneous events can become large, resulting in a large cost for a single causality violation.

Compared to both aggressive and lazy cancellation, dependence list cancellation is very fast and is not costly. It is also selective. For each discovery of an erroneous computation, the cancellation will comb through the simulation system, removing only erroneous events, while leaving "good" ones intact.

Dependence list cancellation can act to prevent rollback explosions. If the computational granularity of the events in a simulation is small, we often see the phenomenon of rollback explosions, in which the number of anti-messages grows exponentially, blocking the communication channels, and bringing the simulation to a standstill. This happens because the chance of these erroneous external events being processed before receiving their anti-messages is high.

However, a rollback explosion will not happen using dependence list cancellation, because the cancellation of erroneous external arrival events is done via the dependence list, not via anti-messages. Anti-messages are used to spread the cancellation wave only. Consequently, the maximum cost of each rollback and cancellation is bounded.

3.5 Event Filtering Function

Normally it is not easy to determine if an event will cause an erroneous computation before processing it. If this is possible, however, there is a tremendous benefit to the simulation system as it will avoid the processing of these events. We call the ability to predict the future behavior of an event the *event filtering function.*

To provide this filtering, cancelled events are not removed immediately, but remain in the system until fossil collection removes them (details later). When an event forms a cycle by coming back to a cluster, the processor in the cluster looks at the status of its ancestor. If the ancestor is a normally processed event, a dependence link is formed between the ancestor and descendent. If, however, the ancestor is a cancelled event, the processor then concludes that this future descendent is erroneous. Hence the processor cancels that descendent, preventing the propagation of potentially erroneous computation. The processor acquired an "*immunity*" over the passing of a cancellation wave such that it will reject the future coming of an erroneous computation wave which a cancellation wave has been trying to catch.

The cancelled events serve as "*anti-bodies*", providing "immunity" for the processors. By this we mean that all descendents of erroneously computed events use themselves cancelled. As long as the cancelled events are allowed to remain in the system, the processor will be able to identify all of their descendents by looking at the attached vector tables.

This cancellation and filtering ability eliminates the "*dog chasing its tail*" problem [Fuji 89] which aggressive cancellation has found hard to tackle. The "dog chasing its tail" problem can be briefly explained as an erroneous computation wave circling around among a few processors at a rapid rate. A cancellation wave is in some distance behind it, trying to outrun it. If the cancellation wave does not spread faster than the computation wave, the computation wave may not be caught. With the dependence list, however, the computation wave stops in the first round because the cancellation wave has "immunized" the processors such that when an erroneous computation wave reaches one of these processors, it is stopped there and prevented from traveling any further.

As mentioned before, the fossil collection of cancelled events ("anti-bodies") is delayed. Otherwise, the event filtering function could *"leak"*, meaning that erroneous future events escape from cancellation by the filtering function. To avoid leaks, the cancelled events are left in the system. These events can be kept either in the input queue, or in a separate queue dedicated for this purpose. During fossil collections, only those older than GVT are discarded.

In addition, during fossil collection, the collection of cancelled events should wait until all of the anti-messages resulting from their cancellation have arrived at their destinations. Otherwise, a leak may still be possible.

3.6 Minimizing the Sending of Anti-messages

We wish to minimize the sending of anti-messages, as doing so can have a significant impact on the performance of the simulation. Our current approach is for a cluster to refrain from sending an anti-messages back to the cluster which sent it. We rely on direct cancellation to eliminate the descendents of an incorrectly processed event. This situation is illustrated in Figure 6.

In the event that the ancestor information in the attached vector table is older than the *GVT* value the information may not be valid, and neither dependence list cancellation nor the filtering function will cause the event to be cancelled. An anti-message has to be sent in this case, even if the destination processor has been visited by a cancellation wave. With this precaution, correctness of the algorithm is guaranteed.

In our implementation, we also utilize vector tables in anti-messages. In each element of vector table, there is only one field, a flag, which is used to indicate whether or not the cluster has been visited by the cancellation wave.

3.7 The Weakness of Dependence List Cancellation

In this paper, our concentration has been on the speed of the simulation. Less focus has been placed on another important aspect of simulation: memory usage. Because of the memory requirements to establish the dependence list, more memory is used than in other method (see the experimental results in the subsequent section). This is the shortcoming of the dependence list. The following are the areas where extra memory is used:

The pointers that make up the dependence list. This extra memory is indispensable for the dependence list. It has a cost of $O(n)$, where n is the number of events in the simulation.

The attached vector table. Our current implementation has assigned a vector table to each event for convenience. But the number of vector tables can be reduced. There is no use for attached vector tables for internal events other than passing the contents of these tables to external events. In this case, keeping vector tables in internal events is no longer necessary. If we assign vector tables only to external events, the cost will be $O(n_e)$ rather than $O(n)$. where n_e is the number of external events in the simulation.

The cancelled events kept in the system for the purpose of event filtering. As we have suggested earlier, some kind of data structure may be used to replace the actual events, which could save considerable memory.

4 Experiments

4.1 The Environment

Our experimental platform consists of five dual processor Pentium III processors connected by a high speed network. Each of the processors has 256 Megabytes of internal memory. The workload of the two processors inside each machine is automatically distributed by the operating system. Our network is a Myrinet (< *http : //www.myri.com* >), a fast network having a link capacity of one Gigabyte per second. We employ PVM (< *http : //www.epm.ornl.gov/pvm/pvm_home.html* >) as the software communication platform. A PVM system consists of a *pvmd*, a daemon process which handles message transmission, and a set of interface routines. PVM provides a reliable mechanism for sending and receiving messages.

We have implemented two dependence list methods: **DEP**, a method that has dependence list cancellation and event filtering functions and **MIN**, a method that, in addition to the functions contained in **MIN** also minimizes the sending of anti-messages. We compare these methods to Time Warp.

Our test environment is VLSI circuitry. The circuits we make use of are from the ISCAS'89 Benchmarks. They are relative small; the largest of our circuits is s38584, which only has 20995 gates. Its simulation time is about 2 seconds in one machine, which is too short to demonstrate the performance of our algorithms. Therefore we created our own circuit s10000, which consists of four s38584 and nine s386 circuits, having the total of 85681 gates.

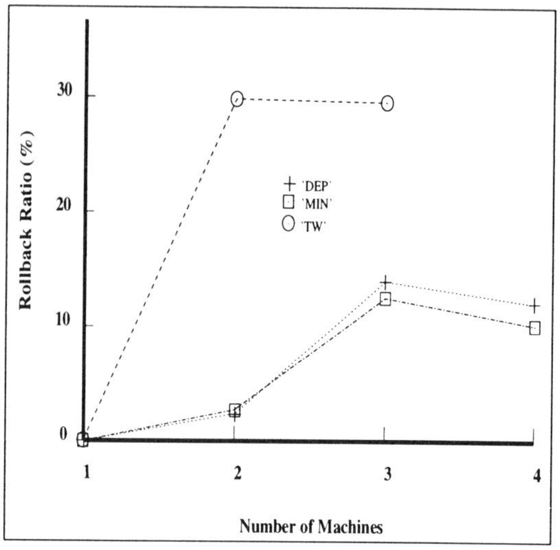

Figure 4: Rollback Ratio *vs.* Number of Machines (circuit s10000, number of vectors = 50)

In our experiments we compare the rollback behavior, throughput, simulation time and memory utilization of the above three methods. We present results for an input vector of length 50. Each data point represents the average of simulation runs.

4.2 Rollback Ratio

We define the *rollback ratio* as the ratio of the number of events rolled back to the total number of events processed.

Figure 7 shows the rollback ratio *vs.* the number of machines. As we can see, both of the proposed algorithms have a far smaller rollback ratio than Time Warp.

In Figure 7, there is a general trend of increasing rollback ratios with an increase in the number of machines for all methods. This phenomenon is expected since the chance of causality errors being introduced in the simulation is higher as the number of machines running asynchronously increases. However, the increase in the rollback ratio is sharper for Time Warp. When the number of machines is 3, the rollback ratio value reaches 29.7% for Time Warp, while the rollback ratio values are 12.1% and 10.8% for DEP and MIN respectively, which is about 60% fewer rollbacks than Time Warp. The rollback ratio value for Time Warp is not recorded when the number of machines is 4 as a rollback explosion occurs and the simulation cannot be sustained. In a rollback explosion, the number of anti-messages grows faster than the machines' ability to process them. Anti-messages are accumulated in the buffer of the *pvmd* process, and eventually uses up all of the available memory, causing the simulation to die. In our experiments, DEP and MIN do not experience such a rollback explosion, just as our theoretical analysis has predicted.

We credit these low rollback ratios for DEP and MIN to the dependence list, which provides early cancellation of erroneous events and which prevents the propagation of "bad" events once the cancellation has started.

4.3 Throughput and Goodput

We define *throughput* as the total number of events processed per second and *goodput* as the number of non-rolled back (or committed) events processed per second.

Figures 8 and 9 show the throughput and goodput respectively *vs.* the number of machines. We can see that both the throughput and goodput increase for DEP and MIN with an increase in the number of machines. The throughput values from 12,700 and 13,100 events per second for DEP and MIN in 1 machine rise to 20,200 and 20,300 events per second in 4 machines respectively. Similarly, the goodput values increase from 12,700 and 13,100 events per second in 1 machine to 18,900 and 19,000 events per second in 4 machines. These increases result from the benefit of workload being shared among machines. The slight drop of throughput and goodput in 3 machines is due to the rollback ratio increase (see Figure 5.1). The benefit of sharing workload is cancelled by the cost of rollback.

Also from Figure 8 and Figure 9, we can see that both throughput and goodput values for Time Warp are higher than those for DEP and MIN in 1 machine. This is because dependence list methods have the overhead of establishing the dependence list, and take a longer time to process an event than Time Warp does. Time Warp's throughput and goodput drop significantly for 2 machines, the result of a large increase in the number of rollbacks.

The throughput and goodput for Time Warp cannot be obtained in 4 machines as a rollback explosion prevents the simulation from terminating normally.

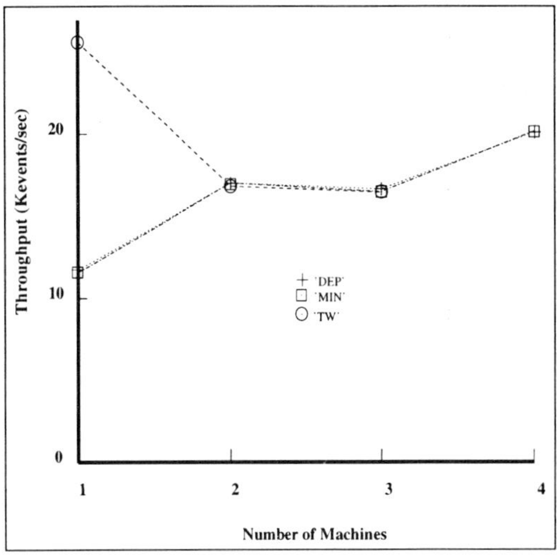

Figure 5: Throughput *vs.* Number of Machines (circuit s10000, number of vectors = 50)

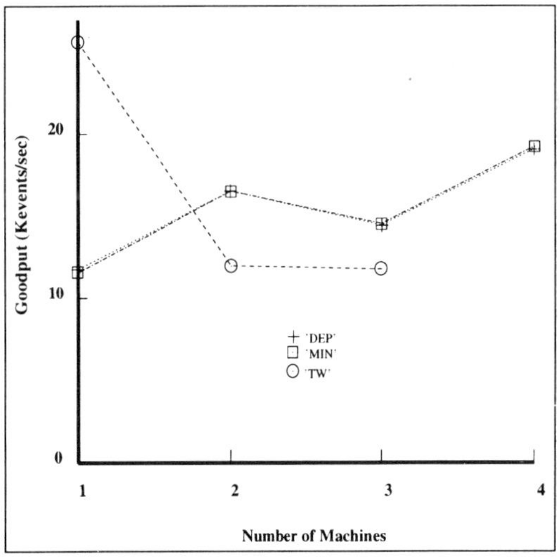

Figure 6: Goodput *vs.* Number of Machines (circuit s10000, number of vectors = 50)

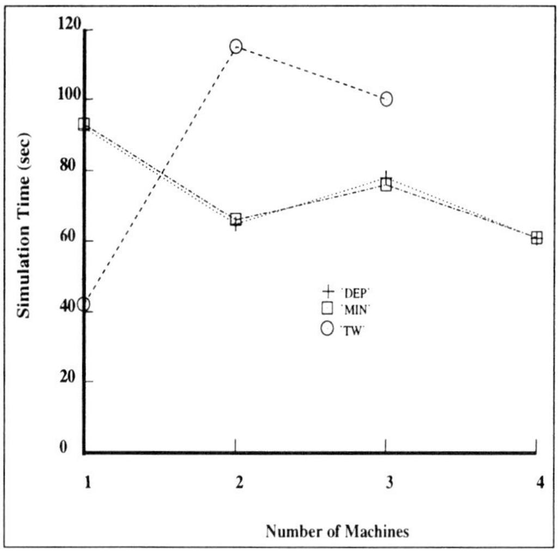

Figure 7: Simulation Time *vs.* Number of Machines (circuit s10000, number of vectors = 50)

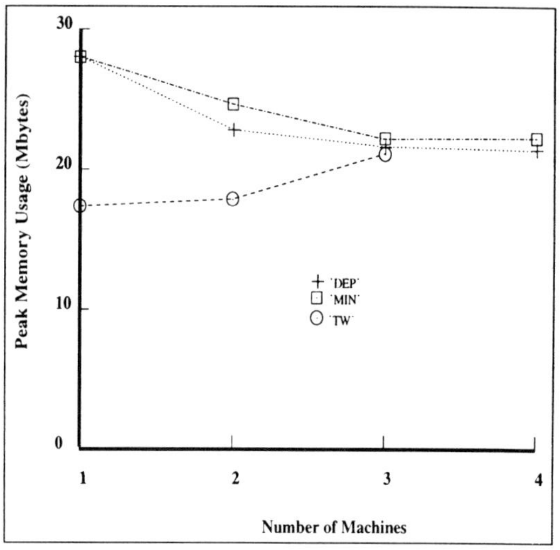

Figure 8: Memory Usage *vs.* Number of Machines (circuit s10000, number of vectors = 50)

4.4 Simulation Time

Figure 10 shows the simulation time *vs.* the number of machines. Both /bf DEP and /MIN experience a sharp decrease in the simulation time when two processors are employed, and an increase in simulation time going from 3 to 4 processors. We attribute the decrease in simulation time to the sharing of workload and the increase from 2 to 3 processors the result of an increase in the rollback ratio. Utilizing 4 processors, there is a 30% savings in the simulation time compared to 1 processor.

For the Time Warp method, the simulation time cannot be improved for both input vector values. This is because the goodput deteriorates with an increase in the number of machines, which, in turn, is the result of high rollback ratios.

From the above figures, we can clearly see that rollback ratio plays a significant role in determining the performance of simulation. Minimizing the cost of rollback processing allows a simulation to benefit from sharing the workload, thus goodput (and/or throughput) increases and simulation time decreases. In our experiments, the dependence list methods, DEP and MIN, exhibit far fewer rollbacks than Time Warp. Hence they have a better performance in terms of goodput and simulation time.

4.5 Memory Usage

We define *peak memory usage* as the maximum of all of the machines' maximal memory usage. Figure 11 shows peak memory usage *vs.* the number of machines. As we can see, the proposed methods use more memory than Time Warp. In experiments with input vectors of length 15, we observed as high as 80% more peak memory usage for DEP and MIN. As previously explained, the extra memory is used in three areas: the pointers which make up the dependence list, the attached vector table, and the storing of cancelled events. We also note that some high peak memory usage points correspond to high rollback ratio values (see Figure 5.1), such as 2 and 3 machines for Time Warp.

5 Conclusion

The biggest facing Time Warp is that of containing the overhead of causality correction. For each occurrence of a correction, the simulation system suffers a setback in terms of simulation progress. The cost of this correction is also unpredictable. It may explode in some situations.

In this paper, we have proposed relating events together as a way of attacking this problem, making use of a fundamental relationship of events, the event dependence relationship. We have attempted to systematically establish the concept of a dependence list, and have developed algorithms that makes use of the dependence list to efficiently correct causality errors. Our method is oriented towards a distributed memory system, e.g. a network of workstations.

Our experimental results establish the success of the dependence list in reducing the number of rollbacks to which Time Warp is prone. This leads to an improvement in the goodput and a decrease in the simulation time. However, the penalty for these improvements is an increase in the amount of memory used by Time Warp. However, as we have seen from our experiments, the dependence list can also cause a simulation which could not terminate under Time Warp to run to completion, rendering this disadvantage moot.

Our current work on the dependence list is very primitive. It has been mainly used to increase the efficiency of rollback and cancellation. However, using the information in the dependence list may lead to improvements in algorithms for GVT estimation, artificial rollback and checkpoint determination.

References

[Avril 95] H. Avril, C. Tropper, "Clustered Time Warp", Proceedings of the Workshop on Parallel and Distributed Simulation, pp. , IEEE Computer Society Press, Lake Placid, New York, 1995

[Das 94] S. Das, R. Fujimoto, K. Panesar, D. Allison, and M. Hybinette. "GTW: A Time Warp System for Shared Memory Multiprocessors". Proceedings of the 1994 Winter Simulation Conference, 1994.

[Deel 97] E. Deelman and B.K. Szymanski. "Breadth-First Rollback in Spatially Explicit Simulations". Proceedings of the 11th Workshop on Parallel and Distributed Simulation, pp. 124-131, IEEE Computer Society Press, 1994.

[Fuji 89] R. Fujimoto. "Time Warp on a Shared Memory Multiprocessor". Transactions of the Society for Computer Simulation, Vol. 6, No. 3, pp. 211-239, July 1989.

[Jeff 85a] D.A. Jefferson. "Virtual Time". ACM Transactions on Programming Languages and systems, Vol. 7, No. 3, pp. 404-425, July 1985.

[Wiel 89] F. Wieland, L. Hawley, A. Feinberg, M. Di Loreto, L. Blume, P. Reiher, B. Beckman, P. Hontalas, S. Bellenot, D. Jefferson, "Distributed Combat Simulation and Time Warp: The Model and its Performance". Proceedings of the 3rd Workshop on Parallel and Distributed Simulation, pp. 14-20, IEEE Computer Society Press, 1989.

Learning Not to Share *

Jason Liu David Nicol
Department of Computer Science
Dartmouth College
Hanover, NH 03755
{jasonliu,nicol}@cs.dartmouth.edu

Abstract

Strong reasons exist for executing a large-scale discrete-event simulation on a cluster of processor nodes (each of which may be a shared-memory multiprocessor or a uniprocessor). This is the architecture of the largest scale parallel machines, and so the largest simulation problems can only *be solved this way. It is a common architecture even in less esoteric settings, and is suitable for memory-bound simulations. This paper describes our approach to porting the* **SSF** *simulation kernel to this architecture, using the Message Passing Interface (MPI) system. The notable feature of this transformation is to support an efficient two-level synchronization and communication scheme that addresses cost discrepancies between shared-memory and distributed memory. In the initial implementation, we use a globally synchronous approach between distributed-memory nodes, and an asynchronous shared-memory approach within a SMP cluster. The* **SSF** *API reflects inherently shared-memory assumptions; we report therefore on our approach for porting an* **SSF** *kernel to a cluster of SMP nodes. Experimental results on two architectures are described, for a model of TCP/IP traffic flows over a hierarchical network. The performance on a distributed network of commodity SMPs connected through ethernet is seen to frequently exceed performance on a Sun shared-memory multiprocessor.*

1. Introduction

Strong reasons exist for executing a large-scale discrete-event simulation on a distributed memory architecture. Distributed memory machines are cost-effective and therefore more accessible to general simulation practitioners. Very large simulation models are typically memory bound, and benefit enormously from distribution. The very largest parallel computers in the world are built with this architecture. Significant projects establishing this trend include Network-of-Workstations (NOW) [1] and Beowulf [6].

While distributed memory systems can be cost-effective and extensible, shared memory systems have much lower memory access latency and allow for simpler synchronization within the same memory space. There exist systems that are made of a distributed memory cluster of processing nodes, each of which is a shared-memory multiprocessor. At the high end of parallel computing, there are supercomputer clusters. For example, the Compaq AlphaServer Supercomputer consists of hundreds of AlphaServer 4-processor SMP nodes interconnected via ultra-low-latency, high-bandwidth network switch. At the low end is a lab with dual processor machines on desktops, connected by ethernet.

This combination of shared and distributed memory in a single architecture creates interesting challenges for parallel simulation. In particular, the synchronization approach one uses to coordinate SMP nodes can—and frequently *should*—be different from the synchronization method one uses among independent timelines (i.e., "logical process" in historic PDES terminology) within an SMP node.

For two years we have been developing and tuning **SSF** (Scalable Simulation Framework) kernels, and developing network models that run on them[1]. The **SSF** API defines a process-oriented, conservatively synchronized parallel simulator, designed primarily for simulating large-scale multi-protocol communication networks [2]. The **SSF** API assumes shared-memory; the question we are most frequently asked is "when will **SSF** run on a cluster of workstations?". This paper describes our first approach of porting an **SSF** kernel to distributed memory, where we use the MPI (Mes-

*This research is supported in part by DARPA Contracts N66001-96-C-8530 and N66001-00-C-8065, NSF Grant ANI-98 08964, NSF Grant EIA-98-02068, Dept. of Justice contract 2000-CX-K001, and a Marion and Jason Whiting Foundation Fellowship.

[1] Please see www.cs.dartmouth.edu/research/DaSSF for extensive information on the Dartmouth implementation of the API, and www.ssfnet.org for extensive information on the SSFNet networking layer that augments it.

sage Passing Interface) to manage the inter-node communication. In doing this we have made two contributions. First, we demonstrate the viability of a hierarchical approach to synchronization. Our implementation uses global synchronization to coordinate SMP nodes, and shared-memory-based asynchronous channel-scanning within an SMP. Second, we develop a strategy for moving an existing shared-memory simulator to distributed memory. Rather than fundamentally change the shared-memory interface (which can still be used within an SMP node), we address the global naming problems introduced by distributed memory in a front-end that interprets model files, partitions the model among SMP nodes, and builds the system. The best way to visualize the result is as a set of shared-memory simulators, coordinated at a high-level through message-passing.

Hierarchical approaches to synchronization have been considered in other contexts. In [5], the authors introduced a scheme that combines a conservative time window synchronization with the Time Warp. This approach and others ([7, 8]) combine conservatism and optimism in an effort to overcome the limitations of either one of them used alone. Time management for HLA [3] can also be viewed as a hierarchical approach. A hierarchical *scheduling* algorithm for shared memory is proposed in [9]. Our work is distinguished by its focus on using hierarchical synchronization to deal with communication and synchronization discrepancies between shared memory and distributed memory architectures.

2. Multilevel Synchronization

The problems of porting our shared-memory API to distributed memory forced us to consider how synchronization might be done differently between SMP nodes than it is within a node. Our implementation employs an asynchronous algorithm to coordinate simulation processes within an SMP node. The algorithm is based on key concepts of of the Critical Channel Traversing [9] approach, as follows. The simulation model is viewed as a directed graph whose nodes are timelines and where an edge (channel) from node i to j reflects the fact that timeline i can send a message to timeline j. A timeline governs its progress as a function of lower bounds on future message times on these channels. Each channel has a minimum delay between the simulation time a message is written into the channel and the simulation time at which it is received. The channel's source timeline maintains a lower bound on the time of the next message it may send over the channel, called a *channel time*. Typically the source records the channel time as the sum of its own simulation clock and the channel's minimum delay. When a timeline is scheduled to run it first computes its safe time t as the minimum of channel times among all channels it reads. It executes all events (if any) up to t, sets its own clock to t, and updates the channel times of each of its output channels. When a timeline suspends, it counts the number of *critical* channels—those whose times equal t— writes this count into a shared variable and marks the critical channels. These marks serve as flags; immediately after a timeline updates a channel time it looks for a critical flag there. If the flag exists, the timeline decrements the number of critical channels the recipient is blocked on, and schedules the recipient to run if that count is reduced to zero.

Each Unix process (one per processor) runs a simulation process scheduler that implements this CCT-like strategy. The scheduler's interaction with the global synchronization mechanism is relatively straightforward. The SMP's submodel is allowed to run as far ahead as it is able[2]—until there are no runnable simulation processes. During this execution burst the channel times on all channels that cross between SMPs remain constant. Once all schedulers in a node have exhausted the available work, the node sends all cross-node messages generated during the burst, and engages in a barrier synchronization and flushing operation with all other nodes. After the barrier is complete, each node has received all the external messages for its timelines needed to execute safely for another D units of time, where D is the minimum delay on any channel that crosses between nodes. The schedulers advance the channel times on all cross-node channels ahead D units, put every timeline that is blocked on such a channel on the runnable list, and continue.

The solution we use is just one of many possible. In some cases it is advantageous to synchronize globally within an SMP node, in order to avoid high scanning costs when timelines have high connectivity. In such a case it is relatively easy to interleave the global synchronizations in with the local synchronizations. It may sometimes be advantageous to synchronize the SMP nodes using an asynchronous algorithm—this happens if it is unavoidable exposing a channel with very small minimum latency across nodes. It may still be advantageous to treat the SMP's submodel synchronously, or to treat it asynchronously. We choose to use global synchronization at the MPI level principally because our past experience with MPI suggested it would be easy and less error-prone than an asynchronous approach. The main point to be made is that the hierarchy of communication costs in a cluster of SMPs forces one to think hierarchically about synchronization.

3. Porting SSF to Distributed Memory

The principle design goal of **SSF** was to provide a simple, unified, object-oriented interface for parallelizable

[2]We do impose flow control here.

discrete-event simulation. Emphasis was placed on the API—not a specific simulator—with the idea that its simplicity should promote multiple implementations (there are 4 such now), and that any simulation model using that API should be able to run on any **SSF** -compliant implementation. **SSF** was originally designed for shared-memory multiprocessor architectures, and the API reflects shared-memory assumptions. Because there is now a body of **SSF** models, one goal of the kernel port is to make manageable the transition of existing **SSF** models to the distributed memory domain. In this section we specifically outline what shared-memory assumptions are in the API, how we approached the problem of the port, and what new support is required of an **SSF** modeler to develop models to run on a distributed memory kernel.

3.1. Problems in the SSF API

Our **SSF** implementation is built by combining C++ source code with an **SSF** library and API. **SSF** implements the process-oriented simulation world-view. An **SSF** model defines threads—called *processes*—of independent execution. Processes communicate with each other through message passing; a process may suspend itself until a message appears for it, or it may suspend for a stated period of simulation time.

The **SSF** API defines five base classes. The essential features of the **Process** class were described above. The **inChannel** and **outChannel** classes describe communication endpoints; a process sends a message by calling an **outChannel** method and receives a message by calling an **inChannel** method. The **Entity** class is essentially a wrapper class. It holds general state data, instances of the **Process** class and instances of the **inChannel** and **outChannel** classes. (Each instance of these classes declares an **Entity** instance as "owner" at construction). Messages between processes are instance of classes derived from the **Event** base class.

Because essential process semantics are based on message passing, an **SSF** model is for the most part not dependent on shared-memory assumptions. Entities are organized into *alignment groups* (also known as *timelines*), within which events are processed in monotone non-decreasing timestamp order. The intention is that timelines interact with each other solely through message passing. In fact the **SSF** API specifically declares as undefined any reference to model state in a non-co-aligned entity. Nevertheless, there is an important dependency on shared memory, which manifests itself explicitly in two method calls. If **oc** is a variable containing an instance of an **outChannel** and if **icp** is the address of an instance of an **inChannel**, the call **oc.mapto(icp)** creates a communication channel between these endpoints. This call can be legally made by **oc**'s owner, or any entity which is co-aligned with that owner. While subsequent semantics describing message-passing from **oc** to ***icp** make no assumptions about memory, the **mapto** method explicitly requires **oc** and **icp** to be in the same memory space, even though the endpoints involved may exist in entities that are simulated in parallel. Similarly, the **Entity::alignto(Entity*)** method declares that the entity whose method is called should join the timeline of the entity indicated in the argument. Like **mapto**, an **alignto** call is not legally made by any entity not co-aligned with the one whose method is called. Both **mapto** and **alignto** may be called at any point in the simulation, and both reference two objects that exist in the same memory space.

Another aspect of the **SSF** API is not so explicitly tied to shared memory, but is supported much more easily in shared than distributed memory. The **main** body of the program is executed serially; in the initialization phase a model is built by calling constructors, **mapto**, and **alignto**. Parallel execution starts after **main** calls the **startAll** method, and serial execution begins again following a call to **joinAll**, after the simulation finishes. Data gathering and analysis typically occurs in the second serial phase. Distributed memory support of these semantics would be possible by distributing copies of submodels across a distributed memory system at a **startAll** call, and bringing back copies of the modified submodels to a single memory space at a **joinAll** call. Needless to say, the paradigm is more easily implemented in shared-memory.

The **SSF** API reflects the fact that after initialization, **mapto** and **alignto** calls cannot take effect instantaneously in simulation time, as this would be equivalent to messages with zero delay between processors, at least as far as synchronization is concerned. Both calls return a simulation time (strictly ahead of the time at which the call is made) after which the kernel guarantees the action to have taken place. The API says that the time returned is implementation dependent, e.g., it is legitimate for an implementation to return a simulation time beyond the termination time, and so never effectually support **mapto** or **alignto** calls after initialization. Because of this, **SSF** models tend to use **mapto** or **alignto** calls only during initialization.

With respect to a distributed memory implementation, most problems occur at initialization. There are myriad problems associated with getting submodels into different memory spaces, and there are problems in naming objects that reside in different memory spaces. As we considered using MPI to handle inter-node communication, we identified additional problems with supporting the serial-parallel-serial model of **main**. While the problems are numbingly technical, the implications were clear—identifying submodels to run in separate memory spaces needs to happen *before* the simulation is started, and construction of those submodels needs to happen on the nodes which will host those submodels.

The general form of a solution suggested itself to us. Our technical problems are minimized if we develop and enforce a methodology for model description that provides a coherent global naming strategy *outside* of the **SSF** kernel. A front-end to the kernel can analyze and partition a static description of a model's topology, and provide to the kernel a partitioned model with global naming problems already resolved. We need then only augment the **SSF** API slightly to provide a few necessary "hooks" needed at model build time, modify the kernel to build its models from these pre-partitioned descriptions, and then coordinate across memory spaces using MPI. The subsections to follow develop this solution.

3.2. DML

The Domain Modeling Language (DML) is used extensively already as part of the SSFNet modeling project [2]. Our approach to a distributed memory **SSF** implementation is based on a DML front-end to the kernel, and so we first sketch the rudiments of DML.

At the most basic level, a DML model is described as a recursively defined list of attribute-value pairs. The model can be thought of as a database, and will be queried like a database. An attribute is a name used to reference its associated value, which may itself be a list of attribute-value pairs. A DML model can always be represented as a tree of attributes. If the attribute is simple, the tree node contains its value; if the attribute is a list of attribute-value pairs, the tree node just serves as the parent to each of attributes in that list. The tree structure reflects the necessarily hierarchical structure of definition; systems described in DML can of course have arbitrary topology. The tree structure will provide us with a needed global naming strategy.

A quite rich description can be embedded in this simple framework. To illustrate, the example below is a snippet of a DML model in the SSFNet distribution.

```
Net [
  frequency 100000000
  AS_status boundary
  ospf_area 0

  traffic [
    pattern [
      client 1
      servers [port 10
       nhi_range
         [from 1:2(0) to 1:5(0)]]
    ]
    pattern [
      client 2
      servers [port 10
       nhi_range
         [from 1:6(0) to 1:10(0)]]
    ]
  ]

  Net [id 0 cidr 0
   _extends .networks.network0.Net]
  Net [id 1 cidr 1
   _extends .networks.network1.Net]
  ...
]
networks [
 network0 [
  Net [
   router [ id 0
    graphics [ x 300 y 200]
    interface [ id 0
      _extends .dictionary.1Gb ]
    interface [ id 1
      _extends .dictionary.1Gb ]
   ...
```

`Net` is a hierarchical network description. Attributes `frequency`, `AS_status`, `ospf_area` have simple values. Attribute `traffic` has a list of two lists as its value. The list values associated with `nhi_range` reflect an iterative numbering scheme, but that scheme is not part of DML semantics. The domain-specific initialization code that reads this file *interprets* the `from` and `to` attribute-value pairs, implements whatever iteration is intended as part of the model build process. The key point is that the DML framework does not impose any interpretation on the attributes or values that are expressed.

DML does contain a handful of keywords that simplify model construction. For example, keyword `_extends` causes a DML submodel to be inserted at the point of the keyword. The string following `_extends` identifies the position of this submodel, in terms of the inherent tree structure. `.networks.network0.Net` refers to the subtree rooted in the node found through attribute `networks` of the tree base, then attribute `network0` of the value list associated with `networks`, then attribute `Net` in the value list associated with `network0`. `_extends` is simple short-hand to save us the trouble of recopying model patterns that are re-used.

A basic DML system has a model parser with a simple API, supporting queries. After opening a DML file the parser returns a pointer to the model's root node. Subsequent queries on the database are done through pointers to tree nodes; given the name of an attribute, the query returns a list of tree nodes whose attribute name match, and which are children of the tree node through which the query is performed. As a consequence of this generality, one designs DML model methodologies for different modeling domains, and writes separate model interpreters for different domains as well.

Applied to the problem of building an **SSF** model, a model domain interpreter uses its domain knowledge to identify entities that are tacitly expressed in the model. For instance, in the example above, `router` might correspond to an **SSF** entity, with the structure and state of the entity described by the list of attributes associated with attribute `router`. The interpreter, parsing the DML tree in a breadth-first fashion, reads configuration and initialization data from the database, calling constructors, `mapto` calls, and `alignto` calls as a function of the model description.

We saw that the DML framework could be used to solve our key problem, that of cross-memory-space naming. The DML tree structure can be used to give a global name to every entity, outchannel, and inchannel in the system, in terms of paths through the tree (same-name attributes in a list—like Net in the example above—can be disambiguated, e.g., by order of appearance in the file). We can in essence replace memory pointers with strings as a way of referencing model components. In the SSFNet example above, the line

```
servers [port 10
  nhi_range [from 1:2(0) to 1:5(0)]]
```

uses the SSFNet-wide NHI naming convention to describe a set of "servers" in the model. In **SSF** these are mapped ultimately to memory addresses, here they are a model-domain specific way of referencing global objects.

Given a domain-specific methodology for DML model description, one writes an interpreter which queries the DML database, reading textual descriptions and translating them into actions which construct and initialize an **SSF** model. To support a distributed memory implementation we saw that we needed to develop such a methodology, and write *two* interpreters for it. One interpreter is responsible for partitioning the model, the second is responsible for loading and initializing the model. Figure 1 illustrates the process. The methodology we developed requires that DML objects which are to be transformed into **SSF** entities identify themselves through a specific attribute (*instance_of*) -name (**SSF** *Entity class type*) pair. It requires that such DML objects identify how their outchannels are to be mapped to inchannels, and how the entities are to be aligned. From this information the first interpreter is able to construct a timeline graph, and run a graph partitioner upon it (e.g., we use the METIS system from University of Minnesota, see **www-users.cs.umn.edu/~karypis/metis/metis.html**). Partitioning results are combined with runtime information and architecture information to produce a single DML file, read by the second interpreter, in each node. This file is structurally equivalent to the first, with the additional of partitioning and run-time information.

At run-time, the DML file produced by the first interpreter is read by every MPI process in the system. The second interpreter is identical to the first in its recognition of entities, `mapto` directives, and `alignto` directives. Its response is different however, proceeding in two passes. In the first pass, as each entity is recognized a factory method for it is called to produce an instance. All entities are created in the first pass. The second pass executes all the `alignto` directives, and all the `mapto` directives involving endpoints in the same memory space. `mapto` statements that would cross memory-space boundaries result in the construction of proxies at both endpoints—at the output side an **inChannel** proxy is constructed in the same memory space and on the input side an **outChannel** proxy is constructed. Proxies are necessary to support the **mappedto** methods of classes **inChannel** and **outChannel**, and **unmap** method of **outChannel**. The results of further access *through* the pointers returned is undefined in the normal **SSF** spec. However, the pointer values can be used by **SSF** models as identifiers. The kernel intercepts **write** calls on channels that cross memory boundaries. Thus, the platform on which an **SSF** model is executing is transparent to the model.

For synchronization purposes, the minimum channel delay D among all channels crossing memory boundaries is computed by each processor. This establishes the synchronization window for the cross-processor synchronization performed in MPI.

3.3. Kernel Support

Several modifications to the **SSF** kernel were needed. When the system is run, one MPI process on each node of the distributed system is created. That process—called the root—will serve both as a simulation process and the representative MPI process for the submodel assigned its node. As a function of the DML file (which identifies how many processors will be used at this node) the root creates the rest of the processes and the shared memory space between them all. At this point, if p processors are to be used at this node, then p processes will have been created. At this point the DML model file is read and the model is built. During the simulation run, each process runs a scheduler which dispatches runnable timelines, each corresponding to a timeline in the **SSF** model.

The **write** method for **outChannels** is rewritten to note when a target **inChannel** lies in a different memory space. When it does, the event being sent is buffered temporarily in shared memory, in a buffer dedicated to the target node, with a code identifying the **inChannel** at the receiving end which should receive the event.

The timelines on a node synchronize with each other us-

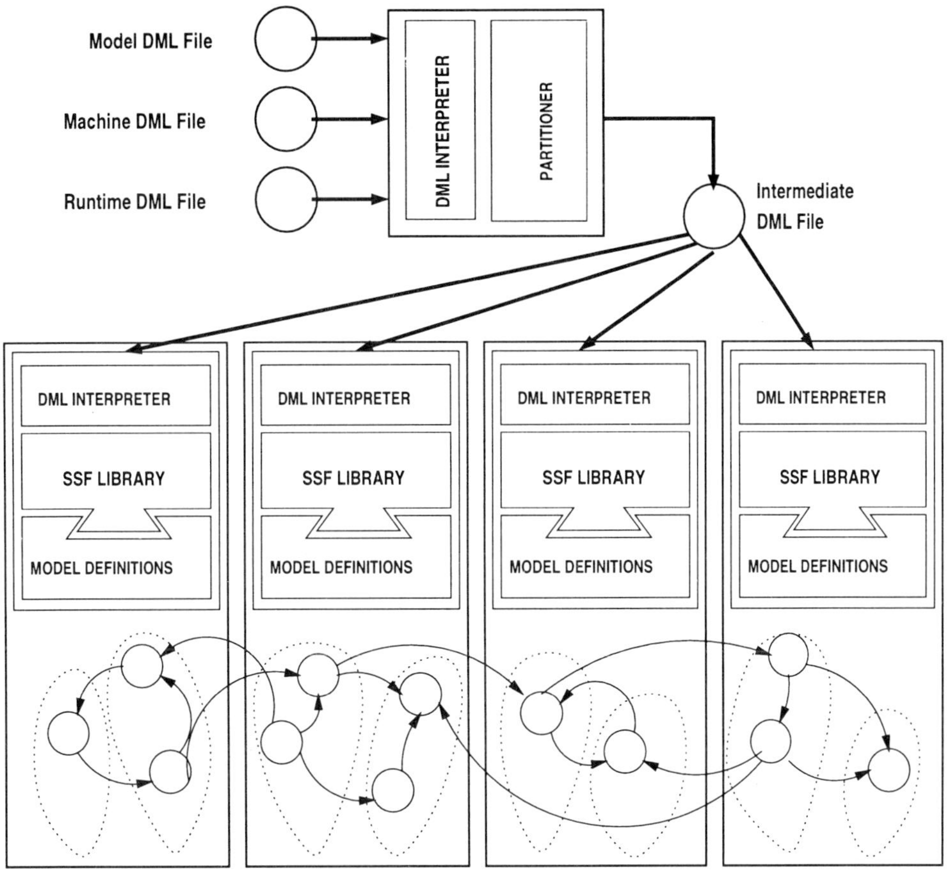

Figure 1. The structure of distributed SSF .

ing a channel scanning method very much like the CCT approach. In this method there is no notion of global synchronization. However, the channels whose endpoints lie in other memory spaces are not updated. The net result is that a node will run timelines until the runnable lists of every scheduler in the node are empty. At this point the root process writes out buffered events to each of the other nodes. Following this, the process uses a non-committal barrier to flush the communication channels and synchronize with all other root processes [4]. Following the barrier, a processor unbundles all the messages just received, reconstructs **SSF** events and inserts them in the event lists of the targeted timelines, and updates the channel times of channels that deliver messages from other SMP nodes, increasing those times by at least D (the minimal channel delay among all cross memory-space channels). After this all is accomplished the schedulers all put on the runnable list precisely those timelines which were blocked on incoming channels from other memory spaces (and possibly others which are blocked due to flow control concerns).

3.4. User Support

The kernel needs help from the user in identifying **SSF** objects and their names. The extended API requires that any **Entity** using an *instance_of* attribute "register" a factory method with the kernel, along with the same **Entity** name string as appears in the DML file. This combination allows the initialization procedure to forge the link between textual name (in the DML file) and memory address (from the associated factory method, which when called returns a pointer to a newly constructed instance of that **Entity** class). Similarly, an **Entity** constructor registers textual names of its channels to facilitate interpretation of **mapto** directives embedded in the DML model description.

Another key area where the kernel needs help from the user is in bundling and unbundling messages across memory spaces. When an event is sent by MPI, it is merely a sequence of bytes. At the receiving node, it must be reconstructed into an event recognizable by C++ as an instance of the user defined class. Unlike Java, C++ has no native serialization methods. Therefore the message will have to contain a code identifying the event's type, and the user will have to provide a method that turns an event into a sequence of bytes, and turns a sequence of bytes into an event. Because event structure can be arbitrarily complex, only a user can write these methods. Consequently, the kernel requires that any event class whose instances may be transmitted across memory-space boundaries have a method named **pack**, which the kernel can call at the point it builds an MPI message containing events; **pack** returns a simple sequence of bytes that represent the event. The extended **SSF** provides methods that help generate an architecture-independent byte string. A second needed component is a marker that identifies the event type of the byte sequence. A global mapping of event type to marker is easily created by requiring the user to give each event type a unique string name and register the name with a callback function that creates an instance of the event. The callback function accepts a byte sequence and from this creates and returns an instance of the class.

The extended API requires an **Entity** to provide a method named **wrapup**. This function is called for every entity at the end of the simulation to compute whatever statistics and data analysis is necessary, and write it out to files or print it on a terminal.

4. Experiments

To demonstrate the viability of our approach we implemented a model of a communication network running TCP/IP applications. The network topology consists of many hosts connected by several levels of routers. The topmost level of routers are interconnected as a fully-connected graph. These model border gateway routers between autonomous systems in the global internet. Each autonomous system is modeled as a tree structure with the gateway router as the tree root. The leaves of the tree are hosts and internal nodes are routers. The number of autonomous systems, the number of levels, and the number of routers for each level within an autonomous system are all configurable. The hierarchy structure represents a simplified but representative internetworking topology.

Each host in the network generates TCP sessions according to an on-off stochastic process. The host waits for an exponentially distributed off-time before it initializes a TCP session with a randomly chosen host. The number of IP packets generated by the TCP session is also a random variable. To model heavy-tailed traffic, we use a Pareto distribution to randomly generate the number of IP packets per TCP session. The TCP model is realistic in that both sender and receiver of a TCP session implement sliding windows for packet re-transmission and acknowledgement to deal with possible losses along the way. Each router in the network has its own routing table. When a packet is received, the router sends it to the right output buffer according to its destination (represented by a simplified form of IP address). A packet is discarded if the buffer becomes full. A buffered packet waits until the channel is freed from transmitting all previous packets ahead of it in the queue. The delay for the packet to reach the other end of the wire is determined according to the real hardware transmission delay (time across the wire) and bandwidth (time to load the wire).

In our experiments, the network is configured with 24 autonomous systems with 10G bps bandwidth interconnection. Each packet sent between the gateway routers experiences a 200 ms transmission delay. Each autonomous system contains 8 routers at the second level with 1G bandwidth and 10 ms transmission delay (to model inter-domain communications). Each second level router connects 8 hosts with 100M bandwidth and 0.5 ms transmission delay (to model an LAN). The mean off-time between TCP sessions is 25 seconds. The full model contains 216 routers and 1536 hosts. The simulation runs for a total of 100 simulated seconds. The model can be configured with one of two traffic distribution models. One model creates *Local Peers*, in that the peers in a TCP session are likely to be relatively close in the network topology, and hence likely to be within the same memory space. In this model we use a truncated discretized exponential distribution to sample the distance of a TCP session from the source, if the hosts are considered to be enumerated in a ring. The second mode generates *Scattered Peers*, by choosing the destination peer uniformly at random from among all hosts. It is easy to see that the second mode has much higher communication demand across the AS router subnetwork, and hence across the MPI subsystem. When the network is simulated on p nodes, on average fully $(p-1)/p$ of TCP connections cross memory-space boundaries. Among symmetrically balanced workloads, this is a worst-case scenario. For the experiments we report here the traffic volume across memory-space boundaries is about 100 times higher in the second model than in the first. From the point of view of the **SSF** kernel, almost all of the MPI communication in the first mode is strictly for synchronization, while most of the MPI communication in the second mode is data-bearing. Comparison of the two helps to isolate synchronization cost from native (and inescapable) traffic cost.

Every data point we show is the sample mean of 10 simulation runs. The 95% confidence interval on execution time is less than 2% of the point estimate in every case, and so we show no error bars on the graphs.

Our first experiments were designed to compare the performance of our mixed-synchronization scheme with that of a pure shared-memory implementation, in order to see what additional synchronization overheads are induced by using MPI. We conducted them on a Sun Enterprise 6500 with 14 UltraSPARC-II (400MHz) processors, having a total of 7 GB memory. Each processor is equipped with

8 MB secondary cache. The system chassis consists of 7 CPU/Memory boards interconnected by high-speed bus with a peak data transfer rate of 2.88 GB per second. MPI is installed on this system; we used the Gnu C++ compiler at optimization level 3. For all experiments shown here, the configuration of a simulation run is denoted by AxB, where A is the number of MPI processes and B is the number of processors utilized by each MPI process for local shared-memory synchronization. The total number of processors used by the simulation is therefore AxB. By varying A and B for a fixed number of processors we come to some understanding of the costs and tradeoffs of the hierarchical scheme. The pure shared-memory case ($1 \times N$) exercises none of the cross-memory logic, it is "traditional" **SSF** .

Figure 2 shows the speedup curves as we vary the number of processors from 1 to 12, comparing the pure shared-memory ($1 \times N$) and pure distributed memory ($N \times 1$) approaches. The serial version against which speedups are computed is the parallel version run on one processor. This is significantly faster than running the whole simulation from a single event list (which we can also do in **SSF** with a command-line switch), because partitioning the model into timelines that synchronize is, in this case, more efficient than the higher costs of a single event-list. The raw performance of the simulator is reflected in measuring the number of "packet-events" per unit execution time. A packet-event is defined to be the act of a host generating or receiving a packet, or the act of a router receiving or sending a packet. For this data the packet-event rate on one processor for local peers is 152,216 packet-events/second, and for scattered peers it is 150,948 packet-events/second. The execution time on one processor are 159 seconds for local peers, and 329 seconds for scattered peers, for 100 simulated seconds. Bear in mind that **SSF** is process oriented, and so these packet-events represent more work done at the kernel level per packet-event than would be done on in an event-oriented model. We believe the model-dependent notion of packet-event better conveys the delivered performance than would some kernel-specific rates such as context switches or kernel events.

In case of local peers the pure shared-memory synchronization achieves a speedup of 9.34 on 12 processors, whereas using message passing we achieve 7.67. Because the submodels are partitioned at the fully connected inter-AS level, as the number of processors used grows, the total volume of communication grows as the *square* of the number of processors (and the volume of communication handled by one node increases linearly). The raw cost of pushing bytes grows, as does the support cost of packing and unpacking messages for communication across memory space. Even though the Solaris MPI implementation takes advantage of shared memory, a noticeable performance price is paid.

Under the scattered peers distribution, the increased communication between distributed subsystems quickly reveals itself. The speedup for pure message passing drops to 4.74 on 12 processors, while it only introduces a slight change for shared-memory synchronization. Analysis of the results shows a dramatic increase in the time taken at barrier window synchronization, which is where all the cross-memory space overhead accumulates.

The next experiment shows the benefits of exploiting shared-memory parallelism within a multiprocessor node, on an actual distributed memory cluster. We ran this same simulation on a network of six PCs running Linux. Each machine has dual 750 MHz Intel Pentium III processors and 512 MB memory. The machines are connected by a 100M Ethernet network. Again we use the Gnu C++ compiler at optimization level 3. The lower portion of figure 2 shows the results of running the model using from one to six workstations. We compare the speedup as we utilize one or two processors on each workstation for local synchronization.

The figure shows good speedups in the case of local peers. For example, with 6 Linux workstations and one processor per machine (i.e. 6×1), we achieve a speedup of 5.51, whereas using the extra processor as well (6×2) we see a speedup of 9.69; doubling the number of processors used nearly doubles the speedup. Observe that the performance gain due to doubling the number of workstations in the $N \times 1$ case (from 1 to 2, from 2 to 4, from 3 to 6) is virtually identical to the performance gain due to using the extra processor (the difference between the $N \times 1$ and $N \times 2$ lines at 1, 2, and 3). It is also worth noting that the raw performance on this model using 12 processors ($9.69 \times 256K = 2.48M$ packet events/second) is almost twice that on the shared-memory machine ($9.34 \times 152K = 1.42M$ packet-events/second). Needless to say, the price of these six workstations and the ethernet network is significantly smaller than the price of the large multiprocessor. For these experiments the raw packet-event rate for one processor was 256,240 packet-events/second on the local peer model, and 291,600 packet-events/second on the scattered peer model.

The cost of high communication shows itself again however when we consider scattered peers. Using only one processor per machine, the model on 6 machines runs only 3.11 times faster than that on just one machine. Addition of the extra processor per node improves speedup, but only marginally. The execution cost is dominated by the message-exchange phase, which does not benefit from the extra computing power used. Even in the face of increased communication costs, the raw performance of the cluster is almost that of the multiprocessor: the 6×2 configuration delivers $4 \times 291K = 1.16M$ packet-events per second whereas 12 Solaris processors yield $8.8 \times 151K = 1.3M$ packet-events/second. Comparison of results using just six

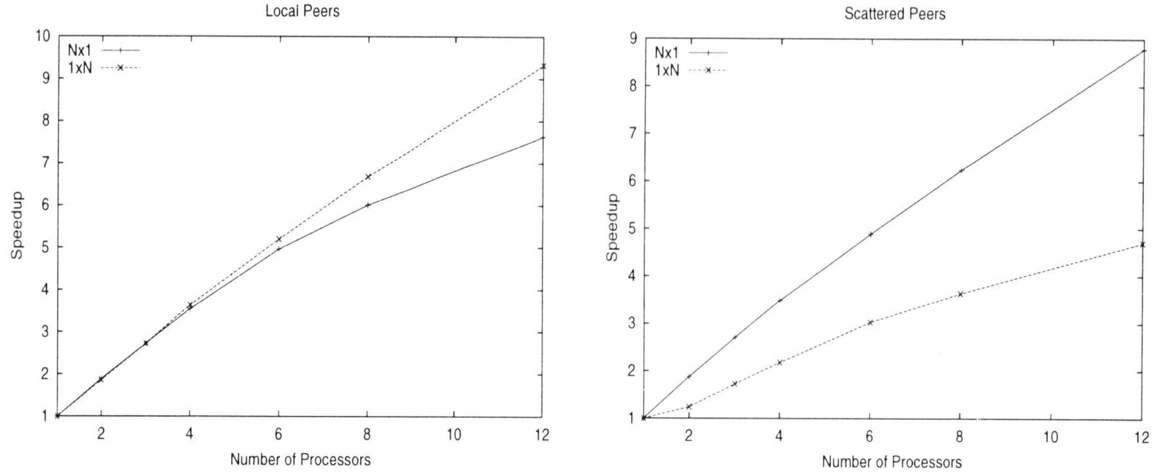

Speedup on Sun Enterprise 6500.

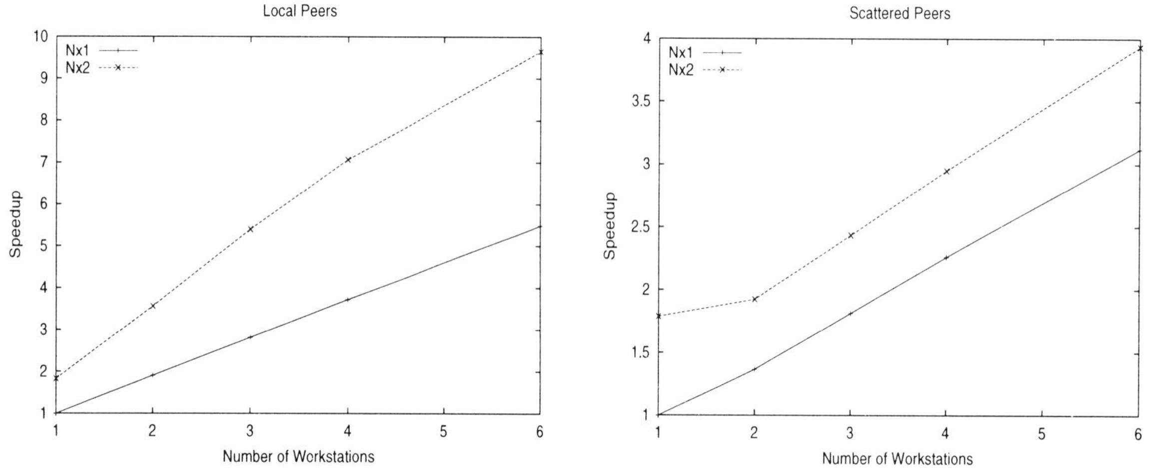

Speedup on a cluster of Linux SMPS.

Figure 2. Speedups on Two Architectures

processors shows better raw performance on the distributed system; the 1×6 Solaris performance is $5 \times 151K = 755K$ packet-events/second and the 6×1 workstation performance is $3.1 \times 291K = 901K$ packet-events/second. Of course the ability of the distributed architecture to deliver such performance is due to its much faster CPUs. The point is that the distributed architecture is built entirely of commodity products—it is the network of the desktop machines in our lab. The promise of high performance simulation on ordinary equipment is fulfilled. The execution on one CPU is 95 seconds for local peers and 170 seconds for scattered peers. In both cases, using the extra processor in the PC nearly doubles performance, and so in both cases we have better than real-time simulation of a substantial model, running a non-trivial application, on a commodity PC.

We also considered comparing 2 separate MPI processes per node ($2N \times 1$) with the combined approached already considered ($N \times 2$). While we observed virtually no difference in performance in the case of local peers, the difference was dramatic in the case of scattered peers. We traced the root cause of this behavior to the way MPI is implemented. Whenever MPI is run a separate kernel process is created to manage all communication traffic; this is separate and distinct from the application process that uses MPI services. We know already that a great deal of time is spent by the application processes at the message exchange phase. When we have two distinct MPI application processes on a node, at a message exchange they contend with the kernel's MPI process for CPU time; three processes, all with much to do, contend for two CPUs.

We also noticed that the model runs faster on four workstations using one processor per workstation (4×1) than on two workstations using two processors each for local shared-memory synchronization (2×2). This is also the case for 6×1 versus 3×2. We instrumented the code and it shows that the message-exchange phase costs in 2 and 3×2 cases are significantly higher than their counterparts. The simple explanation is that this application is communication bound, and using more workstations better exploits parallelism in processing the messaging overhead—communication costs are serialized at the node level. One node in the 3×2 system handles communication for almost a third of the entire model, whereas one node in the 6×1 case handles it for a sixth of the model.

In fairness it should be noted that a major advantage of shared-memory over distributed memory is that it is much easier to do dynamic load-balancing on such a platform than it is on distributed memory. The model we study is almost perfectly balanced, and so does not reveal that advantage.

5. Conclusions

This paper considers problems associated with executing a large-scale discrete-event simulation on an architecture comprised of a cluster of shared-memory multiprocessors. We propose and implement a two-level synchronization scheme, where the synchronization method used to coordinate between SMP nodes is different from the method used to coordinate within a node. We study performance on a Sun Solaris multiprocessor for the purpose of baseline comparison and analysis of inherent communication/synchronization overheads in the most benign environment. We see there that that on a significantly sized model, the inherent overhead induced by a second level of MPI based synchronization is not large relative to workload. However, the overheads of moving large amounts of data across memory-space boundaries are seen to be significant. We also study performance on a distributed network of dual-processor desktop PCs in our lab. Here too we see that the inherent overhead of using MPI to synchronize is not comparatively large when running a large model, but that performance can be severely degraded when the traffic across memory boundaries is very high. Nevertheless, we observe that on the experiments we perform, raw performance on the network of PCs almost always exceeds that of the much more costly multiprocessor.

In order to get to the point where we could study performance on a distributed network of SMPs, we had first to port our **SSF** simulator to run on that architecture. The fundamental problem we had to address was to connect objects that reside in different memory-spaces. We addressed this problem by introducing a front-end to the simulator that allows development of a text-based global naming methodology, and translates objects and connections expressed in that methodology into simulation objects and connections between them, crossing memory space boundaries as dictated by the partition. Under this solution the distributed memory approach is transparent to the **SSF** model, except for model configuration at initialization. Consequently the task of porting existing **SSF** codes to this new platform is greatly simplified.

Load-balancing is the largest problem faced by a distributed memory solution, and is one we have yet to deal with. However, the framework we propose is one that is well-suited for dynamic load-balancing solutions, because the global synchronization framework gives us natural points to to place load-balancing logic. Furthermore, the **SSF** kernel already measures the distribution of time spent in various activities; it is straightforward to recognize when load-imbalance exists. Finally, the mixed approach to synchronization is one that can be extended to within an SMP node. It can be advantageous to synchronize some parts of a node's submodel synchronously and others asynchronously. We are currently investigating such an approach.

References

[1] T. E. Anderson, D. E. Culler, D. A. Patterson, and the NOW team. A case for NOW (network of workstations). *IEEE Micro*, 1994.

[2] J. H. Cowie, D. M. Nicol, and A. T. Ogielski. Modeling the global internet. *Computing in Science & Engineering*, 1(1):42–50, 1999.

[3] R. Fujimoto and R. Weatherly. Time management in the DoD high level architecture. *Proceedings of Symposium on Parallel and Distributed Tools*, pages 60–7, 1996.

[4] D.M. Nicol. Non-commital barrier synchronization. *Parallel Computing*, 21:529–549, 1995.

[5] H. Rajaei, R. Ayani, and L.-E. Thorelli. The local time warp approach to parallel simulation. *1993 Workshop on Parallel and Distributed Simulation*, pages 119–26, 1993.

[6] D. Ridge, D. Becker, P. Merkey, and T. Sterling. Beowulf: Harnessing the power of parallism in a Pile-of-PCs. *Proceeding of IEEE Aerospace*, 1997.

[7] L. Sokol, D. Briscoe, and A. Wieland. MTW: A strategy for scheduling discrete simulation events for concurrent execution. *Distributed Simulation, 1988. Proceedings of the SCS Multiconference on Distributed Simulation*, pages 34–42, 1988.

[8] S. Turner and M. Xu. Performance evaluation of the bounded time warp algorithm. *6th Workshop on Parallel and Distributed Simulation (PADS92). Proceedings of the 1992 SCS Western Simulation MultiConference on Parallel and Distributed Simulation*, pages 117–26, 1992.

[9] Z. Xiao, B. Unger, R. Simmonds, and J. Cleary. Scheduling critical channels in conservative parallel discrete event simulation. *Proceedings of the 13th Workshop on Parallel and Distributed Simulation*, pages 20–8, 1999.

Semi-Asynchronous Checkpointing for Optimistic Simulation on a Myrinet Based NOW

Francesco Quaglia and Andrea Santoro
Dipartimento di Informatica e Sistemistica
Università di Roma "La Sapienza"
Via Salaria 113, 00198 Roma, Italy

Abstract

Great effort has been devoted to the design of optimized checkpointing strategies for optimistic parallel discrete event simulators. On the other hand there is less work in the direction to improve the execution mode of any single checkpoint operation. Specifically, checkpoint operations are typically charged to the CPU, thus leading to freezing of the simulation application while checkpointing is in progress, i.e. the execution mode of the checkpointing protocol is typically synchronous. In this paper we focus on improvements of the execution mode and present a software architecture, designed for myrinet based Network of Workstations (NOWs), to avoid application freezing during any checkpoint operation, thus moving the execution itself towards an asynchronous mode. This is done by charging checkpoint operations to a hardware component distinct from the CPU, namely a DMA engine. On the other hand, totally asynchronous checkpointing could suffer from data inconsistency whenever the content of a state buffer is accessed for further modifications while a checkpoint operation involving it is not yet completed. To avoid this, the architecture includes functionalities for resynchronization on demand. We have used these functionalities to implement an execution mode of the checkpointing protocol we refer to as semi-asynchronous. By the results of an experimental study we argue that the semi-asynchronous mode can be an effective solution to almost completely remove the delay associated with any checkpoint operation from the completion time of the simulation.

1 Introduction

It is widely recognized that the performance of optimistic parallel discrete event simulators can be strongly dependent on the way checkpoint operations are executed. For this reason, a number of optimized checkpointing schemes have been designed with the aim at keeping low the final overhead due to both saving of state information and state recovery.

However, whether they are based on the scattered recording of the whole state vector of the logical process (LP) (see for example [2, 4, 11, 13, 15, 16]) or on the incremental recording of portions of the state vector (see for example [1, 18, 19]), or even on a combination of previous strategies (see for example [5, 9, 17]), they exhibit the common feature that checkpoint operations are totally charged to the CPU. The consequence of this approach is that the simulation application is actually frozen while checkpointing is in progress, thus yielding a *synchronous* execution mode of the checkpointing protocol.

In this paper we present a solution to charge operations associated with checkpointing to other components of the hardware architecture so that the simulation application does not need to be frozen while checkpointing is in progress. Therefore, unlike most previous solutions, our focus is not on optimizing the strategy but on optimizing the execution mode of the checkpoint protocol.

The basic idea underlying our solution is that checkpointing is actually a problem of memory-to-memory data transfer, therefore a well suited component, distinct from the CPU, to support checkpoint operations is a DMA engine. In other words, in our perspective checkpointing means activation of a DMA engine to transfer the LP state vector into a checkpoint buffer. The feasibility of this solution relies on the fact that DMA data transfer should produce minimal BUS interference with the CPU due to the presence of the cache memory.

To our knowledge there has been only an attempt into the direction of avoiding application freezing during checkpoint operations [14]. That solution exhibits strong differences from what we propose. Specifically, the idea behind that solution is to use the instructions performed during the execution of an event as part of the checkpointing protocol, thus aiming at reducing the total number of checkpointing instructions that actually cause application freezing. However, the effectiveness of such an approach depends on the structure of the event code and on the extent to which instructions within the code can be used as part of the checkpointing protocol. In other words, the effectiveness of the approach strongly depends on the code structure of the specific simulation application. Furthermore, unless compiler supports are used, there is a reduction of transparency to the application programmer. By its nature, our proposal removes both previous problems.

Actually, also the work in [7] presents a solution to speedup the execution of the checkpointing protocol. However, that work is only marginally related to our solution

0-7695-1104-X/01 $10.00 © 2001 IEEE

since it makes use of special purpose hardware.

We have developed a software architecture, coupled with a proper API, to support DMA based checkpointing over a cluster of PCs running LINUX, interconnected by a high speed myrinet switch. Specifically, each myrinet card is equipped with an easily programmable DMA engine having the capability to support data transfer between distinct buffers into the host memory, thus being well suited for our purposes.

Actually, DMA based checkpointing moves the execution of the checkpointing protocol towards an asynchronous mode. However, totally asynchronous checkpointing could originate data inconsistency whenever the state vector currently being transferred through DMA is accessed by the LP during the simulation execution for further modifications of some state variables. For this reason we have included in the software architecture functionalities to suspend the execution of the simulation program on demand whenever there is the need to wait for the completion of a pending DMA data transfer. Therefore these functionalities allow data consistency maintenance by implementing a resynchronization point between CPU and DMA, whenever required. The combined use of DMA based checkpoint operations and resynchronization yields an execution mode of the checkpointing protocol we refer to as *semi-asynchronous*.

We have embedded the semi-asynchronous mode into a Time Warp [10] based simulation engine and we have used parameterized synthetic benchmarks for evaluating and comparing this solution to the classical synchronous mode. The collected data have shown that semi-asynchronous checkpointing outperforms synchronous checkpointing on all the workloads tested. The performance gain is evident even for small sizes of the state vector of the LPs, case in which the synchronous mode is expected to perform well.

The remainder of this paper is structured as follows. In Section 2 we provide hints on the hardware architecture of myrinet cards. In Section 3 we describe the implementation of the software architecture for semi-asynchronous checkpointing and present the API to be used at the application level. Section 4 illustrates the main structure of the Time Warp simulation engine embedding semi-asynchronous checkpointing. The performance data are reported in Section 5. Pointers to future developments are discussed in Section 6.

2 Myrinet Card Hardware Architecture

This section provides a description of the hardware structure and of the potentiality of myrinet cards, designed for use in combination with myrinet switches based on wormhole technology. Before entering the description we recall that myrinet based NOWs are actually emerging architectures for parallel applications due to cost vs performance reasons and also to expansibility/modifiability.

The software architecture we have developed has been designed for the M2M-PCI32C card, based on the LANai 4 chip [12]. However, porting the architecture on newer chip versions does not require any programming effort. The

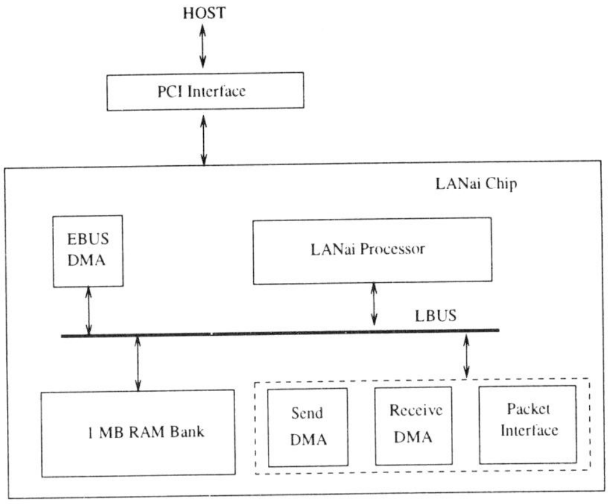

Figure 1. High Level Structure of the Chip.

LANai 4 chip is a programmable communication device consisting of:

- An internal bus, namely LBUS (Local BUS), clocked at twice the chip-clock speed.
- A programmable RISC processor connected to the LBUS, which we will refer to as LANai processor. This processor runs a control program that typically supports exclusively data transfer operations between the host and the network. The program can be structured according to the specific requirements of the overlying application.
- A RAM bank of 1 Mbyte (internal memory), connected to the LBUS, which is used for storing both data and the control program run by the LANai processor. This memory can be mapped into the memory address space of the host so that the host itself can perform read and write operations on it. These operations take place through a proper circuitry between the host and the LANai chip. For the M2M-PCI32C card such a circuitry consists of a PCI bridge.
- A packet interface between the myrinet switch and the LANai chip, accessible by the LANai processor.
- Three DMA engines used respectively for: (i) packet-interface/internal-memory transfer operations (receive DMA), (ii) internal-memory/packet-interface transfer operations (send DMA), and (iii) internal-memory/host-memory transfer (or vice-versa) operations (EBUS DMA, namely External Bus DMA).

The high level structure of the chip is schematized in Figure 1.

As already mentioned, the LBUS is clocked at twice the chip-clock speed, therefore, two memory cycles for every clock cycle can be performed. Each DMA or host access to the internal memory can request a maximum of one memory access per clock cycle. The LANai processor can request up to two internal memory accesses per clock cycle (instruction

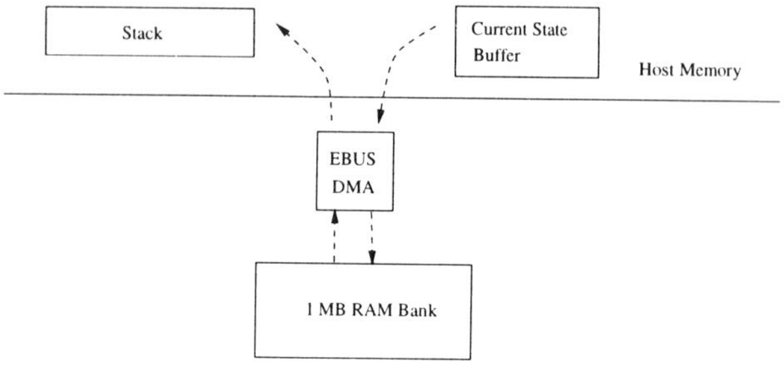

Figure 2. Basic Idea.

fetch and data access). The bus cycles are assigned based on the following priorities (highest to lowest): host and EBUS DMA, receive DMA, send DMA, LANai processor. Finally, we note that the LANai processor cannot access the host memory directly. Nonetheless, it can program the EBUS DMA to perform data transfer to/from that memory.

3 Semi-Asynchronous Checkpointing

3.1 Basic Idea and Basic Problem

As already pointed out in the Introduction, our basic idea for the implementation of semi-asynchronous checkpointing is to use data transfer potentiality offered by DMA components on the myrinet card. Specifically, the DMA of interest in our context is the EBUS DMA.

Basically, in our perspective checkpointing is an operation to be performed by the EBUS DMA, which involves data transfer from the LP current state buffer (located into host memory) to the stack of checkpointed states of the LP (also located into host memory). The LANai internal memory is used as a temporary buffer for the transfer operation. This perspective is shown in Figure 2. In other words, a checkpoint operation issued at the application level actually means requesting the LANai processor to program the EBUS DMA for the data transfer.

The basic problem with this solution is that the simulation application typically manages only virtual addresses, while data transfer through the EBUS DMA requires knowledge of the physical addresses of both the LP current state buffer and the checkpoint buffer into the stack. This is because the EBUS DMA supports data transfer operations based exclusively on physical addresses. How we have tackled this problem is described in the next section where we present the complete software architecture we have developed.

3.2 Software Architecture

The software architecture consists of three distinct parts: a Kernel Module (KM), a software layer (SL) accessible by the simulation application through an API, and a specialized control program (CP) for the LANai processor. Details on each part are separately reported in the following paragraphs.

KM. KM has been introduced just to solve the problem raised in previous section. Specifically, we have decided to solve that problem by reserving blocks of physical memory pages for both the current state buffers of the LPs and their stacks of checkpointed state vectors. Therefore, KM has the functionality to reserve those blocks, and to record both the physical address of the first page of each block and the block size. In our implementation, EBUS DMA based checkpoint operations will involve data located only on physical memory pages associated with these blocks.

The current version of KM has been designed for LINUX 2.0.32. Porting the software architecture for semi-asynchronous checkpointing on other operating systems involves the use of operating system dependent features to implement the current functionality offered by KM.

Reservation of blocks of pages takes place through the function `__get_free_pages()` internal to the kernel. Any reserved page will never be swapped-out from the physical memory. These pages can be mapped in the virtual address space of any application. Therefore, each LP can refer the content of its current state buffer (located on these pages) through virtual addressing. This allows maintenance of transparency at the application programmer level.

SL and its API. SL can be seen as composed by two sets of functions which are used, respectively, for the initialization and for the management of semi-asynchronous checkpoint operations.

Initialization Functions. Upon the startup of the simulation, reserved physical memory blocks must be mapped into virtual address space, so that each LP can access its current state buffer through virtual addressing. We have implemented the mapping in the way that blocks of physical memory pages are seen as grouped into a single block of contiguous virtual memory pages. Then, the reserved memory is partitioned in order to assign a specific portion to each LP hosted by that machine. As already outlined, the portion associated with any LP is used for both the current state buffer of the LP and the stack of checkpointed state vectors. Mapping and partitioning are activated through the function `ckpt_init(int num_LPs, int state_size)`. Actually, this function performs the previously described mapping using the LINUX/UNIX system call `mmap()` on the device file `/dev/mem`. This shows that also this function is dependent on the host operating system. Porting the software onto different operating systems requires partial rewriting of this function.

The execution of this function has also the effect to initialize data structures that, for each LP hosted by the machine, keep track of the busy entries in the stack of checkpointed state vectors. The physical memory destined to the stack is actually managed as a circular buffer, therefore keeping track of the busy entries means, in practice, keeping track of two indexes.

Once mapping and partitioning have been executed, the LP retrieves the virtual address associated with its current state buffer through the function `status *get_status_pointer(int LP_id)`.

Before ending the description of the initialization functions, we would like to outline two limits of the current implementation of ckpt_init(). (i) Only a single state size value can be specified, therefore, in case of different state vector sizes among distinct LPs, buffers destined to state vectors could be oversized. (ii) The reserved physical memory space is divided into equal parts among the LPs, therefore there is no mechanism to grant it dynamically on the basis of the real memory usage of the LPs. We are currently working on the implementation in order to remove these limits.

Checkpointing Management Functions. Each time a semi-asynchronous checkpoint operation needs to be activated, the LANai processor must be notified it must program the EBUS DMA for the corresponding data transfer operation. This involves communicating to the LANai processor the physical addresses of both the current state buffer of the LP and the selected checkpoint buffer. Such a communication takes place through the function semi_asynch_ckpt(int LP_id, time_type simulation_clock). This function accesses the previously mentioned data structures (i.e. data structures maintaining information on the mapping of virtual addresses into physical addresses and keeping track of the busy entries into the stack), identifies the two physical addresses, and communicates them to the LANai processor by writing their values into specific locations of the LANai internal memory. Identification and communication of these two addresses is done in a totally transparent way to the application.

SL includes also the function ckpt_wait() that can be used to freeze the simulation application on demand in case there is the need for waiting the termination of a pending checkpoint operation. This function can be used for data consistency maintenance whenever there is the possibility for an LP to modify the content of its current state buffer while an EBUS DMA based checkpoint operation involving the content of that buffer is not yet completed. Also, the current implementation does not support concurrent execution of multiple EBUS DMA based checkpoint operations, therefore ckpt_wait() must be used to freeze the simulation application each time a new checkpoint operation must be activated while a previously activated one is still in progress. ckpt_wait() returns immediately if no EBUS DMA based checkpoint operation is still in progress. Basically, to verify whether a previously activated checkpoint operation, if any, is not yet completed, this function checks the content of a specific byte into the LANai internal memory.

State recovery in case of rollback occurrence takes place through the function recover_status(int LP_id, time_type recovery_time) that accesses the stack and reloads the earliest checkpoint with simulation clock less than or equal to recovery_time into the current state buffer of the involved LP. This function works with virtual addresses determined by the mapping performed in the initialization phase. Reloading is implemented as a memcpy() call.

Finally, the function prune_stack(int LP_id, time_type fossil_collection_time) included in the API allows storage recovery of busy stack entries associated with obsolete state vectors. Also this function adopts virtual addressing for information access.

CP. The control program run by the LANai processor has the following basic structure:

```
While (1)
  do receive_packet();
      if (EBUS DMA programming required)
         program_DMA();
  while ( no packet to send );
  if (packet to send)
       start_send_packet();
  while( send not done ) receive_packet();
```

(The function receive_packet() has the effect to program the receive DMA in case a message must be transferred from the packet interface to the LANai internal memory. CP is not suspended while DMA based receive is in progress.) As explained before, invocation of the function semi_asynch_ckpt() means setting the values of data structures maintained into the memory on board of the LANai chip to indicate to the LANai processor that a semi-asynchronous checkpoint operation must be executed. In the current implementation, any checkpoint operation is executed through a sequence of invocations of the function program_DMA(). We have made the engineering choice that each invocation has the effect to program the EBUS DMA for the transfer of up to 1024 bytes from/to the LANai internal memory. Therefore, checkpointing state vectors of up to 1024 bytes requires only two successive invocations of program_DMA(). The first invocation has the effect to program the EBUS DMA to transfer the data from the current state buffer, located into host memory, towards the LANai internal memory (intermediate buffering). The second has the effect to program the EBUS DMA for transferring the data from the LANai internal memory towards the stack of checkpointed state vectors of the LP, located into host memory. Obviously, checkpointing state vectors larger than 1024 requires more than two invocations of program_DMA().

The reason for the previous engineering choice is twofold. (i) EBUS DMA data transfer (from/to the LANai internal memory) of a very large data block in a single chunk could excessively delay the access to the LANai internal memory of at least one among send and receive DMAs (this is because the LBUS supports at most two memory accesses for each LANai clock cycle, therefore, at most two DMA engines can be granted access to the LBUS in each clock cycle) with possible interference on communication delay. (ii) In the current implementation of message passing functionalities, buffering of the message content at both send and receive sides is performed into the LANai internal memory, then messages are transferred into the host memory (receive case) or onto the network (send case). Since transferring the message content between the host memory and the LANai internal memory (and vice versa) involves access to the PCI bridge, the EBUS DMA should not keep the bridge busy for long periods, therefore it should not perform transfer of very large data blocks in a single chunk. Otherwise there could be relevant increase in message passing overhead.

The fact that the LBUS supports at most two memory accesses for each LANai clock-cycle is also the reason why, during the send phase (lines from 6. to 8. of CP), no additional programming of the EBUS DMA is performed even if a requested checkpoint operation is not yet completed. Otherwise there could be non-minimal intervals during which all the three DMA engines require access to the LBUS. This potentially penalizes the send DMA that has lower priority.

We have selected the value 1024 bytes for each EBUS DMA transfer operation based on some benchmarks we have run in order to estimate the real interference of EBUS DMA based data transfer with access operations to the LANai internal memory issued by the host and by both send and receive DMAs. We have noted that up to 1024 bytes per single transfer actually provides minimal interference. At the same time, dividing the EBUS DMA transfer into portions of 1024 bytes does not produce relevant transfer delay, as compared to transfer into a single chunk, for data size of up to several Kbytes. Anyway, we are currently investigating on the possibility to determine dynamically the chunk size depending on current system conditions.

4 A Time Warp Engine Based on Semi-Asynchronous Checkpointing

We have embedded semi-asynchronous checkpointing into an existing Time Warp engine whose execution flow is based on the following loop (for sake of simplicity GVT calculation and fossil collection are not included in the description):

```
1. while(not end)
2.    <receive messages>
3.    LP = schedule_next();
4.    if (rollback required for LP) rollback();
5.    if (checkpoint required for LP) checkpoint();
6.    next_event_execution();
7.    <send messages>;
```

(Rollback is implemented using aggressive antimessage sending [8].) By the loop structure, the need for checkpointing the state vector of the scheduled LP is tested prior to the execution of its next event (see line 5.). The test in this point permits the use of checkpointing strategies in which the decision on whether a checkpoint of the state vector of the LP must be taken is based also on features associated with the next event of that LP, such as the event timestamp (see for example [13]).

To embed the semi-asynchronous execution mode, we have decided to move the test in line 5. just after the event execution in order to activate the checkpoint operation, if required, right after the event execution itself. We have done this because semi-asynchronous checkpointing does not avoid application freezing anytime a checkpoint operation is activated after the processor scheduling phase and this operation involves the state buffer of the currently scheduled LP. This is because the LP could modify the content of that buffer, therefore access to that buffer must be granted only after the checkpointing protocol terminates.

With this modification in the loop, semi-asynchronous checkpointing can be combined only with checkpointing strategies in which the decision on whether a checkpoint must be taken does not rely on features associated with the next event of the currently scheduled LP. As an example, it can be combined with classical periodic strategies that make checkpoint decisions based only on the number of executed events from the last checkpoint.

Moving the test in that point requires two distinct resynchronizations between CPU and EBUS DMA (i.e. two distinct invocations of `ckpt_wait()`), thus yielding the following final structure:

```
1. pending_LP = no_LP;
2. while(not end)
3.    <receive messages>
4.    LP = schedule_next();
5.    if (LP = pending_LP)
6.          ckpt_wait();
7.          pending_LP = no_LP;
8.    if (rollback required for LP) rollback();
9.    next_event_execution();
10.   if (checkpoint required for LP)
11.         ckpt_wait();
12.         pending_LP = LP;
13.         semi_asynch_ckpt();
14.   <send messages>;
```

The resynchronization point in line 6. takes place only if the currently scheduled LP is associated with a pending semi-asynchronous checkpoint operation. This allows data consistency maintenance into the stack of checkpointed state vectors of that LP.

The resynchronization point in line 11. actually freezes the simulation application only in case a new checkpoint operation must be issued while the last issued one is still in progress. This is required since, as already outlined, the current version of SL does not support concurrent execution of multiple EBUS DMA based checkpoint operations.

As a final point we would like to outline a possible optimization that we have not yet implemented. In case resynchronization in line 6. leads to application freezing and the scheduled LP must rollback, it would be better to abort the pending checkpoint operation involving the current state vector of that LP. This is because, the content of the current state buffer of that LP represents incorrect information to be discarded in the rollback phase. Therefore checkpointing the content of that buffer actually results in a useless checkpoint.

5 Performance Analysis

In this section we report experimental results demonstrating how semi-asynchronous checkpointing can actually lead to a strong increase of the execution speed of the simulation. The experiments were all performed on a cluster of 4 Pentium II 300 MHz (128 Mbytes RAM - 512 Kbytes second level cache). All the PCs of the cluster run LINUX (kernel version 2.0.32) and are equipped with M2M-PCI32C myrinet cards.

The reference point for our analysis is the classical synchronous checkpointing mode, implemented as a `memcpy()` call having the effect of copying the content of the current state buffer of the LP into the stack. To ensure fairness in the comparison, also for the synchronous mode we have located both the stack and the current state buffer of the LP into reserved pages of physical memory that will never be swapped out. In this case, we can effectively test if one execution mode of the checkpointing protocol outperforms the other due to its proper nature and not to the effects of the underlying virtual memory system.

We have considered also a third type of execution mode, which is actually a simulation of the synchronous mode realized through the API for semi-asynchronous checkpointing. Specifically, in this mode any checkpoint operation results in an invocation of `semi_asynch_ckpt()` immediately followed by an invocation of `ckpt_wait()`, thus yielding artificial freezing of the application while EBUS DMA based checkpointing is in progress. We have decided to include this mode in the analysis since it can provide hints on the real impact of memory-to-memory EBUS DMA based data transfer operations as compared to memory-to-memory data transfer operations supported by the CPU.

We have tested previous execution modes in combination with the copy-state-saving strategy (i.e. checkpoint at each event). This strategy yields the maximum amount of checkpoint operations per event, thus resulting in an extreme case well suited to test the real impact of an optimized execution mode of the checkpointing protocol.

As a benchmark, we have used a classical PHOLD model [6], consisting of 32 LPs evenly distributed among the 4 machines in the cluster. The message population has been fixed at 5 messages per LP, which represents a workload enough saturated to minimize the likelihood of idleness of any machine due to absence of events in the pending event queues of the LPs. If this does not occur, then it would be difficult to judge the real impact of optimizations in the execution mode of checkpointing since the occurrence of idle periods would produce interference on the final performance observed. In the PHOLD model we have used, messages are equally likely to be forwarded to any LP and the timestamp increments follow an exponential distribution with mean 10 simulation time units.

In the experiments we have varied the size of the state vector of the LPs between 100 bytes and 5000 bytes. We believe this interval is representative since several real world simulation applications exhibit LP state vector size within these boundaries.

We have considered two different configurations for the structure of the event routine. (i) A first configuration in which the event routine is a simple CPU busy loop. We set the length of the loop in order to obtain loop completion within about 150 microseconds when there is no other active user load (such a delay can be considered as an intermediate event granularity for parallel simulation applications). (ii) A second configuration in which the event routine consists of a loop that performs `memset()` calls circularly issued on contiguous sets of entries of a vector of chars of size 2 Mbytes. Since the machines we have used have second level cache of size 512 Kbytes, this originates RAM accesses for memory updating. Also in this case, we set the length of the loop in order to obtain loop completion within about 150 microseconds when there is no other active user load.

The configuration in point (i) allows us to test semi-asynchronous checkpointing when there is minimal RAM access due to event execution, thus yielding minimal interference on the host internal BUS between EBUS DMA operations and operations associated with event execution. This represents a favorable case for semi-asynchronous checkpointing. The configuration in point (ii) allows us to test semi-asynchronous checkpointing in the converse scenario, i.e. when there is a non-minimal amount of RAM accesses due to event execution, which possibly originate interference on the BUS, thus yielding a non-favorable case for semi-asynchronous checkpointing.

We report measures related to the following parameters. (i) The efficiency, that is the ratio between the number of committed events and the total number of executed events. This parameter allows us to point out whether different execution modes of the checkpointing protocol produce relevant variations of the amount of rollback of the simulation. (ii) The event rate, that is the number of committed events per time unit. This parameter indicates how fast is the simulation execution with a given checkpointing mode, therefore it is representative of the final performance perceived.

Furthermore, for the case of semi-asynchronous checkpointing we report also the frequency of resynchronization occurrence at the resynchronization points in line 6. (resynchronization after scheduling) and in line 11. (resynchronization before checkpoint) of the previously described Time Warp engine. This frequency has been evaluated as the ratio between the number of times the application is actually frozen due to a call to the function `ckpt_wait()` and the number of semi-asynchronous checkpoint operations issued. Low values for this frequency indicate low probability of application freezing when the semi-asynchronous mode is adopted.

We report the average observed values of previous parameters, computed over 5 runs that were all done with different seeds for the random number generation. At least 3×10^6 committed events were simulated in each run.

The obtained results, reported in Figure 3 and in Figure 4, indicate two major tendencies regardless of the fact that event execution produces RAM access or not. The first tendency is that, once fixed the LP state size, all the tested checkpointing modes exhibit almost the same values for the efficiency. This result is an indicator that, using the semi-asynchronous mode, communication seems to not suffer from the fact that data transfer operations associated with checkpointing are charged to the EBUS DMA. Specifically, if relevant interference on communication would have been produced, then we could have noted an increase in the amount of rollback since delaying the delivery of messages/antimessages might mean higher likelihood of incorrect computations [3].

Checkpointing Mode	Efficiency vs State Vector Size					
	100	1000	2000	3000	4000	5000
synchronous	0.92	0.92	0.93	0.91	0.92	0.93
simul. synchronous	0.93	0.93	0.94	0.90	0.93	0.93
semi-asynchronous	0.93	0.93	0.94	0.90	0.92	0.94

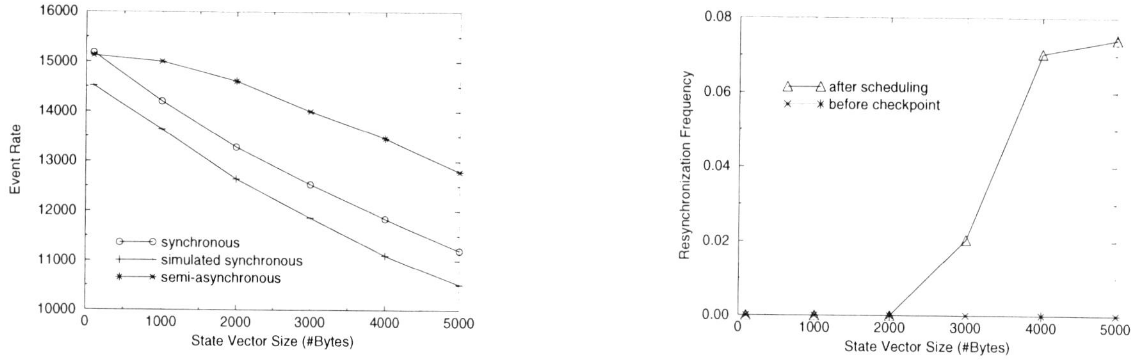

Figure 3. Results for the Case of Event Structured as a Busy Loop.

Checkpointing Mode	Efficiency vs State Vector Size					
	100	1000	2000	3000	4000	5000
synchronous	0.93	0.93	0.93	0.93	0.92	0.92
simul. synchronous	0.92	0.93	0.93	0.94	0.93	0.93
semi-asynchronous	0.93	0.93	0.93	0.94	0.94	0.94

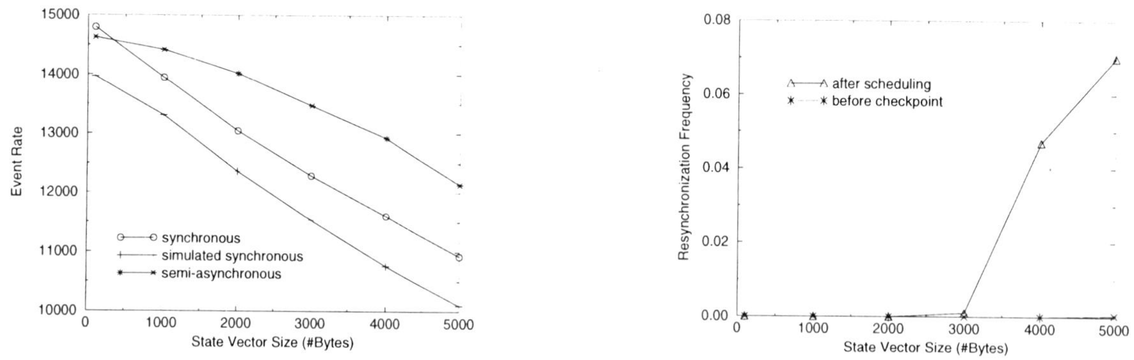

Figure 4. Results for the Case of Event Structured as `memset()` Calls.

The second tendency is that, for the case of minimal state vector size (in the order of 100 bytes), the semi-asynchronous mode produces about the same event rate of the synchronous mode. Instead, as soon as the state vector size becomes non-minimal, it actually yields strong performance improvements, with gain that increases vs the state vector size. This is a tendency we expected to observe since the semi-asynchronous mode should be likely to produce real advantages for any application in which the synchronous mode actually produces long application freezing intervals anytime a checkpoint operation is activated.

Another interesting point to note is that the resynchronization frequency associated with the resynchronization point after scheduling remains practically null for state vector size up to 2000 bytes, and grows up to a maximum of about 7% for larger sizes. Instead, the resynchronization frequency associated with the resynchronization point before checkpoint is null regardless of the state vector size. In practice this means that, adopting the semi-asynchronous mode, the application is rarely frozen while checkpointing is in progress, and this might occur only if the state vector size is large and multiple consecutive times the scheduler selects the same LP for running. We expect that, for applications with a larger number of LPs hosted by a single machine the freezing problem is likely to disappear since, unless the simulation model exhibits strong locality of event occurrences over a period of simulation time, the probability for any LP to be scheduled for running multiple consecutive times is likely to decrease. On the other hand, increase of the resynchronization frequency should be likely to appear for smaller models, characterized by fewer LPs hosted by any machine.

The fact that the resynchronization frequency remains null even for non-minimal state vector size is one of the reasons why, in case of event structured as a busy loop with minimal RAM access, the plot of the event rate for the semi-asynchronous mode remains almost flat for values of the state vector size up to 2000 bytes. Specifically, flatness derives from the fact that, up to 2000 bytes state vector size, checkpointing does never freeze the application (being the resynchronization frequency null) and does not interfere with event execution in respect to the access to the host BUS (due to the structure of the event code). A similar trend can be noted for the case of event structured as a loop performing `memset()` calls. This demonstrates that possible interference with event execution in respect to the host BUS access does not produce relevant changes in the execution dynamics.

As a final point we would like to stress that the performance produced by the simulated synchronous mode is no more than 10% worse, as compared to the performance produced by the synchronous mode. This points out the fact that EBUS DMA based memory-to-memory data transfer operations do not result much penalizing, as compared to CPU based transfer. This supports the feasibility of the basic idea underlying the solution we propose. In respect to this point we would like to recall that the PCI bridge on the card we have used supports data transfer at 33MHz, while newer versions of the card allow data transfer at 66MHz. Using those versions should be likely to further reduce the gap between EBUS DMA based and CPU based transfers.

6 Pointers to Future Work

There is a point that has not been touched in the previous analysis. Specifically, we have studied the performance offered by the semi-asynchronous mode only in combination with a "non-optimized" checkpointing strategy, namely copy-state-saving. It would be interesting to design and test optimized strategies well suited for coupling with the semi-asynchronous mode. We recall that the need for new optimized strategies comes out from the fact that some existing optimized strategies are likely to not yield real benefits when combined with the semi-asynchronous mode (see the discussion presented in Section 4), and some others are based on assumptions that might not hold in case of semi-asynchronous execution of the checkpointing protocol. As an example, a common assumption in models underlying several periodic strategies is that the variance of the CPU time for the synchronous execution of a checkpoint operation is relatively small, i.e. the variance of the length of the application freezing interval due to checkpointing is relatively small. This assumption might not hold for the case of semi-asynchronous checkpointing since the real freezing effect due to resynchronization depends on proper dynamics of the application, therefore the length of the freezing interval could exhibit high variance.

Finally, the implementation we have presented relies on the use of blocks of physical memory pages destined for the current state buffer and for the stack of checkpoints of any LP hosted by the machine, hence these blocks are no longer under the control of the memory manager. As respect to this point, an investigation on possible decrease in memory performance, which might arise in some circumstances, needs to be carried on.

References

[1] H. Bauer and C. Sporrer, "Reducing Rollback Overhead in Time Warp Based Distributed Simulation with Optimized Incremental State Saving", *Proc. 26th Annual Simulation Symposium*, pp.12-20, March 1993.

[2] S. Bellenot, "State Skipping Performance with the Time Warp Operating System", *Proc. 6th Workshop on Parallel and Distributed Simulation (PADS'92)*, pp.33-42, January 1992.

[3] C. D. Carothers, R. Fujimoto and P. England, "Effect of Communication Overheads on Time Warp Performance: An Experimental Study", *Proc. 8th Workshop on Parallel and Distributed Simulation (PADS'94)*, pp. 118-125, July 1994.

[4] J. Fleischmann and P.A. Wilsey, "Comparative Analysis of Periodic State Saving Techniques in Time Warp Simulators", *Proc. 9th Workshop on Parallel and Distributed Simulation (PADS'95)*, pp.50-58, June 1995.

[5] S. Franks, F. Gomes, B.W. Unger and J. Cleary, "State Saving for Interactive Optimistic Simulation", *Proc. 11th Workshop on Parallel and Distributed Simulation (PADS'97)*, pp.72-79, June 1997.

[6] R.M. Fujimoto, "Performance of Time Warp Under Synthetic Workloads", *Proc. Multiconf. Distributed Simulation*, Vol.22, No.1, January 1990.

[7] R.M. Fujimoto, J.Tsai and G.C. Gopalakrishnan, "Design and Evaluation of the Rollback Chip: Special Purpose Hardware for Time Warp", *IEEE Transactions on Computers*, Vol.41, No.1, pp.68-82, January 1992.

[8] A. Gafni, "Space Management and Cancellation Mechanisms for Time Warp", *Tech. Rep. TR-85-341*, University of Southern California, Los Angeles (Ca,USA).

[9] F. Gomes, B.W. Unger, S. Franks and J. Cleary, "Multiplexed State Saving for Bounded Rollback", *Proc. 1997 Winter Simulation Conference*, pp.460-467, December 1997.

[10] D. Jefferson, "Virtual Time", *ACM Transactions on Programming Languages and Systems*, Vol.7, No.3, pp.404-425, July 1985.

[11] Y.B. Lin, B.R. Preiss, W.M. Loucks and E.D. Lazowska, "Selecting the Checkpoint Interval in Time Warp Simulation", *Proc. 7th Workshop on Parallel and Distributed Simulation (PADS'93)*, pp.3-10, May 1993.

[12] MYRICOM, "LANai 4", *Draft*, February 1999.

[13] F. Quaglia, "Combining Periodic and Probabilistic Checkpointing in Optimistic Simulation", *Proc. 13th Workshop on Parallel and Distributed Simulation (PADS'99)*, pp.109-116, May 1999.

[14] F. Quaglia, "Fast-Software-Checkpointing in Optimistic Simulation: Embedding State Saving into the Event Routine Instructions", *Proc. 13th Workshop on Parallel and Distributed Simulation (PADS'99)*, pp.118-125, May 1999.

[15] R. Ronngren and R. Ayani, "Adaptive Checkpointing in Time Warp", *Proc. 8th Workshop on Parallel and Distributed Simulation (PADS'94)*, pp.110-117, May 1994.

[16] S. Skold and R. Ronngren, "Event Sensitive State Saving in Time Warp Parallel Discrete Event Simulations", *Proc. 1996 Winter Simulation Conference*, December 1996.

[17] H.M. Soliman and A.S. Elmaghraby, "An Analytical Model for Hybrid Checkpointing in Time Warp Distributed Simulation", *IEEE Transactions on Parallel and Distributed Systems*, Vol.9, No.10, pp.947-951, October 1998.

[18] J. Steinman, "Incremental State Saving in SPEEDES Using C Plus Plus", *Proc. 1993 Winter Simulation Conference*, pp.687-696, December 1993.

[19] B.W. Unger, J. Cleary, A. Covington and D. West, "External State Management System for Optimistic Parallel Simulation", *Proc. 1993 Winter Simulation Conference*, pp.750-755, December 1993.

Session 4

HLA

Hierarchical Federations: An Architecture for Information Hiding

Wentong CAI Stephen J. TURNER
School of Computer Engineering
Nanyang Technological University
Nanyang Avenue
Singapore 639798
{aswtcai, assjturner}@ntu.edu.sg

Boon Ping GAN
Gintic Institute of
Manufacturing Technology
71 Nanyang Drive
Singapore 638075
bpooi@gintic.gov.sg

Abstract

In a distributed simulation, simulation components of various types are executed at geographically different locations, forming a simulation federation to create a common virtual environment. Under the High Level Architecture (HLA), information that will be produced and consumed by a simulation component is defined in its object model, and how that information is produced and consumed is well encapsulated inside the simulation component's implementation. However, in the current implementation of the HLA's Runtime Infrastructure (RTI), information hiding between groups of simulation components in a simulation federation is not addressed. In this paper, we discuss how hierarchical federations architectures can be used to tackle this problem. The hierarchical federations architecture adopted in this paper differs from the existing architectures in that it is based on a hybrid approach for interoperability between simulation federations. To demonstrate the information hiding using the architecture, a distributed semiconductor supply-chain simulation is also described in the paper.

Keywords: distributed simulation, hierarchical federations, information hiding, semiconductor supply-chain simulation.

1 Introduction

Distributed simulation is an important strategic technology for linking simulation components of various types at multiple locations to create a realistic and complex "virtual world" for the simulation of highly interactive activities [3]. It originated in military applications, where geographically distributed simulators from different types of forces were connected to form full battle situations. Other applications include training, entertainment, logistics, emergency planning and distributed cooperative work.

With the advances of Internet technologies, experiments with a complex distributed simulation become highly feasible. To facilitate interoperability among simulations and promote reuse of simulation components, the High Level Architecture (HLA) for Simulation [2] was developed under the auspices of the US Defense Modeling and Simulation Office (DMSO) as a worldwide standard. Under the HLA, a combined simulation system is called a *federation* and the individual simulation components are called *federates*. The Runtime Infrastructure (RTI) is software, conforming to the HLA standard, that is used to support a federation execution. It provides a set of services available to the federates for coordinating their operations and data interchange during an execution.

Two most beneficial features of the HLA are *reusability* and *interoperability*. The issue of reusability is addressed in the HLA by the Object Model Template (OMT). Each federate has a *Simulation Object Model* (SOM) that describes the information that the federate can produce or consume. A federation has a *Federation Object Model* (FOM) which defines the union of certain parts of the participating federates' SOMs that will be used in the federation. With its capability well defined in the SOM, a federate then could be reused in different federations. The issue of interoperability is addressed by the Interface Specification which specifies the interface between federates and the RTI. Federates in the same federation do not communicate with each other directly, but rather through the RTI via a standard interface.

Using the HLA, information that will be produced and consumed by the federates in a federation is defined in the SOM and FOM. How the information is produced and consumed is well encapsulated inside the federates' implementations. However, in addition to the *information hiding* between individual federates, some applications may also require that certain information could only be shared among a group of federates, not all the federates in a federation. For example, in a battlefield simulation, some strategic move information should only be known by the battalions of the same side, and in a distributed supply-chain simulation that crosses enterprise boundaries, information about certain products should only be available to the factories that belong to the same company or group of companies.

Superficially, information hiding between groups of federates could be realized by having federates subscribe only to the information that they require. However, this cannot be enforced, in general. There are situations where federates could not be trusted to access only the information that they need. In the current implementation of the RTI, once the information is published, it will be accessible by all federates within the federation. There is no way to ensure that the information is only visible to a subset of federates. Thus, using a single level of federation, information hiding between groups of federates cannot be realized.

Hence, our research objective is to develop an *hierarchical federations architecture* that supports secure information hiding. In this paper we propose a new architecture and demonstrate its feasibility using a distributed semiconductor supply-chain simulation. The paper is organized as follows: Section 2 will briefly summarize some related work on hierarchical federations. Section 3 will introduce our proposed architecture and describe its advantages in terms of information hiding. Section 4 will explain a distributed semiconductor supply-chain simulation model and demonstrate how our proposed architecture can be applied to provide information hiding in such an application. The paper will conclude with directions of our future work in Section 5.

2 Hierarchical Federations

A *federation community* is a group of federations and RTIs working together to achieve a common goal [10]. The term *hierarchical federations* refers to a special type of federation community in which federations are organized into hierarchies so that a federation appears as a federate in an upper level federation.

Various issues on interoperability and heterogeneity of a federation community have been addressed by the *RTI Interoperability Study Group* [10]. Four approaches to supporting interoperability among federations in a federation community are proposed in [11]:

- *Federation Gateway*: A federation gateway does not belong to any federation. It is a process that interconnects two or more federates and performs translation functions between different federations (see Figure 1).

- *Proxy Federate*: A proxy federate is a federate that joins more than one federation simultaneously (see Figure 2). In a similar way to the gateway process, it performs translation functions, making information from one federation available to the other federations in the federation community.

- *RTI Broker*: An RTI broker is a process that interacts directly with RTIs. It passes not only federate level data but also RTI internal state information between two (or more) RTIs. Different from a proxy federate, an RTI broker does not belong to any federation.

- *RTI-to-RTI Protocol*: Instead of using an RTI broker, a lower level RTI-to-RTI protocol can be developed so that it can be used directly within an RTI implementation to communicate federate level data and RTI internal state information to other RTIs.

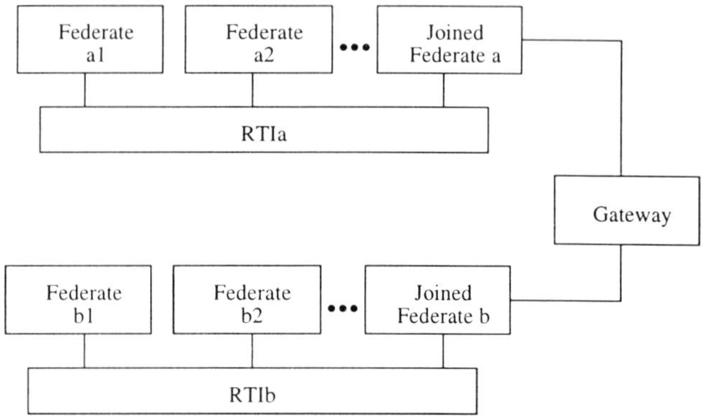

Figure 1. Gateway Architecture

The first two approaches, which are more related to our proposed architecture, provide a solution for constructing hierarchical federations at the application level. The last two approaches may need RTI developers to be involved at the systems level.

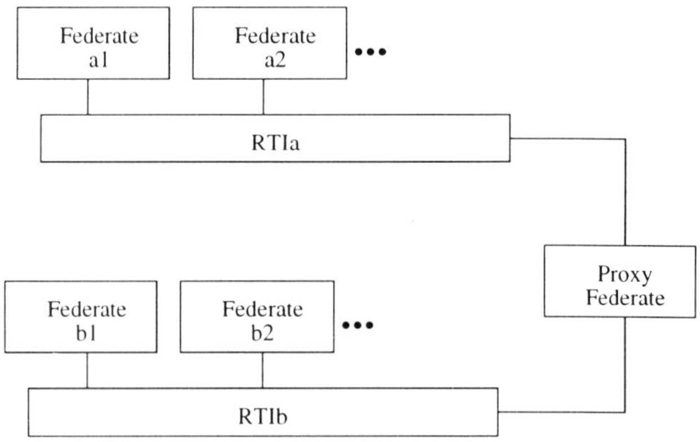

Figure 2. Proxy Architecture

The gateway approach is usually used to provide interoperability between an HLA federation and a legacy simulation network protocol (such as DIS, SIMNET or

ALSP) [14]. However, a federation gateway, as described above, can also be used to create an communication path between different HLA federation executions [11]. As illustrated by the *security guard federate* in [4], a gateway process can provide one federation with state information about another federation as well as performing information hiding between federations to filter out sensitive information.

Since a proxy federate (also called a *bridge federate* [1]) must join more than one federation, a separate RTI Ambassador and Federate Ambassador[1] must be created for each federation joined. The proxy federate can perform some functions similar to those carried out by the gateway process, such as data transformation, but not information hiding. This is because the proxy federate belongs to multiple federations and therefore cannot be completedly trusted by either federation. Although it provides connectivity between federations, it may also create a security loophole.

In general, the advantages of hierarchical federations are:

- supporting interoperability between heterogeneous federations and heterogeneous RTIs and enabling large-scale simulations to be developed using existing (possibly legacy) federations.
- improving the scalability of large and complex applications by reducing the bandwidth requirements through the partitioning of network load and the filtering out of irrelevant data between federations.

Hierarchical federations are also studied in [7, 8]. Previous work has mainly focused on the issues of interoperability and heterogeneity. How secure information hiding can be provided using an hierarchical federations architecture is the focus of this paper and it will be discussed in detail in the following sections.

3 An Hierarchical Federations Architecture for Information Hiding

The hierarchical federations architecture used in this paper is illustrated in Figure 3, where two user federations (federation a and federation b) form a super-federation. It adopts a hybrid approach using a combination of both gateway and proxy for interoperability between simulation federations. In this architecture, conceptually there is a separate RTI session for each participating federation in a super-federation execution. For example, in Figure 3, federation a is supported by the RTI session RTI_a and federation b is supported by the RTI session RTI_b. Federates in federation a, for instance, interact with other federates in the same federation through RTI_a, whereas they interact with federates in federation b through *gateway federates*. Gateway federates themselves form a *gateway federation* whose execution is supported by a dedicated RTI session (e.g., $RTI_{Gateway}$ in Figure 3).

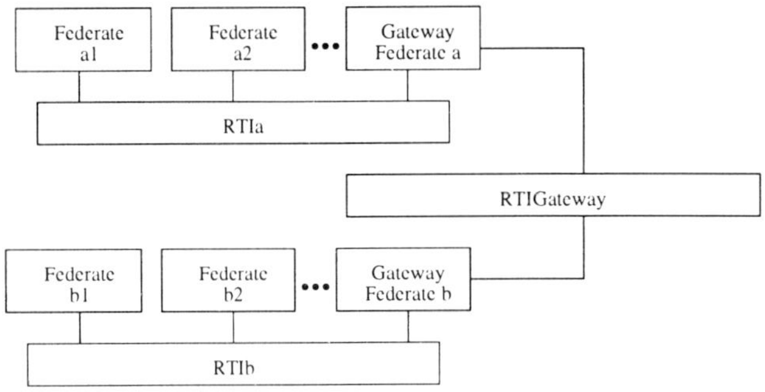

Figure 3. Our Architecture

Our architecture is different from the gateway architecture since it does not have a dedicated federation gateway process. It is also different from the proxy architecture since in our architecture there does not exist a federate that is directly attached to more than one participating user federation in the super-federation. Our architecture is a combination of gateway and proxy architectures because:

- The gateway federate performs some of the activities performed by the gateway process in the gateway approach (for example, data translation and information hiding).
- The gateway federate also acts as a proxy between a participating federation and the gateway federation, providing connectivity between different federations.

Compared to the gateway approach, the implementation of our gateway federate is much simpler, since the connectivity is provided through the gateway federation. First, it is not necessary to define any special protocols for communication through the gateway. Instead, the gateway federate can make use of the standard services of the $RTI_{Gateway}$ to send and receive interactions or update the simulation state. Secondly, whereas the gateway approach may require a gateway to provide communication between multiple federations, in our approach, a gateway federate joins exactly two federations (one of which is the gateway federation).

In the proxy approach, connectivity is achieved by allowing the proxy to join two or more user federations. This means that the proxy federate is able to subscribe to all of the information available within each of these federations. It is therefore impossible to achieve information hiding with the proxy approach. In our architecture, the gateway federate is not connected directly to more than one participating

[1] A federate invokes operations on the RTI Ambassador whenever it needs RTI services and the RTI invokes operations on the Federate Ambassador whenever it needs to call the federate.

user federation. Therefore, information that is confidential within a federation can be filtered out at the gateway federate. Each user federation still has its own FOM and a gateway federate can be trusted since it is associated with a particular user federation. The union of the subsets of the individual FOMs forms the super-FOM that is used by the gateway federation.

As the gateway federate always joins exactly two federations, it has a simple and regular structure. It is therefore feasible to generate the required code for data conversion and information hiding automatically, given an appropriate specification of the mapping between the FOM and super-FOM. Needless to say, our proposed architecture also supports hierarchical federations with any number of levels.

To demonstrate the information hiding using our architecture, a distributed semiconductor supply-chain simulation is studied. The performance of our hierarchical federations architecture, compared to a single-level federation implementation, is also presented in the next section.

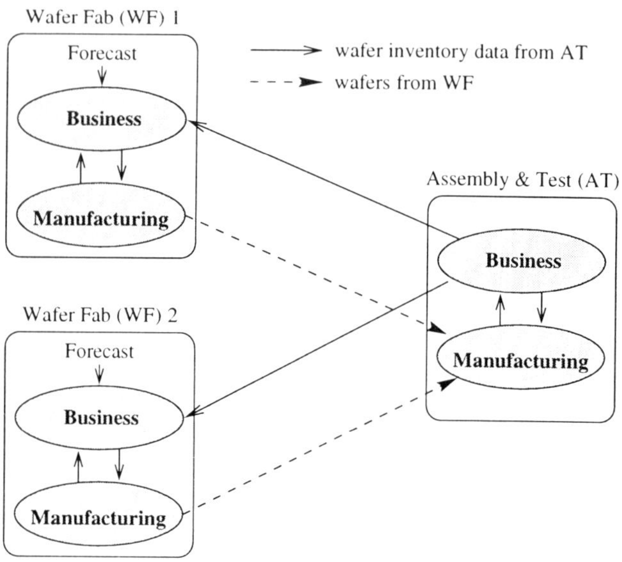

Figure 4. Semiconductor Supply-chain (SC)

4 Feasibility Study

Supply-chain (SC) management covers the planning and management of material and information flow from the manufacturer, through the distributors, and finally to the customer. Simulation of a supply-chain enables the companies to examine the feasibility of alternative inventory control policies. The best option can then be deployed to reduce operating costs and improve customer services.

4.1 Semiconductor Supply-chain Model

As shown in Figure 4, a supply-chain in semiconductor manufacturing may comprise of multiple *wafer fabrication* plants that supply wafers to an *assembly & test* facility. In this model, each factory consists of two basic processes: *manufacturing* and *business*. The manufacturing process simulates the transformation of raw materials into finished products. For the wafer fabrication plant, this means the production of wafers from silicon. In the case of the assembly & test facility, the wafers are converted into integrated circuit units. The business process simulates production and inventory planning. Forecasting is used in the planning to improve lead times by having strategic products in storage so that they are ready for servicing customer orders. It is based on factors such as forecasted demand information, inventory information and work-in-progress information [6].

The simulation in the above semiconductor supply-chain model is driven by the customer orders received by the assembly & test facility, which projects the actual consumption of products against the forecasted demand. Inventory information flows from the assembly & test facility to the wafer fabrication plants. From each wafer fabrication plant, wafers are shipped to the assembly & test facility. The transportation of materials and the transmission of information between the various factories are modeled as short delays.

4.2 Distributed Semiconductor Supply-chain Simulation

In our distributed supply-chain simulation, each factory is a federate [13]. There are two events that are external to a factory. They are ShipmentEvent and InventoryInfoEvent. The ShipmentEvent simulates the material flow from the wafer fabrication plant to the assembly & test facility, and the InventoryInfoEvent simulates the information flow from the assembly & test facility to the wafer fabrication plant. These two events are represented by two interaction classes, InventoryInfo and Shipment, in the distributed simulation (see Figure 5).

Figure 5. Interaction Classes in Distributed SC Simulation

For each interaction class, the parameter is a long string consisting of the list of product IDs and the list of corresponding product quantities. In the interaction sent from the wafer fabrication plants to the assembly & test facility,

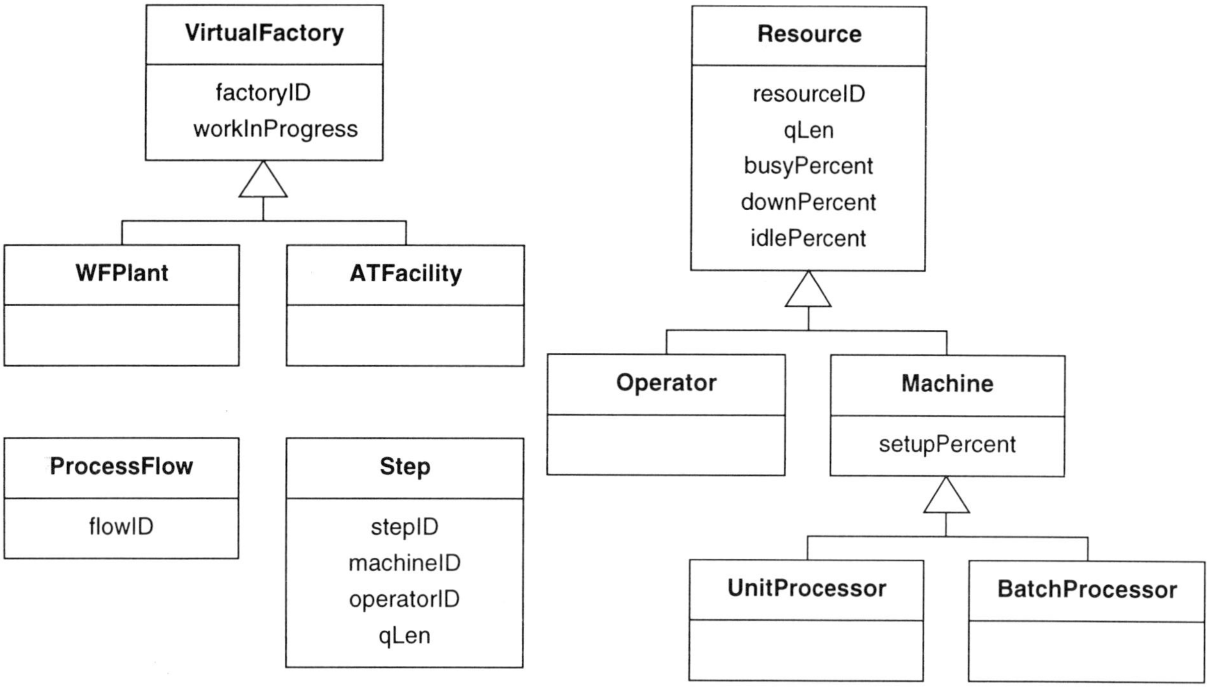

Figure 6. Object Classes in Distributed SC Simulation

the quantities are the number of wafers shipped, while in the reverse direction the quantities represent the inventory information.

Each factory (federate) could also make some (but generally not all) its internal data available to other factories. The internal data are represented by the object classes shown in Figure 6 and are organized into three levels: Factory level, ProcessFlow/Step level and Resource level. There are two sub-classes at the factory level for the two types of factories: WFPlant and ATFacility.

In our semiconductor supply-chain simulation, the format of data to create the manufacturing process follows the Sematech Modeling Data Standard (MDS) [12], where a factory is made up by a number of ProcessFlows. Each process flow consists of many different processing Steps arranged in the order in which they occur in the manufacturing of the product. Each process step is represented by a record that contains information for that step. There are two types of resources: Machine and Operator. A machine can be either a UnitProcessor that processes one wafer-lot at a time or a BatchProcessor that processes multiple wafer-lots at a time.

4.3 Information Hiding in Supply-chain Simulation

Information hiding is very important in supply-chain simulation, since factories involved in the simulation may not all belong to the same company. In a simple situation, all factories participating in the supply-chain simulation might be from different companies. So, sensitive information inside a factory, for instance, the information at process flow and resource levels, should not be made available to other factories. This can be easily handled in the current HLA/RTI by simply removing object classes ProcessFlow, Step and Resource (and their sub-classes) from the SOM and FOM.

However, in a more complex situation, there might be a number of factories, under one company, participating in a supply-chain simulation with factories that do not belong to the same company. In this case, factories within the same company may share some sensitive data that should not be visible to other factories. For example, in our semiconductor supply-chain simulation, a company may own a number of wafer fabrication plants that produce different types of wafers for the assembly & test facility. Information about process flows and resources should be shared among these wafer fabrication plants so that scheduling within each plant could be optimized. However, these data should not be available to wafer fabrication plants in the supply-chain belonging to other companies, since the rival companies could use that information to minimize their risk and optimize their performance. Unfortunately, information hiding as described above, that is between a group of factories (federates), is currently not addressed by the HLA/RTI. Using a single-level federation, once an object class is defined in the

FOM, the corresponding information will be available to all the federates in the federation.

To demonstrate our proposed architecture and its advantages with respect to information hiding, we consider the following scenario: there are two factories (federates) in a supply-chain simulation. One is a wafer fabrication (WF) plant and the other an assembly & test (AT) facility. For each factory, there is a monitoring federate that monitors the performance of the factory. Thus, information at the process flow and resource levels of a factory should be made available to its corresponding monitoring federate. However, process flow and resource information of the wafer fabrication plant should not be visible to the monitoring federate of the assembly & test facility and vice versa.

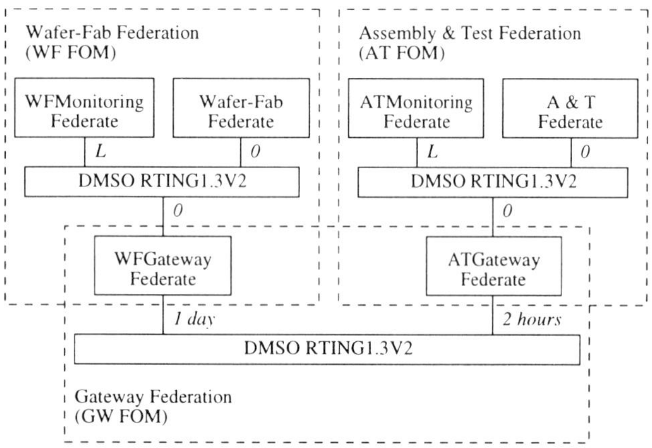

Figure 7. Hierarchical Federations of SC

To apply our proposed architecture, two levels of federations are created (see Figure 7). There are two federations at the first level (i.e., *Wafer-Fab Federation* and *Assembly & Test Federation*), each consists of a factory, a monitoring federate and a gateway federate. The two gateway federates form the second level federation (i.e., *Gateway Federation*). There are three FOMs, one for each federation (i.e., WF-FOM, AT-FOM and GW-FOM). GW-FOM contains the union of the subsets of WF-FOM and AT-FOM. Object classes defined in each FOM are given in Table 1. The two interaction classes shown in Figure 5 are defined in all the FOMs.

Each factory federation (i.e., wafer-fab federation or assembly & test federation) is represented by a gateway federate in the gateway federation. The gateway federate (i.e., *WF Gateway* or *AT Gateway*) forwards InventoryInfo and Shipment interactions from one factory federation to the other. Since only VirtualFactory and its subclasses are defined in the GW-FOM, information at process flow and resource levels will be filtered out by the gateway federates. Only information at factory level will be forwarded. So, detailed information of a factory is now encapsulated inside each factory federation and information hiding between groups of federates is achieved.

Table 1. Definition of FOMs

WF-FOM and AT-FOM	VirtualFactory	WFPlant	
		ATFacility	
	Resource	Operator	
		Machine	UnitProcessor
			BatchProcessor
	ProcessFlow		
	Step		
GW-FOM	VirtualFactory	WFPlant	
		ATFacility	

Note that the same object classes are defined in the WF-FOM and the AT-FOM. Although the wafer-fab federate publishes the Step object class and the assembly & test federate subscribes to the same object class, for instance, updates on process steps in the wafer-fab federate will not be forwarded to the assembly & test federate. This is because the factory federations are connected only by the gateway federation and this information is filtered out by the gateway federates.

4.4 Implementation of Gateway Federates

A gateway federate is attached to two concurrently executing federations. It joins both a factory federation and the gateway federation, and basically performs information filtering and forwarding. A gateway federate may also need to perform data transformation operations. However, in our case, it is not necessary since both factory federations use the same factory level definitions in the FOMs.

The HLA supports a number of time management schemes [5]. Our semiconductor supply-chain simulation uses conservative synchronization, whereby no federate is allowed to advance its simulation time unless the RTI can guarantee it will not receive any events in its past. In our simulation, the lookahead value from a wafer fabrication plant to the assembly & test facility is 24 hours, which is the simulation time assumed for shipment of wafers. In the reverse direction, the lookahead from the assembly & test facility to a wafer fabrication plant is 2 hours, which is the simulation time assumed for sending the inventory information and updating the business node.

In the hierarchical federations architecture, a federation appears like a federate, represented by a gateway, in the federation above it. So, in the gateway federation, the lookahead values of WF Gateway and AT Gateway federates are 1 day (i.e., 24 hours) and 2 hours respectively (see Figure 7). In a factory federation, the monitoring federate is a pacing federate that decides how fast the factory simulation can progress. Thus, the lookahead of the monitoring federate is set to a non-zero value (L). Since the monitoring federate cannot run ahead of the corresponding factory federate, the lookahead of the factory federate is set to zero. The lookahead of the gateway federate, when it is in a factory federation, is also set to zero.

After enabling its time switches, each factory federate can start to simulate the events on its own internal event-list. Since the initial events on the event-list of each factory (to release lots into the process flows) assume a starting simulation time of zero, it is important that both factory federates start executing their simulation at this same simulation time. However, a federate that is late in joining the federation may not be granted the initial simulation time it requested. To synchronize the starting of the federates, an hierarchical synchronization mechanism is required. A federation synchronization point is used in the gateway federation to synchronize the gateway federates. These, in turn, control the starting of the factory federates through synchronization points in the two factory federations.

4.5 Performance Comparison

In order to evaluate the performance of our proposed architecture, the hierarchical federations architecture is compared with a single-level or "flat" federation consisting of the two factory federates and the two monitoring federates. The experiments were carried out using RTI1.3NG-v2 on a platform of five Sun UltraSparc II workstations, running Sun Solaris 2.6 and interconnected by a 100 Mbps Ethernet. For both versions, each factory or monitoring federate was placed on a separate workstation. In the case of the hierarchical federations, each gateway federate is placed on the same workstation as its associated factory federate. In all cases, the RTIExec and FedExec processes execute on a fifth workstation separate from any of the federates.

For these experiments, both monitoring federates subscribe to the most detailed level of information (i.e., information at the Resource level, including all subclasses). As both monitoring federates subscribe to the same object classes, Data Distribution Management (DDM) [9] services are used in the flat federation to ensure that each monitor only receives information from the particular factory it is monitoring. This allows a fair comparison, as the monitoring information received by a particular monitor is then the same in both the hierarchical and flat versions. Note that in the hierarchical federations architecture, we avoid the complications associated with the use of DDM as the routing of information from the factory federate to its own monitoring federate follows naturally from the hierarchical structure.

Table 2 shows the execution time (in seconds) of the two factories for a simulation of 150 days using both versions.

Table 2. Execution Time (secs)

Version	Wafer-Fab	A & T
Hierarchical	3268.44	3223.92
Flat	6675.89	6672.69

It can be seen that there is a significant improvement in the execution time with the hierarchical federations architecture. This improvement cannot be due to a reduction in communication, as the use of DDM in the flat federation means that the bandwidth requirements of the two versions are very similar.

Further analysis was conducted by artificially varying the lookahead values in both the hierarchical and flat versions. This showed that the improvement in performance is mainly due to a more effective *Lower Bound on Time Stamp (LBTS)* calculation in the hierarchical federations architecture. There are two reasons for this:

- In a flat federation, a federate must specify a single *lookahead* value for all other federates in the federation. This means that the factory federates in our model must have zero lookahead because of the communication between factory and monitor. However, in the hierarchical federations architecture, the gateway federate may specify separate lookahead values for the user federation and the gateway federation (as shown in Figure 7).
- The hierarchical federations architecture involves three separate LBTS calculations, whereas in the flat federation there is a single calculation which involves both of the factory federates (each with zero lookahead) and the two monitoring federates. This means that the factory federates in the hierarchical version are more loosely synchronized.

Both of these reasons can contribute towards a more effective LBTS calculation, with a corresponding improvement in execution time.

5 Conclusions

Information hiding is a very important issue in distributed simulations. This paper has demonstrated the advantage of using an hierarchical federations architecture for information hiding. The architecture is based on a hybrid gateway/proxy approach. In addition to the advantage of information hiding and other advantages of hierarchical federations (as mentioned in Section 2), the experiments also show that the hierarchical federations architecture will improve the performance of applications where a more effective LBTS calculation can be achieved through better use of lookahead or more loosely synchronized federates.

Our future work will investigate other issues concerned with hierarchical federations, e.g., the construction of the super-FOM and the mapping between individual FOMs and the super-FOM. This will include the automatic generation of the code for data conversion and information hiding that is required in a gateway federate. Although this is not an easy task, it is simplified by the fact that our hierarchical architecture has a regular structure, with a gateway federate always joining exactly two federations. With super-FOM independence, a user federation will be able to participate in the super-FOM with no modification to its constituent federates.

Acknowledgements

This research is supported by National Science and Technology Board, Singapore, under the project: Parallel and Distributed Simulation of Virtual Factory Implementation. It is a collaborative project between the School of Computer Engineering in Nanyang Technological University, Singapore and Gintic Institute of Manufacturing Technology, Singapore. The project is located at the Centre for Advanced Information Systems at Nanyang Technological University.

References

[1] C. Bouwens, D. Hurrell and D. Shen. "Implementing Ownership Management with a Bridge Federate." in Procs. of 1998 Spring Simulation Interoperability Workshop, pp. 1126-1131, paper no. 98S-SIW-197, Orlando Florida, USA, March 1998.

[2] Judith Dahmann, Frederick Kuhl, and Richard Weatherly. "Standards for Simulation: As Simple As Possible But Not Simpler – The High Level Architecture for Simulation." *Simulation* 71:6, 378-387, 1998.

[3] DIS Steering Committee. "The DIS Vision, A map to the Future of Distributed Simulation." Technical Report IST-SP-94-01, Institute for Simulation and Training, Orlando Florida, USA, 1994.

[4] J. Filsinger. "HLA Security Guard Federate." In Procs. of 1997 Spring Simulation Interoperability Workshop, pp. 1015-1023, paper no. 97S-SIW-163, Orlando Florida, USA, March 1997.

[5] Richard Fujimoto. "Time Management in the High Level Architecture." *Simulation* 71:6, 388-400, 1998.

[6] Sanjay Jain, Chu-Cheow Lim, Boon-Ping Gan and Yoke-Hean Low. "Criticality of Detailed Modeling in Semiconductor Supply-chain Simulation." In Procs. of 1999 Winter Simulation Conference (WSC'99), pp.888-896, Phoenix, Arizona, USA, December 1999.

[7] Tom Lake, Colin Rayment and Kwok Wong. "A Component Framework for Hierarchical Simulation", In Procs. of 2000 Fall Simulation Interoperability Workshop, paper no. 00F-SIW-083, Orlando Florida, USA, Sept. 2000.

[8] Gerry Magee, Graham Shanks and Pete Hoare. "Hierarchical Federations", In Procs. of 1999 Spring Simulation Interoperability Workshop, paper no. 99F-SIW-085, Orlando Florida, USA, March 1999.

[9] Katherine L. Morse and Jeffrey S. Steinman. "Data Distribution Management in the HLA." in Procs. of 1997 Spring Simulation Interoperability Workshop, paper no. 97S-SIW-052, Orlando Florida, USA, March 1997.

[10] Michael D. Myjak, Duncan Clark and Tom Lake. "RTI Interoperability Study Group Final Report." In Procs. of 1999 Fall Simulation Interoperability Workshop, paper no. 99F-SIW-001, Orlando Florida, USA, Sept. 1999.

[11] Michael D. Myjak and Sean T. Sharp. "Implementations of Hierarchical Federations." In Procs. of 1999 Fall Simulation Interoperability Workshop, paper no. 99F-SIW-180, Orlando Florida, USA, Sept. 1999.

[12] Sematech. "Modeling Data Standards." Version 1.0, Technical Report, Sematech Inc., Austin, TX 78741, USA.

[13] Stephen J. Turner, Wentong Cai and Boon Ping Gan. "Adapting a Supply-chain Simulation for HLA." In Procs. of 4th IEEE Workshop on Distributed Simulation and Real-time Applications, pp. 71-78, San Francisco, USA, Aug. 2000.

[14] Douglas D. Wood and Mikel D. Petty. "HLA Gateway 1999." in Procs. of 1999 Spring Simulation Interoperability Workshop, paper no. 99S-SIW-051, Orlando Florida, USA, March 1999.

An Agent-based DDM for High Level Architecture*

Gary Tan and Liang Xu
School of Computing
National Univ of S'pore
Singapore 119260
gtan@comp.nus.edu.sg

Farshad Moradi
Swedish Defense Research
Agency (FOI)
172 90 Sweden
farshad@foi.se

Simon Taylor
Dept of Info. Sys. & Computing
Brunel University
Uxbridge UB8 3PH, UK
simon.taylor@brunel.ac.uk

Abstract

The Data Distribution Management (DDM) service is one of the six services provided in the Runtime Infrastructure (RTI) of High Level Architecture (HLA). Its purpose is to perform data filtering and reduce irrelevant data communicated between federates. The two DDM schemes proposed for RTI, region-based and grid-based DDM, are oriented to send as little irrelevant data to subscribers as possible, but only manage to filter part of this information and some irrelevant data is still being communicated. In a previous paper [3], we employed intelligent agents to perform data filtering in HLA, implemented an agent-based DDM in RTI (ARTI) and compared it with the other two filtering mechanisms. This paper reports on additional experiments, results and analysis using two scenarios, the AWACS sensing aircraft simulation and the air traffic control simulation scenario. Experimental results show that compared with other mechanisms, the agent-based approach communicates only relevant data and minimizes network communication, and is also comparable in terms of time efficiency. Some guidelines on when the agent-based scheme can be used are also given.

1. Introduction

The High Level Architecture (HLA) provides the specification of a common technical architecture for modeling and simulation in the US Department of Defense (DoD), its primary goals being to facilitate interoperability among simulations and to promote re-use of simulations and their components. The HLA is composed of three major components: (i) HLA rules; (ii) HLA interface specification; and (iii) HLA object model template [1].

The services of the Runtime Infrastructure (RTI) are described by the HLA interface specification. The RTI is a collection of software that provides common services required by multiple simulation systems. These services fall into six categories: *federation management*, *object management*, *declaration management*, *ownership management* , *time management* and *data distribution management* [1].

The data distribution management (DDM) services are employed by federates to assert properties of their data or to specify their data requirements in terms of user-defined spaces. The DDM controls the efficient routing of information between federates to reduce the amount of irrelevant data sent between federates and cut network communication cost [1, 2]. The two traditional DDM mechanisms, i.e., the region-based mechanism and grid-based mechanism, are both oriented towards this purpose, but still suffer from several drawbacks. In a previous paper [3], we try to avoid these drawbacks by using agents to do accurate filtering so that the RTI routes only relevant information and minimizes communication. In our method, each time a federate subscribes to some data, intelligent mobile agents are launched to publishers of those data. These agents will fetch the updated data, perform data filtering and then send the subscriber the exact information that they require. We implemented an agent-based DDM in the RTI (ARTI) and compared it with the other two filtering mechanisms. This paper reports on additional experimental results and analysis using two scenarios, the AWACS sensing aircraft simulation scenario and the air traffic control simulation scenario.

This paper is organized as follows. Section 2 describes the two DDM mechanisms employed in RTI, while section 3 describes the agent-based DDM filtering mechanism and the design structure of ARTI. The implementation issues of ARTI are discussed in section 4. Section 5 describes the two experiment scenarios, the AWACS sensing aircraft and Air Traffic Control scenarios, used to compare the three DDM mechanisms. The experimental results and analyses are also provided in this section. The conclusion is given in section 6.

* This research is supported by the NUS-MINDEF collaboration GR6757

2. DDM filtering mechanisms

The two main DDM data filtering mechanisms currently employed in RTI are the region-based filtering and the grid-based filtering, which are described briefly here. The reader is referred to [3] for a more detailed description.

2.1. Region-based filtering

The region-based filtering method uses a fundamental construct called the *routing space*. The routing space is a multi-dimensional coordinate system through which a region is specified. A federate tells the RTI to deliver only the data which fall within the extents of the region by specifying a subscription region. By specifying an update region with a particular object, a federate promises that the data within the extents of this region will be published when it tells the RTI to update its values/attributes.

When an update region and subscription region of different federates overlap, the RTI adds the subscribing federate into the receiving federate group connected to the update region. The data updated will be delivered to the subscribing federate. Each time an update region (or subscription region) is modified, the RTI does the matching again and accordingly updates the receiving federate group.

Every update region must be compared with all the subscription regions to determine if they should be updated. If the number of subscription regions and update regions is high, the number of matches is also high.

2.2. Grid-based filtering

In grid-based filtering, the routing space is partitioned into a grid of cells. Cells are used to efficiently specify the overlapped part between a subscription region and an update region. For each cell, a multicast group containing subscribers whose regions overlap with that cell is maintained. When a publisher's update region overlaps with a cell, the data associated with the update region will then be delivered to the multicast group for that cell. As in the region-based approach, during the simulation runtime execution, the RTI will perform matching again and adjust the multicast groups of the cells when it is notified that a region is modified.

One problem with this method is that irrelevant data may be sent due to subscription and update regions of federate overlapping with a cell, but do not themselves overlap.

2.3. Drawbacks of current approaches

Before DDM was introduced in the RTI, the data distribution in HLA was based mainly on *class* specification by employing the Declaration Management (DM) services. Irrelevant information was generally discarded at the receiving simulations in order to reduce local processing loads. The region-based filtering mechanism and grid-based filtering mechanisms define federates' interest in data as value-based. They however have some obvious drawbacks. These are excessive cost of critical network communication resources because of irrelevant information, and inexact routing causing extra processing in filtering at the receiving simulations' side.

2.4. Related work

There has been much research done on the two main DDM mechanisms, region-based DDM mechanism and grid-based DDM mechanism. For example, Cohen and Kemkes discussed various ways of using the DDM services and studied their impact on performance [4]. Rak and Van Hook gave evaluation of the grid-based relevance filtering [5]. Rizik's research work [6] tried to find an optimal geographic routing space cell size for a specific simulation model. Boukerche et al [7] uses a fixed grid, sender-based hybrid to reduce the multicast groups to improve performance.

In a previous paper [3], a new DDM filtering mechanism based on agents was proposed. This mechanism attempts to overcome the drawbacks discussed previously. Influenced by the popularity of intelligent agents, we noticed that the various properties of agents, including autonomy, mobility, intelligence, sociability and etc, may help to improve the efficiency of the data filtering in the DDM and to overcome these drawbacks. We incorporated the agent technology to the DDM approach and implemented an agent-based DDM filtering mechanism.

In this agent-based filtering mechanism, the RTI delivers to data consumers exactly what they want by using agents to perform exact data filtering in HLA. No irrelevant information will be distributed in this new DDM mechanism. Thus, the network communication is minimized and the extra cost of the local processing resources consumed to filter out irrelevant data is eliminated.

Employing agents in the RTI data distribution framework is previously discussed by Van Hook et al [8, 9]. But in their work, agents are mostly used as an auxiliary part of the data distribution system to collect some useful information and to help form the multicast group. One of their papers [9] mentions that mobile agents may go to publishers' LRC from subscribers' to fetch relevant data, but it gives no detail or method.

The simulation group at Brunel uses a novel agent-based service distribution model called *Thin Agents* to reduce network bandwidth in GRIDS, a generic run-time infrastructure for distributed simulation [10].

3. Agent-based DDM

3.1. Architecture

The description of the agent-based RTI (ARTI) can be found in [3]. We briefly describe the architecture here again for clarity and completeness. We employed a totally distributed RTI structure and the RTI services are implemented in the RTI ambassador of each federate. The design structure of the ARTI is shown in figure 1.

In the HLA, federates make subscriptions to declare their interest in the object attributes or interactions that other federates own. When a subscription is made, intelligent mobile agents are launched to the publishers of those attributes and interactions. Whenever the publishers update their object attributes or interactions, those agents associated with them will fetch the data, perform data filtering and then send the subscriber exactly what it wants. At the same time, agents keep their internal filtering parameters updated by receiving notification from the subscribing federate once a region modification is made.

When a federate calls the DDM services to subscribe to some object class attributes or interaction classes with a region, *Sub_children* are launched to the places where they are most likely to find those data. That means the *Sub_children* are sent out to the federates which publish those data, according to the internal record of the system's publication information. A *SubMaster_agent* is built to manage those *Sub_children*.

When they have reached the (publishing) federates, *Sub_children* communicate directly with the federate environment, fetch the published/updated data, perform filtering for their owners (i.e., the subscribers which launch them), then send the filtered results to the subscribers.

In the ARTI, federates can change their subscription regions by notifying their *Sub_children* of the new subscription region. Upon receiving the notification of region modification, the *Sub_children* modify their internal filtering parameters accordingly. *Sub_children* employ the new filtering parameters the next time they perform data filtering. As a result, only the information that falls into the new subscription region will be routed to the subscribing federate.

It should be noted that no update regions exist in the agent-based DDM. Since the agent deals with all the updated data and deliver the data to its owner federate if the data exactly fall into the subscription region of its owner federates, no update region needs to be defined to clarify the area where updated data will fall into. It is different from the situation in region-based DDM and grid-based DDM, where the data receiving federate group is decided by the matching result between update and subscription regions.

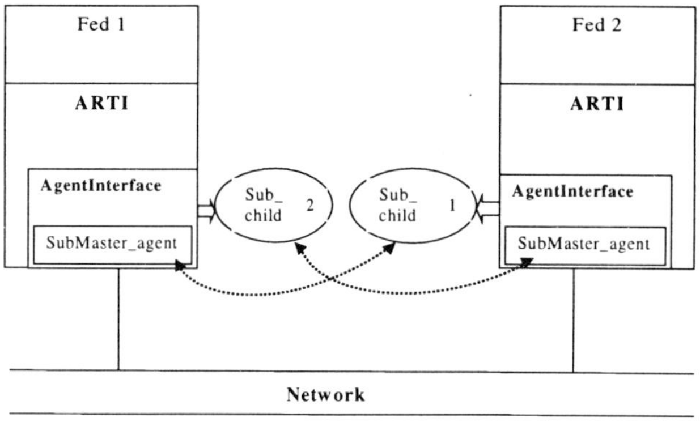

Figure 1: Design structure of agent-based RTI

3.2. Discussion

Compared with the other data filtering mechanisms, by incorporating agent technology in the RTI,

- Extra processing which has been devoted to filtering by the receivers now is done by agents at the physical location of senders, i.e., the publishing federates, on behalf of the receivers.
- Exact filtering by agents at the location of senders leads to exact routing for the data from publisher to subscriber.
- Critical network communication is minimized, by communicating only relevant data.

However, the agent-based DDM mechanism has some disadvantages. Firstly, the internal table of other federates' publishing interest costs storage space. But compared with the changing update regions and subscription regions, it is only a very small cost. Secondly, launching agents to other federates needs a period of time which may delay the program execution. Fortunately, agents are launched only in the initialization period of a simulation, and it will not affect the federation execution progress.

Another disadvantage of the agent-based DDM occurs in large-scale simulations. For a federation with large numbers of federates, hundreds or thousands of filtering agents may be sent out to one federate as a result of the initial matching operation based on the DM services. These large numbers of filtering agents, residing on one federate machine and performing filtering from time to time, will cause a heavy load to the federate machine. The agent-based DDM mechanism will become very inefficient in such cases of large-scale simulations.

4. Implementation issues

Our implementation is built on an MPP – the Fujitsu AP3000/32, UNIX (r) System V, Release 4.0, and the language used is C/C++. The communication architecture is TCP based on the Fast Messages (FM) interface provided by the Federated Simulations Development Kit (FDK RTI-Kit) [11]. The agents are created and act in the environment of D'Agents 2.0 [12]. The Federated Simulations Development Kit (FDK) is a software system that has been developed at Georgia Tech. It comprises composable modules for building RTIs. D'Agents is a mobile-agent system that is under development at Dartmouth College and is used in several information-retrieval and work-flow applications. D'Agents is based on the scripting language Tcl7.5 and Tk4.1 and runs on standard Unix platforms.

The D'Agents system is still under development. Currently, the agents' communication is restricted to between agents, and agents cannot communicate freely with other environment resources. The primitives for agents' activity are also limited. This causes our agents to be not as "intelligent" as it is desired especially when they act against the changes of surrounding environment and communicate with it. Because of this limitation, we employ the socket method for the communication between agents and other processing environment. A federate process writes data to a socket, and the agents fetch data from the socket.

Another implementation technical problem is that the only variable format supported by Tcl agents (D'Agents) is STRING, as TCL/TK is a descriptive language. We have to transform all the data of complex C/C++ data structures to strings before transferring them to Tcl agents, and vice versa. This method is slow and inefficient and will degrade performance.

Because of the above technical problems, currently the ARTI still has some limitations, especially in the time latency when reflecting updated information at the subscriber federates. These limitations need to be overcome in the future by either improving the agent interface, or by writing a custom-built agent tool-kit.

5. Experiment Scenario

The AWACS sensing aircraft [4] simulation scenario and Air Traffic Control (ATC) [14] simulation scenario were used to test the ARTI and to compare the efficiencies of agent-based DDM filtering mechanism with the other two traditional DDM mechanisms.

5.1. Experiment scenario 1: AWACS

In the AWACS sensing aircraft scenario, as described in [4], there are several aircraft and an AWACS circling over an area. When some aircraft happens to fly into the sensor range of the AWACS, it is discovered by the AWACS and its position is noticed by the AWACS.

5.1.1. Experiment assumptions

We assume all aircraft and the AWACS fly at different randomly generated speeds from a randomly generated initial position. Two federates are used, one represents the AWACS, and the other represents the aircraft. The subscription region of the AWACS can be defined from its sensor range. In region-based and grid-based DDM mechanisms, an update region is defined around each aircraft's position (there is no need for an update region in the agent-based filtering mechanism, as agents do exact filtering at the physical locations of the publishers). The AWACS federate subscribes to the aircraft information, but does not publish anything, and the aircraft federate publishes its position, but does not subscribe to any data.

The scenario is performed as a time-stepped simulation [13]. What the simulator calculates is the system status at each time step but not the continuous system moving process. Therefore the update and subscription regions have to be carefully defined to avoid missing the objects falling into the AWACS sensor range in the period between two discrete time steps. In our geographic routing space, we define the subscription region to be equal to the sensor region plus the maximum moving distance of the AWACS during the time between two subsequent subscription region modification requests. The update region is equal to the aircraft's maximum range during the time between two subsequent update region modification requests.

In the simulation, the object attribute values (i.e., the positions of the aircraft) are updated at each time step, but the subscription region and the update regions (only for region-based and grid-based DDM mechanisms) are modified once per k time steps. The frequency of region modification depends on the value of k.

5.1.2. Experimental results

Simulations are performed using ARTI, RTI with only DM, RTI with region-based DDM and RTI with grid-based DDM using different k values and the number of communicated messages after filtering is observed. The simulations are run on a Fujitsu AP3000 32-node multiprocessor running Unix (r) System V, Release 4.0. The AWACS federate and aircraft federate are run on different nodes. Both federates are written in C++.

Table 1 gives the parameter sets used in the simulations (for set A: k =1, set B: k=2, and set C: k=3). The speeds of AWACS and aircraft are generated randomly based on a fixed maximum speed. Their initial positions are also randomly generated in the initialization procedure. When testing the grid-based filtering mechanism, the routing space is divided into a number of grid-cells.

Parameter	Value		
No. of Aircraft	40		
Max Speed - Aircraft	900.0 (km/h)		
Max Speed -AWACS	450.0 (km/h)		
Sensor Range	15.0 (km)		
Subscription Region (km^2)	2025.0 (k=1)	8100.0 (k=2)	22500.0 (k=3)
Routing Space	600*600(km^2)		
Simulation Time	100 (time-steps)		

Table 1: Parameter table

5.1.3. DM vs. agent-based DDM

A simple comparison is made between the agent-based DDM and the DM, which employs only a class-based filtering without any DDM mechanisms. Table 2 gives the test results. The simulation period is 100 time steps. K is set to 3 in the agent-based filtering mechanism. Without employing any DDM filtering mechanism, the DM is no doubt much less efficient than the agent-based DDM and communicates much more redundant messages.

Filtering mechanism	No. of messages
DM	4000
Agent-based DDM (k=3)	146

Table 2: Results of DM vs. agent-based DDM

5.1.4. Grid vs. region vs. agent-based

Simulations were conducted using the three DDM mechanisms at different k values. For the grid-based DDM, since its filtering efficiency largely depends on the cell size, we tested different cell sizes and chose the one that gave the least number of communicated messages [3]. Because at each run of the simulation the initial positions and speeds of all the objects are randomly generated, the filtering results for each run of simulation are not the same. We therefore took replications for each parameter set and calculated the average filtering results. Figure 2 shows the results of the three DDM mechanisms.

5.1.5. Analysis

As seen in the figure, as k increases, the number of communicated messages of both the region-based and grid-based DDM increases. This is because the subscription region and the update region become larger when k increases, thus increasing the possibility of area overlap. This results in more messages being sent.

From the figure we can clearly see that much less information is sent when using the agent-based DDM filtering mechanism than by using grid-based or region-based DDM mechanisms. The grid-based DDM and region-based DDM may deliver irrelevant information in addition to the data the subscribers require. However, the agent-based DDM communicates only relevant data and not redundant information. Thus, the agent-based DDM mechanism improves the filtering efficiency of DDM and minimizes network communication.

The number of communicated messages of agent-based DDM for the different k values as shown in figure 2 are similar and increases slowly when k increases from 1 to 3. As in the cases of the region-based and grid-based DDM, the increasing messages result from the increasing subscription region. As the subscription region becomes larger, the possibility for the aircraft falling into the subscription region increases. However, since the agent-based DDM routes only the required messages, the numbers of routed messages do not vary much for different k values for the same simulation scenario.

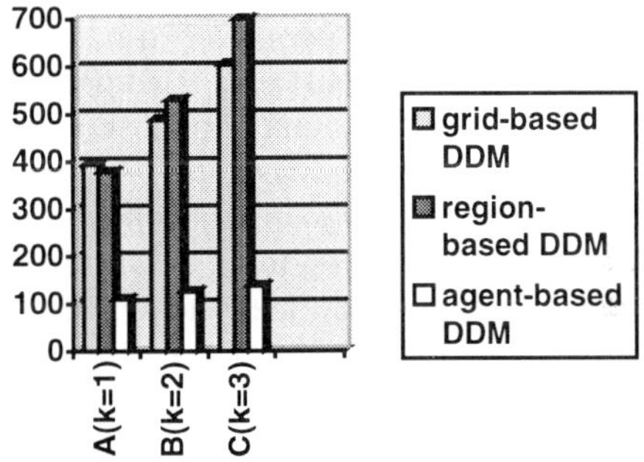

Figure 2: Number of communicated messages for parameter sets A, B, C

The following table 3 shows the simulation processing times of running the simulation with different DDM mechanisms for k = 1. These processing times are collected by running the simulations exclusively on the nodes of Fujitsu AP3000, using the unix command *time*. Compared with the other two mechanisms, the simulation with agent-based DDM takes a longer time. This time latency comes mainly from the time costs for launching agents in the initial period of simulation and the technical problems we mentioned earlier in section 4. Although the simulation with agent-based DDM has a longer processing time than both the grid-based and region-based DDM, they are at least of the same time order. We anticipate that an improvement can be expected if we can address these problems. From table 3, we see that the grid-based DDM mechanism takes more time than the region-based DDM mechanism. This can be attributable to the processing cost of updating the multicast groups of the cells when both the update regions and subscription regions change dynamically over time in the grid-based DDM.

DDM mechanism	Simulation processing time (s)
Agent-based	30.513
Grid-based	27.914
Region-based	23.537

Table 3: Simulation processing times (set A)

5.2. Experiment scenario 2: air traffic control

The air traffic control simulator is a non-military HLA federation designed and developed to simulate air traffic control (ATC) in a distributed environment [14]. In this simulation model, each airport (denoted by APi in figure 3) is represented by a federate and controls a set of aircraft objects. A radar is located at each airport and the radar range (denoted by Ri) covers a portion of the routing space. The aircraft (denoted by Ai) stays at an airport for a random period of time, takes off, flies and lands at its destination airport. At the destination, it stays again for a random period of time, selects the next destination, takes off and lands. This process is performed repeatedly. When some aircraft flies into the radar range of any airport other than its own controller, it is discovered and its position is noted by the airport.

This scenario differs from the first one in that the subscribers (airports) are static and hence their subscription regions do not change.

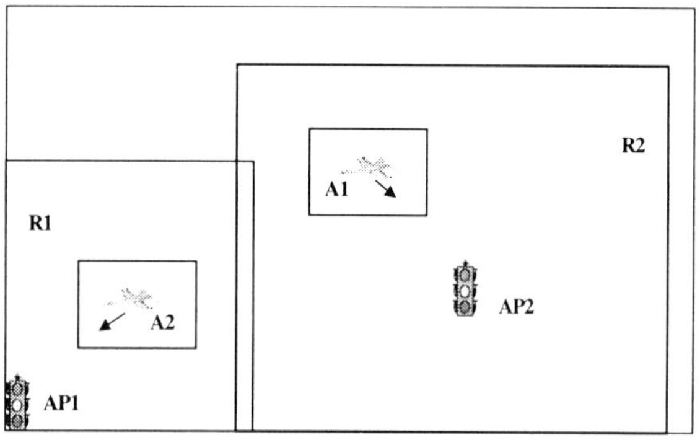

Figure 3: Air traffic control scenario

5.2.1. Experiment assumptions

In the experiment, we assume a simulation scenario of two airports (AP1 and AP2), where each airport controls one aircraft. Two federates are designed for this scenario, each federate representing one airport. The objects (the aircraft) fly at a fixed speed, 100 km per time step, starting from their controller airport. The radar range of the airport is defined by the subscription region of the airport federate. In the region-based and grid-based DDM mechanisms, the update region is defined around the aircraft's current position. The airport federate subscribes to the information of the aircraft controlled by the other federate with its radar range. At the same time, it publishes the position of the aircraft that it controls.

For the example depicted in figure 3, AP1 has control of aircraft A1 and AP2 has control of A2. AP1 subscribes to A2's position with its subscription region R1. At the same time, AP1 publishes the position of aircraft A1. Also, AP2 subscribes to A1's position with its subscription region R2, and at the same time, it publishes the position of aircraft A2.

The experiment is performed as a time-stepped simulation [13]. In the routing space, we define the update region equal to the aircraft's maximum moving range during the time between two subsequent update region modification requests. The subscription region is the radar range of the airport.

In the simulation, the object attribute values (i.e., the positions of the aircraft) are updated at each time step, but the update regions (only for region-based and grid-based DDM mechanisms) are modified once per k time steps. The frequency of update region modification depends on the value of k. The subscription region is unchanged during the simulation.

During the air traffic control simulation, the radar ranges of the airports are unchanged. Thus after the initial setting up of the subscription region, there is no need to modify the subscription region of the airport during the simulation loop. This is different from the algorithm for the AWACS sensing aircraft scenario, where the subscription region of the moving AWACS is changed once for each k time steps.

5.2.2. Experimental results

The same set of experiments is performed using this scenario. The airport federates are run on different nodes, the aircraft are considered objects owned by the airport federates.

Table 4 gives the parameters we used in the simulations. The initial positions of the aircraft are set in the initialization procedure as the positions of their controller airport. When testing the grid-based filtering mechanism, the routing space is divided into a number of grid-cells. Different values of k are used in the tests for region-based and grid-based DDM mechanisms.

Routing Space (km^2)	10000.0*10000.0
Positions of airports (km, km, km)	AP1(10.0, 0.0, 0.0); AP2(7500.0, 2000.0, 0.0)
Radar Range (km)	4000.0
Subscription region(km^2)	4000.0*4000.0
Speed of Aircraft (km/time step)	100.0
Sim Time (time steps)	300
k (time steps)	k=1, 2, 3

Table 4: Parameter table for ATC

5.2.3. DM vs. Agent-based DDM

The agent-based DDM is first compared with the DM. The results when run for different simulation times are listed in table 5. From the table it is easy to see that the agent-based DDM again communicates much less messages than the DM (about 50%). Agents in the agent-based DDM send an airplane's attributes only when the airplane is in the radar range of the subscribing airport. This is roughly half the time of the simulation, since the aricraft fly from one airport to the other airport.

Simulation time (Time steps)	300		200		100	
DM	300	299	200	199	100	99
Agent-based (ADDM)	168	161	96	99	58	57
ADDM/DM(%)	56	54	48	50	58	58

☐ messages received by AP1 ☐ messages received by AP2

Table 5: Results of DM vs. agent-based DDM

5.2.4. Grid vs. region vs. agent-based

We performed the air traffic control simulation using the three DDM mechanisms using different k values. As in the case of the AWACS sensing aircraft scenario, for grid-based DDM, we divide the routing space into different numbers of cells, and choose the one that gives the least number of communicated messages.

5.2.5. Analysis

Figure 4 illustrates and summarizes the number of received messages by AP1 and AP2 after filtering using the grid-based, region-based and agent-based DDM filtering mechanisms. For either airport, less information is delivered by using the agent-based DDM filtering mechanism than by using the grid-based or the region-based DDM mechanisms. It is again shown that the agent-based DDM mechanism uses minimal communication network resources by sending only relevant information.

In the air traffic control scenario, although the number of communication messages in the agent-based DDM is less than in the grid-based DDM and the region-based DDM, the improvement is not that great. This is because of the unchanged subscription region and the aircraft's line of flight. The subscription regions are kept unchanged during the simulation time. Only when the aircraft flies close to the subscription region of its subscribing airport will its update region overlap with the subscription region, and the data of its attributes are then delivered. Soon after this, the aircraft enters the radar region, agents in agent-based DDM route the relevant data of its attributes. Thus the time when the RTI begins to deliver the required information in the grid-based DDM and the region-based DDM is close to the time in the agent-based DDM. So is the time when RTI stops delivering information when the aircraft leaves a subscription region. In such cases, the three mechanisms differ little in the number of communicated messages. However, in the grid-based and region-based mechanisms, the frequent modification of update regions is still a big cost, but does not give rise to any additional network messages.

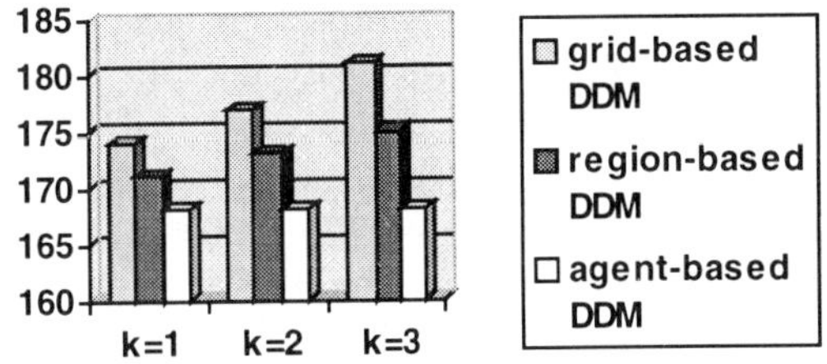

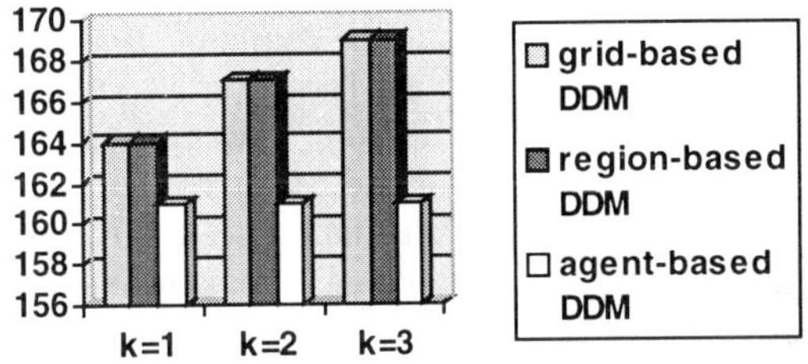

Figure 4: Received messages by AP1 (top) & AP2 (bottom) using different k values

Table 6 gives the simulation processing times of running the air traffic control simulation with the different DDM mechanisms for k = 1. These times are collected by running the simulations exclusively on the nodes of Fujitsu AP3000, using the unix command *time*. The timing trend is similar to the AWACS sensing aircraft scenario. The simulation using the agent-based DDM runs for a longer time than the grid-based and the region-based DDM mechanisms. Although it performs worse than the grid-based DDM and takes twice as long as the region-based one, it is still of the same time order. As we mentioned in the AWACS sensing aircraft scenario, this time latency is attributable to the inefficiencies of interfacing the agents with the RTI environment. Improvements for the agent-based mechanism can be expected by improving this interface.

Another reason is because in this scenario, the subscription regions do not change, and they are much bigger than the update regions. The update regions also overlap with the subscription regions for approximately half the time, since the aircraft fly between airports. For the grid-based DDM, this translates to less frequent updates of the multicast groups, and hence less processing overheads. For the region-based case, the number of matching is low due to the small number of objects.

DDM mechanism	Simulation processing time (s)
Agent-based	15.992
Grid-based	11.612
Region-based	7.028

Table 6: Simulation processing times for k = 1

6. Conclusion

The agent-based DDM filtering mechanism has been proposed to overcome the drawbacks of region-based and grid-based DDM by filtering only relevant information. This paper has compared the three DDM filtering schemes using two different scenarios, the AWACS sensing aircraft and the air traffic control simulation scenarios. In the AWACS sensing aircraft scenario, the experimental results showed that the communicated messages using the agent-based DDM were significantly less than the messages of the region-based and grid-based DDMs (less than one third of the communicated messages of the other two mechanisms). The agent-based DDM was much more efficient in filtering, routing only relevant information and minimizing the network communication. In the air traffic control simulation scenario, where the subscription regions were large and remain fixed, and the number of objects was small, the benefit of the agent-based DDM was not that great compared to the first scenario.

The agent-based DDM mechanism spends more processing time than the other two mechanisms, attributable to the inefficiency of the agent interface. An improvement in time cost can be expected by improving this interface. The performance is worse in the second scenario where the overlap frequency between subscription and update regions was low.

Thus the agent-based DDM is useful for scenarios where the subscription regions change dynamically over time, and the update and subscription region overlap frequency is high. In such cases, the overheads associated with updating multicast lists and sending irrelevant messages will come into play.

During the implementation and testing of ARTI, we observed that the information reflection at the subscriber federates is delayed. This is mostly caused by the technical problems discussed in section 4. The time latency for information reflection limits the application of the agent-based DDM in real time systems. In addition, the agents in our implementation model can be more "intelligent" and more flexible, providing a more complete agent environment tool.

Other further work concerns the scalability of the agent-based DDM. For the agent-based scheme to be viable, its scalability when used in large-scale simulations must be investigated. Improvements need to be made on the design of ARTI to answer this question.

7. References

1. U.S. Department of Defense, "High Level Architecture Interface Specification", Version 1.3, 2 April 1998. http://www.dmso.mil/
2. Katherine L. Morse, Jeffrey S. Steinman, "Data Distribution Management in the HLA, Multidimensional Regions and Physically Correct Filtering", in Proceedings of the Simulation Interoperability Workshop, Spring 1997.
3. G.Tan, L.Xu, F.Moradi and YS Zhang, "An Agent-based DDM Filtering Mechanism", in proceedings of MASCOTS, San Francisco, USA, Aug 2000.
4. Danny Cohen and Andreas Kemkes, "User-Level Measurement of DDM Scenarios", in proceeding of the Simulation Interoperability Workshop (SIW), Spring 1997.
5. Steven J. Rak and Daniel J. Van Hook, "Evaluation of grid-based relevance filtering for multicast group assignment", in Proceedings of the Distributed Interactive Simulation, 1996.
6. Pete Rizik et al., "Optimal geographic routing space cell size in the FEDEP for prey-centric models", in Proceedings of the Simulation Interoperability Workshop (SIW), Spring 1998.
7. A.Boukerche, A.Roy & N.Thomas, "Dynamic Grid-Based Multicast Group Assignment in Data Distribution Management", proceedings of 4th Workshop on Distributed Simulation and Real-time Applications, San Francisco, USA, August 2000.
8. Daniel J. Van Hook, Steven J. Rak, James O. Calvin, "Approaches to RTI Implementation of HLA Data Distribution Management Services", the 15th Workshop on Standards for the Interoperability of Distributed Simulations, September 1996.
9. Van Hook, Daniel J., David P. Cebula, Steven J. Rak, Carol J. Chiang, Paul N. DiCaprio, James O. Calvin, "Performance of STOW RITN Application Control Techniques", 14th Workshop on Standards for the Interoperability of Distributed Simulations, March 1996.
10. R.Sudra, T.Janahan, S.Taylor, "Distributed Supply Chain Simulation in GRIDS", proceedings of 2000 Winter Simulation Conference, Florida, U.S.A., December 2000.
11. Georgia Tech Research Corporation, "FDK-Federated Simulations Development Kit", November 1998. http://www.cc.gatech.edu/computing/pads/fdk.html
12. Dartmouth College, "D'Agents", November 1999. http://agent.cs.dartmouth.edu
13. Gary Tan, Rassul Ayani, Yusong Zhang and Farshad Moradi. "Grid-based Data Management in Distributed Simulation", in Proceedings of 33rd Annual Simulation Symposium, Washington, U.S.A., April 2000.
14. Farshad Moradi, Rassul Ayani, Gary Tan, "Object and Ownership Management in Air Traffic Control Simulations", in Proceedings of IEEE Distributed Interactive Simulation –Real Time '99, Maryland, U.S.A., October 1999.

A Causality Based Time Management Mechanism for Federated Simulation

Bu-Sung Lee, Wentong Cai, Junlan Zhou
School of Computer Engineering
Nanyang Technological University, Singapore
ebslee, aswtcai, ejlzhou@ntu.edu.sg

Abstract

One of the six categories of management services provided in the Run Time Infrastructure (RTI) to federated simulations is Time Management. Currently, it provides only two message ordering policies, that is, time stamp ordering and receive ordering. Temporal anomalies occurred during the execution of federation due to the heterogeneous latencies in the communication network are not handled in receive ordering. While time stamp ordering eliminates the temporal anomalies entirely, it incurs great communication latency and huge bandwidth requirement. This paper presents a new time management mechanism which provides a less costly message ordering service, namely causal ordering, to federates. It does not require the specification of lookahead and allows federates that do not require stringent message ordering properties to achieve much more efficient execution. A series of experiments has been carried out to benchmark the performance of this new time management mechanism and the results show that it incurs a slight overhead compared to receive ordering mechanism but achieves significant performance improvement over time stamp ordering mechanism.

Keywords: *distributed simulation, time management, causal order delivery, direct dependency, happen-before relationship, time stamp ordering, multicasting.*

1. Introduction

The High Level Architecture (HLA) is proposed by Department of Defense (DoD) to support the reusability and interoperability of the simulations. It provides a technical framework where simulation components (federates in the HLA) interact via the services of the HLA Runtime Infrastructure (RTI) [4] according to a set of HLA rules to achieve a combined large scale simulation (a federation in the HLA). Services provided in the RTI are divided into six categories, Federation Management, Object Management, Declaration Management, Time Management, Ownership Management, and Data Distribution Management.

Time Management (TM) is important in distributed simulations as different federates normally utilize different internal time advancement schemes. Time Management services coordinate the exchange of messages among federates and control the time advancements of federates so that they can interoperate in a consistent timely order.

Currently, only two message ordering policies, receive ordering and time stamp ordering, are provided in the RTI TM architecture. Receive ordering is the most straightforward ordering mechanism which has the lowest latency and communication overhead. Messages are processed by federates in the order that they are received. Temporal anomalies, such as receiving a message that happened in the past in simulation time, are not handled in receive ordering. Such anomalies are eliminated entirely with time stamp ordering. Time stamp ordering associates each message with a specific time stamp and guarantees that messages are received by federates in time stamp order.

Time stamp ordering requires a federate to specify a quantity, named lookahead, and that the time stamp of a message is no less than the federate's current time plus lookahead. A federate has to make a time advancement request from the RTI whenever it wishes to advance its simulation time. The RTI grants the time advancement request of the federate after it ensures that no message with a time stamp less than the requested time will be received by that federate in the future. An important feature of time stamp ordering is that all federates receiving a common set of messages will receive those messages in the same order, that is, a total ordering is provided [3]. However, time stamp ordering has several disadvantages. First of all, it generally incurs high latency and requires high transmission bandwidth on the system. Secondly, modifying the simulation model to exploit lookahead is, in general, time consuming and difficult. Furthermore, it performs poorly when the model has little or zero lookahead.

Alternatively, a less stringent but much more efficient message ordering mechanism (that is, causal ordering) that ensures a "cause-effect" relationship among events, is sufficient to eliminate the anomalies in many situations. It was first defined by Lamport [9] in the context of distributed systems. A distributed system is composed by a group of asynchronous processes cooperating to achieve a common goal by exchanging messages. The processes do not share any memory and there is no common clock. The action of each process is modeled as three types of events, internal event, message send event, and message receive event. Causal order establishes a "happen before" relationship, denoted as "$\longrightarrow$", among the events. It is formally defined as follows:

1. if e and f are the events occurring at the same process and e occurs before f, e happens before f (or $e \longrightarrow f$).
2. if e is the send event of a message and f is the corresponding receive event, e happens before f (or $e \longrightarrow f$).
3. if $e \longrightarrow f$ and $f \longrightarrow g$, $e \longrightarrow g$.

If neither $e \longrightarrow f$ nor $f \longrightarrow e$, e and f are said to be concurrent.

Causal order delivery is defined using the happen before relationship as follows: if the send event of message M_1 happens causally before the send event of M_2 and M_1 and M_2 are sent to the same destination federate P_i, M_1 should be delivered to P_i before M_2. Messages with their send events not causally related can be delivered to a common destination federate in any order. Compared to time stamp ordering, causal ordering enables the relaxation of unnecessary synchronization constraints and thus is very useful for simulations which are expected to run as asynchronous as possible to achieve high degree of concurrency and high speed of execution. Federates can proceed with their simulation without waiting for other participating federates and still have messages delivered to them in causal order.

This paper will present a new TM mechanism which provides a causal message ordering service to federates. It uses a Modified Schiper-Eggli-Sandoz protocol to ensure the causal order delivery of messages. The remainder of this paper is organized as follows: Section 2 describes the modified Schiper-Eggli-Sandoz protocol that is proposed by the authors [14]. Section 3 discusses the implementation of the proposed causality based TM mechanism using Federated Simulations Development Kit [2]. Section 4 describes the benchmarking experiments conducted on the proposed TM mechanism and presents the results obtained. Section 5 summarizes the results of this paper and addresses the direction of our future work.

2. A causal order delivery protocol

At the heart of any causal ordering mechanisms is the computation of control information that are appended with messages to enforce their causal deliveries in asynchronous communication environment. Generally speaking, the size of this information is in the order of N^2, where N is the number of processes in a distributed system. Some representative causal ordering algorithms are the ISIS sytem [5], the algorithm proposed by Raynal-Schiper-Toueg in [11], and the Schiper-Eggli-Sandoz (SES) protocol [12]. The SES protocol sends each message with a matrix of size N^2. The destination process uses the associated matrix to determine when it is safe to process the message. A major drawback of the SES protocol is that it only works in unicast environment.

By exploiting the topology of underlying communication network and the communication pattern of the application , it is possible to reduce the size of the control information to the order of N. For example, in the algorithm proposed by C.Sun [13] for shared editing systems where broadcasting is assumed in the inter-process communication, it is enough to attach an array of size N with each message to maintain the causal order among messages.

Another approach to reduce the control information is based on the direct dependency tracking technique, where only the immediate causal predecessors of message M not known to be delivered are tracked and propagated with M. The principle advantage of the direct dependency tracking technique is that it achieves optimality without relying on assumptions over the underlying communication network and thus is feasible for a wider class of applications. Although the upper bound of the space complexity of the control information appended with messages using the direct dependency tracking technique is still $O(N^2)$, the size of the control information is likely to be much smaller on the average. Algorithms using the direct dependency tracking technique include the algorithm proposed by Prakash for mobile computing in [10], the algorithm proposed by Ajay in [8] and the Modified Schier-Eggli-Sandoz (MSES) protocol proposed by the authors in [14].

The algorithm proposed by Prakash has sub-optimal situations where redundant control information such as non-immediate causal predecessors and immediate causal predecessors known to be delivered are attached with messages and propagated to the remote processes. The MSES protocol extends the original SES protocol to works in multicast and broadcast environments. It is more efficient than the algorithm proposed by Prakash and free of the sub-optimal situations of Prakash's algorithm. Simulation experiments have been conducted to measure the communication overhead of the MSES protocol with respect to Prakash's algorithm and the original SES protocol in various situations and the results attest the efficiency of the MSES protocol [14]. The algorithm proposed by Ajay in [8] is equivalent to the MSES protocol in terms of eliminating non-immediate causal predecessors or immediate causal predecessors known to be delivered, despite the different encapsulations of the control information in these two algorithms. A meticulous comparative study of the above three algorithms can be found in [14].

In the MSES protocol, each process P_i keeps an array of size N, VT_{P_i}, to track its vector time [6]. Besides VT_{P_i}, a causal vector CV_{P_i} is also maintained at P_i to track the most recent messages sent to other processes in P_i's knowledge. It will be updated whenever P_i sends or receives a message. CV_{P_i} consists of up to N pairs of (P_l, MVT), where MVT (minimized vector time) is a set of tuples. Each tuple in MVT represents a message sent to P_l. For example, the tuple (k, x) represents a message M' generated by process P_k when $VT_{P_k}[k]$ is equal to x. M' is not known to be delivered to P_l yet. For the convenience of discussion, we denote the MVT in the entry of CV_{P_i} corresponding to P_l as $CV_{P_i}[l]$ in the rest of the paper. When sending a message M, P_i attaches the current contents of VT_{P_i} and CV_{P_i} with M as VT_M and CV_M respectively. When a remote process P_j receives M, it compares $CV_M[j]$ with VT_{P_j}. If each tuple in $CV_M[j]$ is not greater than the corresponding element in VT_{P_j}, M is delivered to P_j immediately. Otherwise, M is placed in an internal buffer because there must exist at least one message M' such that M' precedes M and that M' has not yet been delivered to P_j.

3. A causality based TM mechanism

3.1. Federated Simulations Development Kit (FDK)

The Federated Simulations Development Kit (FDK) [2] was developed at Georgia Institute of Technology by the research group led by Professor Richard Fujimoto. It comprises a collection of libraries designed to support development of RTIs for parallel and distributed simulations, in particular, federated simulations running on high performance compute platforms. Each library can be used separately, or together with other FDK libraries. They can also be embedded into the existing RTI to add more functionality or to increase performance by utilizing a high speed interconnect. The "library-of-libraries" approach of the FDK [7] facilitates the optimization of specific modules as well as the integration of new functionalities. Therefore, the FDK is chosen as the development platform of the causality based TM mechanism.

Figure 1 shows the architecture of the FDK. The DRTI realizes a subset of the RTI services defined in the HLA [4]. The MCAST provides group communication services to the DRTI. If a federate wishes to use a TM protocol for its communications with other federates, calls will be generated by the DRTI to the TM-Kit to utilize the corresponding TM services. The TM-kit and MCAST both require the use of basic communication services defined in the FM-Lib. The

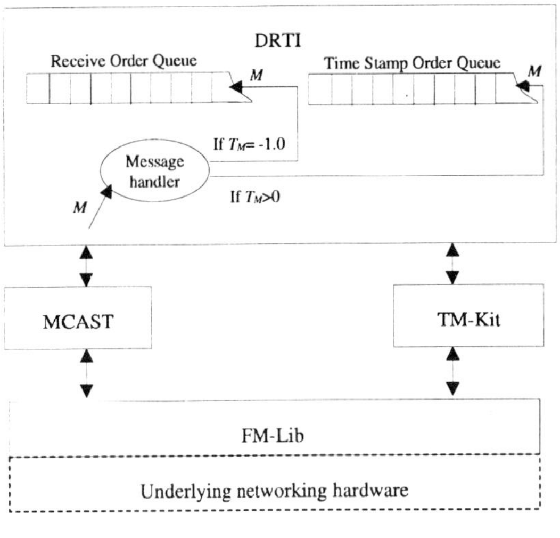

Figure 1. Architecture of the FDK

current implementation of the FM-Lib utilizes an API based on the Illinois Fast Messages software [1] for its basic communication services.

Two message queues, Time Stamp Order (TSO) queue and Receive Order (RO) queue, are maintained by the DRTI at each federate to keep incoming attribute updates and interactions. Attribute updates or interactions that meet time stamp ordering criteria are placed in the TSO queue according to their time stamps. Attribute updates or interactions specified as receive-ordered are placed in the RO queue in FIFO manner. Only one message handler is provided for both types of messages. The ordering is determined by the timestamp of the received message. If it is -1.0, the message is placed in the RO queue, else in the TSO queue.

The TM-Kit provides the basic service primitives necessary for ordering messages exchanged between federations according to time stamp order. At the heart of the TM-Kit are the algorithms for computing LBTS, i.e, a lower bound on the time stamps of future messages that can be received by a federate. It is computed using a "butterfly" like interconnection graph [2]. This allows LBTS to be computed and distributed to all federates in $logN$ time and $NlogN$ messages in the absence of a centralized controller, where N is the number of federates. Whenever a time advancement request is made by a federate, a global LBTS computation will be performed among the federates and the result will be compared with the requested time to determine whether the request of the federate should be granted.

3.2. Integration of causality based TM mechanism into the FDK

At present, only two message ordering mechanisms, receive ordering and time stamp ordering are provided in the

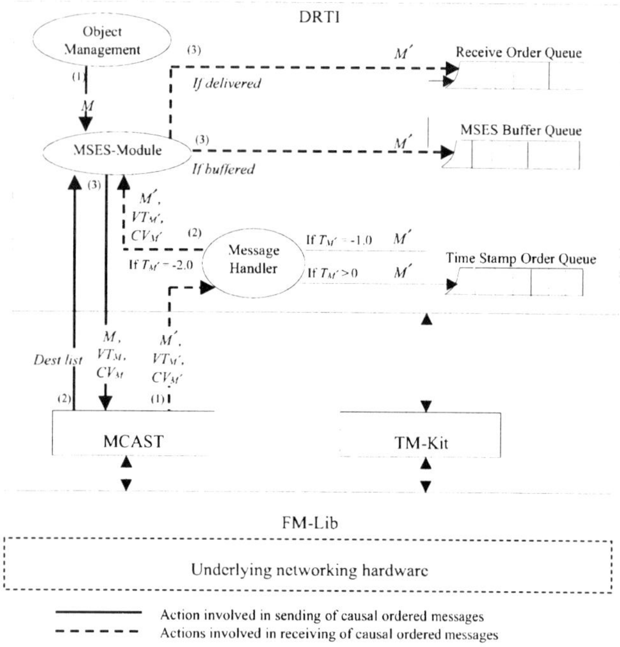

Figure 2. A Causality Based TM Mechanism

FDK. As mentioned before, time stamp ordering has many disadvantages, such as high communication overhead and high latency. $NlogN$ messages and $logN$ pair-wise minimum operations are used per LBTS computation. To enhance the execution speed of simulations and exploit maximum parallelism in distributed simulations, a new module named MSES-Module is developed and incorporated into the FDK. It provides a Causal Ordering (CO) mechanism to federations. CO mechanism will benefit federates to which minimizing latency is of greater importance than adhering to stringent message orders. Figure 2 illustrates the integration of CO mechanism with the FDK.

As illustrated in the diagram, causal ordered messages generated by the local federate is assigned with a time stamp equal to -2.0, to be differentiated from receive-ordered and time stamp ordered messages. The DRTI in the receiving federates determines the ordering of incoming messages according to their time stamps. Receive-ordered messages are placed in the RO queue in FIFO manner and ready for delivery to the local federate immediately. Time stamped messages are placed in the TSO queue in ascending time stamp order and delivered to the local federate only when it is guaranteed that no messages with smaller time stamp will be received. Causal ordered messages will be passed to the MSES-Module for further processing.

The heart of the MSES-Module is the algorithm of the MSES protocol. It provides a layer with the functionality to ensure the causal order delivery of the messages among federates. The MSES-Module has two fundamental interface processes. One processes the sending request from the local federate; while the other the incoming messages. An incoming message is either buffered at the MSES Buffer Queue or directly passed to the local federate if the delivery condition is satisfied (see Section 2).

When the local federate (denoted as P_i) invokes a service call of the DRTI to send a causal ordered message M (see Figure 2), the DRTI will pass it to the MSES-Module and then return to handle other service requests from the federate immediately. The MSES-Module will accomplish the rest of the work, including calculation of control information attached with M, sending M to the remote federates using the MCAST, and updating the control information (i.e., VT_{P_i} and CV_{P_i}) of the federate. As shown in Figure 2, first of all, the MSES-Module at federate P_i queries the MCAST of the destination federates of M as all the subscription and publication information of the federate is kept within the MCAST. Secondly, it increments $VT_{P_i}[i]$ and augments M with VT_{P_i}, CV_{P_i} and the destination list of M. The augmented message is then passed to the MCAST module for sending. Finally, the MSES-Module updates CV_{P_i}, that is, set $CV_{P_i}[k]$ to $(i, VT_{P_i}[i])$ for each destination federate P_k of M.

When an in-coming message M' is received from federate P_j by the MCAST and passed to the message handler in the DRTI, the message handler determines the ordering requirement of M' according to the time stamp of M' as mentioned before. If the time stamp of M' is -2.0, it is forwarded to the MSES-Module. Depending on the comparison between $CV_{M'}[i]$ and VT_{P_i} (as described in Section 2), the MSES-Module will determine whether to buffer M' or to deliver it directly to the local federate P_i. If M' is to be delivered to P_i, the control information will be detached from the augmented message, while the original message is flushed into the Receive Order Queue for delivery. The detached control information of M', including $VT_{M'}$, $CV_{M'}$ and the destination list of M', is used to update CV_{P_i} and VT_{P_i} in the following order:

- update VT_{P_i} using $VT_{M'}$;
- for each destination federate P_k of message M', except for P_i, update $CV_{P_i}[k]$;
- remove tuples in $CV_{P_i}[j]$ that corresponds to messages preceding M'; and
- for each federate P_k that is neither a destination federate of M' nor the sending federate of M' (that is, P_j), perform garbage collections on $CV_{P_i}[k]$ using the information from $CV_{M'}[k]$.

After updating CV_{P_i} and VT_{P_i}, the MSES-Module scans the MSES Buffer queue for the messages ready for deliveries. CV_{P_i} and VT_{P_i} need to be updated each time a message is delivered. This process is repeated until no ready messages can be found in the MSES Buffer Queue.

4. Benchmarks and results

To evaluate the efficiency of the proposed Causal Ordering (CO) mechanism, experiments are conducted to benchmark the performance of this new TM mechanism with respect to the existing Time Stamp Ordering (TSO) mechanisms implemented in the FDK. Receive-ordering (RO) mechanism is used as the reference, which achieves the fastest execution speed, however, without any message order constraints.

Benchmark results always vary with different hardware configurations. To justify and validate the benchmark results, the hardware configuration used for benchmarking, specifically, the network topology and equipment, is shown in Figure 3.

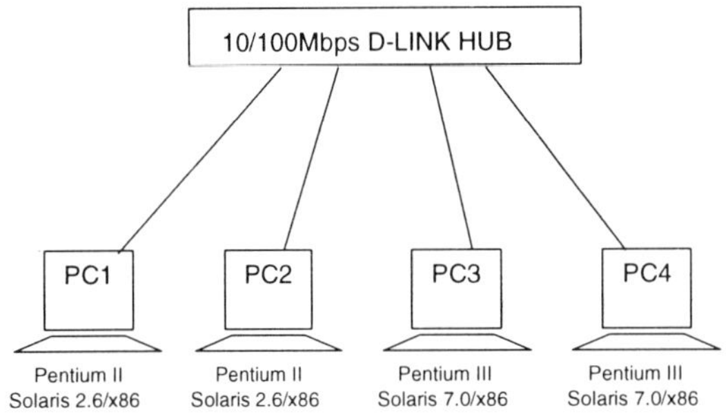

Figure 3. Benchmark Hardware Configuration

To benchmark the performance of the CO Mechanism against TSO and RO mechanisms under various situations, three scenarios are created. Each of these scenarios is designed with a different degree of inter-federate dependency. The first scenario depicts a loosely coupled federation, where each of the federates is running autonomously. The second scenario depicts a closely coupled federation, where federates interact with each other frequently. The third scenario depicts a mixed coupled federation, which comprises a mixture of autonomous federates and interacting federates.

4.1. Loosely coupled federates

In the first scenario, the dependencies among the federates are reduced to the minimum so that only the order of the messages sent by the same sender to the same receiver is maintained. This is the best case where federates are executed as fast as possible and dependencies among the federates are ignored. In this scenario, each federate in the federation sends an interaction periodically using the reliable TCP/IP connection. Under the TSO mechanism, each federate requests to advance its time 1.0 second further after it sends an interaction and it will continuously call tick() until its time advancement request is granted by the DRTI before it sends the next interaction. The lookahead of federates is set to 0.1 second. The time stamp of interactions is set to the current time of the local federate plus 1.0 second. A fixed spin loop is executed at the federates after each out-going message to account for the CPU time used by local simulation tasks, so as to make the simulation more realistic.

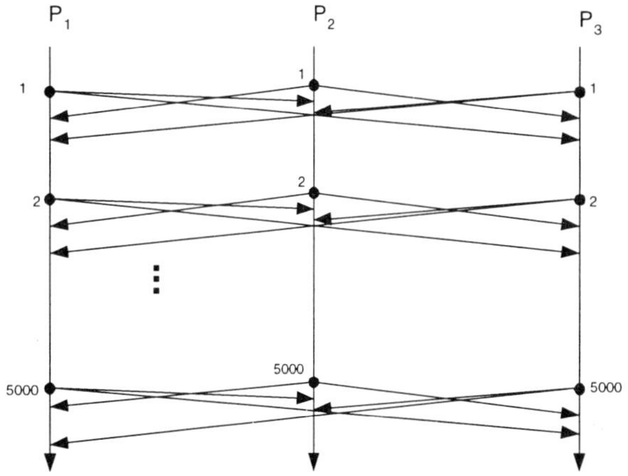

Figure 4. Execution of Loosely Coupled Federates

The execution of a loosely coupled federation is further illustrated in Figure 4. In this federation, activities of different federates are independent on each other. Thus, for a federate P_i, temporal relationships of two messages received from different remote federates are of no interest. The only requirement for P_i is that the ordering of messages from the same federate must be maintained so that it could view the activities of the federate in a timely manner. Both CO and TSO could guarantee this ordering requirement. However, both of them would incur communication overhead and latency. Although RO does not guarantee the ordering of messages from the same source explicitly, such ordering requirement is satisfied when TCP/IP is used as the underlying network communication protocol. Hence, RO is sufficient in this scenario to satisfy the ordering requirement without any extra communication overhead and latency. It is the most efficient TM mechanism for a federation with independent federates.

To evaluate the impact of CO and TSO on the performance of federate execution in this scenario, experiments are carried out to measure the average execution time of federates, i.e. the mean duration between the time when a federate start sending the first interaction and the time when the federate finishes sending 5000 interactions and quits the

Average federate execution time			
TM Mechanism	Number of Federates		
	2	3	4
RO	12.67954s	14.58417s	15.56844s
CO	12.61791s	14.75345s	15.87068s
TSO	13.96927s	21.38334s	38.51876s

Table 1. Execution Time of Loosely Coupled Federates

federation. Another factor affecting the performance of federation execution is the size of the federation, or the total number of federates. Thus, an array of simulation experiments has been conducted with various combinations of time management mechanisms and federate sizes. Each combination has been repeatedly tested five times and the average is used. The results are given in Table 1.

It can be seen from Table 1 that the CO mechanism incurs only a slightly higher latency with respect to the RO mechanism. The latency experienced by the federates using the TSO mechanism is rather small when there are two federates in the federation. This is because each LBTS computation only requires one pair-wise minimum operation with two message passings between the two federates in the federation. The federates using the CO mechanism execute much faster than those using the TSO mechanism when there are more than two federates in the federation. The computation overhead of the CO mechanism is almost negligible for a federation population smaller than five. Furthermore, the latency of the computation overhead generated by the CO mechanism is overshadowed by that of the vast inter-federate communications generated by the LBTS computations of the TSO mechanism.

Therefore, the CO mechanism has a small influence over the performance of federation execution in loosely coupled federations. However, federates experience rather high latency and communication overhead when the TSO mechanism is used. In addition, the execution time of federates using the TSO mechanism grows much faster than that of federates using the CO mechanism when the federation population increases.

The total CPU time elapsed in the spin loops during the execution of the federates is 11.594665 seconds in average for the experiments conducted in Table 1. Experiments have also been conducted to study the effect of the event granularities of federates on the total CPU time used by other activities of the federates rather than the local simulation tasks (that is, the execution time of the federates without the CPU time used by the spin loops). By varying the average total CPU times elapsed in the spin loops from 11.594665 to 134.1803 seconds, we did not observe any significant differences in the total execution time elapsed on other activities, irrespective of the TM mechanisms and the total number of federates in the federation.

4.2. Closely coupled federates

While the first scenario creates the least causally related federates in a federation, the second scenario creates the most causally related federates. In this scenario, the causal orderings are exploited to the extreme that each message sent out by a federate is dependent on the previous messages received from all other federates. In a federation execution using RO or CO mechanism, federates will execute similar programs as the first scenario except that after sending an interaction a federate will continuously call tick() until it receives an interaction from each of other federates before it sends the next interaction.

In a federation execution using TSO mechanism, it is guaranteed that federates will not receive messages occurring in the past. If all the federates are time-stepped federates with the same time-step size, dependency among federates in the closely coupled federation is implicitly realized. A federate will ask for advancing simulation time to the next time step after sending an interaction without explicitly waiting for replies from other federates. In this scenario, federates using TSO mechanism executes the same program as that in the first scenario. The time step of federates is set as 1.0 second, lookahead 0.1 second and time stamp of messages the current time of the local federate plus 1.0 second.

In the closely coupled federation, activities of different federates are highly inter-related with each other. The TSO mechanism provides a total ordering service to federates but the CO and RO mechanisms do not provide such a service to federates. So, when the CO or RO mechanism is used, to ensure the close and consistent interoperation among the federates, federates have to execute additional synchronization activities among them explicitly, such as handshakes among federates in this scenario (i.e., waiting for reply after sending an interaction). A total ordering service is provided in TSO mechanism, but at the cost of increased communication overhead and latency. To investigate the trade-off between efficiency and degree of ordering, experiments have been carried out to measure the average execution time of federates in federations using the RO, CO and TSO mechanisms under various situations (i.e., different combinations of time management mechanism and federation population). The results of the experiments are shown in Table 2.

It can be seen from Table 2 the latency experienced by the federates using the CO mechanism or RO mechanism increases much slower than the federates using the TSO mechanism when the federation population increments. The latency experienced by the federates using the TSO mechanism is close to that by the federates using the CO mechanism only when there are only two federates in the federation. This is because each LBTS computation costs only one pair-wise minimum operation in a two-federate federation and additional synchronization activities to ensure the dependency of federates are not needed in TSO mechanism. As the federation population increases, the latency incurred by the TSO mechanism raises rapidly and becomes much higher than the latency experienced by federates using the CO or RO mechanism. Thus although the TSO mechanism eases the burden of providing additional synchronization code in the federates, it is not very efficient to use in large federations.

Average federate execution time			
TM Mechanism	Number of Federates		
	2	3	4
RO	13.95665s	16.52154s	20.15819s
CO	13.89454s	16.38024s	20.22069s
TSO	13.96927s	21.38334s	38.51876s

Table 2. Execution Time of Closely Coupled Federates

In this scenario, the experiments have also been conducted with a variety of event granularities of federates. The results show that the execution time of the federates without the CPU time used by the spin loops varies little with different event granularities.

4.3. Mixed coupled federates

The aforementioned two scenarios illustrate the performance of federations in two extreme cases: one with zero inter-federate dependency; while the other with maximum inter-federate dependency. The results show that the federate execution time has a positive relationship with the inter-federate dependency. Since these two scenarios are rarely seen in practical simulations, another scenario is studied with moderate inter-federate dependency. In this scenario, three federates make up a "war-fare" federation. One federate is simulating an aircraft, another federate is simulating a tank, and the third federate is simulating an observer. The "aircraft" federate broadcasts an update message to the other two federates periodically. It also "fires" at the "tank" federate sometimes. When receiving a "fire" interaction, the "tank" federate broadcasts a "hit" update message to the other two federates. Except when reacting to the "fire" interaction initiated by the "aircraft" federate, the "tank" federate does not send any messages. The "observer" federate receives messages from the "aircraft" and "tank" federates and does not send messages itself. Experiments were conducted with the inter-fire interval of the aircraft federate changing from 100 update messages to 10 update messages. Similarly as before, a fixed spin loop is executed at the "aircraft" federate after each message is sent.

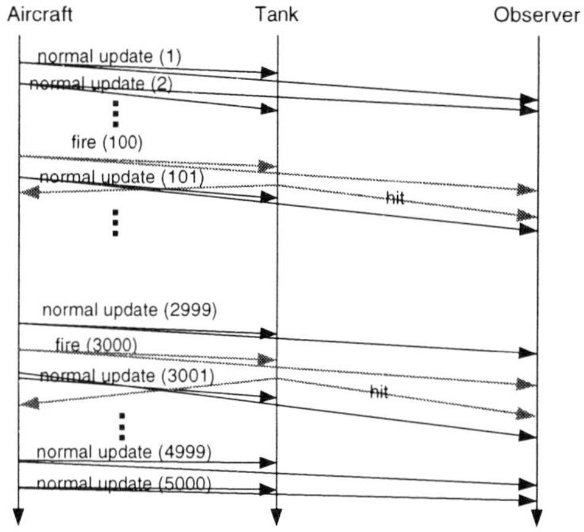

Figure 5. Execution of Mixed Coupled Federates

A typical execution of the "aircraft" federate, "tank" federate and "observer" federate is shown in Figure 5. In this federation, the fire interval of the aircraft federate is 100 update message. As the "hit" message is causally dependent on the "fire" message, the CO mechanism ensures that the observer sees the tank being "fired" and "hit" thereafter. It also ensures that the updates from the "aircraft" are received by the "tank" and "observer" in order. Thus CO mechanism fulfills all the ordering requirements of federates in this scenario. Since the observer may see the "hit" event of the "tank" occurs before the "fire" event if RO mechanism is used, RO mechanism cannot be used for this scenario. However, TSO mechanism is applicable in this scenario. Experiments are conducted to measure the execution time of federates in a mixed coupled federation execution using TSO or CO with different fire frequencies. Results are shown in Table 3.

Average federate execution time				
TM Mechanism	Fire Interval			
	10	25	50	100
CO	13.16066s	13.10884s	12.99197s	12.96808s
TSO	37.88004s	37.09594s	37.08293s	36.5227s

Table 3. Federate Execution Time in Mixed Coupled Federation

The results shown in Table 3 further proved the efficiency of CO mechanism compared to TSO mechanism in federation executions with moderate inter-federate dependencies. It can be seen that CO mechanism demonstrates a more than 60% performance improvement over the TSO mechanism. Event granularities are also found to have little impact over the execution time of the federates without the CPU time used by the spin loops.

5. Conclusions and future works

Exploiting a "happen before" relationship among the events occurred in the system, causal ordering maximizes the parallelism of the distributed simulations while maintaining a message order consistent with the requirements of simulations. Causality is particularly useful for collaborative applications or groupware real-time applications, such as multi-player Internet game and shared window systems, where participants need to exchange real-time data (messages) over a communication network. Such applications need good interactivity and may tolerate a message ordering less stringent than time stamp ordering. Furthermore, a great number of the participants in such applications may have zero lookahead as some messages they generate represent the events occurring immediately.

The causality based TM mechanism proposed in this paper uses a Modified Schiper-Eggli-Sandoz (MSES) protocol that minimizes the size of the control information propagated with messages using the direct dependency tracking technique. It has been implemented with the FDK and its performance is studied using federations with minimum, moderate and maximum inter-federate dependencies. The causality based TM mechanism demonstrates a significant performance improvement over the TSO based TM mechanism in almost all of the experiments. The experiments also show that the proposed TM mechanism works almost as efficiently as RO mechanism with only a small communication and computation overhead.

Due to the limited hardware resources, the federation used for benchmarking consists of at most four federates. The overhead of the causal ordering is almost unnoticeable for such a small federation size. In the future, we will measure the overhead of the CO mechanism in a much larger federation. Another dimension of our future works is toward the applicability of the proposed causal ordering mechanism. While causal ordering is sufficient to avoid certain causality anomalies, it is not sufficient in all situations (e.g., if ordering relationships of concurrent events are important). The simulations that only require causal ordering will be categorized in our future research. Extensions of causal ordering will be investigated to cater for the simulations with more stringent ordering requirements than causal ordering. Finally, an important issue to be addressed is how the causal ordering can be applied to the simulations where the time stamp ordering is needed for some messages.

Acknowledgements

The authors wish to thank Dr. Stephen John Turner of School of Compuer Engineering at Nanyang Technological University, Singapore, for providing valuable comments and suggestions on this study. This research is supported by SINGAREN (the Singapore Advanced Research and Education Network) and Network Technology Research Center of Nanyang Technological University, Singapore.

References

[1] Fast Messages. http:://www-csag.ucsd.edu/projects/comm /fm.html.

[2] Federated Simulations Development Kit (FDK). *Georgia Institute of Technology*. http://www.cc.gatech.edu/computing /pads/fdk.html.

[3] HLA Time Management Design Document, version 1.0. *U.S. Department of Defense*, August 1996.

[4] High Level Architecture interface specification, version 1.3. *U.S. Department of Defense*, April 1998.

[5] K. Birman, A. Schiper, and P. Stephenson. Lightweight causal and atomic group multicast. *ACM Transactions On Computer Systems*, 9(3):272–314, August 1991.

[6] C. J. Fidge. Timestamps in message-passing systems that preserve the partial ordering. *Australian Computer Science Communication*, 10(1):56–66, February 1988.

[7] R. Fujimoto. RTI-Kit V0.2 Specification. *Georgia Technological University*, (18), March 1998.

[8] A. D. Kshemkalyani and M. Singhai. Necessary and sufficient conditions on information for causal message ordering and their optimal implementation. *Distributed Computing*, 11:91–111, 1998.

[9] L. Lamport. Time, clocks, and the ordering of events in a distributed system. *Comm. of ACM*, 21(7),:558–565, July 1978.

[10] R. Prakash, M. Raynal, and M. Singhal. An adaptive causal ordering algorithm suited to mobile computing environments. *Journal of Parallel and Distributed Computing*, pages 190–204, March 1997.

[11] M. Raynal, A. Schiper, and S. Toueg. The causal ordering abstraction and a simple way to implement it. *Information Processing Letters*, 39(6):343–350, 1991.

[12] A. Schiper, J. Eggli, and A. Sandoz. A new algorithm to implement causal ordering. *Proceedings of the International Workshop on Distributed Algorithms Springer-Verger New York*, LNCS Vol 392:219–232, 1989.

[13] C. Sun, Y. Zhang, Y. Yang, and C. Chen. Distributed concurrency control in real-time cooperative editing systems. *Proceedings of the 1996 Asian Computing Science Conference*, Springer-Verlag, Singapore:84–95, December 1996.

[14] J. Zhou. A causality-based time management mechanism, Master Thesis. August 2000.

The Resource Sharing System: Dynamic Federate Mapping for HLA-based Distributed Simulation

Johannes Lüthi and Steffen Großmann
Institut für Technische Informatik
Universität der Bundeswehr München
85577 Neubiberg, Germany
luethi@informatik.unibw-muenchen.de

Abstract

Networks of workstations have become a popular architecture for distributed simulation due to their high availability as opposed to specialized multiprocessor computers. Networks of workstations are also a well-suited framework for distributed simulation systems based on the High Level Architecture (HLA). However, using workstations in a distributed simulation system may eventually effect the availability of computing resources for the users who need their computers as working tools. Thus, for coarse grained distributed simulation it may be desirable to let the users control to what extent their workstations should participate in a distributed simulation. In this paper, we present a resource sharing system (RSS) that provides a client user interface on each potentially participating workstation. With the RSS clients, users of workstations can control the availability of their computer for the HLA simulation federation. An RSS manager keeps track of available computing resources and balances the participating HLA federates among the available workstations.

Keywords: Fault tolerance, high level architecture, load balancing, network of workstations

1 Introduction

The High Level Architecture (HLA), developed by the U.S. Defense Modeling and Simulation Office (DMSO) provides a general software architecture for distributed simulation [13], [1]. The HLA is defined by its three components: the HLA rules, the object model template, and the interface specification. Its primary purpose is to serve as a tool for the common execution of a composable set of interacting simulations with the goal of increasing model reusability. However, the Run Time Infrastructure (RTI), which is the implementation of the HLA interface specification, can also be used as a building block for parallel simulation on high-performance computers [18]. Furthermore, also a network of workstations (NOW) may be used for HLA-based distributed simulation. Using a NOW is often preferred to implementations on specialized parallel hardware because of its higher availability. This is especially useful, if an existing network of workstations which are used for other purposes, can additionally be used for simulation. Thus, it is not surprising that recently it has become popular to use NOWs for distributed simulation. Some examples for distributed simulation on a NOW can be found in [15], [16], or [9].

However, if the computers in a NOW are concurrently used for simulation as well as conventional (interactive) computer work, the (non-simulation) users may desire to be able to decide during which periods of time they want to make their workstations available for participation in the distributed simulation. A similar approach, using automated control of computing resources is followed in the search for extra terrestrial intelligence (SETI), where computers connected via the internet collaborate in analyzing huge amounts of measured data [2]. In the *SETI@home* project, the clients automatically make their resources available as soon as the screen-saver activates (i.e., as soon as the real user does not do any interactive work at the computer). For distributed simulation using the HLA, existing systems for distributed computing and load sharing such as PVM (Parallel Virtual Machine) [11] or *Condor* [4], [10] are not appropriate for various reasons. PVM cannot be used in this context because in PVM the available computing nodes have to be known in advance whereas the desired system should support dynamic participation of resources. Another problem with non-HLA specific solutions is that in contrast to distributed jobs in Condor, HLA federates are not independent. Since they may only communicate via the RTI, the RTI has to keep track of every migration. Furthermore, time management and synchronization issues of distributed sim-

0-7695-1104-X/01 $10.00 © 2001 IEEE

ulation are not taken care of in these general purpose load management systems.

Another important motivation for our work is that the proposed resource sharing system (RSS) can be used as a first step in the direction of fault tolerant distributed simulation with the HLA. Currently, the HLA does not include a formal failure model [6]. Furthermore, to the best of our knowledge, existing RTI implementations do not support fault tolerance in distributed simulation. With the exception of the work reported by Agrawal and Agre [3] and Damani and Garg [7], also for distributed simulation without the HLA, only little has been done to increase the amount of software-based fault tolerance for distributed simulation systems. Following concepts for fault tolerant distributed simulation proposed in [14], it is planned to extend the RSS presented in this paper with checkpointing management, fault detection, and error processing mechanisms. In ongoing work it is planned to design a *fault tolerance system* that can be wrapped around existing HLA federations. The proposed RSS will be a key component of such a fault tolerance system managing migration activities for federation reconfigurations during fault recovery. Thus, the performance aspects of distributed simulation with the RSS are not the main focus of this work. For example, the implemented load balancing mechanism is very elementary because for the current RSS prototype a principle load balancing functionality is more important than performance optimization.

In this work, we present the resource sharing system (RSS) which allows the users of workstations connected as a NOW to control the availability of their computers for an HLA-based distributed simulation. Typical use cases include the following:

1. During the course of a distributed simulation run, the user of a workstation would like to offer his/her computing resources to the distributed simulation system. If possible, parts of the simulation are moved to that computer. If not needed at the moment, it is registered that this workstation is available for load migration in the future.

2. A user (of a workstation) notifies the RSS of his/her desire to gain back control over the computing resources, i.e., to quit the participation in the distributed simulation. The simulation federates running on that workstation have to be migrated to other computers currently participating in the distributed simulation run.

3. A simulation user requests to participate at the distributed simulation with a new simulation federate. The new federate has to be integrated in the distributed simulation as well as in the RSS.

Three main objectives of the proposed architecture and implementation are (a) to intervene with the RTI functionality as little as possible (i.e., to use as many existing methods as possible), (b) to require only a minimum adaptation effort for existing HLA federates to participate at an RSS-controlled distributed simulation federation, and (c) to guarantee repeatability of simulation experiments independently from federate migration during the course of the simulation run (this claim only applies to simulations that guarantee repeatability without using the RSS).

The paper is organized as follows. In the next section, the architecture of the resource sharing system (RSS) is presented including a detailed discussion of its three main components. In Section 3, the communication mechanisms of the RSS are considered. Section 4 deals with the way information about the distributed simulation system and participating computing resources is maintained by the RSS. Implementation issues including requirements for participating HLA federates and restrictions for the distributed simulation system are discussed in Section 5. Section 6 summarizes the results and points out how our work concerning the RSS is going to be continued in the future.

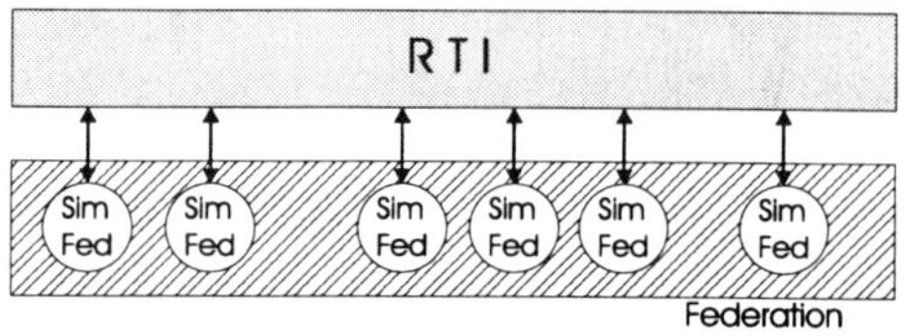

Figure 1. HLA-based distributed simulation architecture.

2 RSS Architecture

In the HLA, a distributed simulation is referred to as a *federation* of a number of simulation *federates*. All simulation specific communication between the federates is supposed to be performed via the *run time infrastructure* (RTI) of the HLA. This basic architecture is depicted in Figure 1 (simulation federates are denoted by "SimFed"). For the desired flexibility in federate-to-workstation mapping, it is necessary to be able to redistribute federates in the NOW during federation runtime. Such load balancing and migration functionality is not provided by the HLA and its RTI. A migration of an HLA federate at process level is not feasible with reasonable adaptation effort under MS Windows NT (which serves as our development platform). Thus, migration at federate level has been chosen: on request, federates save their state and are restarted using the saved state file on another node. An additional infrastructure component, the *RSS manager* is introduced for that purpose. Furthermore, on each workstation a *client program* is executed, provid-

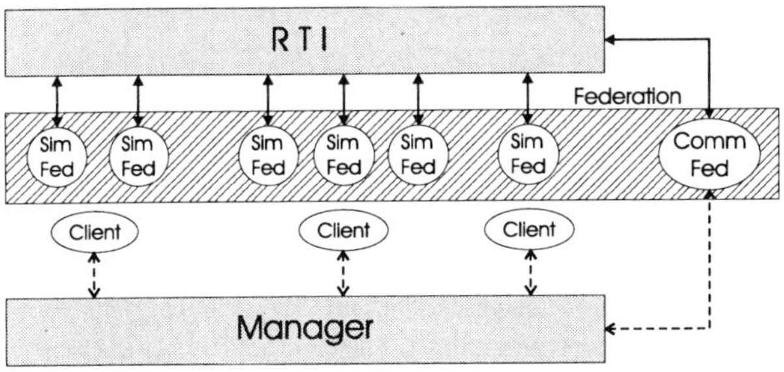

Figure 2. Architecture for HLA-based distributed simulation with the RSS.

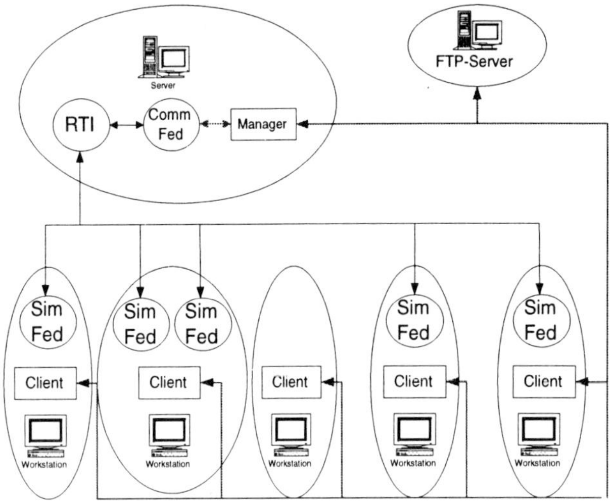

Figure 3. Mapping of RSS components to nodes.

ing the user interface that allows the user of a workstation to control the availability of the workstation for simulation computations. To keep the adaptation effort for the simulation federates as low as possible, the simulation federates do not communicate with the manager directly. In contrary, all communication between the manager and the simulation federates is performed via the so-called *communication federate*. Communication between simulation federates and the communication federate is done via the RTI along the lines of the HLA rules [17].

The resulting architecture is depicted in Figure 2. Communication external to the RTI is plotted using dashed lines. Figure 3 shows the mapping of the simulation components to a NOW: the components *RTI*, *RSS manager*, and *communication federate* are located on a *server* node. However, these components could as well be located on different nodes. On each *client* node, the client program as well as a number of simulation federates reside. An ftp-server located on an arbitrary node is used for data transport during federate migration processes. The total of these components is referred to as the *resource sharing system* (RSS). In the following, the main components of the RSS are discussed in more detail.

2.1 Manager

The manager is the central component of the RSS. Its main tasks include: (a) processing incoming requests from the clients, including connection and disconnection requests, (b) performing migration decisions for simulation federates, (c) balancing the load of federates among connected nodes, and (d) controlling the migration operations.

At the start of a simulation federation, all federates are executed at the server node. The manager keeps track of client nodes joining the RSS and distributes the federates among the available client nodes. Thus, all mapping information is maintained at the manager. Every time, a client node joins the RSS or cancels its participation at the RSS, the manager decides whether or not simulation federates are supposed to migrate from one node of the RSS to another. Associated migration control information is passed to the communication federate, which communicates the migration directions to the federates via the RTI.

Every time a migration is necessary, the manager performs a load balancing decision. In its current implementation, the RSS follows relatively basic load balancing rules: as soon as there are client workstations available, no simulation federate runs on the server node. If there is more than one client, it is tried to have approximately the same number of federates on every client node. This is obtained by passing migration directions to as many federates such that finally the number of federates on the new client node equals the rounded average number of federates per node. When a simulation federate leaves the federation, no load balancing is performed. This strategy is implemented to avoid migration cascades at the end of the whole simulation at the cost of unbalanced situations if there is a high variation in the end-of-simulation-time among the federates. This is a very basic load balancing strategy that does not take into account structural information about the whole simulation federation or observations of the data flow among the various federates. Since for the current prototype it is more important to provide some elementary load balancing functionality than to optimize performance, this relatively naive mechanism is implemented. In later versions, techniques to combine flow control with load balancing as described by Choe and Tropper [5] or load balancing strategies that use structural model information such as e.g. the load balancing method for spatially explicit problems by Deelman and Szymanski [8] or the locality-preserving load-balancing mechanism by Vee and Hsu [19] might be integrated in the

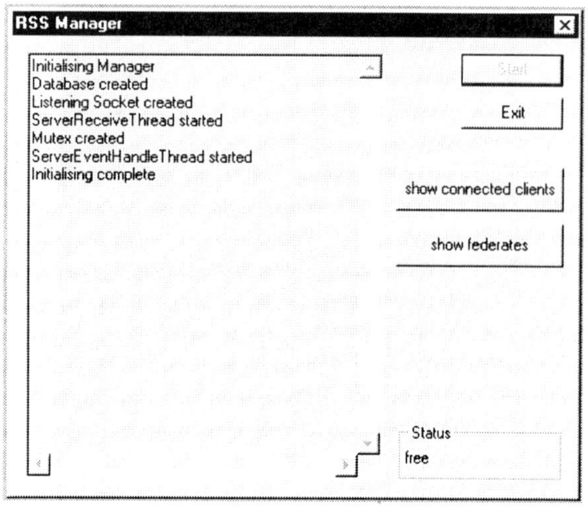

Figure 4. Screen shot of the RSS manager.

load-balancing functionality of the RSS manager.

Time management conflicts during migration of a federate are avoided by bounding the simulation time of all federates to the global virtual time (GVT) of the whole federation at the beginning of the migration activity. Although this is a rather brute force method it may be sufficient for coarse-grain simulations since relative to the total simulation time the number of migration events is not too high.

To allow the parallel processing of an arbitrary number of external requests, the manager is implemented as a multithreaded server [12]. Every connection request spans a *ServerReceiveThread* which checks the syntax of incoming events, categorizes them into expected and unexpected events, and inserts the events in corresponding manager event lists. Access to the manager event lists is mutual exclusive because the processing of manager events is done by another thread, the *ServerEventHandleThread*. Currently, the event lists are processed sequentially. In future work, the manager event lists may be used for the load balancing mechanism, in a way that all currently known manager events are considered during the load balancing decisions.

Figure 4 shows the screen shot of the RSS manager user interface. A log-window shows important actions. Furthermore, an overview of currently connected RSS clients as well as participating federates can be obtained.

2.2 Clients

On every client workstation that wants to participate in the RSS (i.e., that is willing to make its computing resources available for the distributed simulation) a client program is started. There is one client program per client workstation. The RSS client has two main functions: (a) It provides the user interface that allows the user of a workstation to communicate his/her requests to the RSS manager. (b) The

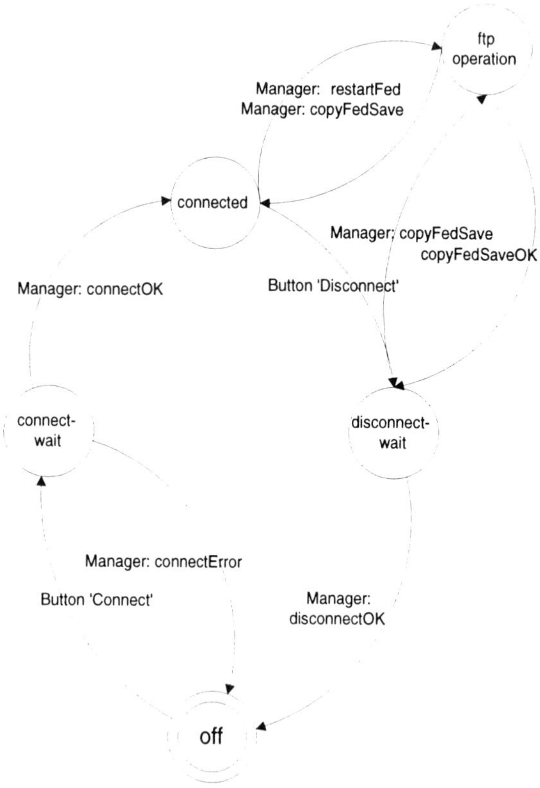

Figure 5. State transition diagram for an RSS client.

client processes directions received by the manager, such as ftp-operations or requests to start federates on the client workstation. Possible user requests are firstly the request to participate in the distributed simulation, i.e., to let one or more federates run at the client computer, and secondly the request to quit participation in the distributed simulation (if e.g. the computing power of the workstation is needed for other purposes).

After successful connection of a client to the RSS, a multithreaded server is also started at the client workstation, which permanently allows the client to receive instructions from the manager. As opposed to the RSS manager, the client does not store incoming instructions in an event list but processes them immediately. Thus, the client can be viewed as a finite automaton, such as depicted in Figure 5. After startup, the client program is in the *off* state. This means that it is not available for distributed simulation. When the *'Connect'* button of the client's user interface is pressed, the client waits to be connected to the RSS. Depending on whether or not it receives a *connectOK* message from the manager

(see Section 3), it either goes to the *connected* state or it returns to the *off* state. While in the *connected* state, the

Message	Sender	Recipient
connect	client	manager
connectOK [ftpServer] [ftpLogin] [ftpPass] [ftpPort]	manager	client
connectError [error]	manager	client
copyFedSave [fedname]	manager	client
copyFedSaveOK [fedname]	client	manager
restartFed [fedname]	manager	client
disconnect	client	manager
disconnectOK	manager	client
disconnectError	manager	client
comFedConnect	comm. fed.	manager
newFed [fedname] [exeFileName]	comm. fed.	manager
exitFed [fedname]	comm. fed.	manager
stopSave [fedname]	manager	comm. fed.
stopSaveOK [fedname]	comm. fed.	manager

Table 1. RSS messages.

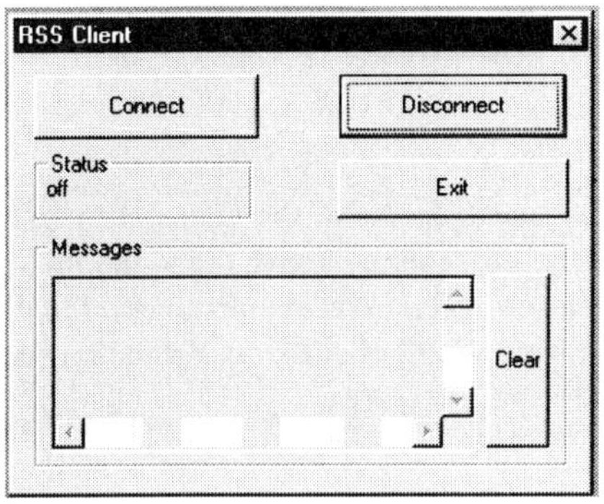

Figure 6. Screen shot of an RSS client's user interface.

client may be requested by the RSS manager to start a federate or to pass responsibility for a federate to the manager. Both situations involve ftp operations. By pressing the *'Disconnect'* button the client may move from *connected* state to the *disconnectWait* state. While being in that state, the client may eventually have to send files belonging to the federates that have been active at the client's node to the ftp server. When the client receives the *disconnectOK* message from the manager, it returns to the *off* state.

Figure 6 shows an RSS client window, that allows the user to pass connect and disconnect requests to the manager. Furthermore, the current status is displayed and a message log scroll-box allows to observe message communication between the client and the RSS manager.

2.3 Communication Federate

The communication federate serves as the interface between the RSS manager and the simulation federates. Since all communication between the communication federate and the simulation federates is done via the RTI using HLA *interactions*, the communication federate can be viewed as a part of the HLA federation. Communication with the simulation federates via a specialized communication federate has been chosen to reduce the adaptation effort for the simulation federates. This way, no non-RTI communication with the RSS manager has to be integrated into the simulation federates. There are basically two types of communication performed via the communication federate: (a) the communication federate passes requests of the RSS manager to the simulation federates via the predefined HLA interaction *requestFederationSave* and (b) information about the participating federation (such as registration or termination of simulation federates) is reported to the RSS manager by the communication federate via the self-defined interaction *federateData*.

3 Communication between RSS Components

Communication between simulation federates (i.e., all communication associated to simulation objects and interactions) as well as the communication between the simulation federates and the communication federate is done via the RTI (as required by the HLA rules [17]). However, all communication involving the RSS manager is not done via the RTI. Instead, sockets based on TCP/IP are employed. In the current C++ implementation, the *CblockingSocket* class is used [12]. This class allows access to an asynchronous stream-socket with timeout surveillance.

3.1 Messages

Information between the manager and RSS clients as well as the communication federate is exchanged by means of messages with associated parameters. For this communication, three distinct ports are used for the RSS manager, RSS clients, and for the communication federate. This allows an easy association of messages and their recipients. Table 1 lists the implemented message types and associated communication partners. Message parameters are listed in brackets. The *connect* message communicates the desire of a client to be connected to the RSS. *connectOK* and *connectError* are positive, respectively negative acknowledgements given by the manager. If the connection is established, the manager passes ftp-server information needed for data transport during later migration activities to the client. *disconnect*, *disconnectOK*, and *disconnectError* are the respective messages associated to disconnection requests. With the message *copyFedSave*, the manager tells a client to transfer the state file of a federate to the ftp server (see Section 4.2). The successful operation is reported to the manager via the message *copyFedSaveOK*. The message *restartFed [fedname]* tells a client to start the federate *fedname* using its save file to continue simulation with the saved state. With the *comFedConnect* message, the communication federate tells the RSS manager of its existence. *newFed* reports the start of a new federate (being observed by the communication federate) to the manager, whereas *exitFed* tells the manager that an existing federate left the federation. Finally, *stopSave* tells the communication federate to trigger a simulation federate to save its state and stop computation. The message *stopSaveOK* reports the successful operation.

3.2 Communication Example

Figure 7 shows an example of a typical communication sequence. In this example, a new client joins the distributed simulation, i.e., it offers its computing power to the RSS. After successful connection, a federate is migrated from an existing RSS client to the new one. This involves the following communication activities: when the user presses the *'Connect'* button at the client's user interface (i.e., in the dialog *CRSSCLientDlg*), the client sends a *connect* message to the RSS manager. The manager acknowledges the connection request by passing back necessary ftp-server information along with the *connectOK* message to the client. *CRSSCLientDlg* is notified of the successful connection. Since the manager decides to migrate an existing federate running at an 'old' client, communication continues as follows: A *stopSave* message is sent to the communication federate. The communication federate transfers this request to the affected client (i.e., the client of the node where the federate to be migrated currently resides) via the RTI (RTI communication is not depicted in the diagram of Figure 7). The successful termination of the simulation federate including generation of a save file is subsequently reported

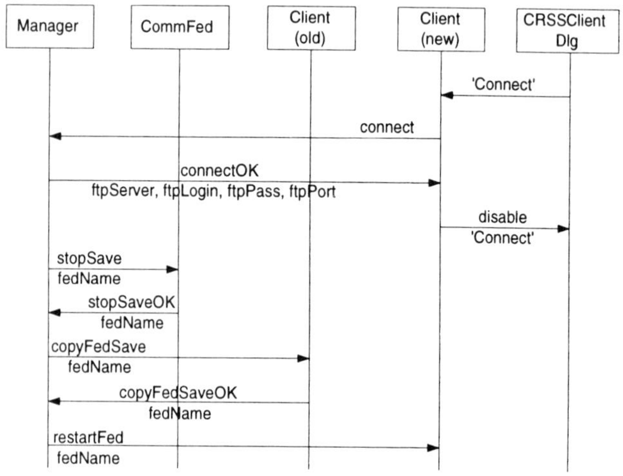

Figure 7. Communication example: a new client joins the RSS, causing a federate migration operation.

back to the manager. Next, the manager instructs the 'old' client to send the federate's save file to the ftp-server (*copyFedSave* and *copyFedSaveOK* messages). Finally, the manager tells the new RSS client to restart the migrated federate via the message *restartFed*.

4 RSS Data Maintenance

To be able to perform the desired actions, the RSS must hold information about participating workstations, the simulation federation, simulation federates, and the participating ftp-server. Most of this information is maintained by the RSS manager. Additionally, some data has to be available for the manager as well as all participating RSS clients. These data and program files are organized as discussed below.

4.1 Internal RSS Manager Data

In the manager, chained lists of objects associated to information about clients, federates, and events are kept. Separate lists for user-triggered events (connect and disconnect messages) and expected events (acknowledgement messages) are held. These objects store the following information: clients are represented by an associated *CRSSClientItem* and are identified by their IP address (only one client per IP address is allowed). A federate is stored as a *CRSSFedItem* with its name, its current residence (execution node), and the name of the associated executable program file. User triggered events (messages) are stored as *CRSSEventItem* which includes type, sender and message parameters. An acknowledgment event is represented as a *CRSSOKEventItem* which includes its type as well as the context it refers to.

4.2 Global RSS Data Files

The following files have to be available to the manager as well as to all clients: executable program files for the simulation federates, save files to store the state of each federate for migration purposes, and federation description files. To guarantee shared access to these files, an ftp-server is chosen as the file resource. Using ftp for file maintenance allows to rely on an existing fault tolerant protocol instead of having to define a new protocol for data interchange. Furthermore, extension of the RSS in the direction of fault tolerance which is planned for future work is also supported: if these essential files are external to the RSS, it is easier to establish redundancy of data as well as data transport.

5 Implementation Issues

The prototype of the RSS was developed for MS Windows NT using MS Visual C++. Thus, in its current state, the RSS can only manage HLA federations based on MS Windows NT.

5.1 Requirements for Simulation Federates

Although one of the design objectives of the RSS is to minimize the adaptation effort for simulation federates to be able to be used with the RSS, some restrictions apply. To enable participation of an HLA federate at the RSS, the following requirements have to be met by the federate.

- At the start and at autonomous termination (i.e., termination independent from an RSS manager request), the federate is supposed to call an associated HLA interaction, called *federateData*. There are three parameters for this interaction: *ready* (reporting whether a federate is started or has finished computation), *saveFile* (the file name for saved states of the federate), and *exeFile* (the file name of the executable code for the federate).

- A reaction to the HLA's *requestFederationSave* has to be implemented. I.e., When instructed by the manager (via the communication federate), a simulation federate must be able to save its state in a way such that it can be restarted after migration using that saved information. This includes information about the internal state of the simulation engine as well as information about which HLA objects have to be created after federate restart.

- The federate must be able to interpret the string parameter provided by *requestFederationSave* as federate name. The federate in question must terminate after successfully saving its state without sending an HLA interaction.

- A simulation federate must be able to be started with the name of a save-file as argument allowing continuation of the simulation after migration.

- The saved data must be sufficient to guarantee the semantically correct continuation of the whole simulation. If repeatability of simulation experiments is to be guaranteed independently from the use of the RSS, the saved state must include additional data to enable maintenance of repeatability in the presence of federate migrations. This may for example include seeds for pseudo random number generators.

5.2 RSS Rules

Currently, also for the whole RSS and the managed HLA federation some additional restrictions apply. These restrictions apply to the prototypical implementation of the RSS and may be dropped in future versions: (a) All federates being part of the HLA federation from the beginning of the simulation have to be started at the server node (i.e., at the node the RSS manager resides). As soon as client nodes are connected, federates may be moved to client workstations. (b) Only a single federation per RTI can be handled by the RSS.

6 Conclusions

Networks of workstations (NOW) are a popular platform for distributed simulation as an alternative to highly specialized multiprocessor architectures. NOWs are also well-suited for distributed simulation with the High Level Architecture (HLA). However, often such workstations in a NOW concurrently serve as working tools for their users while being used for distributed simulation runs. This may sometimes lead to situations where a user may desire to have the ability to control the availability of its computing resources in order to continue work without obstruction. In this work we introduce the Resource Sharing System (RSS) that provides a user interface at the client computers (potential participants in the distributed simulation) to control the availability of their workstations for distributed simulation runs. An RSS manager keeps track of available computers and distributes the simulation load. To reduce the adaptation effort for participating HLA federates, communication of the simulation federates with the RSS is performed via the HLA's runtime infrastructure (RTI) using a specialized communication federate.

An important shortcoming in conventional distributed simulation, including distributed simulation via the HLA, is the lack of fault tolerance. Thus, in future work, the RSS will be extended by fault tolerance mechanisms such as checkpointing management, management of replicated federates, and fault detection. This way, the RSS may additionally serve as the reconfiguration component of a *fault tolerance system* wrapped around existing HLA simulation federations. Future work may also include refinement of the load balancing mechanisms in the RSS manager. Another potential improvement of the RSS may be an extension of the control features at the RSS clients. This may include an automatic mode as well as a more fine-grained control about the amount of computing power that is dedicated to simulation.

Acknowledgements

The work described in this paper has been done in the context of the student project "fault tolerant distributed simulation" performed at the institution of the authors. We gratefully appreciate the help and fruitful discussion of all participants of this project (teaching staff and students). Special thanks in that direction go to Axel Lehmann, Dirk Brade, and Gerald Anders. We also like to thank the anonymous referees of the paper for their helpful and constructive comments.

References

[1] HLA web-page of the U.S. defense modeling and simulation office. http://www.dmso.mil/index.php?page=64.

[2] Seti@home. http://setiathome.ssl.berkeley.edu/.

[3] D. Agrawal and J. R. Agre. Replicated objects in time warp simulations. In J. Swain, D. Goldsman, R. Crain, and J. Wilson, editors, *Proceedings of the 1992 Winter Simulation Conference*, pages 657–664, 1992.

[4] J. Basney and M. Livny. Deploying a high throughput computing cluster. In R. Buyya, editor, *High Performance Cluster Computing*, chapter 5. Prentice Hall PTR, May 1999.

[5] M. Choe and C. Tropper. On learning algorithms and balancing loads in time warp. In *Proceedings of the* 13th *Workshop on Parallel and Distributed Simulation (PADS '99), Atlanta, GA, USA, May 1–4, 1999*, pages 101–108. IEEE Computer Society Press, 1999.

[6] J. S. Dahmann. The high level architecture and beyond: Technology challenges. In *Proceedings of the* 13th *Workshop on Parallel and Distributed Simulation (PADS '99), Atlanta, GA, USA, May 1–4, 1999*, pages 64–70. IEEE Computer Society Press, 1999.

[7] O. P. Damani and V. K. Garg. Fault-tolerant distributed simulation. In *Proceedings of the* 12th *Workshop on Parallel and Distributed Simulation (PADS '98), Banff, Alberta, Canada, May 26–29, 1998*, pages 38–45. IEEE Computer Society Press, 1998. (Simulation Digest, Vol. 28, No. 1, July 1998).

[8] E. Deelman and B. K. Szymanski. Dynamic load balancing in parallel discrete event simulation for spatially explicit problems. In *Proceedings of the* 12th *Workshop on Parallel and Distributed Simulation (PADS '98), Banff, Alberta, Canada, May 26–29, 1998*, pages 46–53. IEEE Computer Society Press, 1998. (Simulation Digest, Vol. 28, No. 1, July 1998).

[9] P. M. Dickens. A workstation-based parallel direct-execution simulator. In *Proceedings of the* 11th *Workshop on Parallel and Distributed Simulation (PADS '97), Lockenhaus, Austria, June 10–13, 1997*, pages 174–177. IEEE Computer Society Press, 1997. (Simulation Digest, Vol. 27, No. 1, July 1997).

[10] D. H. J. Epema, M. Livny, R. van Dantzig, X. Evers, and J. Pruyne. A worldwide flock of condors: Load sharing among workstation clusters. *Journal on Future Generations of Computer Systems*, 12, 1996.

[11] A. Geist, A. Beguelin, J. Dongarra, W. Jiang, R. Manchek, and V. Sunderam. *PVM: Parallel Virtual Machine - A User's Guide and Tutorial for Networked Parallel Computing*. The MIT Press, Camebridge, 1994.

[12] D. Kruglinski. *Inside Visual C++ 6.0*. Microsoft Press Deutschland, Unterschleißheim, 1998.

[13] F. Kuhl, R. Weatherly, and J. Dahmann. *Creating Computer Simulation Systems – An Introduction to the High Level Architecture*. Prentice Hall PTR, Upper Saddle River, NJ, 1999.

[14] J. Lüthi and C. Berchtold. Concepts for dependable distributed discrete event simulation. In R. V. Landeghem, editor, *Proc. Int. European Simulation Multi-Conference (ESM 2000, Ghent, Belgium, May 23–26, 2000)*, pages 59–66. SCS, May 2000.

[15] F. Quaglia and V. Cortellessa. Grain sensitive event scheduling in time warp parallel discrete event simulation. In *Proceedings of the* 14th *Workshop on Parallel and Distributed Simulation (PADS 2000), Bologna, Italy, May 28–31, 2000*, pages 173–180, Los Alamitos, May 2000. IEEE Computer Society.

[16] G. D. Sharma and R. Radhakrishnan. Time warp simulation on clumps. In *Proceedings of the* 13th *Workshop on Parallel and Distributed Simulation (PADS'99), Atlanta, GA, USA, May 1–4, 1999*, pages 174–181–, Los Alamitos, May 1999. IEEE Computer Society.

[17] SISO. High-level architecture rules version 1.3. U.S. Department of Defense, draft 2 of IEEE standard 1516 (IEEE Architecture Management Group), http://www.dmso.mil/index.php?page=121, 1998.

[18] J. S. Steinman, G. Berliner, G. E. Blank, J. S. Brutocao, J. Burckhardt, M. Peckham, S. Shupe, K. Stadsklev, T. Tran, R. Van Iwaarden, and L. Yu. The speedes-based run-time infrastructure for the high-level architecture on high-performance computers. In A. Tentner, editor, *Proceedings of the High Performance Computing Symposium – HPC'99*, pages 255–266. SCS, April 1999.

[19] V.-Y. Vee and W.-J. Hsu. Locality-preserving load-balancing mechanisms. In *Proceedings of the* 14th *Workshop on Parallel and Distributed Simulation (PADS 2000), Bologna, Italy, May 28–31, 2000*, pages 131–138, Los Alamitos, May 2000. IEEE Computer Society.

Session 5

Applications

A Parallel Object-oriented Manufacturing Simulation Language

Ye ZHANG   Wentong CAI   Stephen J. TURNER
School of Computer Engineering
Nanyang Technological University
Nanyang Avenue
Singapore 639798

Abstract

When used to simulate manufacturing systems, most existing parallel simulation languages cannot easily implement some features of those systems, such as the scheduling rules of a machine or the sharing of operators by multiple machines. This paper presents the design and implementation of a Parallel Object-oriented Manufacturing Simulation Language, called POMSim. A POMSim simulation is developed by using the concept of classes (entity-types) and inheritance to support iterative design of efficient simulation models. POMSim completely hides all the details of parallel simulation, and provides simple and direct constructs to efficiently model the scheduling rules in manufacturing simulation. It also provides asynchronous method invocation and synchronous function call. POMSim libraries predefine a set of basic classes for manufacturing simulation, each of which represents a particular component in the physical manufacturing system.

Keywords: *parallel simulation language, object-oriented simulation, semiconductor manufacturing, Sematech Data Modeling Standard, POMSim, PARSEC.*

1 Introduction

Parallel Discrete Event Simulation (PDES) [4] has been widely researched in recent years. A number of PDES languages and libraries have been developed to support parallel execution of simulation models [6]. However, most of the PDES languages have been developed for general simulation applications. When applied to a specific area, they often cannot provide a direct and efficient solution. For example, in manufacturing simulation, one of the reasons that the construction of the simulation is difficult is the realization of the scheduling rules [14] for processing a product. Most PDES languages do not provide the mechanisms to model these rules directly. The objective of this research is thus to design a parallel simulation language especially for the manufacturing domain.

The manufacturing model we describe in this paper is for wafer fabrication processes, and follows the Sematech Data Modeling Standard (DMS) [10]. The Sematech datasets provide information containing actual factory parameters from some existing anonymous wafer fabrication facilities. The model described by a Sematech dataset generally consists of a number of process flows, a number of machine sets and operator sets, a generator that releases initial wafer-lots into all process flows and a collector that gathers all the finished wafer-lots. Each process flow is made up of a number of steps. At each step, a machine from a machine set is required to perform the relevant work. In some models, each step also requires an operator from an operator set and this may result in an operator set being shared by multiple machine sets.

Each machine set has associated with it some scheduling rules that specify the way a wafer-lot is processed. Setups are required when different types of operations can be performed on a machine, but the machine must be reconfigured (setup) in order to perform the new operation. A *setup rule* is a set of criteria for deciding if the setup of a free machine within the machine set should be changed when allocating a wafer-lot. A *dispatching rule* is used by the machine set to decide the relative priority of waiting wafer-lots. An example of a complex scheduling rule is given in section 3.2.

In this paper, we present a Parallel Object-oriented Manufacturing Simulation Language, called POMSim. Using the object oriented paradigm, a POMSim program is designed as a collection of entity-types. An entity-type is similar to a class, and models a type of machine set, operator set, generator, or collector in a manufacturing simulation. POMSim provides constructs to ease the implementation of the setup and dispatching rules. It also provides both asynchronous and synchronous communication among simulation entities. The synchronous communication mechanism allows operator sets to be directly shared by multiple machine sets.

This paper is organized as follows: Section 2 gives an overview of related work. Section 3 describes the language constructs of POMSim and presents the organization of the system classes in the POMSim libraries. Section 4 describes the structure of the POMSim simulator. In Section 5, we evaluate POMSim by simulating some Sematech datasets and comparing our results with those obtained using an existing simulator for wafer fabrication [5]. Finally, Section 6 gives our conclusions and outlines future work.

2 Related Work

To encourage the adoption of PDES in the real world, many parallel simulation tools have been provided in the last decade. A full survey of PDES languages can be found in [6]. Parallel simulation tools may be classified based on the generality of their programming interface. Available tools range from general-purpose parallel simulation languages to domain-specific simulation tools. This section gives a brief overview and discussion of several existing PDES languages.

A PDES language can provide the user with either a traditional structured programming approach, such as PARSEC [1], Maisie [2] and YADDES [9], or an object-oriented programming approach, such as TeD [8], APOSTLE [13], and MOOSE [12].

PARSEC and Maisie are C-based general-purpose PDES languages that were developed to support a number of different simulation protocols, including conservative and optimistic. PARSEC is derived from Maisie, with several enhancements incorporated and language constructs rewritten. YADDES is a simulation-specification language, which also provides support for a variety of synchronization protocols. It requires users to provide a specification of the desired simulation in the form of a specification source file.

With regard to event scheduling, YADDES provides a simple scheduling construct to model the passing of time, while PARSEC provides a more complete scheduling construct – the *guard*. The guard is expressed by the keyword **when**. It may suspend an entity until the guard expression is satisfied. Using the guard, some simple scheduling rules in the manufacturing domain can be simulated. But, for more complex scheduling rules, considerable effort is still needed. Moreover, none of these languages have achieved total transparency with regard to the synchronization protocol. For instance, PARSEC requires users to provide the communiction topology and lookahead information when it uses a conservative algorithm.

TeD, APOSTLE and MOOSE all have the common features of object-oriented languages, such as data encapsulation, object communication, and inheritance. TeD is an application-specific PDES language for modeling telecommunication networks. APOSTLE is based on an optimistic protocol, whereas MOOSE is the object-oriented version of Maisie and supports a number of different simulation protocols. Entities in MOOSE communicate with each other asynchronously by invoking the methods defined in other entities. APOSTLE supports both asynchronous and synchronous communication. In APOSTLE, method invocation itself is synchronous. However, any expression containing one or more statements or method invocations may be executed asynchronously [13]. While MOOSE provides a similar guard construct to PARSEC, APOSTLE supports an *interrogative scheduling* [3] mechanism that is used to model the passing of time of a simulation entity, or the situation that a simulation entity waits for an event to happen.

Although the languages surveyed provide some constructs useful for implementing manufacturing simulation, they still do not allow direct and easy specification of all features, for example, complex scheduling rules. In order to solve these problems, we have designed a parallel simulation language called POMSim, especially for the manufacturing domain. In order to simplify the design, we extend one of the existing PDES languages and add some new constructs specific to manufacturing simulation. PARSEC is chosen as the intermediate language of POMSim as a number of simulation models in diverse domains have been developed using PARSEC and good performance has been obtained. Since object-oriented design can reduce development time and provide better code management and reusability, the object-oriented approach is adopted in the design of the new language.

3 Language Constructs of POMSim

In this section, we describe the language constructs of POMSim. Several concepts were borrowed from MOOSE and APOSTLE, such as the guard of MOOSE and the asynchronous and synchronous communication that APOSTLE supports. The language has the following characteristics:

- It supports object-oriented features – encapsulation, inheritance and polymorphism in order to facilitate hierarchical structure and behaviour description.
- It is fully transparent with regard to the underlying parallel protocols. Using POMSim, users need not worry about the connections among LPs (logical processes) and the mappings from LPs to physical processors.
- It provides easy and direct constructs to simulate the setup rules and dispatching rules in the manufacturing models.
- It allows both asynchronous and synchronous communication among entities. The synchronous communication will allow information to be shared among entities.

```
entity Name
{
    declaration portion
    initialization {
        ......
    }
    method portion
    function portion
    finalization {
        ......
    }
}
```

Figure 1. Components of an entity-type

A POMSim source program consists of a collection of entity-types which model the machine sets, operator sets, generator and collector in a manufacturing model. Here, an entity-type is similar to a class in C++. An entity-type is composed of five portions: the *declaration* portion, *initialization* portion, *method* portion, *function* portion and *finalization* portion.

3.1 Entity-types

The definition of an entity-type begins with the **entity** keyword, followed by a name for the entity-type. The appearance of an entity-type is given in Figure 1.

The variables declared in the declaration portion can be accessed within the other four portions. POMSim supports all C declarations. In addition, an entity name can be used as a data type to declare a reference to an entity of that entity-type, as follows:

entity *M1 m;*

It declares *m* as a reference to an entity (instance) of entity-type *M1*. The reference is normally initialized by calling a library function. We will discuss the creation of entities in Section 4.

The initialization portion initializes the variables declared in the declaration portion. It may include a set of C and POMSim statements. The finalization portion may also include a set of C statements to collect some statistics when the simulation is terminated. The initialization and finalization portions are executed automatically when an entity of an entity-type is created and the simulation terminates respectively. Any of the five portions may be omitted.

3.2 Method – Asynchronous Communication

The *method* portion of an entity-type consists of a set of method definitions. A method definition includes a method name, a set of parameters and a body, but no return type. The parameters may be empty. A method and its parameters implicitly define a message-type that has the same name as the method. The body of a method consists of a set of POMSim statements and C statements and describes one of the simulation behaviours of the entity to which the method belongs.

POMSim supports implicit communication via method invocation. An entity asynchronously executes a method defined in another entity by executing an **invoke** statement. This is similar to the corresponding message being sent from one entity to another entity in PARSEC. After invoking the method, the entity continues execution. The **invoke** statement must specifiy the identifier of the destination entity and provide the name and actual parameters for the method being invoked. An entity can reference its own identifier using the keyword **self**. The syntax of the **invoke** has one of the following forms:

invoke *identifier* **with** *method-name*
invoke *identifier* **with** *method-name*
  after *period*
invoke *identifier* **with** *method-name* (*args*)
invoke *identifier* **with** *method-name* (*args*)
  after *period*

The first two statements are used when the method invoked has no parameters. The **after** causes the method to be scheduled after a period of simulation time.

Figure 2 defines two entity-types, *E1* and *E2*. *E1* declares an instance of *E2*, called *e* and defines a method called *start*. The initialization portion of *E1* starts the execution of the program by invoking its own method *start*. *E2* declares a variable named *units* that stores the number of available units, and defines two methods – *allocate* that allocates a resource and *free* that returns a resource to *E2*. The initialization portion of *E2* initializes the total number of units with 10. *E1* invokes the *allocate* method and the *free* method of *E2* at different simulation times. The execution of an **invoke** statement simply deposits the messages – *allocate* and *free* – in the message buffer associated with the destination entity *e*. The messages are removed from the buffer only when *e* reaches the corresponding simulation time and executes the corresponding method.

A method may additionally be associated with a *guard* expression or *ranker* expression, or both. The two expressions may reference the method parameters and the variables declared in the declaration portion. The two expressions allow many complex conditions such as the setup and dispatching rules of manufacturing simulation to be expressed in an easy manner. The guard is an optional boolean expression, which can suspend an entity until a certain condition becomes true. A guard expression is identified by the keyword **when**. A ranker expression is also an optional expression, which allows a method to be executed only when the message corresponding to the method makes the value

```
entity E1
{
  entity E2 e;
  initialization {
    e= ...; // e is the reference to an instance of E2
    invoke self with start;
  }
  start() {
    invoke e with allocate;
    ......
    invoke e with free after 10;
    ......
  }
}

entity E2
{
  int units;
  initialization {
    units=10;
  }
  allocate() {
    units−−;
  }
  free() {
    units++;
  }
}
```

Figure 2. An example of the use of methods

```
entity E3
{
  int units;
  initialization {
    units=10;
  }
  allocate(int num) when (units>=num)
    bymin (num) {
    units=units-num;
  }
  free(int num ) {
    units=units+num;
  }
}
```

Figure 3. An example of the use of guard and ranker

of the ranker expression maximum or minimum. A ranker expression is identified by the keyword **bymax** or **bymin**.

Figure 3 gives an example that illustrates the use of guard and ranker. It defines an entity-type, *E3*. The *allocate* can only be executed when the number of units it requires is available. The *allocate* message which requires the smallest number of units is first removed from the message buffer.

In general, in the manufacturing simulation domain, the setup rules are implemented using guards, while the dispatching rules are implemented using rankers. POMSim supports simultaneous use of **bymax** and/or **bymin** to achieve a combination of several dispatching rules. Suppose the method to process a lot is associated with three dispatching rules, as follows:

```
lot(int flow, int step) when (numof machines> 0)
   bymin (setup_time(flow, step))
      bymax (comp_ratio(flow, step))
         bymin (due_date(flow, step))
```

In order to process the lot, a machine must be available. The *lot* message with the smallest *setup time* is favoured. When two *lot* messages have the same setup time, the *lot* message with the largest *completion ratio* (computed as the current step number divided by the total number of steps in the process flow) is favoured. In case there is a tie in the first two rules, the *lot* message with the smallest *due date* is favoured.

3.3 Function – Synchronous Communication

The function portion of a POMSim entity-type consists of a set of functions. A function by default has full access to the variables declared in the declaration portion of an entity. It can modify or read those variables. A function may be additionally qualified by the keyword **pure**. The variables declared in the declaration portion are not accessible by **pure** functions unless these variables are passed as parameters to the function.

One point worth noting is that a method definition has no return type, while a function definition must have a return type (which may be **void**). A function call is synchronous and the calling entity waits until the function returns. A function is called in one of the following ways:

identifier.function-name (args)

function-name (args)

In the first statement, the dot operation is adopted. The *identifier* represents the identifier of an entity. The simulation time of this entity is the same as that of the calling entity. If the function is defined in the same entity as its caller, the second statement is used. In some cases, a method invocation and a function call may both be semantically correct. In this case, the function call is recommended, because it can be executed immediately. For instance, in Figure 4, we redefine the two entities *E1* and *E2* that were defined in Figure 2. The *allocate* method is replaced by the *allocate* function. Invoking the *allocate* method is also replaced by *e.allocate*().

```
entity E1
{
  entity E2 e;
  initialization {
    e= ...; // e is the reference to an instance of E2
    invoke self with start;
  }
  start() {
    e.allocate();
    ......
    invoke e with free after 10;
    ......
  }
}

entity E2
{
  int units;
  initialization {
    units=10;
  }
  free() {
    units++;
  }
  void allocate() {
    units--;
  }
}
```

Figure 4. An example of a function call

3.4 Inheritance

In POMSim, code reuse is typically provided by *class-based* inheritance. A new entity-type can be derived from an existing entity-type. The derived type will have all the portions of its base type. The keyword **inherit** is used when a new derived entity-type is defined. For instance, entity *B* is derived from entity *A*. It has the following statement:

entity *B* **inherit** *A*

The derived type will typically define additional data declarations, methods and functions. It may also override the implementation of the initialization portion, a method, a function or the finalization portion defined in the base entity-type and replace it with its own. When the derived entity-type only appends new code to the old code of the base type, the keyword **super** can be used to represent the old code of the base type in the new implementation. Figure 5 illustrates how to use **inherit** to define a derived entity-type and how to use the **super** statement to represent the same code as defined in the base entity-type. *E5* is inherited from *E3* defined in Figure 3.

POMSim only supports a form of inheritance known as single inheritance in which a new entity-type can be derived from only a single entity-type. POMSim also does not support the overloading technique in which the same method or function name may be declared with different arguments.

```
entity E5 inherit E3
{
  allocate(int num) {
    super;
    printf("The num units are released.");
  }
}
```

Figure 5. An example of inheritance

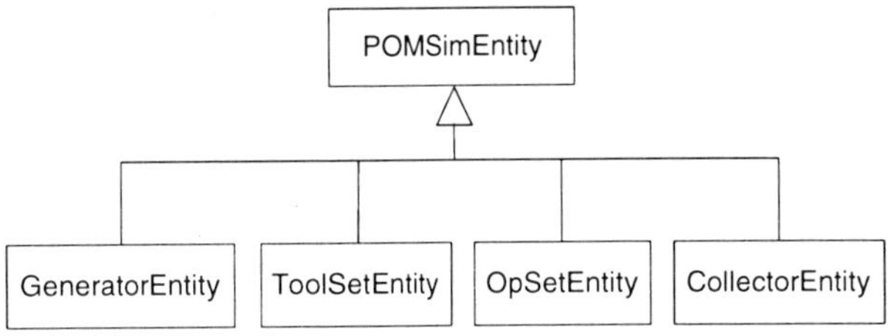

Figure 6. The hierarchy of system classes

3.5 POMSim Libraries

The POMSim libraries consist of the *POMSim source library* and the *POMSim run-time library*. The POMSim source library predefines five system entity-types (classes) written in POMSim as shown in Figure 6. They are structured as a hierarchy of classes, where the basic and general functionality is defined in the root class, and more specific functionality is defined in the derived classes. The class *POMSimEntity* is the root class that has four derived classes – *ToolSetEntity*, *OpSetEntity*, *GeneratorEntity* and *CollectorEntity*. Each class defines a set of functions especially for it. No methods are defined in the five classes.

The *POMSimEntity* defines a number of predefined functions, such as the function *now* to get the current simulation time and functions for the POMSim random number generators. Any entity-type defined by users is derived from the root *POMSimEntity* by default, if the keyword **inherit** is omitted in the entity-type definition. *GeneratorEntity* models the generator which releases the original products into the production lines. *CollectorEntity* models the collector that collects the finished products.

ToolSetEntity is a basic class for the machine sets in the manufacturing model. Any class modeling a machine set is inherited from *ToolSetEntity* either directly or indirectly. It defines some new functions especially for machine sets, such as the functions *get_mset* and *get_opset* which return references to entities for the machine set and the operator

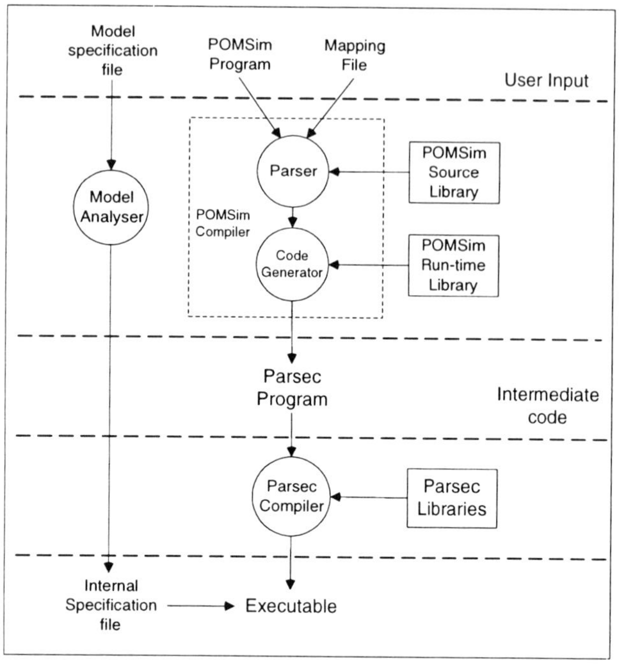

Figure 7. Structure of the POMSim simulator

POMSim source program	Mapping file
entity *LotRelease* **inherit** *GeneratorEntity*	*LotRelease*
{	*LotShipment*
}	*OPS*:
entity *LotShipment* **inherit** *CollectorEntity*	*OP 1-2*
{	*TS*:
}	*M 1-5*
entity *OP* **inherit** *OpSetEntity*	
{	
}	
entity *M* **inherit** *ToolSetEntity*	
{	
}	

Figure 8. Entity types and mapping file

set used at a certain step of the process flow respectively. *ToolSetEntity* also declares a variable named *MAXWAIT*. POMSim provides a default *setup rule* that uses *MAXWAIT* as a parameter. Finally, *OpSetEntity* defines a basic entity-type for all the operator sets. All derived entity-types that model operator sets are inherited from this entity-type either directly or indirectly.

The POMSim run-time library predefines several system files written in PARSEC that will be used by the POMSim compiler when the PARSEC programs are generated, as described in the next section.

4 Structure of the POMSim Simulator

The conceptual structure of the POMSim simulator is shown in Figure 7. When using POMSim to write a simulation program, users need to provide three input files – a *POMSim source program*, a *mapping file* and a *model specification file*. The POMSim compiler translates the POMSim source program and the mapping file into an intermediate program (i.e., a PARSEC program). This PARSEC program is subsequently compiled into an executable file by the PARSEC compiler. The executable file reads the internal specification file that is generated by the *model analyser* from the *model specification file*. POMSim does not support the creation of entities (instances) of entity-types in its source programs. Instead, POMSim only allows references to entities of entity-types to be declared. Using the mapping file, the entities of POMSim entity-types will be created automatically by the POMSim compiler.

The mapping file declares instances of the entity-types defined in the POMSim source program. The first line specifies the entity-type of the generator. The second line specifies the entity-type of the collector. The subsequent lines declare instances of the entity-types for the operator sets and the machine sets. The operator sets and machine sets are identified by their integer identifiers. Those integer identifiers correspond to the ones used in the model specification file. In Figure 8, the POMSim program on the left defines four entity-types – *LotRelease*, *LotShipment*, *OP* and *M*. The model includes two operator sets that have the entity-type of *OP* and five machine sets that have the entity-type of *M*. The mapping file is shown on the right in Figure 8.

The *model specification file* describes static aspects of the simulation model. Our current model is for wafer fabrication processes and is based on the Sematech datasets [10]. These datasets are not suitable for direct use in POMSim, because the Sematech datasets are very complex and large. So, we first translate them into a simple internal specification file using the *model analyser* (see Figure 7). Another reason we define an internal specification file rather than directly using the Sematech datasets is that it allows the model specification file to take different data formats in future. Thus, the POMSim program is independent from the model specification file as long as the latter can be translated to the internal specification file.

We have extended the C-to-C translator [7], developed at MIT, to implement the POMSim compiler, because POMSim and PARSEC are both C extension languages. The POMSim compiler is divided into two phases – the parsing phase that translates each entity-type defined in the POMSim program into an intermediate representation and the code generation that outputs the PARSEC program. The POMSim source library is written in POMSim and the

POMSim run-time library is written in PARSEC. They are used by two phases of the POMSim compiler respectively when a PARSEC program is generated.

In designing the POMSim compiler, one decision to be considered is the modeling approach to be taken by the generated PARSEC programs. This decision is important as it directly affects the way that the simulation program is generated. The decision is made by the compiler and is hidden from the user of POMSim. In the simulation model without operator sets, the resource modeling approach is adopted. This approach takes each machine set and maps it to a PARSEC entity (LP). In a simulation model with operator sets, the conflict set modeling approach [11] is used. The approach takes a conflict set and maps it to a PARSEC entity. A conflict set consists of a set of operator sets and machine sets. If different machine sets require an operator from the same operator set, or operators from different operator sets may operate the same machine, then these machine sets and operator sets are grouped into a conflict set. The conflict sets are calculated by the model analyser.

5 Evaluation

In order to evaluate the correctness and performance of POMSim, we present results for the simulation of the Sematech datasets using POMSim in this section. The experiment was carried out on a 4-CPU (250MHz) Sun Enterprise 3000 SMP, running Solaris 2.5. The simulation model built from the Sematech datasets consists of a number of process flows. The generator releases the initial lots into the process flows at different release rates. At each step of a process flow, a free machine is required to process a lot. In some models, a free operator is also required at a process step. After being processed at a process step, the lot is passed to the next step. Finally, the finished lot will be accepted by the collector.

The POMSim program used for the evaluation defines four entity-types for the generator, the collector, the machine sets and operator sets. The intialization portion of the generator starts the simulation by invoking itself with a message that releases the initial lots into different process flows. The finalization portion of the generator calculates the total number of lots released. The collector accepts all the finished lots. The number of lots received and the average cycle times are calculated in the finalization portion. The cycle time is the total time a completed lot spends in the manufacturing process, inclusive of the time spent queueing for resources. The average cycle time is the average cycle time of all finished lots in a particular process flow.

In Tables 1, 2 and 3, we compare the number of lots finished and the average cycle time we obtained using POMSim with the results provided by a PDES simulator [5] that has previously been validated against Factory Explorer [14]. The Sematech datasets 1, 2 and 6 are used in the experiments. (Note that the model built from Sematech dataset 1 does not include operator sets.) The PDES simulator has the same number of lots started as POMSim. The results are almost identical, showing the correctness of the POMSim simulator. The minor differences are mainly due to the way simultaneous events are resolved by the two simulators.

Table 1. Validation of POMSim (dataset 1)

Sematech dataset 1 (without operator sets)					
	POMSim			*PDES*	
Product	Lots Started	Lots Finished	Ave. Cyc. Time(hr)	Lots Finished	Ave. Cyc. Time(hr)
1	16575	8552	12253.9	8550	12228.9
2	8288	1280	21359.3	1282	21355.2

Table 2. Validation of POMSim (dataset 2)

Sematech dataset 2 (with operator sets)					
	POMSim			*PDES*	
Product	Lots Started	Lots Finished	Ave. Cyc. Time(hr)	Lots Finished	Ave. Cyc. Time(hr)
1	4755	3130	8626.3	3129	8620.7
2	3704	1403	15620.0	1404	15605.7
3	2432	1394	10758.0	1394	10747.0
4	6343	4791	6215.9	4786	6211.1
5	8220	3105	15702.5	3108	15694.8
6	2630	2628	38.9	2627	39.1
7	3244	2447	6262.0	2446	6267.3

Table 3. Validation of POMSim (dataset 6)

Sematech dataset 6 (with operator sets)					
	POMSim			*PDES*	
Product	Lots Started	Lots Finished	Ave. Cyc. Time(hr)	Lots Finished	Ave. Cyc. Time(hr)
1	1642	48	24726.2	47	24484.2
2	538	131	19120.6	130	19094.0
3	1139	560	12859.3	559	12891.2
4	1373	82	23645.4	82	23843.3
5	4581	274	23727.0	271	2369.5
6	2905	708	19076.1	704	19092.4
7	1050	256	19074.2	255	19115.3
8	1217	297	19057.3	295	19103.1
9	1418	698	12849.2	697	12889.7

Figure 9 shows the speedup of simulating the three datasets. Speedup is defined as T_s/T_p, where T_s is the sequential execution time and T_p the parallel execution time using the conservative *null message* algorithm. The speedup

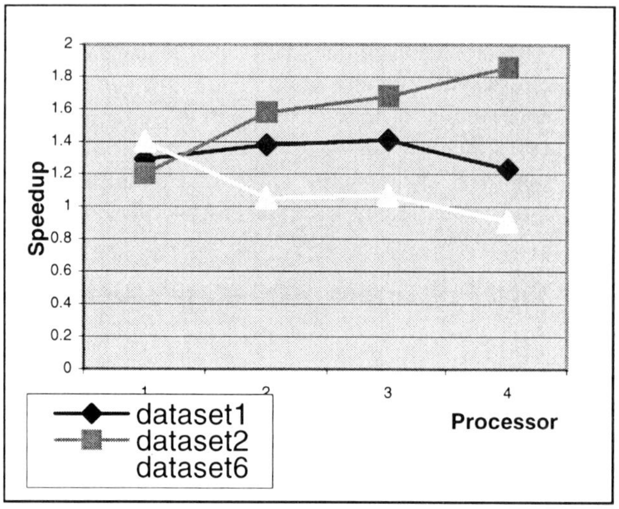

Figure 9. Speedup for POMSim

for dataset 2 increases with the number of processors. When executed on 4 processors, the speedup is very close to 2. But, the speedup for dataset 6 decreases with the number of processors. These datasets have different number of conflict sets (*LP*s). They are 23, 97 and 7 for datasets 1, 2 and 6 respectively. There are two reasons that result in different speedups among these three datasets. One reason is that a model with a large number of conflict sets provides more opportunities for events to be executed in parallel. The other reason is that PARSEC takes the round-robin policy to map *LP*s to physical processors. So, it may cause load imbalance for datasets with a smaller number of conflict sets.

6 Conclusions

This paper has described a parallel object-oriented manufacturing simulation language called POMSim. POMSim allows users to develop manufacturing simulation models using object-oriented principles. The input to the POMSim simulator consists of a POMSim source program, a model specification file and a mapping file. A POMSim program consists of a collection of entity-types (classes) that model the generator, collector, machine sets and operator sets in the physical manufacturing domain. The model specification file describes static aspects of the simulated manufacturing model. The mapping file specifies the mapping of entity instances to the entity-types defined in the POMSim program. A POMSim method of a POMSim entity describes the dynamic behaviours of a simulation entity. When associated with the *guard* and *ranker* expressions, a POMSim method can implement complex setup and dispatching rules of manufacturing systems.

In the continuing development of POMSim, we will extend our programs to include the simulation of batch processing (in this case, multiple lots are processed as one operation) and other more complicated features of manufacturing simulation. Here we can take advantage of the powerful facilities in POMSim for expressing complicated scheduling rules. We will also generalize the POMSim compiler to support more advanced features of polymorphism.

References

[1] R. Bagrodia, *PARSEC User Manual Release 1.1*, UCLA Parallel Computing Lab, Department of Computer Science, Los Angeles, 1998.

[2] R. Bagrodia and W.T. Liao, *Maisie User Manual Release 2.2*, UCLA Parallel Computing Lab, Department of Computer Science, Los Angeles, 1995.

[3] J.B. Evans, *Structures of Discrete Event Simulation: An Introduction to the Engagement Strategy*, Ellis Horwood Ltd., Chichester, 1988.

[4] R.M. Fujimoto, *Parallel and Distributed Simulation Systems*, Wiley, New York, 2000.

[5] C-C. Lim, Y-H. Low, B-P. Gan, S.J. Turner, S. Jain, W. Cai, W-J. Hsu and S-Y.Huang, "A Parallel Discrete-Event Simulation of Wafer Fabrication Processes", Proceedings of 3rd High Performance Computing (HPC) Asia, September 1998, Singapore.

[6] Y-H. Low, C-C. Lim, W. Cai, S-Y. Huang, W-J. Hsu, S. Jain and S.J. Turner, "Survey of Languages and Runtime Systems for Parallel Discrete Event Simulation", *Simulation*, 72:3, pp. 170-186, March 1999.

[7] MIT Laboratory for Computer Science. *C-to-C Translator*, ftp://theory.lcs.mit.edu/pub/c2c/

[8] K. Perumalla and R. Fujimoto, *A C++ Instance of TeD*, GIT-CC-96-33, Technical Report, College of Computing, Georgia Institute of Technology, Atlanta, 1996.

[9] B.R. Preiss, *YADDES – Yet Another Distributed Discrete Event Simulator: User Manual*, Department of Electrical and Computer Engineering, University of Waterloo, 1990.

[10] Sematech, *Modeling Data Standards, version 1.0*, Technical report, Sematech Inc., Austin, TX78741, 1997.

[11] S.J. Turner, C.C. Lim, Y.H. Low, W. Cai, W.J. Hsu and S.Y. Huang. A Methodology for Automating the Parallelisation of Manufacturing Simulations", Proceedings of the 12th Workshop on Parallel and Distributed Simulation (PADS'98), pp. 126-133, May 1998.

[12] J. Waldorf, R. Bagrodia, "MOOSE: A Concurrent Object-Oriented Language for Simulation", *International Journal of Computer Simulation*, 4:2, pp. 235-257, 1994.

[13] P. Wonnacott and D. Bruce, "The APOSTLE Simulation Language: Granularity Control and Performance Data", Proceedings of 10th IEEE/ACM/SCS Workshop on Parallel and Distributed Simulation(PADS'96), pp. 114-123, May 1996.

[14] Wright Williams and Kelly, *Factory Explorer version 2.6, User's Guide Reference Topics*, Technical report, Wright Williams and Kelly, Pleasanton, California, 1998.

Practical Parallel Simulation Applied to Aviation Modeling

Dr. Frederick Wieland
Center for Advanced Aviation Systems Development
The MITRE Corporation
1820 Dolley Madison Dr., McLean, VA 22102
fwieland@mitre.org

Abstract.

This paper analyzes the Detailed Policy Assessment Tool (DPAT) as an example of a practical real-world aviation simulation that uses optimistic simulation technology. We present a review of analyses that have used DPAT results to support their conclusions, and discuss the design and performance of the system in the context of parallel simulation. The thrust of this paper is to explain how DPAT avoids some of the problems associated with optimistic simulation, while exploiting its strengths. A key conclusion is that parallel simulation technology, particularly optimistic synchronization, needs to be built into the product from its conceptual design through implementation, as opposed to adding it afterwards.

1. Introduction and Background

Designing parallel simulations that are optimistically synchronized is more of an art than a science. While there are some heuristics for good performance, such as maximizing granularity and lookahead while minimizing the coupling between logical processes (LPs), combining these heuristics together with a useful model to produce simulations that are both practical and well-performing has rarely been done. Compounding the problem is the myriad of difficulties that surround optimistic simulation that are absent in sequential systems, such as managing concurrent threads of execution, verifying correct execution, and handling risky events that may cause severe difficulties. Despite these apparent difficulties, the MITRE Corporation has developed a useful and high performing optimistically synchronized parallel simulation for the analysis of air traffic control. The simulation, called the Detailed Policy Assessment Tool (DPAT), is fully optimistic. There is no throttling of optimism, and yet it is devoid of rollback explosions, cascading rollbacks, and other problems that have been widely publicized in the parallel simulation literature.

That DPAT has had a significant and positive contribution on the aviation community is unassailable. Over twenty analysis projects used DPAT during the last four years, some of them reported in the popular press. An analysis of the proliferation of regional jets and their impact on airspace and airport congestion using DPAT can be found in the magazine "Air Traffic Management"; the remarkable accuracy of the predictions from this study have been lauded by industry leaders [1]. Prediction of future airport bottlenecks in the Asia-Pacific region using DPAT is outlined in a publicly available report [2]. The United States Federal Aviation Administration (FAA) has itself performed a detailed validation study of DPAT [3]. The results show that the model produces credible answers that are consistent with actual data collected from FAA's own systems. At the time of this writing, they are continuing to use the model for infrastructure investment analysis. Additionally, DPAT results have been used for testimony before the United States Congress [4].

While these reports are all publicly available, there have been many more proprietary studies using DPAT. The model has been used to study the impact of reducing required airplane separation, and its impact on system wide throughputs and delays [5]. It has also been used to study the tradeoffs between enroute and terminal-area efficiency improvements [6]. One of the most impressive non-public studies simulated each of the 365 days in 1997, with actual traffic and weather conditions, *twice,* one time with a proposed avionics system and once without. The analysts used the results from the 730 model runs to determine the annual cost/benefit of the proposed avionics improvement [7].

DPAT has been the subject of papers in recent years on its internal representation of the air traffic control system as a queueing network [8], and on its use for system wide analysis [9]. Although these papers mention DPAT's use as a parallel simulation, there are a number of important questions that remain unanswered. How can an optimistically synchronized simulation produce such a great impact on the real world? Are there not major problems with such simulations, including runaway rollback explosions, cascading antimessage chains, risky processing leading to erroneous states that crash the

0-7695-1104-X/01 $10.00 © 2001 IEEE

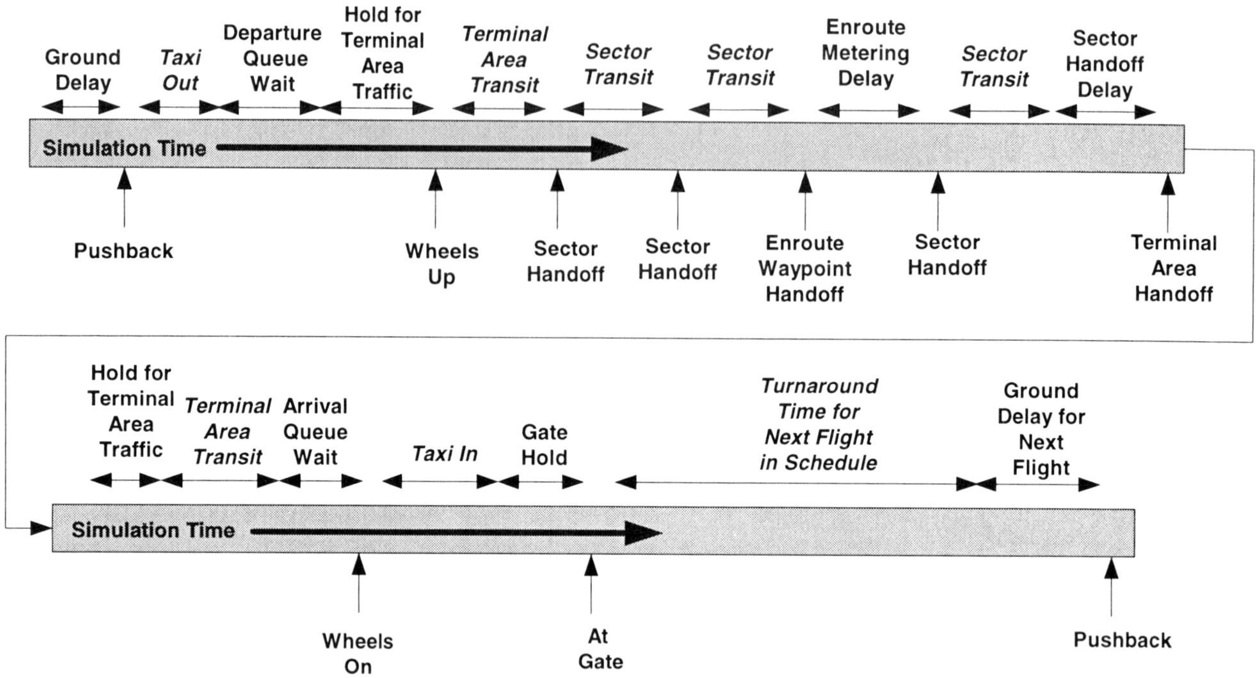

Figure 1. The modeled world. Time starts in upper left and flows to the right.

system? How are these problems avoided, and how do aviation analysts react to a system that processes both forwards and backwards? The remainder of this paper focuses on how the technical problems with parallel simulation are avoided, and the conceptual model exploited, to produce a good simulation.

2. Design Heuristics

Building a successful parallel simulation—whether conservative or optimistic—requires a creative blend of technical knowledge of parallel simulation and domain acumen about the physical system under study. Technical knowledge without any domain acumen produces "toy" simulations; domain acumen without any technical knowledge produces poorly performing, frequently crashing systems that are neither scalable nor useful for basic analysis.

On the technical side, it is well known that a number of factors contribute to good performance. Proper event granularity and good lookahead are both necessary ingredients. "Proper" event granularity is difficult to quantify, as it depends upon hardware characteristics, network performance, and whether an SMP or distributed system is employed. Studies of lookahead have shown that it influences greatly the probability of rollbacks and therefore the efficiency of the simulation engine. Generally, the greater the lookahead the greater the efficiency.

But there are other, more subtle, performance parameters that must also be considered. Most notably, computations in the model need to be "smoothed out" in three dimensions: simulation time, real time, and space (memory). In simulation time, it is well known that zero lookahead is to be avoided. Additionally, major computations should be staggered in simulation time. Instead of one event computing everything, the computation should be staggered among several events at different times. This can often be accomplished without compromising the integrity of the model, by merely changing its implementation. In real time, event explosions should be eliminated. An event explosion occurs when the minimum number of events that are needed to advance GVT by one time unit is very large. Finally, in space (i.e. memory), computations need to be as independent as possible, so that LPs do not need much knowledge of other LPs' states in order to compute an event.

3. The National Airspace System (NAS)

At its peak, the United States air traffic control (ATC) system currently handles 100,000 passengers per hour on 4,000 aircraft, or about 650 million passengers per year [10]. The volume is increasing at least as fast as the general economy, and yet the number of airports and runways are increasing more slowly, and the volume of airspace is (obviously) static. The result can be unusually large delays when the system is stressed. About 70% of delays are due to bad weather; the remainder occurs for a variety of other factors.

DPAT is designed to predict system-wide delays resulting from congestion, weather-related problems, system outages, growth in air traffic volume, or any combination of these. It is built to handle worldwide air traffic, taking as input the airports, airspace, flights, routes, and system capacities that constitute the ATC system under study. The data can represent past historical days, the current situation, or future hypothesized scenarios. The current situation can be input from live data feeds provided by ATC authorities; for historical and future information, DPAT reads data files in a well-documented format. The DPAT User's Manual [11] explains the capabilities of the model as well as the input and output data provided.

4. The Modeled World

DPAT represents the ATC system as a network of queues. Flights acquire and release a predictable set of resources as they travel gate-to-gate from their origin to their destination. The resources can be gates, taxiways, runways, blocks of airspace, waypoints in space called "fixes," and so forth, and the set of resources modeled by DPAT is shown in the time diagram of Figure 1. In that figure, simulation time is advancing from left to right. Below the gray bar, discrete events are shown, while above the gray bar, intervals representing activities occurring during a flight are shown. The intervals listed in *italic font* represent quantities that DPAT reads directly from a data file. Examples are the taxi in and out times, as well as minimum transit times in terminal areas and sectors. These times are always nonzero. Intervals listed in normal font are computed by DPAT as a result of congestion; examples include the various delays and holding patterns that occur during a flight. These times may be zero, depending upon congestion. The particular timeline shown in Figure 1 is for illustrative purposes. Some flights in an actual DPAT scenario may have as many as twenty (or more) enroute sectors, others might have no computed delay anywhere along their timeline, and still others may have excessive delays in some areas and none in others.

While the set of resources required by a flight is predictable, the interaction of these flights with other flights is unpredictable, and may result in delays. The resources themselves are the servers in the queueing system. Some of the resource capacities are specified as service rates, while others are specified as maximum queue lengths or a combination of queue length limits and the number of input queues. These rates can be a time varying function of random variables such as the weather, system outages, and closures. Flow control mechanisms can be applied on the ground or en-route, further reducing service rates and increasing delays. Many of the service rate changes are input to the model, while some are derived by DPAT itself and applied as the simulation evolves.

The net effect of these factors causes the queueing network to be analytically intractable. The most expedient way to analyze the system is to simulate actual flights traversing the network of resources, and to compute the resulting throughputs and delay at each point. It is this computation that is realized by the DPAT model.

5. Parallel Decomposition

Central to any parallel simulation system is the decomposition of the model into logical processes (LPs) that interact in parallel. Criteria for making this decision involve considerations of LP independence and scheduling overhead. It is desirable for the parallel LPs to be as independent as possible; this maximizes the amount of parallel computation and minimizes communication and synchronization costs. There is also a tradeoff between parallelism and scheduling overhead. The more parallel LPs that exist per processor, the greater the scheduling overhead but also the greater potential that the processor will have useful work to do.

In DPAT, stationary objects are implemented as LPs, while moving objects are implemented as messages passed among the stationary LPs. Practically, this means that airports, terminal airspace, enroute airspace, and enroute waypoints called "fixes" are modeled as LPs, while the flights are messages that move among these LPs.

Several criteria were used in making this decision. First, it maps to the physical system nicely: airplanes move among stationary resources, much as messages are moving among stationary LPs. Secondly, it allows easy proximity detection. The moving objects that are near each other will be located in one LP. Because LP boundaries are precise, it is easy for LPs to share information with their neighbors to resolve inter-LP proximity.

There is a potential drawback with this approach. Because the number of airports and airspace sectors is potentially large, the number of LPs will correspondingly be large. On a small number of processors, this might increase the scheduling overhead and therefore negatively impact performance.

For scenarios that concentrate on North American airspace, DPAT is typically configured with 500 airports, 20 additional "super source/sink" airports, and about 730 enroute airspace sectors, for a total of 1250 LPs. Some scenarios require speed restrictions to be placed enroute; these scenarios would add about a dozen "fix" logical processes. The largest DPAT scenario ever built consisted of over 1800 LPs representing global air traffic; the smallest consisted of only 30 LPs modeling East Asian traffic. DPAT performs well at both extremes.

6. Performance Measurements

The performance measurements presented below are from a standard DPAT scenario. The standard scenario uses traffic from May 6, 1993, with 520 modeled airports and 730 modeled airspace sectors, for a total of 1,250 LPs. There are 487,238 committed events. This scenario is typical of those used for actual analysis with DPAT; most scenarios contain between 400,000 and 600,000 events. Each LP contains state ranging from one to two kilobytes, and the state is incrementally saved. The message sizes are only a few hundred bytes, as the messages (which represent flights) contain pointers to static read-only data (such as flight itineraries, aircraft performance, and so forth). Because DPAT runs on a shared memory SMP, the use of pointers is nonproblemmatic.

The system is measured on a six processor Sun SPARC SMP with 450 MHz processors and four gigabytes of memory. The parallel simulation system used is the Georgia Tech Time Warp (GTW) system, which is composed of about 20,000 lines of "C" code and uses multiple threads on an SMP as the basis for parallelism [12]. Each performance measurement was computed five times, to get an idea of the standard deviation around the mean results.

6.1. Granularity Measurement

It has been shown that larger granularity can produce better performance, particularly if the LPs are somewhat independent. DPAT is a queueing-based model, so its granularity is relatively small. Because we are using GTW on an SMP system, the small granularity impacts performance only slightly.

The granularity distribution is shown in Figure 2, and has a high variance as well as being highly skewed. There appears to be no regularity in the length of events in DPAT. Although the model is fundamentally a queueing network, the servers have different traffic patterns, with different routing characteristics, queue lengths, service times, and internal decision algorithms. Thus a particular

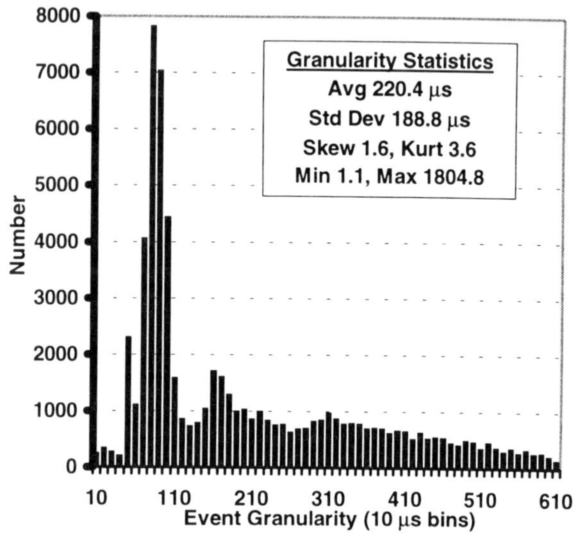

Figure 2. Event Granularity, 10 microsecond bins.

type of event at one LP takes a different amount of real time than the exact same type of event at a different LP. In terms of performance modeling, the high variance combined with the skewness of the distribution means that it is difficult to characterize using a standard probability distribution. In fact, different DPAT scenarios manifest different granularity distributions.

6.2. Lookahead Exploitation

Among the most sensitive indicators of parallel performance is the amount of lookahead in the model. Figure 3 is a histogram of the lookahead in the sample scenario for DPAT. The histogram is given in logarithmic units. Each bin spans a factor of ten, and there are 65,523 events that are sampled for this distribution from a total count of 487,238 committed events for this run of DPAT. The sample was taken from a sequential run of DPAT, and thus is not influenced by out-of-order risky event processing introduced by parallelism. Because DPAT yields the same number of committed events for both parallel and sequential runs, the data here are a valid look at a DPAT scenario.

Like the granularity, the lookahead of the model is highly skewed. The model runs for a total of 3,000 simulation time units, however the model completes 95% of its total events by time 2,000. Thus the average lookahead value of 62.6 represents a lookahead of about 2% of the total simulation time, or about 3% of the bulk of the simulation activity. The variance of the distribution is quite high, with a coefficient of variation of about 2.9.

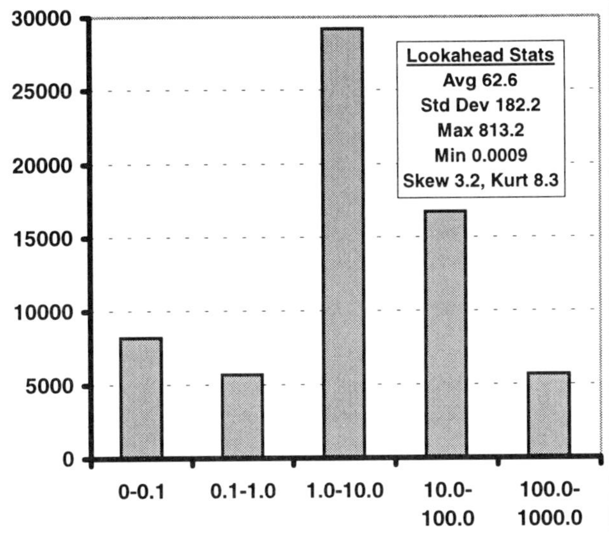

Figure 3. Lookahead histogram (logarithmic x-axis).

The distribution is highly skewed and is leptokurtotic. The maximum lookahead is 813 units of simulation time.

Figure 4 shows the lookahead probability from the same run. It is essentially a magnification of the histogram for the first 20 minutes of lookahead. The probability is binned into 0.125 simulation minute intervals, and the distribution is cut off at a lookahead of 20 simulation minutes. This cutoff results in a smaller set of 30,282 events from the total sample of 65,523 events. Within this smaller set, the mode is bin 0-0.125, which occurred 20.7% of the time (this value is truncated in Figure 4 because of the vertical scale); the next most frequently occurring lookahead value is bin 4.5-4.625, which occurred 1.44% of the time. A detailed analysis of the data shows that the true mode is a lookahead of 0.01 simulation minutes, which occurs 4,787 times, which is 15.8% of this smaller data set or 4.3% of the larger sample of 65,523 events. Ignoring the spike at the first bin, this distribution resembles a Poisson distribution.

DPAT is essentially a queueing network applied to aviation. Lookahead characteristics of queueing networks have been extensively studied. In [13], a generalized queueing network is studied wherein each server schedules the arrival of the customer at the next queue immediately upon entering service in the previous queue; the next queue then computes a service time for the new arrival. As with this general model, DPAT also knows the queue to which each aircraft will be routed upon completing service. However, two additional considerations cause it to behave differently than in Nicol's general case. First, it is possible for the receiving queue to *block* the arrival of a new customer; the conditions governing whether the customer is blocked depend upon the number of customers in the receiver's own queue just prior to the attempted handoff. Secondly, the service rates for any queue in DPAT, rather than being sampled from a constant distribution, are sampled from a distribution that varies nonlinearly as a function of queue length, and by simulation time. The variation by queue length models airport configurations when an arrival or departure "push" results from hub-and-spoke scheduling by the airlines. The variation by simulation time allows analysts to model weather events that change service times. These nonconstant distributions allow realism in modeling airport and airspace operations, both of which are sensitive to congestion and local weather conditions.

To exploit lookahead under these conditions, DPAT schedules the next queue arrival when an airplane enters a server, similar to Nicol's model cited above. Unlike this general model, if the next queue blocks the arrival, then a *near zero lookahead* (NZL) message is sent back to the previous server, at the time of the attempted handoff. An NZL message is one whose lookahead time is nonzero but less than 0.01 simulation time units. The receipt of this event causes the airplane to wait at the previous server for an additional amount of time, constituting a queueing delay. At some later time, when the next server has cleared a spot in its queue, a second NZL message is sent to the previous server that moves the airplane between the two queues. These NZL events occur infrequently, from about 3% of the total events for a typical scenario, up to 20% for a pathologically congested scenario. Such NZL events are an anathema to conservatively synchronized simulations, while the optimistic Time Warp engines handle them with little problem.

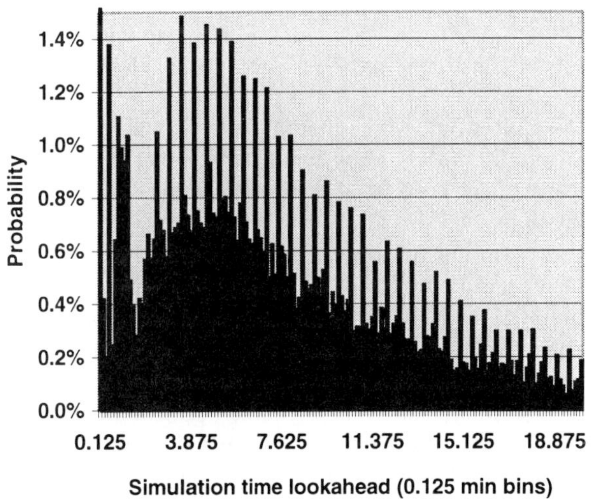

Figure 4. Lookahead probability below 20 minutes.

6.3. Risk Management

Risk management refers to how the optimistic simulation programmer deals with optimistically generated errors. Such errors are the result of out-of-order optimistic processing of events and do not exist in sequential simulations, optimistic but risk-free simulations, or conservatively synchronized parallel simulations. As such, they represent potentially catastrophic behavior unique to the fully optimistic technique that is difficult to predict but very easy to manage.

Risk management has been known since the invention of optimistic simulation by Jefferson and Sowizral in the early 1980's. Awareness of this issue has been recently elevated through a high-profile paper on its dangers [14]. The problem is that the programmer must ensure that events executing in a risky manner avoid errors that bring down the entire simulation. Such catastrophic errors can be caused by floating point over/underflow (such as dividing by zero or taking the logarithm of a negative number); by memory overwrites; by array bounds overflows; and so forth. It is possible to write a simulation that behaves correctly when executed sequentially, but exhibits one or more of these errors when executed optimistically.

In practice these errors are very easy to manage. First, the parallel simulator can itself trap most of the problems (such as floating point exceptions, divide by zeros, over/underflow, and so forth). When these exceptions occur, the state can be marked in error and, if the state is rolled back and executed properly, then the error is effectively "undone." This strategy was employed and implemented successfully in the Time Warp Operating System. Beyond that, the simulation programmer can prevent the conditions that lead to erroneous behavior by putting guards in the code—either explicit conditional tests or constructs like the C++ try/throw block.

A skeptic would argue that the latter is a heavy burden on the programmer. They would argue that the number of guards that need to be placed in the code, plus the possibility of missing one, is such a high cost that it renders optimistic simulation useless. They would further argue that the burden of guarding all function calls, library routines, and so forth makes such implementations impractical. It is certainly true that building an optimistically synchronized parallel simulation is harder than building its sequential counterpart. On the other hand, many of the risk-driven errors are indistinguishable from errors that occur in ordinary sequential simulations, albeit through other mechanisms. For example, how do sequential simulation programmers guard against bad input data that causes a negative logarithm to be computed? A human pushing a key at exactly the wrong time? A combination of events in a scenario that might lead to division by zeros? Buffer overflow from a large data set? The most common method is through validation checks on the input data, assertions throughout the code, and conditional tests that trap such errors, combined with very thorough and careful testing. These are the same techniques that an optimistic simulation programmer would use to resolve risk-generated errors.

In this respect the risky aspect of optimistic simulation actually is a *benefit* to the simulation developer. Each execution on multiple processors generally follows a different code branch—because the set of risky events run in successive replications is usually different. Thus the code is "automatically tested," although in a nontraditional sense. The sequential programmer would have to develop dozens of data sets to discover what an optimistic programmer would find out in only a few runs of the simulation. Such rigorous testing is not normally done in academic environments, and yet it is *necessary* and *forced* when running optimistically.

Our experience is that the only risk-generated errors encountered in a run of DPAT—running out of space in an array or dividing by zero when computing average values—are easily guarded in the code and thus easily avoided.

6.4. Verification

But how do we know if DPAT produces correct answers? How can the DPAT developers guarantee to the analyst that the result is not faulty due to some combination of risky events that were not rolled back properly? The chief verification tool is the observation that the set of committed states from a multiprocessor run of an optimistically synchronized simulation must exactly match the set of states produced by the same simulation when run sequentially. This is the essence of the term "logical correctness." Thus, if a sequential run of DPAT repeatedly produces *identical* output to the parallel run, regardless of the number of processors used, then the system is free of errors that might be caused by optimistic processing.

Verifying that a sequential run is identical to a parallel run is an *enormous* task, even for a small model such as DPAT. However, in ensuring such consistency, many model bugs (that are there anyway—even in a sequential version) are eliminated. In DPAT, inconsistent results are usually due to one of two problems: (1) inconsistent treatment of simultaneous events or (2) roundoff errors when converting from one precision to another. These bugs tend to be *nonrepeatable*—when the state rolls back and re-executes, a different value is generated the second time from the first (and therefore, a different value is generated vis-à-vis the sequential run). These problems are there even in a sequential model, except that there is no mechanism to discover their source, and therefore many extant sequential models latently exhibit these problems. In DPAT, it is true that every run using the same initial random number seeds—regardless of the number of processors that it uses—generates the same number of committed events, and the same exact answer, byte-for-byte.

Beyond verification, there is the additional task of validation—ensuring that the model is producing results that are credible with respect to the physical world it is simulating. Validation is also an enormous task, and has been done several times. Most noteworthy is the validation conducted by the Federal Aviation Administration, which revealed that four of five metrics tested produced results close to the real world [3]. The fifth metric, passenger arrival delay, is influenced by factors that are not modeled in detail by DPAT.

6.5. Execution Time Performance

The performance of DPAT on the standard scenario is shown in Figure 5. Both the run time and the number of rollbacks are included in the figure. The results were computed on a six processor machine. Results are shown up to eight processing elements (PEs) because the GTW system creates threads for each PE. Therefore it is possible to create more PEs than there are physical processors on the system. As can be seen in the Figure, when that occurs (at 7 and 8 PEs), the performance suffers. Not only does the run time begin to suffer, but the variance in the run time from successive executions begins to become large. The larger variance is due to the fact that the operating system is now scheduling more than one thread per processor, and the nonrepeatabilities in such scheduling between successive runs cause different execution times. In all cases, as noted above in the discussion on verification, the result produced to a DPAT analyst is identical. There is about a three fold reduction in run time up to three processors (linear speedup); beyond that, the run time levels off.

6.6. DPAT and the High Level Architecture

The United States Department of Defense has produced a specification for simulation interconnection commonly known as the High Level Architecture (HLA). As DPAT is capable of producing throughputs and delays quickly, federations containing a DPAT component have been proposed. One such federation is a combination of the Sector Design Analysis Tool (SDAT) with DPAT. SDAT allows aviation analysts to reconfigure both the shape and

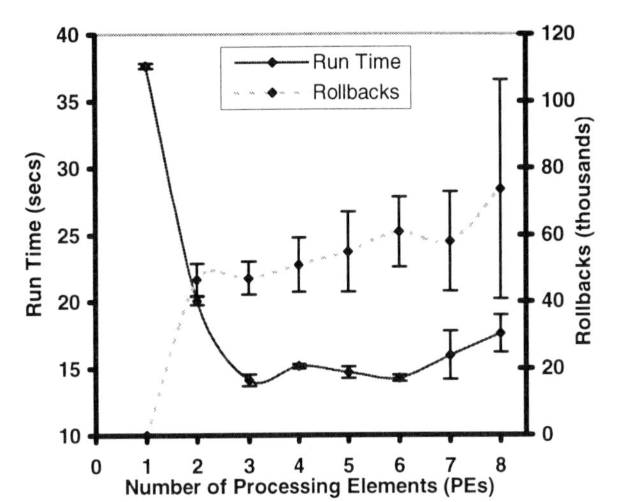

Figure 5. Performance of DPAT.

number of airspace sectors in a region. Airspace geometry affects the workload of controllers in a very profound way: the greater the number of crossing tracks, the more work controllers must do to separate planes. Accordingly, the fewer airplanes a controller will allow in their airspace.

To assess the delays caused by reconfiguring sectors, DPAT has been federated with SDAT. The resulting tool allows analysts to effectively redesign airspace while assessing the affect different traffic loads might have on the results. Federating the models required an initialization sequence, during which the models register their objects and interactions with the HLA's Run Time Infrastructure (RTI), followed by a processing sequence in which SDAT publishes its new routing structure and DPAT then publishes the predicted delays. The interaction diagram for the processing sequence is shown in Figure 6. It should be noted that there are no limit on the number of SDAT federates that can be incorporated in the system, due to the inherent flexibility of HLA.

7. Conclusions

We can make some general statements about why DPAT avoids many of the problems associated with optimistic computation. First, in the hundreds of scenarios run through DPAT, we have observed no "rollback explosion." A typical configuration of DPAT, containing over 1,200 LPs on six PEs, yields an average of 200 LPs per PE. The large number per PE means that each PE will generally see "average" behavior of the system, preventing any one from computing too far ahead or lagging too far behind. The result is a well-balanced, stable system. Secondly, the state size of about 2 kilobytes per LP,

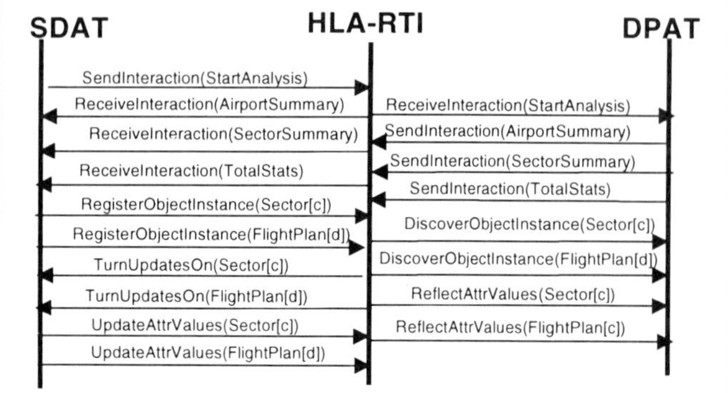

Figure 6. HLA interaction diagram (not in time order).

coupled with the use of incremental state saving, means that the overhead of saving state and rollback is minimized. Thirdly, the messages average a few hundred bytes each, and are passed through pointers in shared memory; this minimizes message communication costs. Fourthly, the software contains only a few places where risk-driven event processing might cause errors, and those places are easily identified and fixed with proper testing. Finally, optimistic computing is not as sensitive to zero-lookahead messages as conservative systems, so modeling blocking queues (as is done in DPAT) can be accomplished with no change to the conceptual design.

Our main conclusion is that it is possible—even desireable—to build a model containing optimistic synchronization that avoids the problems associated with such systems and exploits its main advantages: fast run times and the ability to interconnect with other models easier. The key factor to achieving these goals is to design a system with hundreds to thousands of LP's with small (1-3 kilobyte) states, incremental state saving, to run on only a few processors (so that there are hundreds of LPs per processor). Systems configured in this manner, like DPAT, can be effective vehicles for delivering usable simulations to the analysis community.

8. Acknowledgements and References

We would like to thank Frank Carr for his work on the DPAT-SDAT HLA connection, as well as Dr. Len Wojcik for his support over the years. We would like to thank Dr. Richard Fujimoto's research group at the Georgia Institute of Technology for providing the GTW system.

The contents of this paper reflect the views of the author. Neither the Federal Aviation Administration nor the Department of Transportation makes any warranty or guarantee, or primise, expressed or implied, concerning the content or accuracy of the views expressed herein.

[1] Carroll McCormick, "Jam Tomorrow," *Air Traffic Management*, Euromoney Publications:London, **8**(2), March-April 1999, pp. 42-43.

[2] L. A. Wojcik, et. al. "World Regional Air Traffic Modeling with DPAT," MTR 97W00000070, September 1997.

[3] Daniel Citrenbaum, Nastaran Coleman, Robert Kennington, Bryan Baszczewski, Anh Nguyen, "The Detailed Policy Assessment Tool (DPAT) Validation Report: A Comparison of DPAT Simulation Results to National Data," Federal Aviation Administration, October, 1999.

[4] Dr. George Donohue, "Testimony before US House of Representatives Committee on Science, Subcommittee on Space and Aeronautics: Hearing on the 2001 NASA Budget Request," 106th Congress, April 11, 1999.

[5] "Separation Reduction Impact Analysis: Initial Results," MP 99W0000019, January, 1999 (not for public release).

[6] Suzanne Bradley, et. Al. "Improving NAS Efficiency: Assessment Approach and Initial Analyses," MP 99W0000020, January, 1999 (not for public release).

[7] Jim Cieplak, John DiLeo, Jonathan Hammer, and Stephen Yeh, "Annual DPAT Analysis Capability," briefing, September 1998 (not for public release).

[8] Frederick Wieland, "Parallel Simulation for Aviation Applications," *Proceedings of the 1998 Winter Simulation Conference*, (IEEE) Washington, DC, December 1998.

[9] Frederick Wieland, "Limits to Growth: Results from the Detailed Policy Assessment Tool," in Proceedings of the Digital Avionics Systems Conference, Irvine, CA, IEEE:1997.

[10] "FAA Disputes Airlines' Claim of Outdated ATC System," *Aviation Daily*, McGraw-Hill Publishing Company, July 19, 2000.

[11] Frederick Wieland, "The Detailed Policy Assessment Tool User's Manual," MITRE Technical Report MTR99W00000012 (not for public release).

[12] R. M. Fujimoto, "Time Warp on a Shared Memory Multiprocessor," Transactions of the Society for Computer Simulation, **6**(3):211-239, July1989

[13] David M. Nicol, "The Cost of Conservative Synchronization in Parallel Discrete Event Simulation," *Journal of the Association of Computing Machinery,* **2**(2), April, 1993, pp. 304-333.

[14] David M. Nicol, "The Dark Side of Risk (What your mother never told you about Time Warp)," *Proceedings of the 11th Workshop on Parallel and Distributed Simulation*, June 10-13, 1997 IEEE Computer Society Press:1997.

Using Quad Trees for Parallelizing Conflict Detection in a Sequential Simulation

Dr. Frederick Wieland, David Carnes, Gregory Schultz
Center for Advanced Aviation Systems Development
The MITRE Corporation
1820 Dolley Madison Blvd.
McLean, VA 22102
{fwieland,dcarnes}@mitre.org

Abstract

This paper describes a parallel proximity detection algorithm and illustrates its application to the problem of conflict detection in an aviation simulation. The algorithm invokes a previously designed sequential function in parallel, using spatial information acquired during the traversal of a quad tree, to keep the separate invocations of the function as independent as possible. The method is generally applicable to any function (not just conflict detection) whose arguments are spatially organized. Empirical results show that a single-threaded version of the algorithm sped up the simulation by 57%, while a four-threaded parallel version extracted 30% of the remaining additional speedup. These results are even more noteworthy given that the architecture of the simulation remains intact; we only replace the invocation mechanism for one function.

1. Introduction

Proximity detection is a vexingly difficult problem on parallel computers, and yet its use is ubiquitous throughout the simulation world. Its difficulty is caused by the large amount of distributed position information that must be assimilated to determine proximity. Various algorithms for handling this have been proposed; one such algorithm is embodied as "interest management" within the United States Department of Defense (DoD) High Level Architecture (HLA). In its most general form, it can be used in military simulations for sensing assets of the opposing side, and in civilian simulations for avoiding collisions between moving objects. It is the latter application that we will use in this paper, and we will refer to "proximity detection" as the general algorithm for solving the more specific problem of "conflict detection" between moving objects.

The MITRE Corporation's Center for Advanced Aviation Systems Development (CAASD) is in the process of inserting parallel algorithms into a large existing sequential air traffic control simulation; the simulation contains nearly one million lines of code. One of its main bottleneck algorithms is conflict detection, which involves determining whether, and when, two aircraft are within a threshold radius. If an aircraft pair is found to be in conflict, then the model can invoke vectoring logic determined from a built-in knowledge base of applicable conflict resolution strategies. Conflict detection is a natural algorithm for parallelization, because in some scenarios it can consume up to 50% of the total run time.

One of the constraints in parallelizing the extant simulation is to minimize changes to its source code. As it is installed at a myriad of different sites, it is necessary to insert parallelism with very little change in the architecture. Because of this constraint, most of the extant proximity detection algorithms, which require extensive changes to the architecture of the system, cannot be used. Instead, we have devised a method to parallelize the logic in a manner that requires virtually no change to the underlying software architecture; in fact, this technique is generally applicable to *any* sequential function that contains a geometric component.

Our method is grid-based, employing a quad tree data structure that is normally found in the context of computer graphics [10] and in conflict-free route planning in the field of robotics [4]. The main concern of any proximity detection algorithm is efficient filtering of pairs of moving objects. The detailed geometric calculations determining proximity should only be computed on pairs most likely to be in conflict. In the existing simulation, these filters are applied using bounding boxes around the aircraft's intended flight plan. We have replaced that logic with a quad tree algorithm that geographically filters the flight pairs in a manner unrelated to

0-7695-1104-X/01 $10.00 © 2001 IEEE

the aviation or flight dynamics in the simulation. As we will discuss later, the algorithm can be applied to the movement of objects, updating graphics displays, and other independent functions.

2. Prior Work

Parallel proximity detection has been extensively studied and published in the open literature. The available algorithms fall into two different camps: the so-called *grid based* algorithms, which rely on dividing a simulated space into cells that "tile" the space, and the *region based* algorithms, which rely on defining a region in which an object declares interest. There are advantages and disadvantages to each one. The grid based algorithms require sophisticated protocols for keeping track of objects that are near the grid boundaries, and to hand off the objects from one grid to the next as they move. The region based algorithms require common definitions of regions across objects sharing the same region, and require sophisticated geometric calculations in the simulation engine that, if done in full generality, can add much overhead to the system. Region-based interest management is part of the DoD's HLA. Recently, hybrid algorithms that dynamically size the grids or merge the region and grid based approaches have emerged [3].

Other variations are possible. In [14], a hybrid algorithm is used to combine the best approaches of both the grid and region based filtering in the context of the HLA. In [12], a grid-based algorithm is described where the grid boundaries are extended and overlapped to help minimize problems along grid boundaries. In a later version of the algorithm [13], the spherical virtual space is tiled with grid cells of approximately equal size. Within each cell, a 3-way tree is produced that acts as an index into object positions in 3-space (x, y, z). The three-way tree is a fast indexing mechanism for position.

The current work differs from these previous studies in a number of significant respects. First, this algorithm uses a quad tree as the basis for spatially decomposing the virtual world into unequal-sized grid cells. The basis for sizing is to maintain (approximately) a constant number of objects per cell. Furthermore, the sizes of the cells dynamically change with time as the simulation evolves and as the spatial density of objects changes. Thirdly, load balancing is provided by queueing the potential conflicts for resolution by a separate set of "worker" threads. This technique, discussed later, prevents cells having excessive conflicts from becoming a serial bottleneck in the computation.

Quad trees themselves are not new data structures. Prior work that used quad trees for parallelization mainly focused on scheduling ready processes to available hardware resources efficiently; a good example can be found in [11]. They have also been used as a basis for communication topologies in parallel processors, such as quad-tree-based hypercube communication interconnects [8]. Collision detection of moving objects using quad trees, and their three-dimensional extension to oct trees, has also been studied [5, 15]. The problem of using trees in their generality for geometric proximity problems can be found in [2]. The general problem of conflict detection and resolution in the context of aviation simulation can be found in [16].

Automatic parallelization of sequential simulations, which this research is attempting, also has a long history of study. Some have focused on changing the underlying simulation engine to add constructs that allow modelers to exploit parallelism; a good example of this can be found in [6, 7]. Others have focused on the tasks required to explicitly parallelize a sequential simulation model [1]. In the present study we are inserting parallelism into an existing sequential simulation, with the goal of leaving the existing simulation model and architecture undisturbed. We can neither change the aviation logic, nor can we change the underlying simulation engine. These constraints severely limit our options, and require a creative solution. The goal is similar to others exploiting parallel simulation technology: speeding up the processing of the simulation.

3. Conflict Detection in the Simulation

At regular, user-specified intervals, the simulation passes all airborne aircraft through various filters to create a list of candidate aircraft pairs to be checked for possible conflict. During each interval, the simulation updates the current *flight envelope* for each aircraft, which is a bounding box containing all waypoints in its flight plan, including requirements for lateral separation, from its present position to its destination. Aircraft pairs whose flight envelopes overlap are nominated as candidates for conflict detection, as they may approach each other closely enough to be in conflict. Likewise, existing aircraft pairs whose flight envelopes no longer intersect are removed from the candidate pairs list, as they cannot approach each other closely enough to ever be in conflict. Geometric calculations performed to determine bounding box intersections occupy a substantial part of the simulation run time. Several attempts were made to reduce this time, including an attempt in which the bounding boxes were precomputed at each leg of the flight plan and compared to current aircraft positions to determine potential conflicts, before the quad tree scheme presented here was developed. These earlier optimizations had only a minor effect on reducing run time.

The quad tree software library was designed with two objectives in mind. The first objective is to provide an efficient geographical filter to minimize the number of candidate aircraft pairs that require further checking. The second is to provide a mechanism to perform conflict detection on multiple aircraft pairs in parallel. As finally designed, the quad tree library is useful for performing in parallel *any* function in the simulation that relies on a geometric component, and that requires either a single aircraft or a pair of aircraft. Any function so invoked must be thread-safe, which is an issue as any global data structures that are updated during this process must be identified, and a mechanism for mutual exclusion must be established in order to provide repeatable and accurate parallel operation.

The quad tree is a hierarchical structure that provides spatial decomposition of data such as points, lines, or polygons. In this case, aircraft positions are treated as points in three-dimensional space. A conflict occurs when the Euclidean distance between any two points (i.e. aircraft) in the quad tree falls below the specified lateral and vertical separation thresholds. These thresholds are set by the user, and can vary by the air traffic control sector in which the aircraft is currently flying. Two further possibilities exist: if only conflict detection is desired by the user, then the current position of the aircraft is used to determine where the aircraft will be inserted into the quad tree. The simulation also offers the user a chance to perform automatic conflict resolution. In that case, each aircraft has a list of future positions for that aircraft at discrete simulation time intervals, up to a user-specified maximum. The position at that maximum time is used as the basis for determining the position of an aircraft in the quad tree in order to provide the simulation with a look-ahead capability. This provides the simulation with the opportunity to detect conflicts early enough to invoke automatic conflict avoidance.

Figure 1 illustrates the geometry of a quad tree node. The inner thick rectangle represents the space represented by a node in the quad tree, call it the *parent node.* That node has four children, labeled by their compass points (NE for northeast, and so forth). The outer dotted rectangle encompasses the parent node and the space that is within the *maximum conflict distance* of the edge of the parent node. The maximum conflict distance is the largest distance in the entire simulation (since it can vary by sector) that two planes can be from one another and yet still be in conflict with one another. For aviation simulations, that distance is typically 5 nautical miles. Any node can be decomposed into four child nodes by dividing the inner rectangle into quadrants along the X- and Y- centerlines, represented by the dashed lines. Each child would also have its own exterior area, which would be a subset of the exterior area of the parent, but still containing all the area within the minimum conflict distance for the new child node.

Each node has two lists: an interior list and an exterior list. Any object that falls within a node's inner rectangle is stored in the interior list of that node. Objects that are within the outer bounding box, but not within the inner one, are placed in the exterior list of that node. This insures that conflict detection is performed only on objects near enough to the space contained by a node boundaries to require it, while filtering out objects that are too far away to be in conflict. Each node is responsible for conflict detection between all objects in its interior list, and between the objects in its interior list with those in its exterior list.

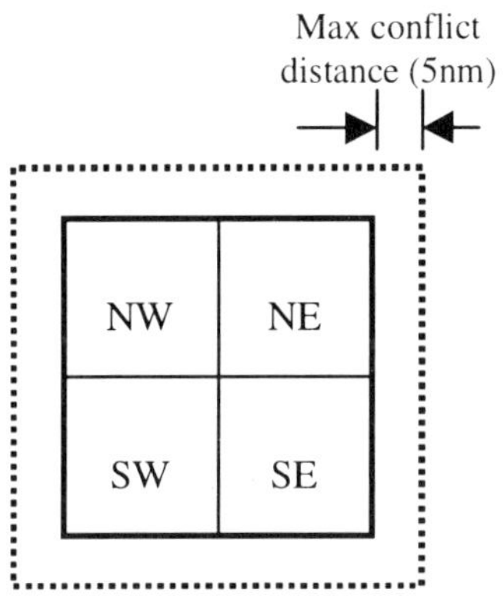

Figure 1. Geometry of the quad tree data structure.

When a conflict detection cycle is performed, a new quad tree is created, which consists of a single root node with no children. The root node encompasses the entire virtual space defined for the scenario. Practically, this means that no aircraft should ever be added into the exterior list of the root node. If this occurs, then the size of the root node is not sufficiently large, and should be extended to include the offending object. When an object is inserted into the quad tree, it is passed to the insert method of the root node. The root node first checks to see if whether the object falls within its extended boundary, and if so, it will pass the object on to its four children. If no children exist, and the boundary conditions for the quad tree have not been met, then the children of the node will be created. The root node will implicitly test for boundary conditions by then checking to see if any children exist. If no children exist, then the boundary conditions for the quad tree have been met and the node is also a leaf node of the tree. If the node is a leaf node, and the object falls within its inner rectangle, then the object is added to its interior list. If the object is not contained in the inner rectangle, then it is added to the exterior list. If a child exists, this procedure is recursively executed until a boundary condition of the quad tree is encountered, and a leaf node created.

Once all airborne aircraft have been inserted into the quad tree, the tree is traversed in order to generate candidate aircraft pairs for conflict detection. The type of tree traversal is not important as long as it only visits each node to process its objects once. When the traversal occurs, the current node will generate a candidate aircraft pair by comparing each aircraft in its interior list with all the aircraft subsequent to it on that list. This prevents each aircraft pair from being nominated twice for checking, as an aircraft can only exist in one interior list in the entire tree. The same aircraft can appear in multiple exterior lists, although it will only occur once in the exterior list for a given node. Then each aircraft on the interior list is paired with the aircraft contained in the exterior list, and nominated for conflict detection. In order to prevent duplicate checking in this case, each aircraft should be given a unique number upon insertion into the quad tree. Only if the first aircraft's number is greater than the second one's should the pair be nominated for conflict detection. If they are not, then when the node containing the second aircraft on its the interior list is encountered, the pair will be nominated. Each unique pair of aircraft (objects) identified will be used as parameters to a callback function, such as the one providing conflict detection, supplied as an argument to the quad tree traversal function. If the callback function only requires a single aircraft, then only the interior list of the node only shall be iterated, and each aircraft encountered will be nominated to the callback function.

As potential conflict pairs are nominated as described above, they are placed in a statically created and sized circular queue. A specified number of worker threads are statically created during simulation initialization, and then block until work (a callback function and the appropriate aircraft as parameters) arrives in the queue. When work is inserted into the queue, the threads are signaled that the queue is no longer empty, and the threads wake and take the next aircraft pair off the queue and invoke the associated callback function. The main thread of execution continues in parallel with the worker threads until all work units (aircraft pair) have been generated from the quad tree traverse, upon which the main thread of execution blocks until all work has been processed. Should the circular work queue fill up, then the main thread will block until the worker threads have opened up some space in the circular queue by processing some work units. The use of a circular queue as an intermediary between the traversal of the quad tree and the invocation of the callback allows a form of load balancing between the threads by preventing worker threads from becoming idle while work still is in the queue. A circular queue also eliminates the overhead for memory allocation and deallocation that would otherwise occur if a standard queue were used.

4. The Algorithm in Pictures

Below is a series of commented diagrams that explain how the algorithm works.

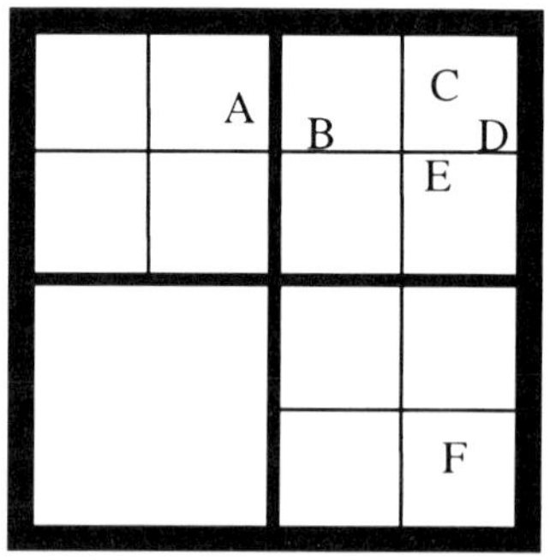

Figure 2. Initial placement of aircraft ('A' through 'F') for this example, and the quad tree overlay.

Figure 2 shows the position of aircraft in the scenario space at a particular point in the simulation. In this simple example, letters "A" through "F" represent distinct aircraft objects. The hierarchical inner bounding rectangles of the quad tree structure is overlaid on their position.

Figure 3 shows the hierarchical representation of the aircraft positions in a quad tree. The leaf nodes collectively contain all the aircraft. Each leaf node contains two lists, the one on the left representing the interior list, and the one on the right the exterior list. NW, NE, SE, and SW represent the four compass point combinations.

The sequence of candidate conflict pairs generated from the quad tree traversal is (C,D), (C,E), (D,E), (B,C), (B,D), (B,E), and (A,B). The quad tree data structure is traversed depth-first. Since only the conflict detection portion of the simulation was converted for use with the quad tree, all work generated for the worker threads was in the form of aircraft pairs used as arguments to the conflict detection callback. As the main thread traverses the tree and identifies unique object pairs, they are queued for processing by the worker threads.

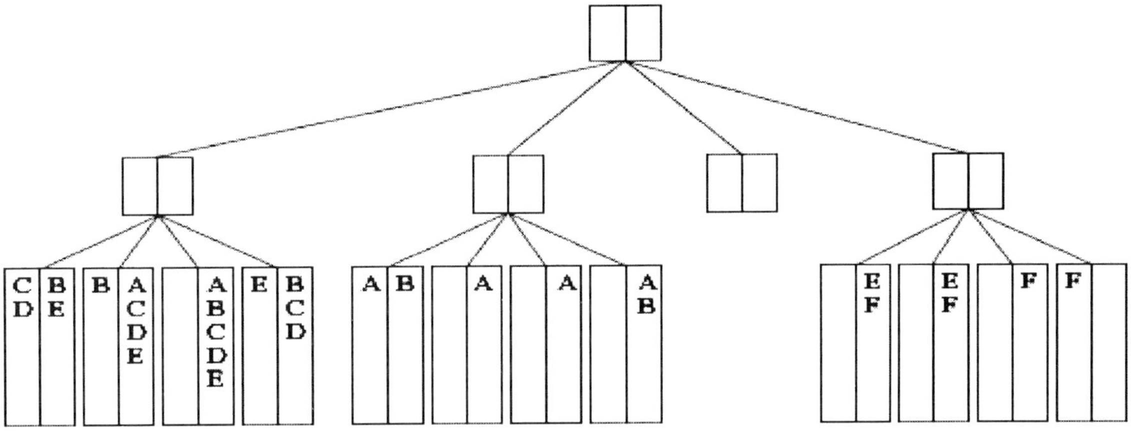

Figure 3. Hierarchical representation of the quad tree for the aircraft positions in Figure 2. The symbols on the left represent aircraft within the boundary of the cell; those on the right represent aircraft outside the cell, but within the conflict detection radius.

The worker threads take the candidate conflict pairs generated by the quad tree traversal, and call (in parallel) the existing sequential function (called "conflict check" in the simulation). In this example if there are four worker threads, then the seven candidate conflict pairs will be evaluated in two units of time (assuming that each call to conflict check takes one unit of time). In the single threaded version, it would take seven units of time to evaluate the pairs. In the unfiltered, unoptimized algorithm that compares every aircraft with every other aircraft, it would take fifteen units of time to evaluate all pairs. However the execution time of conflict check is dependent upon the geometry of the conflict, and thus is different for each candidate conflict pair.

The quad tree boundary conditions can be tuned so that the width (measured as latitude) of the resulting leaf nodes and boundary area is no less than the maximum conflict distance; this configuration is used herein. If the dimension of the root node is the maximum conflict distance, then any aircraft object in a leaf node is within the maximum conflict distance, and therefore is probably in conflict with any others in the same node. Other factors may affect whether a candidate aircraft pair should be forwarded to the conflict detection callback, such as whether the user has enabled conflict detection for a particular flight or the sector in which the aircraft is flying, or whether it has been enabled for uncontrolled airspace.

A reasonable question to ask is the role of the quad tree in this algorithm. If the thrust of the algorithm is to produce a queue of work for the worker threads, then why is a quad tree necessary? Could a flat tiling of the scenario space by equal sized cells work just as well? The quad tree is important for three reasons. First, consider the case where there are N moving objects. The quad tree provides filtering so that the $(N^2 - N)/2$ comparisons that would normally occur are reduced to just those comparisons between objects that are physically close to each other. But even regular grid cells accomplish that reduction. Secondly, and more importantly, the tree is pruned so those cells without objects do not have child nodes that must be processed. When the tree is traversed, only those node containing objects in their interior lists are considered. Finally, and most importantly, the tree structure allows conflicts between objects on opposite sides of the cell boundary to be handled in a consistent and elegant manner. The recursive nature of an insert and the geographical filtering provided by the decomposition of the space naturally directs the aircraft into geographically local groups. These latter two strengths are weaknesses of regular grid cell approaches. Overcoming these weaknesses in the flat grid cell approach causes the algorithm to become more complex and less elegant.

5. Quad Tree Performance

This algorithm was tested on a four processor, 550 MHz Pentium III Xeon SMP with 2 gigabytes of RAM, using the Sun Solaris operating system. The number of worker threads was varied from one to five; at five, there are more parallel threads than there are processors on the machine. Two different scenarios are used, each representing air traffic in the northeast United States. The first scenario (called "one-fifth") represents one-fifth of a day and contains approximately 7,000 flights. The second scenario (called "whole day") represents a whole day and contains approximately 34,000 flights. Both scenarios are an airspace-intensive model of six of the twenty enroute air traffic control centers in the United States, and thus represent good stress tests for conflict detection.

Figures 5 and 6 show the performance of the algorithm for the one-fifth and the whole day scenario. In both figures, the upper dashed line represents the performance of the original conflict detection (CD) algorithm (with the envelope calculation filters), while the lower dashed line represents the original algorithm with conflict detection disabled. The difference between the two times is the amount of real time consumed by the original conflict detection algorithm. Because the original algorithm is sequential, this time does not vary with the number of threads.

The solid line in both figures represents the time taken by the quad tree algorithm, as the number of threads is varied. In both cases the time for the single-threaded quad tree case is substantially faster than the original algorithm. For the one-fifth scenario, the single threaded quad tree algorithm reduces the run time to 46% of the original run time (a speedup factor of 2.18). For the whole day scenario, the sequential quad tree algorithm reduces the run time to 64% of the original (a speedup factor of 1.56). The run time reduction is achieved because the quad tree filtering is more efficient than the envelope filtering, generating a candidate conflict pair list containing fewer entries than the original algorithm. The original algorithm generated many redundant conflict pairs as well as pairs that, when evaluated by conflict check, were not in conflict at all.

The parallel results seem less impressive in figures 5 and 6, in part because of the vertical scale. To compute the maximum possible parallel speedup available, we take the difference between the single-threaded quad tree algorithm (solid line at one thread) and the original simulation without conflict detection (lower dotted line). Of course, no algorithm would ever achieve the maximum speedup, because any conflict detection algorithm would consume a nonzero execution time and therefore run slower than the lower dotted line in the figures.

If we compute the run time reduced through parallelization as a percentage of this theoretical maximum, we get the results in Figure 7. The results show that we are obtaining up to 30% of the maximum possible speedup available. It is encouraging that the larger scenario has greater parallel efficiency. Apparently this algorithm scales well and has good performance characteristics as the problem size increases.

These results are encouraging for a number of reasons. First, as we have merely provided a mechanism to invoke

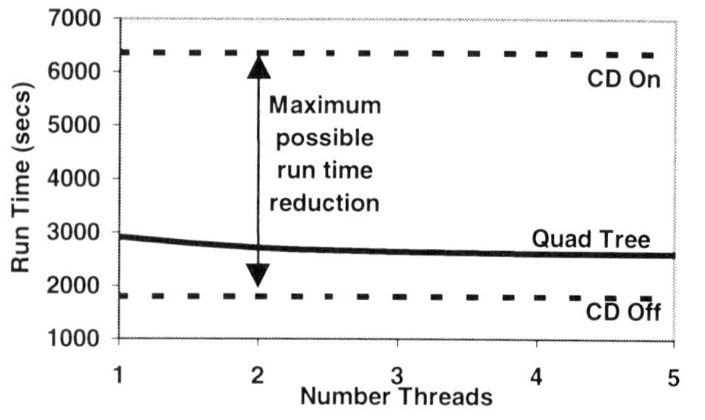

Figure 5. Performance for the one-fifth scenario.

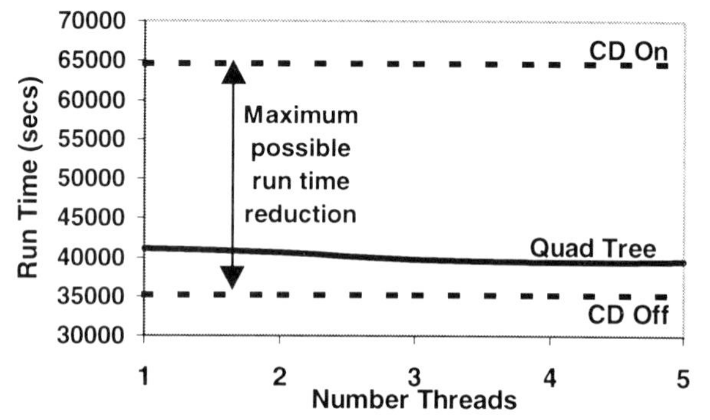

Figure 6. Performance for the whole day scenario.

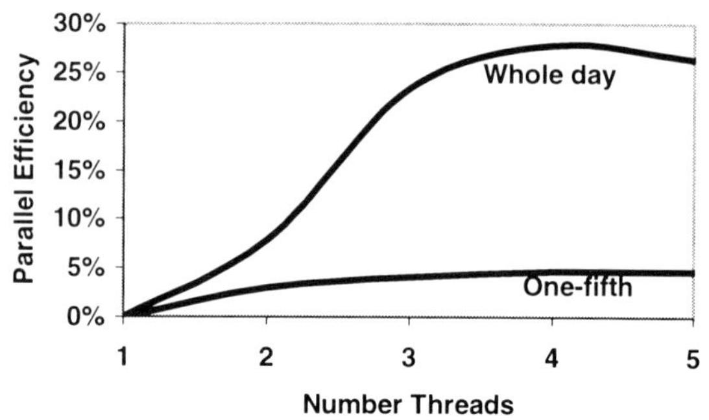

Figure 7. Parallel efficiency for both scenarios.

an existing sequential function in parallel, the fact that we are getting any speedup at all is very encouraging. Secondly, the method of parallel invocation is independent of the air traffic control logic in the simulation, so this mechanism can be used in any simulation in any domain where geographic partitioning can be used to exploit parallelism. Thirdly, we are still exploring mechanisms by which the parallel efficiency can be increased further.

Finally, if you look at the total run time reduction—the original sequential simulation compared to our four-threaded quad tree version—we have obtained an overall speedup factor of 2.4 for the one-fifth scenario and 1.6 for the whole-day scenario. Comparing our total run time reduction to the maximum we could have achieved, the one-fifth scenario achieved 75% of the maximum while the whole day scenario achieved nearly 80% of the maximum.

6. Conclusions

We have shown that it is possible to parallelize an otherwise sequential program by using threaded invocation mechanisms to call a sequential function in parallel. The key is to call the sequential function in separate threads, providing it work that is independent of the work being done by other threads. The geographical nature of many simulations allows a spatially explicit geometric function (such as proximity detection, movement of objects, or drawing them on an output device) to be called in parallel for objects in different regions of the space. The mechanism outlined herein enables such spatial parallelization with elegant handling of objects on opposite sides of cell boundaries, as well as automatic adaptation to scenarios where the objects are spatially clustered.

7. Acknowledgements and References

The assistance of Dr. Paul Wang, who helped with some of the performance measurements, is greatly appreciated. We would like to thank The MITRE Corporation Center for Advanced Aviation Systems Development for sponsoring this work. The contents of this material reflect the views of the authors. Neither the Federal Aviation Administration nor the Department of Defense makes any warranty or guarantee, or promise, expressed or implied, concerning the content or accuracy of the views expressed herein.

[1] Lokesh Bajaj, Rajive Bagrodia, Richard Meyer, "Case Study: Parallelizing a Sequential Simulation Model *13th Workshop on Parallel and Distributed Simulation*, pp. 29-36, IEEE Computer Society Press, 1999.

[2] Julien Basch, Leonidas J. Guibas, and Li Zhang, "Proximity Problems on Moving Points," *Computational Geometry 97*, Nice France, pp. 344-351, ACM:1997.

[3] Azzedine Boukerche, Amber Roy, Neville Thomas, "Dynamic Grid-Based Multicast Group Assignment in Data Distribution Management," *4th International Workshop in Distributed Simulation and Real-Time Applications*, pp. 47-54, IEEE Computer Society Press, 2000.

[4] Koichi Hamada and Yoichi Hori, "Octree-Based Approach to Real-time Collision-free Path Planning for Robot Manipulator," *4th International Workshop on Advanced Motion Control* (AMC '96), IEEE:March 1996.

[5] Yoshifumi Kitamura, Haruo Takemura, Narendra Ahuja, and Fumio Kishino, "Efficient Collision Detection Among Objects in Arbitrary Motion Using Multiple Shape Representations," *12th IAPR International Conference on Pattern Recognition*, IEEE:October 1994.

[6] D. M. Nicol and P. Heidelberger, "On Extending Parallelism to Serial Simulators," *9th Workshop on Parallel and Distributed Simulation*, pp. 60-67, IEEE Computer Society Press, 1995.

[7] "David Nicol, Philip Heidelberger, "On Extending More Parallelism to Serial Simulators," *10th Workshop on Parallel and Distributed Simulation*, pp. 202-205, IEEE Computer Society Press, 1996.

[8] Mahmoud Omri, "Routing in Quad Tree-Hypercube Networks," *2000 ACM Symposium on Applied Computing*, volume 2, pp. 677-681, Association for Computing Machinery, 2000.

[9] Hanan Samet, *The Design and Analysis of Spatial Data Structures*, Addison-Wesley:1990.

[10] Hanan Samet, *Applications of Spatial Data Structures*, Addison-Wesley:1990.

[11] Jeerapron Srisawat and Nikitas A. Alexandridis, "A New 'Quad-Tree Based' Sub-System Allocation Technique for Mesh-connected Parallel Machines," *2nd ACM International Conference on Multimedia*, pp. 279-286, Association of Computing Machinery, 2000.

[12] Jeff S. Steinman, Frederick Wieland, "Parallel Proximity Detection and the Distribution List Algorithm," *1994 Workshop on Parallel and Distributed Simulation*, pp. 3-11, IEEE Computer Society Press, 1994.

[13] Jeff Steinman, Tuan Tran, Jacob Burckhardt, Jim Brutocao, "Logically Correct Data Distribution Management in SPEEDES", *1999 Fall SIW Conference*, Paper 99F-SIW-067, September, 1999.

[14] Gary Tan, YuSong Zhang and Rassul Ayani, "A Hybrid Approach to Data Distribution Management," *4th IEEE International Workshop in Distributed Simulation and Real-Time Applications*, pp. 55-61, IEEE Computer Society Press, 2000.

[15] Costas Tzafestas and Philippe Coiffet, "Real-Time Collision Detection using Spherical Octrees: Virtual Reality Application," *5th IEEE International Workshop on Robot and Human Communication*, IEEE:November 1996.

[16] Alex Vink and Seppo Kauppinen, "Medium Term Conflict Detection in EATCHIP Phase III," *16th AIAA/IEEE Digital Avionics Systems Conference*, IEEE:October 1997.

Session 6

Panel: Large Scale Network Modeling

Session 7

Optimistic Simulation II

Virtual Time Synchronization over Unreliable Network Transport

Kalyan Perumalla
kalyan@cc.gatech.edu
Richard Fujimoto
fujimoto@cc.gatech.edu
College of Computing, Georgia Tech
Atlanta, GA 30332-0280

Abstract

In parallel and distributed simulations, it is sometimes desirable that the application's time-stamped events and/or the simulator's time-management control messages be exchanged over a combination of reliable and unreliable network channels. A challenge in developing infrastructure for such simulations is to correctly compute simulation time advances despite the loss of some simulation events and/or control messages. Presented here are algorithms for synchronization in distributed simulations performed directly over best-effort network transport. The algorithms are presented in a sequence of progressive refinement, starting with all reliable transport and finishing with combinations of reliable and unreliable transports for both time-stamped events and time management messages. Performance results from a preliminary implementation of these algorithms are also presented. To our knowledge, this is the first work to solve asynchronous time synchronization performed directly over unreliable network transport.

1. Introduction

Traditional parallel discrete event simulation research has so far focused mainly on reliable communication platforms. However, in certain application domains, such as Distributed Interactive Simulation (DIS) and High Level Architecture (HLA), it is desirable to execute the simulations directly over unreliable (best-effort) network transport such as User Datagram Protocol (UDP). This is motivated in part by potential performance gains due to the lower overhead afforded by unreliable transport compared to reliable delivery. However, current state-of-the-art parallel/distributed simulation techniques restrict the applications either to using completely reliable communication for all time-stamped ordered event processing, or alternatively to receive-ordered processing of all events irrespective of their timestamps. This is clearly restrictive and points to a need for extending parallel/distributed simulation technology to accommodate unreliable transport in time synchronization and timestamp-ordered event exchange.

Several important issues arise in the context of building simulation infrastructure over unreliable transport: Does time management make sense if time-stamped events sent over unreliable transport can be lost? How should time management be performed in such applications? Are traditional synchronization algorithms that are based on reliable transport less or more efficient than alternative algorithms (such as those presented here) implemented directly over unreliable network transport? Here, we attempt to answer some of these questions by first presenting a parallel/distributed simulation application model that accommodates a combination of reliable and unreliable time-synchronized events, followed by a description of novel algorithms that solve the associated time synchronization problem.

1.1. *Motivation*

In domains such as DIS and HLA, for performance reasons, unreliable message transport services such as UDP are typically employed for exchanging events. In DIS, entity state update events are sent periodically, while intermediate notification events are also sent when the state differs significantly from the dead-reckoned state. Since regular state updates are sent periodically, the applications are designed to tolerate some losses in the intermediate state notifications between the periodic state updates. However, unlike traditional parallel and distributed discrete event simulation (PDES) applications, time synchronization is not performed, partly because of lack of efficient algorithms in the context of unreliable network transport, thus giving rise to potential for anomalies in the simulation. Traditional time synchronization algorithms are not directly useful here, since most of them assume reliable delivery. The algorithms presented here are designed to solve this problem, so that time management can be enabled in such applications.

1.2. *Related Work*

Little literature exists on the use of unreliable network transport for simulation time management. Several global virtual time (GVT) algorithms have been formulated, but almost all of them assume reliable message delivery. In fact, most parallel simulation synchronization algorithms have been presented in the context of reliable delivery.

In [2], fault tolerance at the level of node-failures is addressed in the context of optimistic parallel simulation, whereas we address individual message losses, and are not restricted to optimistic simulators. Specialized hardware-supported techniques for fast reductions are presented in [10], whereas we address unreliability of message delivery in the common communication platforms, such as multi-hop wide-area networks. The work that is closest in relation to our work is the time synchronization algorithms presented in [8] in the context of unreliable delivery in broadcast-based networks. Also, our algorithms have some superficial resemblance to coloring-based GVT algorithms such as Mattern's algorithm[6], although they differ significantly in that unreliable communication is supported in our algorithm.

The solution to the noncommittal barrier synchronization problem presented in [7] in the context of reliable network transport appears to be closely related to the virtual time synchronization problem. We believe that variations of the algorithms presented here can be used to solve the same noncommittal barrier synchronization problem, but in the presence of message losses.

On a more theoretical note, distributed consensus problems such as leader election and termination detection have been previously studied in the context of faulty networks[1]. However, most of that work is theoretical in nature, dealing with less benign node and link failures, and not directly applicable to efficient distributed simulation execution over best-effort networks.

The rest of the paper is organized as follows. A generalized model is described for simulations that exchange time-stamped events over unreliable network transport. This is followed by a description of implementation challenges for providing safe simulation time advances during the course of simulation execution, along with associated definitions. We then present the algorithms and describe their operation, followed by a report on a preliminary performance study. We conclude with a summary of results and description of related open issues.

2. Background

2.1. *Simulation Model*

Here we consider a generalized model of distributed simulations in which the application designates certain events as "reliable" events, and others as "unreliable" events. For our purposes, a message is defined as reliable if it is guaranteed to arrive at its destination within a certain time limit. Both reliable and unreliable events are time-stamped. The difference between the two types is in their (1) potential to be lost (2) potential to violate global simulation time order. Reliable events are never lost, and always delivered to the application in a timely manner in relation to global simulation time. Unreliable events, on the other hand, can be lost, and can arrive sufficiently late to miss their timestamp ordered processing opportunity.

For correctness, the application requires *all* reliable events to be processed in global simulation time order. However, the application is designed to tolerate the loss (non-delivery) of a certain number of unreliable events per unit execution time and still retain simulation model accuracy. Unreliable events could potentially be received with their timestamps being less than the (currently committed) simulation time of the processor.

2.2. *Simulator Implementation Challenges*

The use of unreliable transport in parallel/distributed simulation raises two challenges that are different from traditional PDES: (1) lost time management messages (2) lost time-stamped events.

Time Management (TM) messages: Most parallel and distributed simulators have been implemented on top of reliable network delivery. Such implementations typically fail if the assumption of reliable delivery is violated at any time during the simulation execution. Most existing time synchronization algorithms have this property of failure, and hence cannot be used unmodified over unreliable network transport. Either existing algorithms need to be modified, or new algorithms must be devised to deal with losses in TM messages.

Time-stamped Events: A fundamental problem with unreliable time-stamped events is that it is hard to distinguish between transient events and lost events. The challenge is to resolve this conflict by accounting for as many events as possible within a specified amount of time, and presume the rest of the events are lost. If some of those events indeed arrive late without getting lost, then they could still be used in the application without violating global simulation time order if their timestamps happen to be greater than current simulation time at the received processor. On the other hand, if the timestamps are less than current simulation time, then those events can be passed to the application to be dealt with accordingly. Since applications that use unreliable events typically possess functionality to deal with late events, the late delivery should not be a problem.

In summary, the main trade-off in dealing with unreliable events is to wait sufficiently long for unreliable events to arrive, but not too long to hold up the simulation time advances in case the events never arrive.

2.3. *Lower Bound on Timestamp (LBTS)*

A value called lower bound on timestamp (LBTS) is a useful quantity that can be defined in any parallel/distributed simulation system. At any given moment during simulation execution, the LBTS value at a processor is defined as the timestamp of the earliest event that can be received by that processor in the future from other processors. The LBTS value is useful in conservative parallel simulation to determine which events are safe to execute. In optimistic parallel simulation it is useful in determining when it is safe to reclaim optimistic memory and to commit other irrevocable actions. The faster the LBTS is updated as the simulation progresses, the better is the performance of the simulation. Moreover, it is desirable that the process of computing LBTS value is asynchronous in nature, so that the simulation can continue without stopping while LBTS is being computed in background.

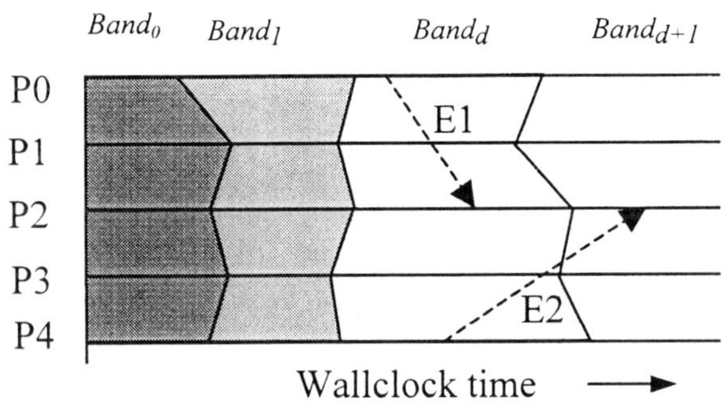

Figure 1: Illustration of wallclock time divided into bands. Event E1 is entirely contained in band d, while E2 crosses band *d* into *d+1*.

In our approach for asynchronous LBTS computation, the wallclock time at each processor is divided into contiguous bands as shown in Figure 1. The bands need not be equi-spaced, but could in fact have a staggered pattern as Figure 1 illustrates. Some events may be in transit across bands, while other events originate and terminate entirely within the same band.

In fact, the end of band $d+1$ is conveniently defined for our purposes by the latest wallclock time at which all events sent from band d are received by their destination processors. In other words, all events sent from band d are fully contained within bands d and $d+1$. All four algorithms presented here preserve this invariance.

2.4. *Definitions*

Every event E is tagged with the ID of the band d during which the event was sent. Thus each event is denoted by $E_d(t)$, or simply by E_d, where d is its sending band and t is its simulation receive time. Further, the transport type, if relevant, is shown as superscript. Thus, E^r denotes an event sent over reliable transport, and E^u denotes one sent over unreliable transport.

Let $\delta_i[d]$ denote the number of events E_d sent minus the number of events E_d received by processor i. Let $\Delta=\sum\delta_i[d]$. Let $\tau_i[d] = min(t)$ of all unprocessed events $E_{d'}(t)$ (uncommitted events, in the case of optimistic simulation) received by processor i, for all $d'<=d$.

Let $LBTS_d$ denote the smallest timestamp of all events $E_{d'}$ that originate in bands $d'<=d$ and received in future bands $d''>d$. In other words, it is the smallest timestamp of any event that is sent from any band $d'<=d$ and received in any band $d''>d$.

Note that $LBTS_d$ can be safely used as $LBTS$ in all bands $d'>d$. Also $LBTS_d<=LBTS_{d-1}$ for all d. In the algorithms presented later, the computation for $LBTS_d$ is performed during the band $d+1$.

Clearly, $LBTS_d = min(\ \tau_i[d]\ )$ over all i, if $\Delta=\sum\delta_i[d]$ equals zero. In other words, if every event originating or contained in band $d' <= d$ has been received at its destination processor, then no event received in future band $d'' > d$ can have timestamp less than $min\ \tau_i[d]$. But how do the processors know when Δ becomes equal to zero? In other words, how can the processors detect that all $E_{d' \le d}$ have reached their destinations?

2.5. *LBTS Computation*

One approach to detect exhaustion of all transient events belonging to band d is to iteratively perform a distributed reduction of all the $\delta_i[d]$ values. Once the sum (Δ) of all the values reduces to zero, the minimum of their corresponding $\tau_i[d]$ directly gives $LBTS_d$! This observation is key to the algorithms presented here. The algorithms are based on the fact that each LBTS computation can be performed as an iterated sequence of distributed reductions. The last reduction in each sequence is one that observes $\Delta=0$. The reductions in this sequence are numbered starting with zero, and every control message (not simulation event) used for reduction belonging to band d and reduction r is identified by its band number and iteration number, and denoted as V_{dr}. Each reduction itself is uniquely identified by its band and iteration numbers.

With every V_{dr}, the value of $LBTS_{d-1}$ is piggybacked, and hence reduction messages are written as $V_{dr}(L_{d-1})$ where L_{d-1} denotes the value of $LBTS_{d-1}$. Note that $LBTS_{d-1}$ is always available when $LBTS_d$ is being computed, for any d.

3. Algorithms

We now present four algorithms corresponding to four different combinations of reliability of time-stamped events and time management (TM) messages.

The first algorithm is designed for the classical PDES model: reliable events coupled with reliable TM messages ($E_R V_R$). The remaining three algorithms are based on the first algorithm and are progressively refined to accommodate unreliability. As a surprisingly simple variation of the first algorithm, we present the second algorithm to deal with lost TM messages, i.e., reliable events coupled with unreliable TM messages ($E_R V_U$). We further refine the second algorithm to give the third algorithm, which is designed for the more general case of applications using both reliable and unreliable events coupled with unreliable TM messages ($E_R E_U V_U$). Finally, as a special case of the third algorithm, we describe the fourth algorithm for an important class of applications that use both reliable and unreliable events coupled with reliable TM messages ($E_R E_U V_R$).

The algorithms are presented from the point of view of processor i's execution. All processors execute the same algorithm. In all four algorithms, reduction messages are identified by their band and sequence identifiers (d,r). When a reduction (d,r) is in progress at a processor, any arriving reduction messages belonging to an older reduction (d',r') are discarded (i.e., if $d'<d$ or if $d=d'$ and $r'<r$). If any reduction messages belonging to a future reduction (d'',r'') are received, they are buffered until the algorithm moves to that reduction (i.e., if $d''>d$ or if $d''=d$ and $r''>r$). Also, whenever a processor i receives a time-stamped event, it immediately adds that event to its local event queue.

As noted previously, all the algorithms are defined in such a way that computation of $LBTS_d$ is started as well as completed entirely within band $d+1$. A corollary is that all events originating in band d are received in bands d or $d+1$ and no later.

Note that in both reliable and unreliable transports, the algorithms do not require message order to be preserved by the network.

3.1. *Reliable Events and Reliable TM Messages*

The algorithm for this model is shown in the following box. This algorithm possesses some resemblance with other coloring-based global virtual time (GVT) algorithms, such as Mattern's algorithm [6]. The band numbers roughly correspond to the colors in those algorithms; however, the use of multiple reductions per band is unique to our algorithm.

Although other well-known algorithms exist in PDES literature for time synchronization over reliable transport, our Algorithm 1 is unique in that the algorithms for unreliable transport follow as natural extensions to this algorithm, as will be seen in ensuing sections.

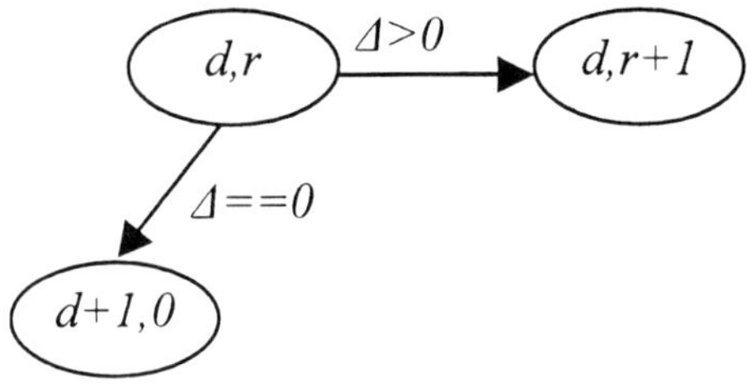

Figure 2: Transitions from reduction *(d,r)* in Algorithm 1.

Algorithm 1: $E_R V_R$ At each processor i:

1. For all d, $\delta_i[d]=0$; $\tau_i[d]=\infty$.
2. $d=0$
3. $r=0$
4. $\tau_i[d]=min(\tau_i[d], MinQ_i)$
5. Start-reduction(d, r, $\delta_i[d]$, $\tau_i[d]$)
6. While not end of reduction(d,r)
   6.1 If $E_d(t)$ is received
   { $\tau_i[d]=min(\tau_i[d], t)$; $--\delta_i[d]$ }
   6.2 If any E is sent
   {tag E as E_{d-1}; $\delta_i[d+1]$++}
7. (Δ,τ)=reduced-value(d,r)
8. If $\Delta>0$ then { r++; goto 5 }
9. Else ($\Delta==0$) { Output $LBTS_d=\tau$; d++; goto 3 }

In line 1, all the $\delta_i[d]$ values are initialized to zero since no events are sent or received during any band at the beginning of simulation. Similarly, all the $\tau_i[d]$ values are initialized to infinity. The algorithm starts with band 0, by initializing d to zero (line 2). For each band, it starts with the sequence of reductions, starting with reduction zero (line 3). The LBTS computation for a band d starts by initializing $\tau_i[d]$ to the smallest timestamp of events in a snapshot of its local event queue ($MinQ_i$) on line 4. This snapshot covers all events that may have arrived before the processor entered the $LBTS_d$ computation. The loop between lines 5 and 9 inclusive is used to iterate through the reduction sequence of band d until $LBTS_d$ is computed.

During each iteration of the loop, a distributed reduction R_{dr} is started (line 5), with $\delta_i[d]$ and $\tau_i[d]$ as processor i's contribution to the reduction values. Note that $\delta_i[d]$ are reduced using the *sum* operator, while $\tau_i[d]$ are reduced using the *minimum* operator. The reduced value is stored in (Δ,τ), where, Δ represents the sum of all $\delta_i[d]$ (the total number of outstanding events in the network that are yet to reach their destinations), and τ is the minimum of all $\tau_i[d]$. If Δ does not equal zero, it implies that not all events generated in band d have been accounted for in τ (some events are in transit). In that case, another reduction is attempted by continuing the loop to move to the next reduction $r+1$ (line 8). If Δ equals zero, then it clear that there are no more outstanding events in transit in the network. Hence τ represents the minimum of all events generated within band d that are not yet processed by the processors, which is nothing but $LBTS_d$. Hence, $LBTS_d$ is generated as output and then the algorithm moves to the next band $d+1$ (line 9). Figure 2 illustrates the transitions from reduction (d,r) to the next reductions.

Even while a reduction is in progress, the simulation could send and/or receive other events, since the LBTS computation is asynchronous. These events are handled in lines 6.1 and 6.2. If an event originating in band d is received, then $\tau_i[d]$ is updated to take the timestamp of the received event into account, and $\delta_i[d]$ is decremented to note the fact that one more event of band d has been accounted for (line 6.2). If an event is being sent, that event is tagged as originating in the next band $d+1$, and the corresponding $\delta_i[d+1]$ is incremented to note the fact that one more event originated in band $d+1$.

It is easy to prove by induction on d that Algorithm 1 correctly computes $LBTS_d$.

3.2. Reliable Events and Unreliable TM Messages

Algorithm 1 requires surprisingly few modifications to deal with lost reduction messages. As such, the second algorithm is a natural extension to algorithm 1 to function in the presence of unreliable reduction messages. The extension is to essentially perform timeouts on incoming reduction messages, and act on timeouts.

Let us examine the effect of a lost reduction message in algorithm 1. First it should be noted that some processors might still be able to complete their current reduction and move on to the next reduction or next band. This is possible, for example, if the message is lost in the last level in a butterfly communication pattern for hierarchical reduction [3]. Other processors fail to complete their current reduction, waiting directly for the lost message, or indirectly for messages that are supposed to be generated based on the lost message.

Thus, three cases arise in Algorithm 1 if a reduction message is lost:

<u>Case 1</u>: All processors fail to complete their current reduction (d,r) waiting for the message that will never arrive.

<u>Case 2</u>: Some processors successfully complete their reduction while others fail. Those processors that do succeed observe that the Δ value has still not reached zero, and hence they move on to the next reduction within the same band, i.e., to $(d,r+1)$. The other failed processors are still waiting for their current reduction (d,r) to complete.

<u>Case 3</u>: Those processors that succeed observe that Δ equals zero, and hence successfully complete the computation of $LBTS_d$ and move on to the next band $d+1$, starting with reduction $(d+1,0)$.

The first two cases can be easily addressed by adding a timeout mechanism to reductions. Upon waiting for a predefined time interval, reductions complete abnormally with a Δ value of ∞. The processors then will continue with the algorithm as though the failed reduction in fact completed with a non-zero value for Δ, making it appear as though some more messages of band d are in transit.

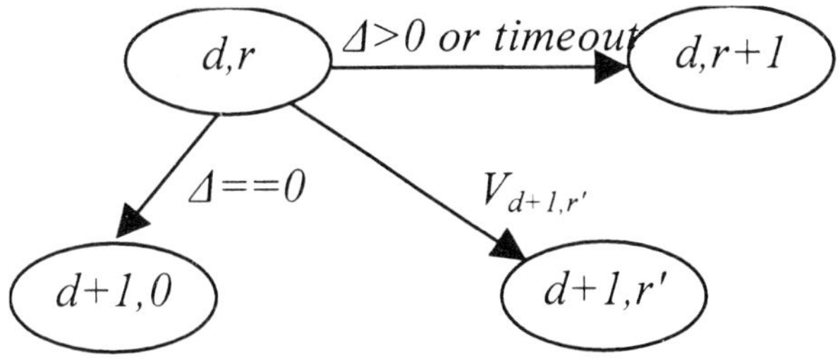

Figure 3: Transitions from reduction *(d,r)* in Algorithm 2.

Now consider case 3. In this case, some processors are still waiting for their current reduction to complete, but might receive reduction messages corresponding to the next band $(d+1,r')$ from the successful processors. Recall that the value of $LBTS_d$ is always piggybacked as L_d in reduction messages, $V_{d+1,r'}$, of band $d+1$. The waiting processor can exploit this fact when it receives a reduction message of $d+1$, by using that L_d value as $LBTS_d$ to immediately terminate its current reduction. Moreover, for the next band $d+1$, it can advance to reduction r' instead of starting with reduction 0. These transitions are illustrated in Figure 3, and the Algorithm 2 is given in the following box, expressed as a modification to Algorithm 1. The modification is to add timeout mechanism to reductions, and to terminate the currently active reduction (d,r) if a future reduction message $V_{d+1,r'}$ is received, and catch up to that future reduction.

Algorithm 2: $E_R V_U$ At each processor i:
Same as Algorithm 1, but with the following added:
6.3 If $V_{(d+1)r'}(L_d)$ is received { Output $LBTS_d=L_d$; d++; $r=r'$; goto 4 }

It is very interesting that tolerance to lost reduction messages can be easily achieved by adding just a couple of lines to the reliable delivery-based algorithm. Thus it can be noted that resilience to network transport unreliability is conceptually very easy to achieve in simulation time management.

3.3. Reliable and Unreliable Events and Unreliable TM Messages

We now turn to the more general case in which applications can send time-stamped events on both reliable and unreliable transports, and also want to perform time management over unreliable transport. All events sent over reliable transport must always be factored into time management; however, there is flexibility with regard to the number of unreliable events that can be missed in time management, which in turn translates into a trade-off for performance optimization.

We exploit this flexibility by introducing two parameters, α and β, using which this algorithm can be tuned to suit the application's performance needs. The parameter α is defined as a limit on the number of reductions performed per band. The parameter β is defined as a limit on the number of unreliable events that the application can tolerate per band, if all those β events (eventually) violate global timestamp order or never arrive. A special case is when $\beta=\infty$, in which case $LBTS_d$ can be advanced without ever waiting for unreliable events.

The parameter α can be viewed as controlling the maximum amount of wallclock time spent waiting for unreliable events, while β can be viewed as controlling the maximum number of unreliable events that can be ignored in the LBTS computation.

The algorithm is shown in the following box. This algorithm follows along the lines of Algorithm 2, except that the conditions for transitions from one reduction to the next are slightly more complex.

Algorithm 3: $E_R E_U V_U$ At each processor i:

1. For all d, $\delta^r_i[d]=\delta^u_i[d]=0$; $\tau_i[d]=\infty$.
2. $d=0$
3. $r=0$
4. $\tau_i[d]=min(\tau_i[d], MinQ_i)$
5. Start-reduction(d, r, $\delta^r_i[d]$, $\delta^u_i[d]$, $\tau_i[d]$)
6. While not end of reduction(d,r)
   - 6.1 If $E_d(t)$ is received
     - 6.1.1 $\tau_i[d]=min(\tau_i[d], t)$;
     - 6.1.2 If E_d is reliable { $--\delta^r_i[d]$ }
     - 6.1.3 Else (unreliable) { $--\delta^u_i[d]$ }
   - 6.2 If any E is sent
     - 6.2.1 Tag E as E_{d-1}
     - 6.2.2 If E is reliable { $\delta^r_i[d+1]++$ }
     - 6.2.3 Else (unreliable) { $\delta^u_i[d+1]++$ }
   - 6.3 If $V_{(d-1)r'}(L_d)$ is received
     { Output $LBTS_d=L_d$; $d++$; $r=r'$; goto 4 }
7. $(\Delta^r, \Delta^u, \tau)$=reduced-value($d,r$)
8. If $\Delta^r>0$ or ($\Delta^u>\beta$ and $r<\alpha$) then { $r++$; goto 5 }
9. Else { Output $LBTS_d=\tau$; $d++$; goto 3 }

First, each $\delta_i[d]$ is split into two terms: $\delta^r_i[d]$ and $\delta^u_i[d]$, where $\delta^r_i[d]$ corresponds to reliable events and $\delta^u_i[d]$ corresponds to unreliable events. Similarly, Δ is split into Δ^r and Δ^u. For correctness of simulation, all processors must necessarily keep iterating for $LBTS_d$ until the total number of transient reliable messages in the system, given by Δ^r, becomes zero for $LBTS_d$ to be correct. Otherwise, $LBTS_d$ could potentially advance further than the timestamp of a transient reliable event that can arrive later. In contrast, by definition, the application can tolerate up to β unreliable events that violate global timestamp order.

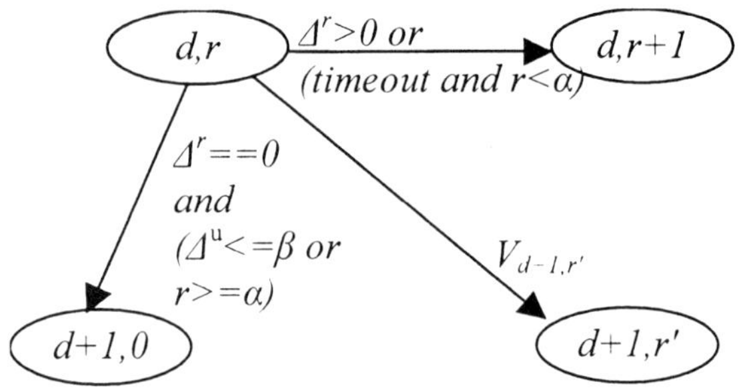

Figure 4: Transitions from reduction *(d,r)* in Algorithm 3.

Except for the way transport types are used for events, this algorithm is similar to Algorithm 2, and differs with it in the following ways: (1) Reductions are performed on triples $(\delta^r_i[d], \delta^u_i[d], \tau_i[d])$, instead of pairs $(\delta_i[d], \tau_i[d])$. (2) Whenever an event is sent or received, the appropriate event counter is updated corresponding to the event's transport type. (3) The termination condition for reduction sequence and LBTS computation for a band are modified appropriately to accommodate unreliable events.

3.4. Reliable and Unreliable Events and Reliable TM Messages

In an important class of applications, such as Distributed Interactive Simulation (DIS), applications utilize a mixture of reliable and unreliable events. Periodic state updates, which contain critical information, are sent over reliable transport, while less critical events are sent over unreliable transport. Time management in such applications can be performed over reliable transport. The last algorithm addresses time management in such applications.

This algorithm, in fact, can be expressed as a special case of Algorithm 3. First, the timeout value for reductions can be set to infinity, since reduction messages sent over reliable transport are never lost. Secondly, α can be set to a value that ensures that the algorithm waits for a fixed amount of time before giving up waiting for any transient unreliable events. Note that α should be not be set to too low a value, since otherwise it could potentially ignore all transient unreliable events. Finally, β can be set to infinity, which essentially translates to the fact that no unreliable events will ever hold up the progress of LBTS.

4. Performance Study

We have completed a preliminary implementation of the algorithms and incorporated them into the time management module of the *Federated Simulations*

Development Kit (FDK) from Georgia Tech[5]. The FDK is a modular set of libraries designed for the development of Run Time Infrastructures (RTIs) for parallel and distributed simulation systems, and includes an RTI that implements a subset of the High Level Architecture (HLA) services.

To study the effects of unreliable transport on the performance of time management, we tested the implementation using two applications. The first is a time-stepped application that exercises simulation time advances in the absence of inter-processor event exchange (i.e., invokes HLA-like *TimeAdvanceRequest* service). The application stresses the speed of asynchronous reduction, with the metric of interest being the number of LBTS computations that successfully complete per second of wallclock time. The second is a TCPI/IP traffic simulation using the Parallel and Distributed NS (PDNS), which uses the FDK for event exchange and synchronization. The PDNS simulation included both time-stamped event exchange and simulation time synchronization. The experiments were run on a network of workstations. In one scenario, the workstations were connected by local area network (Ethernet) at Georgia Tech, and in the other, the workstations spanned Georgia Tech, Dartmouth College and Carnegie Mellon University.

Unfortunately, we observed few message losses in either scenario. The performance of time management (number of LBTS computations per second) remained the same between UDP-based and TCP-based communication. This can be attributable to the fact that TCP can perform as efficiently as UDP in the absence of losses, and the simulation incurs the overhead of TCP connection setup among processors only at initialization time. The absence of losses prevented us from making conclusions about the performance of reliable and unreliable transports, except for the observation that our algorithms performed no worse than reliable transport-based algorithms in the absence of message losses.

As an alternative scenario, we used reliable transport (TCP) and artificially dropped messages (using a uniform random number generator) in the RTI communication module before they are submitted to the time management module. This provided us control on the actual loss probability realized in the network during execution as seen by the time management module.

The experiments were executed on a cluster of 16 Intel Pentium III 550 MHz processors connected by fast Ethernet. The machines were normally loaded when the experiments were executed (i.e., there were other user processes running on the system). The results are shown in Figure 5, comparing the rate of completed LBTS computations for different values of message loss probability q (10%, 1% and 0.1%), against that of reliable delivery (no loss).

As expected, increasing the loss probability decreases the LBTS computation rate. The performance for low loss probability (q=0.1%) is similar to that of no losses, showing that the algorithm is capable of dynamically extracting the superior performance of reliable delivery if the actual observed losses are low. For higher loss probability (q=10%), the reduction algorithm is observed to be not sufficiently robust for larger number of processors. For more than 4 processors, reductions timed out more frequently due to the higher loss probability; degrading the overall LBTS rate. The average number of reduction iterations per band was between 1 and 2.

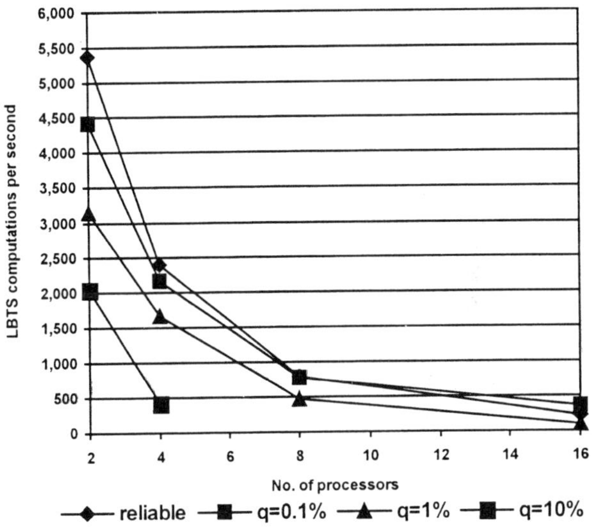

Figure 5: Performance of Algorithm 2 for different values of message loss probability *q*.

Evidently, more extensive performance analysis is needed before conclusive notes on the performance differential between reliable and unreliable transport-based synchronization can be made.

5. Conclusions and Future Work

Time-synchronized distributed simulation over best-effort/unreliable networks is an important problem that has largely gone unresolved so far. Little literature exists that deals with solutions for simulation time management in the presence of event and control message losses. Here, we have presented algorithms to address these issues. To our knowledge, ours is among the first works to address this problem in the context of general best-effort networks. We have first defined a simulation model in the context of unreliable delivery of time-stamped events, which has not traditionally been considered in PDES. We have shown that unreliable delivery of time management messages can be dealt with in a relatively straightforward fashion, as a simple extension of our algorithm for reliable transport. In addition, none of our algorithms assumes that the network preserves message order. Using the algorithms presented here, more complex time-managed applications can be developed using a mixture of reliable and unreliable time-stamped events, and using reliable or unreliable time management messages. It is now clear that unreliable events can in fact be explored for use in real-life applications. Additional work, however, remains in the area of performance analysis, optimization and tuning, as discussed next.

5.1. *Reduction Timeout Value Estimation*

It is clear that the timeout value used for detecting failed reductions affects the rate of LBTS computations. Longer timeouts imply longer time for processors to discover failed reductions, thus wasting time. On the other hand, lower timeout values make the processors timeout too early, thus artificially missing messages that might complete the reduction. The best timeout value is one that is based on dynamically tracking network delays, and varying it accordingly. It is very hard to predict message delays in multi-hop networks; however, a reasonable alternative would be to start the timeout value at a large conservative value, and gradually adjust it based on a history of actual delays observed for the received messages. Dynamic adjustment techniques for an optimal timeout value remain to be investigated. Some of the techniques from networking research, such as TCP timeout mechanisms, could be potentially applied here.

5.2. *Threshold for Unreliable Events*

In applications using both unreliable and reliable time-stamped events, the threshold β determines the time spent waiting for unreliable events in transit to arrive at their destinations. Thus, the β value affects the rate of LBTS computations. Larger β values waste time waiting for the events that will never arrive. Smaller β values advance the LBTS more rapidly than the unreliable events can arrive, potentially advancing LBTS beyond the timestamps of some or all of the outstanding unreliable events. Thus, there is a tradeoff between waiting sufficiently long to receive as many unreliable events as possible, and waiting sufficiently little to not hold up the LBTS computation for receiving the unreliable events that may have actually been lost. Additional research is needed to dynamically estimate and adjust the threshold β to its optimal value.

5.3. *Robust and Scalable Reduction*

Another interesting research item is the design of robust and scalable distributed reduction algorithms that perform well even in the presence of significant number of lost messages. The challenge is to devise a distributed reduction algorithm that scales with the number of processors as well as with message loss probability. When used within the LBTS algorithms presented here, it can improve the efficiency of time management by providing a high degree of probability that a reduction will complete without timing out, despite message losses.

5.4. *Additional Performance Evaluation*

The biggest challenge to a performance evaluation of the algorithms was that we could not control the amount of message losses observed on the network connections. To address this, we are exploring network emulation-based experimentation approaches. We also intend to study the performance of the algorithms on a more extensive set of applications (e.g. *ModSAF*[11]) over wide-area networks using UDP.

6. Acknowledgements

The authors would like to thank David Nicol and Maria Hybinette for providing access to their workstations, at Dartmouth and CMU respectively, for wide area experiments. Thanks also to Mostafa Ammar and George Riley for helpful comments on TCP vs. UDP performance.

7. References

[1] Afek, Y. and M. Saks, "Detecting Global Termination Conditions in the Face of Uncertainty," Principles of Distributed Computing, August 1987.

[2] Damani, O.P., V.K. Garg, "Fault Tolerant Distributed Simulation," the 12th Workshop on Parallel and Distributed Simulation, May 1998.

[3] Fujimoto, R.M., "Parallel and Distributed Simulation Systems," Wiley Inter-science, 2000.

[4] Fujimoto, R.M., "Time Management in the High Level Architecture," Simulation, Vol. 71, No. 6, December 1998.

[5] Fujimoto, R.M., T. McLean, K. Perumalla and I. Tacic, "Design of High-performance RTI Software", Proceedings of Distributed Simulations and Real-time Applications, August 2000.

[6] Mattern, F, "Efficient Algorithms for Distributed Snapshots and Global Virtual Time Approximation", Journal of Parallel and Distributed Computing, 1993.

[7] Nicol, D., "Noncommittal Barrier Synchronization," Parallel Computing, vol. 21, 1995.

[8] Riley, G.F., et al, "Network Aware Time Management and Event Distribution," the 14th Workshop on Parallel and Distributed Simulation, May 2000.

[9] Riley, G.F., et al, "A Generic Framework for Parallelization of Network Simulations",MASCOTS, 1999.

[10] Srinivasan, S., et al, "Implementation of Reductions in Support of PDES on a Network of Workstations," the 12th Workshop on Parallel and Distributed Simulation, May 1998.

[11] Modular Semi-Automated Forces, http://www.modsaf.org.

Consistent Modeling of Distributed Mutual Exclusion Protocol using Optimistic Simulation

Malcolm Yoke Hean Low
Programming Research Group
Computing Laboratory, University of Oxford
mlow@comlab.ox.ac.uk

David M. Nicol
Dept. of Computer Science
Dartmouth College
nicol@cs.dartmouth.edu

Abstract

This paper discusses the problem of risk in optimistic simulation protocols, using as example simulation of a distributed mutual exclusion protocol with strong consistency properties. The simulation model is augmented to detect model inconsistency errors resulting from risky optimistic simulation. While the model runs sequentially without consistency errors, errors occur when the model is executed in parallel optimistically. Some of the errors entirely violate the fundamental mutual exclusion properties of the model itself. To address this problem we extend the optimistic simulation library to eliminate these inconsistencies. We discuss the details of these extensions and the performance trade-off for adding them.

1. Introduction

Optimistic simulation protocols use "*aggressiveness*" and "*risk*" to exploit parallelism in models. As described by Reynolds [7], *aggressiveness* allows events to be executed speculatively, while *risk* allows possibly incorrect state resulting from speculative execution to be exported from one processor to another. It is possible to execute aggressively but without risk, as demonstrated by the Breathing Time Bucket protocol [9]. Most optimistic systems, such as GTW [2] employ both *risk* and *aggressiveness*.

Potential hazards of *risk* in optimistic simulation protocols were examined in [5] by Nicol and Liu. They argue that optimistic simulation systems built by linking a library to native language source code are vulnerable to risk, in that execution behavior which is perfectly legitimate in an optimistic simulation can crash a simulation or silently corrupt the simulation state. They go on to identify two hazards of *risk* with respect to consistency, "rollback inconsistency" and "stale state". Rollback inconsistency occurs when "a completed rollback makes two sampled states inconsistent", and stale state occurs when "an initiated but as yet uncompleted rollback chain makes two sampled states inconsistent". The paper proves that both hazards can be eliminated by requiring a message acknowledgement protocol both for normal event messages and anti-messages.

Nicol and Liu neither give examples of how the consistency errors they describe could occur in a semantically consistent model, nor do they study implementation problems that might arise in implementing their solutions. In this paper we do both of these things. Our objectives are to (a) verify that a semantically consistent model such as the modeling of distributed mutual exclusion protocol can exhibit inconsistent behaviors when executed using an optimistic simulation protocol; (b) describe various extensions to a superstep based optimistic simulation protocol to eliminate rollback inconsistency and stale state; (c) determine the trade-off between performance and consistency in that protocol.

The rest of the paper is organized as follows. Section 2 describes the distributed mutual exclusion model together with a classification of various errors that could arise in an optimistic simulation. Section 3 gives a brief introduction of the SimBSP parallel simulation library and the BSP Time Warp (BSP TW) protocol used to construct the distributed mutual exclusion model.

Section 4 outlines the extensions to BSP TW to eliminate rollback inconsistency and stale state. It considers a sequence of extensions, each motivated by performance deficiencies in previous extensions, until arriving at a low-cost solution. Section 5 highlights some related work and section 6 concludes the paper.

2. Distributed Mutual Exclusion Model

In order to detect inconsistency errors in an optimistic simulation, we choose to simulate a distributed mutual exclusion simulation model that has strong model consistency properties. We added program code to the simulation model

0-7695-1104-X/01 $10.00 © 2001 IEEE

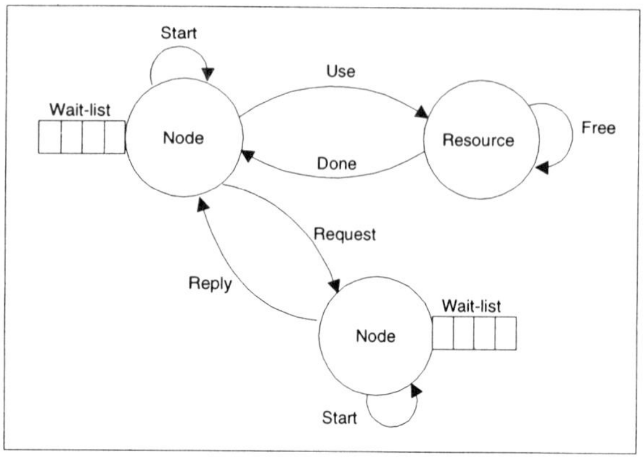

Figure 1: Events Relationship between Node and Resource.

to detect violation of these properties.

The simulation model consists of an n by n grid with each element in the grid being a node or a resource. During the course of the simulation, a node will acquire a resource for a certain period of time. A "radius-of-usage" parameter, r, is defined for the resources in the simulation model to restrict the set of nodes a resource will serve. A resource R_i at grid coordinate (x,y) will service any node N_i with grid coordinate (s,t) if $|s-x| \leq r$ and $|t-y| \leq r$. When the radius-of-usage of two resources overlap, nodes that are within the overlapping regions will be randomly serviced by both the two resources.

A resource is used exclusively by a node during the service period denoted by the service time, t_s, sampled from an exponential distribution with mean 1.0. The distributed mutual exclusion algorithm by Ricart and Agrawala [8] is used to achieve exclusive access to the resources by the nodes. Figure 1 shows the events used to implement the model.

At any point in time, a node N_i can be in one of these states: 1) `RELEASED`: N_i is not using any resource; 2) `WANTED`: N_i has began requesting for a resource; 3) `HELD`: N_i is using a resource. The states for a resource R_i are: 1) `LOCK`: R_i is being used by a node; 2) `UNLOCK`: R_i is not used by any node.

Several types of errors that are semantically inconsistent with the distributed mutual exclusion model are listed in Table 1. For example, error type 5 states that a resource receives a `USE` message from a node but the state of the server is `LOCK`. This means that the resource is currently being used by a node but another node is also trying to use the resource as well. This error is clearly a violation of the semantic of the distributed mutual exclusion protocol which guarantees that a resource will only be used by a node at any one time. For our purposes, the essential point is that knowledge of the model semantics allows us to detect inconsistencies between state and message, at the point a message arrives.

Type	Description of Error
1	A node receives a `START` message but its state is not `RELEASED`
2	A node receives a `REPLY` message but its state is not `WANTED`
3	A node receives a `DONE` message but its state is not `HELD`
4	A node receives a `DONE` message from a wrong server
5	A server receives a `USE` message but its state is `LOCK`
6	A server receives a `FREE` message but its state is `UNLOCK`

Table 1: Description of Errors in Model Consistency.

bsp_begin();
[A] Initialization;
while GVT < SimEndTime;
    [B] Receive external events and process rollback;
    [C] Compute new GVT, perform fossil collection and compute new event limit n every k supersteps;
    [D] Execute n events;
    bsp_sync();
endwhile
bsp_end();

Figure 2: Algorithm for BSP Time Warp.

3. SimBSP Parallel Simulation Library

We examine the problem of preventing rollback inconsistency and stale state in the context of the SimBSP library, available from Oxford University. SimBSP implements a C++ programming API for optimistic simulation and is based on the BSP Time Warp protocol [4]. The algorithm for BSP TW is shown in Figure 2. Each processor manages a group of logical processes (LPs) in the system. LPs in the same processor share a common event-list. Each processor executes a series of supersteps; each superstep is the total work done between calls to **bsp_sync()**, i.e., one pass through the `while` loop. The superstep structure of the BSP TW algorithm allows deterministic execution ordering of simulation models that is not affected by message latency times between processors.

The most distinctive feature of BSP TW is that it throttles optimism and balances load by controlling the number of events n that every processor executes every superstep. Events sent from one processor to another in a superstep are only received at the beginning of the next superstep. Any rollbacks caused by receiving these external events are consolidated and processed in bulk after all external events have been received. Each processor then simulates n events from the sequential event-list. n is adaptively recomputed based on information from fossil collected events after each global virtual time (GVT) computation. This limit makes no distinction between newly received or rolled-back events.

P	l (μs)	g (μs/word)
4	22.7	0.08
9	54.1	0.15
16	121.1	0.23

Table 2: BSP Parameters for 86-nodes 195Mhz (101.03 Mflops) Origin 2000 using Different Number of Processors P.

$\%G$	Low Connectivity	High Connectivity
10	3866222	10466256
30	7070687	17238147
50	5804330	12846059

Table 3: Number of Committed Events in the Distributed Mutual Exclusion Model. $\%G$ is the Percentage of Grid Cell being Resources.

4. Eliminating Risk Hazards

To verify that the distributed mutual exclusion protocol does exhibit inconsistency errors with an optimistic protocol, we conducted experiments on the model using the original BSP TW protocol.

The experiments are conducted using 4, 9, and 16 processors on a 86-node Origin-2000 system. The Oxford BSP Toolset [6] is used as the runtime library. The BSP synchronization cost l and communication cost g for different processor configurations on the Origin-2000 system are shown in Table 2.

The distributed mutual exclusion model has a grid size of 100 by 100. Different percentages of the grid cells as resources ($\%G$) are used. We experimented with two different radius-of-usage values, 1 and 2. A radius-of-usage of 1 represents low connectivity in the network, as each resource will be connected to a maximum of 8 nodes. A radius-of-usage of 2 represents high connectivity with each resource connecting to a maximum of 24 nodes. A spinloop of 25μs is used to model fine event granularity.

The simulation length for all the runs is fixed at 1000 time units. A GVT computation interval of 40 supersteps is used throughout the experiments. A two-dimensional block partitioning is used to assign grid cells (LPs) to processors. The total number of committed events is shown in Table 3. Table 4 shows a breakdown of the different errors detected for the model executed using the original BSP TW protocol. Error types 1 and 6 are not detected in all the runs. The high connectivity model shows significantly higher number of errors compared to the model with low connectivity.

The subsequent sections describe our attempts in developing efficient solutions to eliminate the inconsistency errors. In each case, we verified that all the errors shown in Table 4 are eliminated by our solution.

		Low Connectivity				High Connectivity			
		Error Type				Error Type			
P	$\%G$	2	3	4	5	2	3	4	5
4	10	19	2	0	1	3096	43	0	109
	30	252	10	0	24	2087	29	0	46
	50	352	21	1	27	1516	25	0	22
9	10	254	30	1	8	3677	59	0	117
	30	684	30	0	62	3759	50	0	77
	50	816	51	0	37	3033	47	0	37
16	10	339	45	0	30	4055	71	0	116
	30	1201	46	5	97	4910	72	0	62
	50	1237	80	8	99	3655	56	0	56

Table 4: Number of Errors Detected in the Distributed Mutual Exclusion Model using BSP-TW1 Protocol with Different Number of Processors P.

Description of BSP TW Algorithms	
BSP-TW1	Original BSP TW without anti-message acknowledgement
BSP-TW2	BSP-TW1 with LP suspension and anti-message acknowledgement
BSP-TW3	BSP-TW2 with 25% throttling
BSP-TW4	BSP-TW1 with only anti-message acknowledgement

Table 5: Description of BSP TW Algorithms: BSP-TW1, BSP-TW2, BSP-TW3 and BSP-TW4.

4.1. Anti-Message Acknowledgement

We first turn to the problem of eliminating rollback inconsistencies. In [5], Nicol and Liu proved that rollback inconsistency cannot occur if after an LP sends an anti-message, it suspends until the full effect of that anti-message is propagated through the system. This can be accomplished through an anti-message acknowledgement protocol, in which an LP acknowledges an anti-message to the sender of that anti-message, as soon as all subsequent anti-messages caused by that receipt have themselves been acknowledged. If an LP receives an anti-message which does not cause further anti-messages, it acknowledges the anti-message immediately.

As we began our study, the first implementation considered (we call it BSP-TW2) exhibited dismal performance relative to the base implementation (BSP-TW1). In response to this we analyzed behavior and identified an explosion of rollbacks as reflective of the performance degradation. This led to implementation of BSP-TW3, which employs a throttling mechansim. In addition, in an effort to separate the performance implications of suspending LPs on anti-message acknowledgements and the raw overhead of carrying the additional anti-message acknowledgement traffic, we constructed BSP-TW4, which is identical to the base model, but generates and carries the anti-message acknowledgement traffic. BSP-TW4 does not cause LPs to

	BSP-TW1	BSP-TW2	BSP-TW3	BSP-TW4
No. of supersteps	1189	2993	2993	1189
No. of events rolled-back	517851	15335534	313985	517851
No. of remote messages	469400	897615	436068	469400
No. of remote anti-messages	67457	495672	34125	67457
Average time (sec.)	222.55 (11.17)	469.21 (5.15)	226.03 (8.99)	212.93 (4.80)
Barrier time (sec.)	233.57 (11.31)	527.09 (6.62)	388.79 (14.18)	224.31 (5.12)

Table 6: Performance Comparison between BSP-TW1, BSP-TW2, BSP-TW3 and BSP-TW4 Protocols on 4 Processors for High Connectivity Model with 50% Resources.

suspend. Comparison of BSP-TW1 and BSP-TW4 isolates the message traffic overhead of acknowledgements. Table 5 describes the four variations of BSP TW that will be discussed in this section.

4.1.1 Experimentation with Anti-message Acknowledgement

Our first implementation of anti-message acknowledgements is BSP-TW2. In this version, acknowledgement messages are sent and received just as any other message generated by the simulation is sent and received. This means, in particular, that the full recognition of a rollback tree and full acknowledgement response can take many supersteps, as messages are exchanged between processors only at superstep synchronizations.

As expected, BSP-TW2 eliminates the rollback inconsistency errors found in Table 4. However, the addition of the anti-message acknowledgement mechanism has a significant impact on performance. Table 6 compares certain optimistic simulation statistics under the BSP-TW1 and BSP-TW2 protocols, for the high connectivity simulation model with 50% of the grid cells being resources. Three of these statistics are standard to optimistic simulation. The number of supersteps is peculiar to BSP TW, and counts the number of superstep computations needed to advance the simulation to termination. SimBSP has built-in measurement infrastructure that allows one to measure the time a processor spends in a superstep (excluding waiting for other processors to complete the superstep) and the time processing at the superstep boundary. The "Average time" gives the per-processor average of the sum of this measurement over all supersteps, and so reflects the intrinsic amount of work the simulation is doing. The "Barrier-time" however measures at each superstep the time required by the last processor to finish. Load-imbalance is revealed when the average time and barrier time are significantly different.

For both the average time and barrier time, the timings for the average of five runs are shown. The numbers in parenthesis show the standard deviations for the five runs and reflect variation in system load when the experiments are conducted.

BSP-TW2 has significantly more rollback events and anti-messages than BSP-TW1, and requires significantly more supersteps. The cost of processing all these rollbacks in BSP-TW2 is reflected in the two-fold increase in average time. Furthermore, analysis of the average and barrier times shows that BSP-TW2 has more problems with load-imbalance than does BSP-TW1.

The sudden explosion of rollback events using BSP-TW2 is attributed to the over-optimism in executing events of other LPs while some LPs in the same processor are suspended while waiting for anti-message acknowledgement. For BSP-TW1, the total number of external anti-messages sent is only 14% of the total number of ordinary external messages sent. For BSP-TW2, since each anti-message must be acknowledged, we need to double the number of external anti-messages to take into account anti-message acknowledgements. The total number of external anti-messages and anti-message acknowledgements sent amount up to 110% of the total number of actual ordinary external messages sent in BSP-TW2.

BSP-TW3 attempts to reduce the number of rollbacks by adding a throttling mechanism to BSP-TW2. For each LP that is suspended, the remaining limit to the number of events that can be processed in the current superstep is reduced by 25%. This reduction is maintained across supersteps as long as the LPs remain suspended. The net effect is that a processor with a large number of LPs suspended will be penalised from executing more events.

Table 6 shows that under BSP-TW3 the number of rollbacks and remote anti-messages drop significantly. In fact, both the number of events rolled back and the number of remote anti-messages sent are also lower than that of BSP-TW1. This agrees with the small difference in the average time for BSP-TW1 and BSP-TW3. However, the addition of the throttling mechanism resulted in even higher load-imbalance between processors across supersteps. This is reflected in the long barrier time for BSP-TW3, which is 71% higher than the average time.

The small difference in the average times for BSP-TW4 and BSP-TW1 shows that the overhead in sending anti-message acknowledgements is negligible. The average time and barrier time for BSP-TW1 are in fact worst than BSP-TW4. In general, we would expect BSP-TW1 to perform

%G	BSP-	Low Connectivity			High Connectivity		
		4	9	16	4	9	16
10	TW1	8.9	24.4	44.7	7.5	21.9	39.0
	TW2	20.6	51.3	75.2	12.9	48.7	83.9
	TW3	36.7	92.7	103.2	64.8	110.8	145.4
	TW4	7.5	22.3	44.6	7.8	19.8	39.8
30	TW1	6.4	14.7	24.9	4.7	17.5	19.4
	TW2	16.6	30.6	45.6	13.6	30.5	39.5
	TW3	50.2	84.0	102.7	78.1	118.4	149.7
	TW4	6.3	13.8	22.6	5.0	16.9	19.7
50	TW1	8.4	16.8	23.6	4.9	17.6	20.6
	TW2	18.0	31.8	42.2	12.3	29.9	38.5
	TW3	53.2	81.8	99.2	72.0	115.8	140.8
	TW4	8.2	16.3	23.2	5.3	17.4	19.1

Table 7: Percentage Difference between Barrier Time and Average Time using BSP-TW1, BSP-TW2, BSP-TW3 and BSP-TW4 Protocols.

%G	BSP-	Low Connectivity			High Connectivity		
		4	9	16	4	9	16
10	TW1	0.7	10.5	16.3	8.0	17.6	23.1
	TW2	31.3	74.4	62.1	91.3	132.4	120.8
	TW3	1.3	8.4	10.9	2.7	7.9	15.2
30	TW1	2.1	5.2	9.1	4.7	10.7	14.0
	TW2	70.6	81.8	86.0	133.4	129.1	125.5
	TW3	1.4	3.9	6.9	2.3	5.6	10.6
50	TW1	2.4	5.8	8.7	4.0	9.2	12.2
	TW2	74.2	82.9	86.5	119.4	121.4	115.9
	TW3	1.6	4.0	6.9	2.4	6.3	11.0

Table 8: Percentage of Anti-Messages over Committed Events using BSP-TW1, BSP-TW2 and BSP-TW3 Protocols.

better than BSP-TW4 since BSP-TW4 has to handle anti-message acknowledgements. We attribute this to the variation in system load as indicated by the large standard deviation in both timings for BSP-TW1.

Table 7 shows the load-imbalance in terms of percentage difference between barrier time and average time. Table 8 shows the percentage of anti-messages over the total number of committed events in the system. The statistics for BSP-TW4 are the same as BSP-TW3 and are thus not shown in the table.

As shown in Table 8, the percentage of anti-messages using BSP-TW3 is much lower than that of BSP-TW2. Although there is substantial performance improvement using BSP-TW3 over BSP-TW2, the performance of BSP-TW3 is still significantly worst than that of BSP-TW1. Moreover, Table 7 shows that BSP-TW3 has even worst load-imbalance than BSP-TW2. For most cases using 9 and 16 processors, the barrier takes twice as long as the average time.

There is clearly room for improvement. We were pushed then to re-think our approach.

bsp_begin()
[A] Initialization
while GVT < SimEndTime
  [B1] Receive external events and process rollback
  [B2] Broadcast suspend-messages if any anti-message
    is sent in part B
  bsp_sync();
  [B3] Receive external events and process rollback
  [C] Compute new GVT, perform fossil collection and
    compute new event limit n every k supersteps
  [D] Execute n events. n is set to zero if :
    [1] suspend-message is sent in part B1;
    [2] suspend-message is received in part B3;
    [3] anti-message is sent in part B3;
    [4] anti-message is sent while processing an events.
  bsp_sync();
endwhile
bsp_end();

Figure 3: Algorithm BSP TW with Extended Barrier.

4.2. Extended Barrier

Analysis of BSP-TW2 and BSP-TW3 suggests that load-imbalance due to LP suspension is the root cause of the performance difficulties, and the suspension is due to the high numbers of supersteps needed to push anti-message acknowledgements around in the standard BSP framework. Table 2 shows that the cost of executing a barrier synchronization (**bsp_sync()**) on the SGI Origin is much smaller than the observed cost of load-imbalance. This observation led us to consider a mechanism that would accelerate the anti-message acknowledgement processing, at the cost of additional barriers.

The algorithm in Figure 3 uses a series of supersteps to roll back an entire chain of causally incorrect events whenever external anti-messages are sent from a processor. We compare this algorithm with the original BSP TW algorithm outlined in Figure 2. Part A of the algorithm remains the same. Part B is expanded into three parts. In part B1, all normal messages and anti-messages are received and any rollbacks are processed accordingly. In part B2, a processor broadcasts a suspend-message to every other BSP processor if it sent any anti-message in part B1. The **bsp_sync()** that follows, together with the receipt of events in part B3, delivers the suspend-messages and anti-messages sent in parts B1 and B2 to their destinations. Part C of the algorithm remains the same. In part D, the event limit, n, is set to 0 if one of the following conditions are satisfied: 1) suspend-message is sent in part B1; 2) suspend-message is received in part B3; 3) anti-message is sent in part B3; 4) anti-message is sent while processing one of the n events.

The net effect of the above scheme is that the processors

%G	P	Low Connectivity		High Connectivity	
		BSP-TW5	BSP-TW6	BSP-TW5	BSP-TW6
10	4	13704	35397	348256	389862
	9	163531	197949	641588	972061
	16	339111	405452	1073115	1580840
30	4	60591	127091	437738	721267
	9	140716	270793	928435	1673417
	16	256731	443110	1409948	2603786
50	4	51155	98431	290935	594300
	9	133335	251563	681462	1312950
	16	215710	327548	917059	1696651

Table 9: Comparison between BSP-TW5 and BSP-TW6 in terms of the Number of Anti-Messages.

%G	P	Low Connectivity		High Connectivity	
		BSP-TW5	BSP-TW6	BSP-TW5	BSP-TW6
10	4	21669	53374	566460	681951
	9	220665	269700	1082110	1652469
	16	437982	545274	1803351	2733183
30	4	89081	180633	729065	1163745
	9	203045	382296	1493024	2645103
	16	366679	621089	2284885	4144120
50	4	71739	133516	460798	899032
	9	179900	333402	1061214	1985119
	16	289204	438400	1422109	2580613

Table 10: Comparison between BSP-TW5 and BSP-TW6 in terms of the Number of Rollbacks.

will engage in a series of normal event processing supersteps. The superstep in which an external (between processors) anti-message is sent is followed by a series of supersteps that consist of receiving events and rollbacks, without any event execution.

We call this series of supersteps "extended barriers". The extended barrier works like a special superstep whereby all anti-messages sent while the extended barrier is in effect will be acknowledged. The suspend-messages keep all processors suspended while the anti-messages undo the entire rollback chain. Explicit anti-message acknowledgement is not needed in this algorithm since no normal event processing can proceed while the rollback is going on. This approach therefore takes advantage of the special structure of SimBSP, in its reliance upon barrier-synchronization. We will refer to this variant of extension to BSP TW as BSP-TW5.

4.3. Normal Message Acknowledgement

We have so far concerned ourselves only with anti-message acknowledgements. Nicol and Liu showed that stale state can be eliminated if every ordinary message is acknowledged before an LP sends another, in the same fashion as anti-messages are acknowledged. The fundamental idea is the same—wait until any rollbacks caused by the message have been fully propagated before continuing to process the LP. At face value it would seem that the cost of implementing acknowledgements would be high, as far more ordinary messages are sent than anti-messages. However, once again the structure of SimBSP and our solution to process rollback trees quickly can be leveraged to provide an efficient solution to the stale state problem.

We propose an extension to BSP-TW5, called BSP-TW6, which deals with the threat of stale state. For normal messages sent between LPs on the same processor, no acknowledgements are needed as any rollbacks caused by the messages are immediately performed. If an LP sends messages to LPs in other processors, the LP is immediately suspended for the current superstep. Note that in this case, only the LP that sends out external messages is suspended, co-resident LPs are unaffected. Also, the LP is suspended for only one superstep and any events destined for the suspended LP in the current superstep will be kept in a temporary buffer and will be merged back into the event-list at the end of the superstep.

It is somewhat remarkable that a sending LP need only be suspended for one superstep. The reason is that acknowledgements for the external messages are implicitly received at the start of the next superstep. Any rollback caused by external messages at the receiving LPs would trigger an extended barrier, at the end of which all the rollback-chains initiated by the external messages are removed. Suspension of the LP for a step just ensures that any rollback tree triggered by its message is completely processed before the LP resumes. This is equivalent to receiving explicit acknowledgements. We denote this extension as BSP-TW6.

Tables 9 and 10 show that BSP-TW6 generally has twice the number of rollbacks and anti-messages as BSP-TW5. We saw this same phenomenon comparing BSP-TW1 and BSP-TW2— the suspension of LPs, coupled with the SimBSP instance on executing exactly n events in a superstep, forces unprofitable speculative execution. To correct this we experimented with the same throttling mechanism as mentioned in section 4.1.1 on BSP-TW6. Each time an LP is suspended for sending out external messages, the event limit per superstep, n, is reduced by a fixed percentage. The net effect is that the more LPs that are suspended on a processor in a superstep, the less event the processor gets to execute in that superstep. We experimented with 2 different throttling limits, 25% and 10%. The variant of BSP-TW6 with 25% throttling will be referred to as BSP-TW7 and the one with 10% throttling will be referred to as BSP-TW8.

Table 11 describes these four variants of BSP TW. Table 12 compares the simulation statistics using BSP-TW5 and BSP-TW6 on the high connectivity simulation model with 50% of the grid cells being resources. The numbers

	BSP-TW5	BSP-TW6	BSP-TW7	BSP-TW8
No. of supersteps	1435 (2816)	3280 (6405)	6560 (10179)	3813 (6694)
No. of events rolled-back	460798	899032	96247	93115
No. of remote messages	447877	474252	413456	413443
No. of remote anti-messages	45934	72309	11513	11500
Average time (sec.)	214.11 (4.94)	232.27 (12.71)	215.51 (4.59)	216.40 (8.64)
Barrier time (sec.)	274.49 (4.19)	502.08 (23.73)	296.06 (5.73)	278.55 (10.36)

Table 12: Performance Comparison between BSP-TW5, BSP-TW6, BSP-TW7 and BSP-TW8 on 4 Processors for the High Connectivity Model with 50% Resources.

Description of BSP TW Algorithms	
BSP-TW5	Original BSP TW with Extended Barrier
BSP-TW6	BSP-TW5 with suspension of LP that sends external messages
BSP-TW7	BSP-TW6 with 25% throttling
BSP-TW8	BSP-TW6 with 10% throttling

Table 11: Description of BSP TW Algorithms: BSP-TW5, BSP-TW6, BSP-TW7 and BSP-TW8.

in parenthesis show the actual number of supersteps taken if we expand and count each individual supersteps within each extended barrier.

Comparing Table 12 and the statistics for BSP-TW1 in Table 6, we note that the average times required to complete the simulation using BSP-TW5, BSP-TW6, BSP-TW7 and BSP-TW8 are all close to the average time for BSP-TW1. The mechanisms we propose do not induce a great deal of computational overhead. However, BSP-TW6 shows barrier time which is twice the average time, indicating load-imbalance. This agrees with our observation on BSP-TW2 that suspension of some LPs while allowing other LPs in the same processor to proceed ahead will result in over-optimism, hence leading to load-imbalance.

The significant reduction in barrier time with BSP-TW7 and BSP-TW8 also confirms our observation on BSP-TW3 that the over-optimism can be controlled using some form of throttling. However, we also note that the performance is sensitive to the throttling level used and mechanisms for fine-tuning the throttling parameter are needed; however a study of this issue is beyond the scope of this paper.

At the end of all this the key question asks what the performance cost is of ensuring that a SimBSP simulation is free from rollback inconsistencies and stale state. Figure 4 shows the speedup curves for BSP-TW1, BSP-TW5, and BSP-TW8 on 4, 9 and 16 processors for the models with 50% of the grid cells being resources. Comparison of BSP-TW5 and BSP-TW8 shows that the cost of getting freedom from stale state, once we have freedom from rollback inconsistencies, is not excessive. Comparison of BSP-TW1 and BSP-TW5 shows that the cost of freedom from rollback inconsistency is an increase of about 20% in execution time, which seems quite an acceptable price to pay. Furthermore,

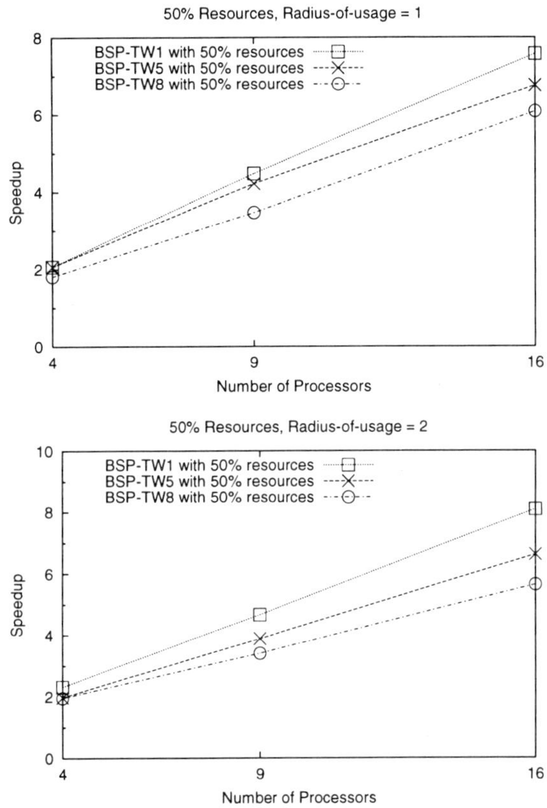

Figure 4: Speedup Graphs using Different BSP TW Protocols.

that cost does not manifest itself as more computational work so much as it manifests itself as load-imbalance. Better techniques for dynamically managing load might conceivably reduce this cost further.

5. Related Work

In this section, we describe two related works relating to this paper. In [1], a fault tolerance rollback-based optimistic discrete event simulation protocol is proposed to allow crash recovery of a distributed simulation. This scheme uses dependency vectors tagged onto normal messages to detect causality violation among LPs and thus eliminates the use of anti-messages. Although the scheme is proven to be free from rollback inconsistency, there is no provision in the scheme for the elimination of stale state.

The BSP-TW8 protocol proposed in section 4.2 closely resembles the "wolf calls" protocol described in [3]. Both schemes use the broadcast of a special control message to stop the spread of incorrect computations. While the BSP-TW8 protocol sends this control message to all the processors, the "wolf calls" protocol determines the set of LPs this control message should be sent to using a "spheres of influence" parameter. This technique is not suitable for BSP-TW8 due to the synchronous nature of the computation. Suspending only some processors in any superstep will only lead to more speculative executions and worsen the load-imbalance among the processors. The "wolf calls" protocol seems to be capable of eliminating rollback inconsistency. However, there is also no mechanism in the protocol to prevent the occurrence of stale state.

6. Conclusion

The potential risk hazards of an optimistic protocol are clearly illustrated in the distributed mutual exclusion model presented in this paper. We have shown that inconsistency errors do occur when the semantically consistent model is executed using an optimistic protocol such as BSP TW. We also verified that by adding anti-message acknowledgement into an optimistic protocol such as BSP TW, rollback inconsistency errors can be eliminated.

Different algorithms to improve the performance of BSP TW with anti-message acknowledgement are considered. We showed that BSP TW with extended barrier can achieve the effect of anti-message acknowledgement with comparable performance to the original BSP TW algorithm. We further extended the algorithm to allow stale state to be eliminated from the simulation.

Experimental results from these algorithms are presented and analyzed. Our study shows that reasonable performance can still be achieved for the algorithms to eliminate rollback inconsistency. However, the further performance degradation that resulted if we try also to eliminate stale state may well deserve some careful considerations.

Acknowledgements

The work of Malcolm Low is funded by the Gintic Institute of Manufacturing Technology (Singapore). David Nicol was supported in part by DARPA Contracts N66001-96-C-8530 and N66001-00-C-8065, NSF Grant ANI-98 08964, NSF Grant EIA-98-02068, Dept. of Justice contract 2000-CX-K001, and a fellowship from the Marion and Jason Whiting Foundation. The authors would like to thank the Oxford Supercomputing Center for the use of their Oscar Origin 2000 system.

References

[1] O. Damani and V. Garg. Fault-tolerant distributed simulation. In *Proceedings of the 12th Workshop on Parallel and Distributed Simulation (PADS '98)*, pages 38–45, Ban, Alberta, Canada, May 26 - 29, 1998.

[2] S. Das, R. Fujimoto, K. Panesar, D. Allison, and M. Hybinette. GTW: A Time Warp System for Shared Memory Multiprocessors. In *Proceedings of the 1994 Winter Simulation Conference*, pages 1332–1339, 1994.

[3] V. Madisetti, J. Walrand, and D. Messerschmitt. WOLF: A Rollback Algorithm for Optimistic Distributed Simulation Systems. In *Proceedings of the 1988 Winter Simulation Conference*, pages 296–305, December 1988.

[4] M. Marin. Time Warp on BSP Computers. In *Proceedings of the 12th European Simulation Multiconference*, 1998.

[5] D. M. Nicol and X. Liu. The Dark Side of Risk (What your mother never told you about Time Warp). In *Proceedings of the 1997 Workshop on Parallel and Distributed Simulation*, pages 188–195, Austria, June 10 - 13, 1997.

[6] Oxford Parallel. The Oxford BSP Toolset and Profiling system (v1.4), 1999. URL : http://www.bsp-worldwide.org/implmnts/oxtool/download.html.

[7] P. F. Reynolds, Jr. Comparative analyses of parallel simulation protocols. In *Proceedings of the 1989 Winter Simulation Conference*, Washington, D.C., December 1989.

[8] G. Ricard and A.K. Agrawala. An Optimal Algorithm for Mutual Exclusion in Computer Networks. *Communications of the ACM*, 24(1):9–17, November 1981.

[9] J. S. Steinman. SPEEDES: Synchronous Parallel Environment for Emulation and Discrete Event Simulation. In *Proceedings of the SCS Multiconference on Advances in Parallel and Distributed Simulation*, pages 95–101, January 1991.

Spatio-Temporal Correlations and Rollback Distributions in Optimistic Simulations

B.J. Overeinder and A. Schoneveld and P.M.A. Sloot
University of Amsterdam
Faculty of Science, Section Computational Science
Kruislaan 403, 1098 SJ Amsterdam
The Netherlands
{bjo,arjen,sloot}@science.uva.nl

Abstract

In this paper we study the influence of spatio-temporal correlations on the dynamic runtime behavior of the optimistic parallel Time Warp simulation method. By using the Ising spin model, we show experimentally that the distribution of the number of rolled back events behaves as a power-law distribution over a large range of sub-critical Ising temperatures and decays exponentially for super-critical Ising temperatures. For critical Ising temperatures, where long-range correlations occur, the computational complexity of Time Warp and physical complexity of the Ising spin model are entangled and contribute both to the runtime behavior in a nonlinear way.

1 Introduction

The increasing interest in the application of discrete event simulation to solve problems from natural sciences, is motivated by the ability of the discrete event simulation to capture the asynchronous behavior that is characteristic to a certain class of models. We are specifically interested in the use of parallel discrete event simulation (PDES) methods, in particular the Time Warp method [5], to study dynamic complex systems modeled by asynchronous cellular automata (ACA) [9, 10]. Asynchronous cellular automata differ from regular synchronous cellular automata (CA) in their update scheme. The danger of simply imposing an update scheme has been considered in an article by Huberman and Glance [4]. They used a spatial version of the prisoner's dilemma to show the remarkable differences between asynchronous and synchronous updating.

The dynamic behavior of many natural systems is strongly imposed by the statistical (spatio-temporal) correlation between the individual components of the system. In particular, critical phenomena in Ising spin systems (i.e., magnetization in ferro-metals) or individual-based population dynamics are explained by spatio-temporal correlations [12]. The fundamental question addressed in this paper is, to which extent the correlations in the simulation model influence the runtime behavior, or dynamics, of the PDES method. To study this phenomenon, both correlated and uncorrelated system dynamics are simulated, and their effect on causality errors in the Time Warp method is examined.

A highly speculative conjecture is made, that the Time Warp dynamics can be characterized as a so-called self-organized critical system [1]. Self-organized critical behavior is found in many complex systems, for example in sandpile and earthquake dynamics. Similar to the Gutenberg-Richter histogram of earthquake magnitudes, the histogram of rollback lengths is very close to a power law. The analog suggests that large rollbacks are related in a scale-invariant fashion to smaller rollbacks, i.e., large rollbacks and small rollbacks are basically different manifestations of the same phenomenon [13].

2 The APSIS Optimistic Simulation Environment

The APSIS environment is a research vehicle for both optimistic simulation protocol design and evaluation, and parallel simulation development of dynamic complex systems [7]. Specifically, requirements for computational science applications are taken into consideration to assess the potential of PDES methods to solve problems originating from, e.g., physics, chemistry, or biology. These requirements put special constraints on the design of the simulation environment and necessitate extensions to the basic Time Warp method.

The design and implementation of *incremental state sav-*

0-7695-1104-X/01 $10.00 © 2001 IEEE

ing in the APSIS environment is an essential feature to effectively support the simulation of dynamic complex systems such as ACA [9]. The state vector of a spatially decomposed ACA can be arbitrarily large, that is, all the cells in the sub-lattice are part of the state vector. Incremental state saving stores not the full state vector, but saves only the changes to the state vector due to the execution of an event, which is only a small fraction of the full state. Besides efficient memory management, incremental state saving also reduces the time overhead related to the memory copy.

A second necessary extension to the basic Time Warp method is *optimism control*, or *optimism throttling*. Uncontrolled optimism may lead to thrashing behavior, where the system experiences excessive long and/or frequent rollbacks. This results in an inefficient execution where correcting causality errors consume more computation time than the forward simulation. An effective method to control optimism is to impose a time window on the events: the events outside the time window are delayed until the time window is updated [11]. The time window bounds the difference between the LVTs of the simulation processes and hence limits the lengths of rollback chains.

3 The Ising Spin Model

We use the Ising spin model to study the influence of spatio-temporal correlations to the dynamic behavior of the Time Warp optimistic simulation protocol. The Ising spin model is a fairly simple model that exhibits complex behavior under the control of one well-defined parameter, the temperature of the system; and as such, the model is ideal for our experiments.

The Ising spin model is a popular model of a system of interacting variables in statistical physics, and was introduced as a model for ferromagnetism. The model is defined on a grid of interacting "spins" that can either have a state "up" ($s_i = 1$) or a state "down" ($s_i = -1$). Spins on adjacent, nearest-neighbor sites, interact with each other in a pair-wise manner with a strength J. When J is positive, the energy is lower when spins are in the same direction and when J is negative, the energy is lower when spins are in opposite directions. The *magnetization* M of the system is the sum of the spin values s_i. The energy of the system is given by the following Hamiltonian:

$$E = -J \sum_{\langle ij \rangle} s_i s_j - \mu_0 H \sum_i s_i \ .$$

The first sum is over all pairs of spins that are nearest neighbors. The second term is the energy of interaction of the magnetic moments, μ_0, associated with the spins with an external magnetic field, H.

At random times, a spin is granted a chance to change the state, a so-called spin flip. The attempted spin flip, or trial, is accepted proportionally to the energy difference ΔE between the new configuration and the old configuration. Using a constant temperature (T) condition the so-called *Metropolis algorithm* can be used to simulate the dynamics. In the Metropolis algorithm, a spin flip is accepted according to the Boltzmann probability distribution $\exp(-\Delta E/kT)$. If the temperature is below a well-defined temperature, known as the critical or *Curie* temperature T_c, a spontaneous non-zero magnetization occurs ($T_c \approx 2.27$, in J/k degrees Kelvin). For temperatures $T > T_c$ the magnetization vanishes abruptly. Hence T_c separates the disordered phase for $T > T_c$ from the ferromagnetic phase for $T < T_c$.

The transition from the ordered ferromagnetic phase to the disordered paramagnetic phase is remarkably sharp, since the order parameter M approaches zero at T_c with infinite slope. Such singular behavior is an example of a "critical phenomenon." The sudden alignment of the spins as $T \to T_c^+$ (T_c^+ denotes from high T) results from correlations that are propagated extensively throughout the entire system: everything depends on everything else.

This tendency to be correlated can be measured using the *correlation function*

$$C(r) = \langle s_0 s_r \rangle \ ,$$

where s_r is a spin that is located r lattice sites away from s_0. Some results for the correlation function are shown in Fig. 1, which shows $C(r)$ at several different temperatures.

In this paper we use a discrete event simulation for the Metropolis algorithm to simulate the Ising spin model at different temperatures T. The parallel discrete event simulation in APSIS exploits the implicit spatial locality present in the Ising spin model, without altering the update history [6].

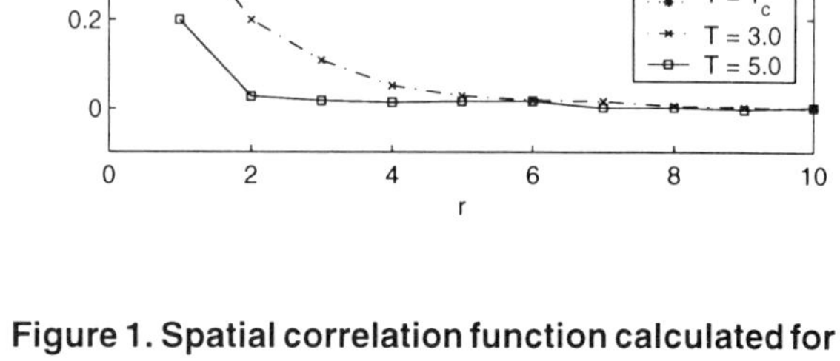

Figure 1. Spatial correlation function calculated for a 32 x 32 lattice at several temperatures.

4 Self-Organized Criticality

4.1 Criticality versus Self-Organized Criticality

Most of the time, equilibrium systems with short-range interactions, exhibit exponentially decaying correlations. Infinite correlations, i.e., scale invariance, can be achieved by fine-tuning some parameters (e.g., temperature) to a critical value [12]. An example of such a system is the Ising spin model of magnetization.

Besides systems exhibiting critical behavior, a large class of non-equilibrium locally interacting, nonlinear systems spontaneously develop scale invariance. Such composite systems with many interacting degrees of freedom may evolve to a critical state in which minor events may trigger a chain reaction that can affect an arbitrary large number of constituents of the system. This state is called *self-organized criticality* (SOC) [1]. The probability of spontaneously generated structures or events, further called avalanches, of many different sizes s show a power-law distribution

$$P(s) \sim s^{-\tau} ,$$

where τ is a critical exponent and most other observables of the system have no intrinsic time or length scale. This implies that we expect to observe scale invariance, or power-law scaling, in the system. The absence of intrinsic length scale is attributed to SOC, where avalanches of all sizes contribute to keep the system perpetually in a critical state. This critical state is robust with respect to any small change in the rules of the system. The size of an avalanche can be defined in different ways. It can be measured by the number of relaxation steps needed for the chain reaction to stop or the total number of sites involved in the avalanche.

Many naturally occurring systems exhibit this kind of scaling- or self-similar behavior, examples are earthquakes, stock markets, and ecosystems. The concept of SOC is developed to explain the behavior of such systems. Self-organized critical behavior was first investigated for sandpile models [1]. In this cellular automata model, a particle is dropped onto a randomly selected lattice point. When a lattice point accumulates four particles, they are redistributed to the four adjacent lattice points, or in case of edge lattice points they are lost from the grid. Redistributions can lead to further instabilities and avalanches of particles in which many particles may be lost from the edges of the lattice. The average number of particles per lattice point is the density that fluctuates about a *quasi-equilibrium* value. One measure of the avalanche size is given by the number of particles lost by the lattice during a sequence of redistributions, or alternatively can be given by the number of lattice points that participate in the redistribution.

4.2 Self-Organized Criticality in Time Warp Dynamics

As the Ising spin model is a critical system, that is for a certain parameter regime the system exhibits fractal structures, it appears an ideal simulation model to study the influence of spatial correlation on the dynamical behavior of the Time Warp protocol. The many degrees of freedom that are interacting show emergent behavior, i.e., magnetization, as the temperature of the Ising spin system approaches T_c^+. This emergent behavior is the result of the correlation length in the system that diverges as the temperature approach T_c, and is even infinite at T_c.

An important characteristic of systems exhibiting SOC behavior is a separation of time scales. It is required that such systems are slowly driven, that is *perturbations* occur on a much larger time scale than the *diffusion* or *relaxation* dynamics. The critical state in SOC systems is furthermore characterized by a stationary state where the driving forces balance the cascades. For example in the sandpile model, adding sand causes on the one hand the pile to grow, on the other hand avalanches. The dynamically stationary state is obtained at the "critical point" where these two effects exactly balance.

A highly speculative analogy could be made with Time Warp: adding events (i.e., perturbations) causes on the one hand the event rate to grow, on the other hand rollbacks to occur (i.e., relaxation). Our experiments show that in Time Warp, the event rate eventually reaches a kind of stationary state with superimposed rollback cascade effects. In Fig. 2, the event rate shows a so-called punctuated equilibrium, which is the hallmark of SOC. We define two time scales in Time Warp: *simulation time* and *protocol time*. The simulation time in Time Warp is updated by the rate at which the system is driven. This driving rate is determined by the dynamics of the simulation. The protocol time, needed to process a rollback, is determined by machine specific parameters. A difference with conventional SOC systems and Time Warp is that there is no explicit separation of time scales, asynchronous updates and rollbacks may intervene. Also rollbacks take place on separate processors instead of an entire lattice of sites.

It is very important to note that, in fact, we are confronted with two kinds of critical behavior. The critical behavior of the first kind is a result of the Ising spin phase transition at the critical temperature T_c. At the Ising spin phase transition, long range spin correlations occur, that probably influence the Time Warp dynamics. We call this critical behavior of the first kind the *physical critical behavior*. The critical behavior of the second kind is conjectured, and is caused by SOC. We assume that in the low temperature Ising regime the Time Warp dynamics reaches a self-organized critical state, which we call *computational*

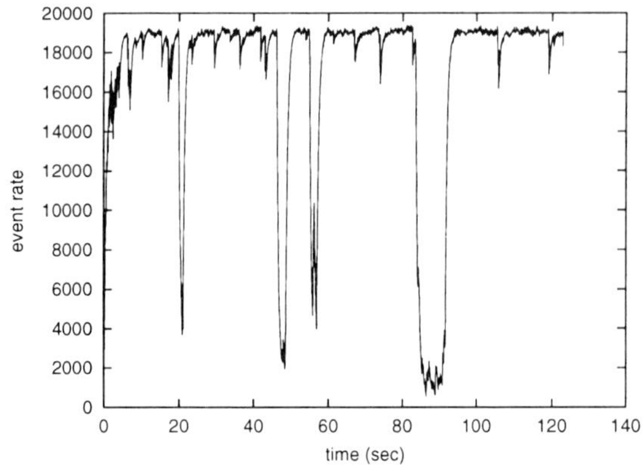

Figure 2. Event rate of one of the logical processes in a PDES Ising simulation, with number of processors $P = 6$ and Ising temperature $T = 1.0$.

critical behavior.

In the next section, the influence of the spatio-temporal correlation on the average rollback length and the rollback length distribution is studied. In the first series of experiments, a correlated and an uncorrelated spin system simulation is used. The other experiments use the correlated Ising spin system simulation. The average rollback length and rollback length distribution is studied at different temperatures in order to determine the influence of the Ising spin phase transition on the Time Warp protocol. It is expected that around the Ising spin phase transition, the long range spin correlations increase the average rollback sizes. In this way, the correlation in the Ising spin system dynamics influences the rollback behavior of the Time Warp simulation protocol. It is well known that these long range correlations result in moving islands of actively flipping spins, located in a sea of inactive spins. This separation of activity can trigger very large rollbacks whenever an active island moves over a processor boundary.

We are interested in rollback length distributions in order to do a first order check of SOC in Time Warp dynamics. Remember that for SOC systems it is well known that many observables scale as power-laws.

5 Experimental Results

5.1 Correlated versus Uncorrelated Systems

A series of experiments are executed using the APSIS parallel simulation environment on the the Distributed ASCI Supercomputer (DAS). (Note that ASCI stands for Advanced School for Computing and Imaging—a Dutch research school.) The DAS consists of four wide-area distributed clusters of total 200 Pentium Pro nodes. ATM is used to realize the wide-area interconnection between the clusters, while the Pentium Pro nodes within a cluster are connected with Myrinet system area network technology. The experiments are performed within one single cluster, thus all communication is via the 1.28 Gbit/s Myrinet. The efficient communication primitives and thread support in the communication fabric allows for low latency, high throughput communication performance over the Myrinet network. The measured null message latency is $\pm 17\ \mu$sec, and the throughput ± 60 MB/s.

The experiments with the parallel simulation of the Ising dynamics use a two-dimensional decomposition of the $L \times L$ square lattice. The decomposition is made up to assure optimal load balance. The individual Ising spins in the sublattices are aggregated into one single Time Warp logical process, resulting in a mapping of one Time Warp logical process onto a processor.

For all parameter instances of the simulation experiments we measure the average rollback length and rollback length distributions. For the first series of experiments in this section we have fixed the lattice size to $L = 220$, the number of processors to $P = 12$, and the bounded time window (BTW) to 3000. A bounded time window of 3000 has been experimentally established. For this window size, the Time Warp simulation of the Ising spin model operates almost optimally [8]. For smaller window sizes, for example 2000, the Time Warp simulation is hampered by the limited number of pending event messages. For larger window sizes, such as 4000 or larger, the simulation is significantly slowed down by the increased number of rollbacks. The rollback strategy used in all the experiments is incremental state saving.

The influence of correlation on the rollback behavior is studied using the correlated Ising spin system simulation and the uncorrelated, "adapted" Ising spin system simulation. In the uncorrelated spin system, the spin flip probability is *only* dependent on the temperature of the system, and not on the spin orientation of its nearest neighbors (thus the change in energy ΔE). In the remainder of the discussion, we drop the adjective "correlated" for the Ising spin system.

Figures 3 and 4 show the rollback distributions for the Ising spin system and the uncorrelated spin system respectively, for temperature range $0.5 - 2.5$. However, for the discussion is the acceptance probability more important. For the Ising spin system, the acceptance probability varies from $p = 0.007$ for $T = 0.5$, to $p = 0.323$ for $T = 2.5$. For the uncorrelated system, the acceptance probability varies from $p = 0.0003$ for $T = 0.5$, to $p = 0.202$ for $T = 2.5$. In Fig. 4, the small acceptance probability $p = 0.0003$, and consequently the small number of events, makes that the rollback data set is too small for proper statistical analysis; hence the staggering line.

Besides the *quantitative* differences between the two fig-

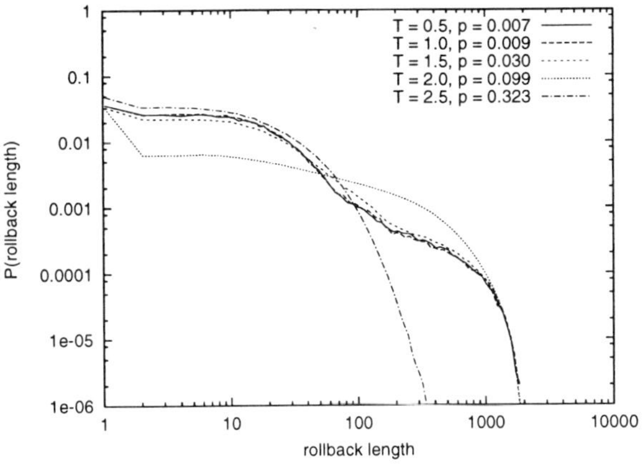

Figure 3. Rollback distribution for the Ising spin system with temperatures in the range 0.5 – 2.5.

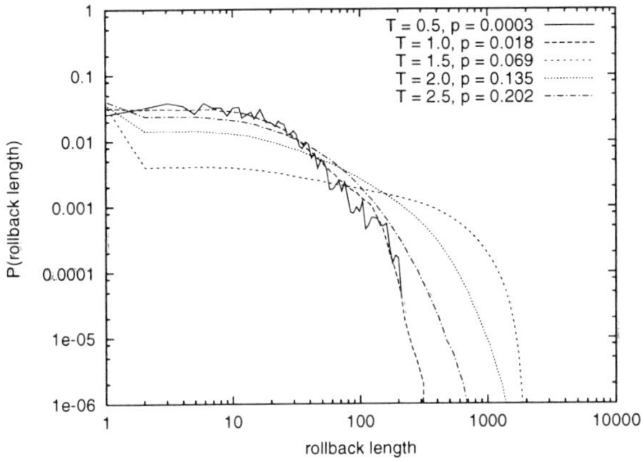

Figure 4. Rollback distribution for the *uncorrelated* spin system with temperatures in the range 0.5 – 2.5.

ures, there is a remarkable *qualitative* difference between the rollback probability distributions for Ising spin and uncorrelated spin systems. For the Ising spin system, simulations with $T \leq 1.5$ result in almost identical distributions, although the acceptance probability varies from $p = [0.007 - 0.030]$ (see Fig. 3). The rollback probability distribution for $T \leq 1.5$ is a so-called fat-tail distribution, which is a power-law with exponential cut-off. Simulations of the Ising spin system with $T \geq 2.0$ give exponential rollback probability distributions. The uncorrelated spin system rollback probability distributions are different for each temperature $T = [0.5 - 2.5]$, and all distributions are exponential (Fig. 4).

Summarizing, for the ferromagnetic phase, the combined Ising spin system and Time Warp simulation mechanism shows power-law rollback distributions, which are different from the exponential rollback distributions in the paramagnetic phase (for Ising spin systems $T > T_c$, and always for uncorrelated spin systems). In the next section, the Ising spin system phase transition between ferromagnetic and paramagnetic is studied in more detail.

5.2 Influence of the Temperature in the Correlated System

In Fig. 5 the average rollback lengths are shown for the temperature range $0.1 - 2.7$. Ideally, rollback avalanches are measured instantaneously over the system, that is over all processors used by the parallel simulation. However, the instantaneous measurement requires freezing the forward simulation, and allowing only rollbacks to occur, i.e., the relaxation in Time Warp. This would fundamentally alter the dynamics of the Time Warp protocol, and is therefore unacceptable intrusive. Hence, each processor records the local rollbacks for analysis. The rollback lengths are averaged over time for all processors. The results of three different runs are depicted in the figure. Close to the Ising phase transition ($T_c \approx 2.27$ for infinite lattices), the expected peak in the average rollback length can be observed. From this figure, three different regimes can be identified: the *physical sub-critical phase* ($< T_c$), the *physical critical phase* ($\approx T_c$) and the *physical super-critical phase* ($> T_c$).

The different phases influence the rollback length distributions. In the physical sub-critical temperature regime $0.1 - 1.4$, power-law scaling is found (see Fig. 6), i.e., the Time Warp dynamics appear to be in a computational critical regime. As the temperature approaches the physical super-critical regime a transition to exponential scaling can be observed (see Fig. 7). Close to the critical temperature, length distributions with "fat tails" (power-law distributions

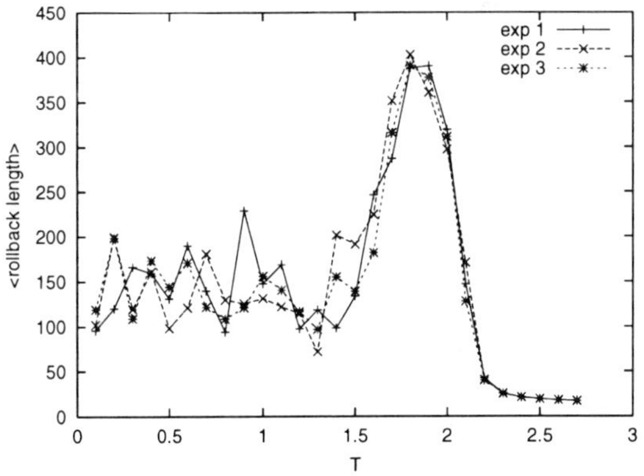

Figure 5. Average rollback length for different temperatures. For each temperature, the results of 3 experiments are shown. Using the parameters $L = 220$, $P = 12$, **and** $BTW = 3000$, **and a 2D decomposition.**

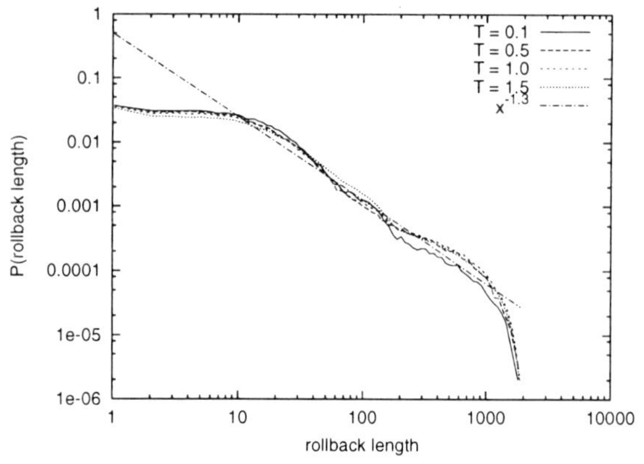

Figure 6. Rollback distribution for temperatures in the range 0.1 – 1.5, fitted exponent has value -1.3 (± 0.03). Using the parameters $L = 220$, $P = 12$, and $BTW = 3000$, and a 2D decomposition.

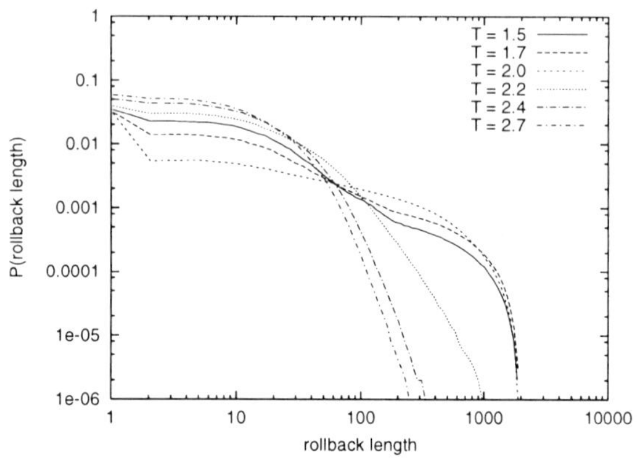

Figure 7. Rollback distribution for temperatures in the range 1.5 – 2.7. Using the parameters $L = 220$, $P = 12$, and $BTW = 3000$, and a 2D decomposition.

with exponential cutoff) develop due to the emergence of long-range spin correlations.

The scaling exponent α in the physical sub-critical regime seems to be universal for all temperatures in this regime. From the experimental data a power law with exponent $\alpha = -1.3$ is fitted. Because the rollback length distribution obeys power-law scaling, we conjecture that the rollback dynamics are in a SOC regime.

The slope of the power function flattens out in the range of its lower magnitude rollbacks with length $1 - 10$. This flattening, rather than remaining double log-linear, occurs because discreteness effects of the rollback lengths come into play. As the rollback cascades approach the size of what is assumed to be the size of a real-world system's component particle, in our study an event, it becomes impossible for the fractal pattern to repeat at this scale [1, 2, 3].

5.3 Varying the Number of Processors

To study the influence of the number of processors on the rollback length distribution in the SOC or computational critical regime, a series of experiments with $P = \{4, 8, 12, 24\}$ using a 2D decomposition has been performed. The lattice size has been fixed to $L = 220$. The rollback distributions of Ising spin simulations at $T = 1.0$ are shown in Fig. 8. Similar results are seen for other temperatures T in the SOC regime. The results indicate that for increasing P the rollback length distributions converge. Again, the scaling exponent α is not influenced by increasing P.

The average rollback lengths for different processors in the range $T = [0.1-2.7]$ are shown in Fig. 10. For 8, 12 and 24 processors, again, a peak around T_c can be distinguished. For $P = 4$, this peak is not present. Apparently, the critical Ising spin dynamics does not reduce the performance of the Time Warp protocol if only 4 processors are used.

From Fig. 8 we observe that for $P = 4$ the rollback length distribution does not show power-law scaling behavior. The cutoff size of the rollback length distributions for processor numbers $P = 8$ and larger is determined by the bounded time window (BTW) size. (This effect is in more detail presented in a research note [8].) In the low temperature regime the *average* rollback length increases with the number of processors P (see Fig. 10).

This is not valid anymore in the high T regime, where the rollback length distributions approximately collapse (see Fig. 9) to the same exponentially decreasing distribution. As a direct consequence, the average rollback lengths will

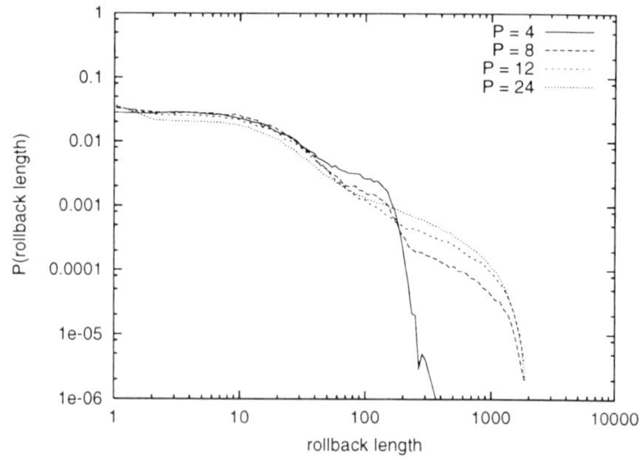

Figure 8. Rollback distributions for $P = \{4, 8, 12, 24\}$ at $T = 1.0$ using the parameters $L = 220$, $BTW = 3000$, and a 2D decomposition.

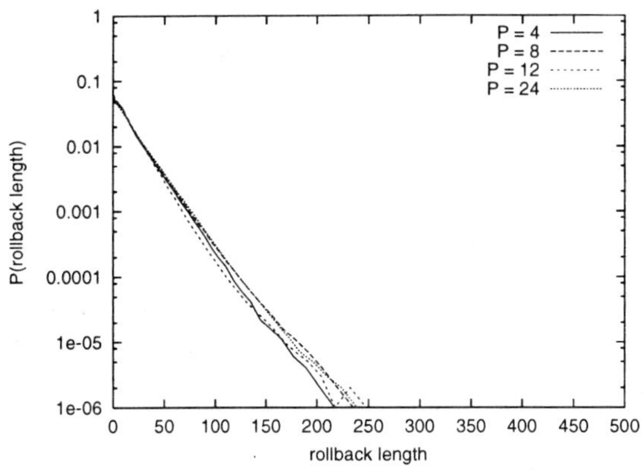

Figure 9. Rollback distributions for $P = \{4, 8, 12, 24\}$ at $T = 2.7$ using the parameters $L = 220$, $BTW = 3000$, and a 2D decomposition. Note that the horizontal axis has a linear scale.

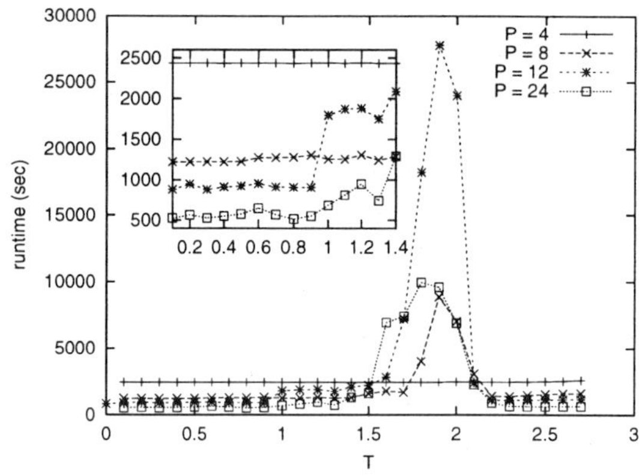

Figure 11. Run times for $P = \{4, 8, 12, 24\}$ for varying T using the parameters $L = 220$, $BTW = 3000$, and a 2D decomposition.

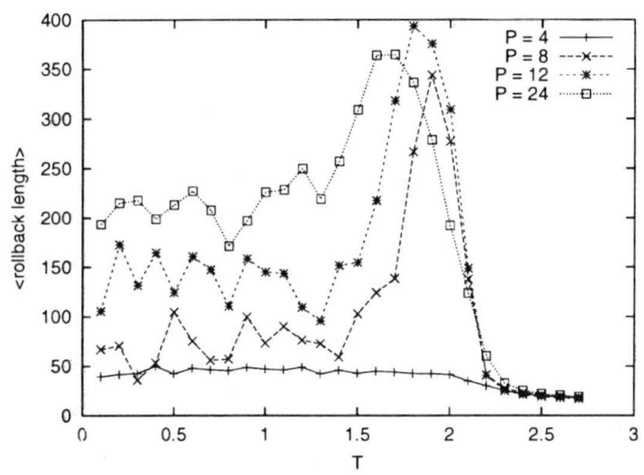

Figure 10. Average rollback lengths for $P = \{4, 8, 12, 24\}$ for varying T using the parameters $L = 220$, $BTW = 3000$, and a 2D decomposition.

collapse (see Fig. 10). In the high T regime the rollback lengths are not influenced by P as in the low T regime. The processors are synchronized frequently in this regime, due to a high acceptance ratio of flipped spins. Therefore, there is hardly any real time to build large simulation time differences between the processors, resulting in only small rollback lengths.

It is interesting to compare the runtimes for different P in the same temperature range. The results are presented in Fig. 11. From the figure one can derive that in the low T regime, the runtime scales down if more processors are used. This is also valid for the high temperature regime. Around T_c, we find non-trivial scaling for the different processors. Obviously, using only 4 processors gives the best result, which could be expected from the significantly lower average rollback length in this regime. Using 12 processors gives the worst results in this case.

For the high and low temperature regimes $P = 24$ gives the best performance results. Even though, in the low T regime, the average rollback length is maximal for $P = 24$, the extra overhead is beneficially applied to efficiently exploit the parallelism present in the simulation.

Although the average rollback lengths in the low T regime are much larger than the average rollback lengths in the high T regime, the execution times are comparable. This is a result of the frequency of rollback events. In the low T regime this frequency is much lower, due to the reduced acceptance probability of spin flips. It seems that, the average rollback lengths and the rollback frequency are balanced to approximately similar execution times for the low and high T regimes.

In other studies [8] using a 1D data decomposition, we have found similar results as reported in this section. This indicates that the robustness of the phenomena, which persists over different number of processors and different decompositions in 1D or 2D.

6 Discussion and Conclusions

In this paper we have studied the influence of spatio-temporal correlations on the dynamical behavior of the Time Warp protocol for parallel discrete event simulations. As a simulation case we considered the Ising spin model, which is basically a cellular automata model. A property of the Time Warp protocol is the appearance of so-called rollbacks whenever a causality error occurs. This rollback mechanism can trigger a cascade of events that need to be undone. The local rollbacks are recorded by the simulation process, as the instantaneous global cascaded rollbacks cannot be administered without unacceptable intrusion to the Time Warp dynamics.

From the experiments in Section 5.3, we see that the optimistic simulation of the Ising spin system scales linearly with the number of processors for temperatures at sufficient distance from the critical temperature T_c. However, it is found that the Ising spin phase transition influences the rollback behavior, and consequently the runtime. Around the critical temperature (physical critical behavior) T_c, the average rollback lengths increase dramatically, as well as the simulation runtimes, due to long-range spin correlations.

For the rollback dynamics three different phases can be distinguished: *physical sub-critical*, *physical critical*, and *physical super-critical* rollback length scaling behavior. In the sub-critical regime the scaling behavior appears to behave like a power-law, with exponents independent of the temperature. In this regime we conjecture that *computational critical* (SOC) behavior appears. Note that in the sub-critical regime, the Ising spin system is *not* in a critical state. Hence, the application does not need to exhibit critical behavior for the Time Warp simulation protocol to show SOC. Around the critical phase large rollback lengths become more abundant due the long-range spin correlations. Here the computational complexity and the physical complexity are entangled and contribute both to the runtime and rollback behavior in a nonlinear way. In the physical super-critical phase a negative exponential distribution of the rollback lengths is observed.

Obviously a lot of work remains to be done in the study of physical- and computational critical behavior in Time Warp. Other series of experiments with different parameters for the Ising lattice size and bounded time window, support our findings. Complementary studies are necessary, such as the simulation of the dynamic behavior of Time Warp and the Ising spin simulation. The simulation of the model of Time Warp and Ising spin simulation allows for a full statistical analysis of the runtime behavior. In the current study, only local rollbacks are administered. However the sizes of the cascaded rollbacks is another observable of the system and should show power-law scaling behavior.

Besides Ising spin models, other application systems with (long-range) spatio-temporal correlations should be considered for evaluation of SOC behavior. In particular, spatial decomposed problems like population dynamics, forest fire, or damage spreading models are potential candidates. The study of other simulation applications with spatio-temporal correlations will further increase our insight into the power-law rollback behavior and complexity entanglement in the Time Warp simulation protocol.

The results presented in this paper are, to our knowledge, the first series of experiments that have ever been conducted to study the influence and the appearance of critical behavior in Time Warp. The entanglement of the computational and physical complexity, and their non-trivial contribution to the runtime behavior might have consequences for other optimistic simulations.

Acknowledgments

This research is supported in part by the Netherlands Organization for Scientific Research, Massively Parallel Computing Priority Program under grant 95MPR01/1.

References

[1] P. Bak, C. Tang, and K. Wiesenfeld. Self-organized criticality. *Physical Review A*, 38(1):364–374, July 1988.

[2] G. Brunk. Understanding self-organized criticality as a statistical process. *Complexity*, 5(3):26–33, January/February 2000.

[3] V. Frette, K. Christensen, A. Malthe-Sørensen, J. Feder, T. Jøssang, and P. Meakin. Avalance dynamics in a pile of rice. *Nature*, 379(6560):49–52, Jan. 1996.

[4] B. Huberman and N. Glance. Evolutionary games and computer simulations. *Proceedings of the National Academy of Sciences of the United States of America*, 90(16):7716–7718, Aug. 1993.

[5] D. Jefferson. Virtual time. *ACM Transactions on Programming Languages and Systems*, 7(3):404–425, July 1985.

[6] B. Lubachevsky. Efficient parallel simulation of dynamic Ising spin systems. *Journal of Computational Physics*, 75(1):103–122, Mar. 1988.

[7] B. Overeinder. *Distributed Event-driven Simulation: Scheduling Strategies and Resource Management*. PhD thesis, Department of Computer Science, University of Amsterdam, Amsterdam, The Netherlands, Nov. 2000.

[8] B. Overeinder, A. Schoneveld, and P. Sloot. Self-organized criticality in optimistic simulation. *Parallel and Distributed Computing Practices*, 2001. (Research note accepted for publication).

[9] B. Overeinder and P. Sloot. Application of Time Warp to parallel simulations with asynchronous cellular automata. In *Proceedings of the 1993 European Simulation Symposium*, pages 397–402, Delft, The Netherlands, Oct. 1993.

[10] P. Sloot and B. Overeinder. Time-Warped automata: Parallel discrete event simulation of asynchronous CA's. In *Proceedings of the Third International Conference on Parallel Processing and Applied Mathematics*, pages 43–62, Kazimierz Dolny, Poland, Sept. 1999.

[11] L. Sokol, B. Stucky, and V. Hwang. MTW: A control mechanism for parallel discrete simulation. In *Proceedings of the 1989 International Conference on Parallel Processing*, volume III, pages 250–254, Minneapolis, MN, Aug. 1989.

[12] H. Stanley. Scaling, universality, and renormalization: Three pillars of modern critical phenomena. *Reviews of Modern Physics*, 71(2):S358–S366, Mar. 1999.

[13] H. Stanley, L. Amaral, P. Gopikrishnan, P. Ivanov, T. Keitt, and V. Plerou. Scale invariance and universitality: Organizing principles in complex systems. *Physica A*, 281(1-4):60–68, June 2000.

Session 8

Work in Progress

Session 9

Optimistic Simulation III

A Scaled Version of the Elastic Time Algorithm

FRANCESCO QUAGLIA
Dipartimento di Informatica e Sistemistica
Università di Roma "La Sapienza"
Via Salaria 113, 00198 Roma, Italy
quaglia@dis.uniroma1.it

Abstract

Recently a new class of synchronization algorithms for parallel discrete event simulation has been proposed, namely the near perfect state information algorithms, which are based on a notion of error potential to control the optimism of event execution. An algorithm of this class, called elastic time algorithm (ETA), has been instantiated. In this algorithm, the error potential is computed using temporal information (next event timestamp, simulation clocks etc.) and is then translated into event execution delay based on a constant factor. In this paper we present a scaled version of ETA (SETA), in which the error potential is translated into event execution delay based on both a constant factor and an additional scaling factor determined dynamically as a function of the event granularity.

We have implemented versions of ETA and SETA for a cluster of PCs connected by a Myrinet switch and we have established in an empirical study that SETA outperforms ETA if there is difference in the granularity of different event types.

1 Introduction

Several algorithms have been proposed to solve the synchronization problem in parallel discrete event simulation. However, this problem still remains a major issue to tackle. In particular, defining synchronization algorithms that have the capability to perform efficiently for any simulation application is still an open research area.

A common classification separates existing synchronization algorithms into conservative and optimistic. The former ones allow logical processes (LPs) to execute events only after determining the execution does not violate timestamp order at any LP. Instead, the latter ones allow the LPs to execute events without the guarantee of no timestamp order violation, and use a rollback mechanism to recover the system state to a correct value in case real violations are detected. These algorithms allow the exploitation of parallelism anytime it is possible for timestamp order violations to occur but they do not.

Some optimistic algorithms, like classical Time Warp [8], adopt no control at all on the optimism of event execution. Some others adopt controlled optimism (see, for example [1, 2, 3, 9, 10, 15, 19, 21]) in order to keep low the rollback overhead while still exploiting parallelism internal to the application. A classification of these algorithms based on controlling criteria has been presented in [17].

The work in [17] introduces also a new class of algorithms with controlled optimism, namely the *near perfect state information* (NPSI) algorithms. These algorithms use state information to compute an *error potential* (EP) which is then used to control the optimism. The control mechanism consists of delaying the event execution based on the EP value. (Control mechanism based on delayed event execution is commonly referred to as *throttling*). Then the authors instantiate an algorithm of this class, namely the *elastic time algorithm* (ETA), in which the EP of an LP is computed using temporal information (such as the next event timestamp of the LP) and is then translated into event execution delay based on a constant factor.

In this paper we show by discussion how a finer kind of optimism control can be implemented if the EP value is translated into event execution delay based not only on a constant factor but also on execution costs that determine the real rollback penalty. Then we present a *scaled* version of ETA (SETA) in which the translation of the EP value takes into account those costs. This is done by introducing an additional scaling factor in the translation process, which we call Rollback Penalty Factor (RPF).

Actually, for the version of SETA we present in this paper we limit our approach in the construction of RPF by keeping into account exclusively the cost of event execution (i.e. the event granularity). Therefore, other execution costs having an impact on the rollback penalty (e.g. state restoration, antimessage sending) are not included in the definition of RPF. As a consequence this version of SETA is likely to be useful in practice for any application with at least minimum difference in the (expected) granularity of different event types, for which fine tuning of the delay as a function of the event granularity is likely to produce real benefits. (We recall that at least minimum difference is typical of several real world applications, such as battlefield simulations or simulations of mobile communication systems.) Extensions to include additional costs in the definition of RPF could however be envisaged.

We have implemented versions of ETA, SETA, as well as classical Time Warp, for a cluster of PCs connected by a Myrinet switch and we have tested the performance of these algorithms using a classical benchmark. The collected data have pointed out that both ETA and SETA outperform Time

0-7695-1104-X/01 $10.00 © 2001 IEEE

Warp, and that SETA shows better, or at least the same, performance of ETA.

The remainder of this paper is structured as follows. In Section 2 we provide an overview of the NPSI approach and of ETA. In Section 3 we provide a discussion on how optimism control performed by ETA can be improved by exploiting execution cost information. Section 4 presents SETA. The performance data are reported in Section 5.

2 The NPSI Approach and ETA

In the NPSI approach, a function M_1 computes the EP value of the LP using as input state information collected through an adequate feedback system. Once computed EP, a function M_2 uses this value to control optimism by determining the delay in the event execution. In other words, M_2 acts as a translator of EP into execution delay.

The feedback system should provide up to date state information and the function M_1 should be evaluated frequently. This allows NPSI algorithms to be adaptive in that the EP value changes dynamically depending on current system conditions, therefore the delay of event execution changes dynamically as well. Srinivasan and Reynolds defined this approach as the *micro-adaptive* one as opposed to the *macro-adaptive* approach in which parameters having an impact on optimism control are recomputed infrequently.

In the ETA algorithm, the function M_1 computes the EP value associated with an LP using state information (temporal information) related to all the LPs belonging to the predecessor set of that LP ([1]). We denote the predecessor set of LP_i as $PS(LP_i)$.

Denoting with:

σ_i the simulation clock (local virtual time) of LP_i;

ν_i the minimum unreceived message time of LP_i (that is the smallest timestamp of events scheduled by LP_i but not yet incorporated in the event lists of the recipient LPs);

η_i the next event time of LP_i (this value is equal to σ_i while LP_i executes an event);

α_i the minimum between η_i and ν_i (i.e. $\alpha_i = min(\eta_i, \nu_i)$);

α'_i the following value: $min_{LP_k \in PS(LP_i)}(\alpha_k)$.

the function M_1 of ETA computes the EP_i value of LP_i as follows:

$$M_1 : \; EP_i = max(\eta_i - \alpha'_i, 0) \tag{1}$$

The authors called α'_i the *minimum future time* associated with LP_i. It indicates the minimum simulation time from which events not yet executed, or currently being executed, can affect LP_i.

[1]We recall that the predecessor set of an LP is determined by the communication graph defined by the LPs in a way that a directed edge exists from LP_j to LP_i if LP_j can schedule simulation events for LP_i. In particular, the predecessor set of LP_i includes any LP_k such that there exists a directed path from LP_k to LP_i in the communication graph.

The responsibility to calculate the state information α'_i and to provide it to M_1 pertains to the feedback system implementing an adequate reduction model. Implementations of reduction models can be found in [6] for the case of a shared memory architecture and in [18] for the case of a distributed memory architecture. For both ETA and the scaled version we propose, namely SETA, we have used a solution similar to the one in [18], which has been designed for the case of a distributed memory system with a high speed Myrinet switch, that is the type of architecture we have used in the performance study.

The function M_2 of ETA, which translates EP_i into delay δ_i in the execution of the next event of LP_i, is defined as follows:

$$M_2 : \; \delta_i = s \times EP_i \tag{2}$$

where s is a constant factor. The authors pointed out that s is a global static parameter whose value must be determined in an application specific manner. s is a static parameter since the adaptiveness of ETA derives primarily from the dynamic recalculation of EP. They also pointed out how an adequate value for s can be selected automatically during the simulation execution by monitoring the impact of its variation on the rate of commitment of events [16, 17].

3 Comments on the EP Translation of ETA

It is recognized that any optimistic synchronization algorithm incurs three overheads, namely state saving, rollback and memory management. When introducing optimism control in the algorithm, a fourth overhead is originated, commonly referred to as "lost opportunity". It is representative of the performance loss due to the fact that an LP suspends event execution when it is safe to proceed.

However, results in [17] demonstrate that adding any form of optimism control in the algorithm typically yields a strong reduction of the memory consumption of the LPs. As a consequence, the memory management overhead becomes a minor issue. On the other hand, the state saving overhead is not directly related to the level of optimism, but to the way state saving is performed (e.g. how frequently). Therefore, any refined optimism control mechanism should pursue the objective to minimize the function obtained by the sum of the rollback overhead and the lost opportunity overhead. We denote this function as Total Overhead function (TO). It is formally defined as:

$$TO = RO + LOO \tag{3}$$

where RO and LOO indicate rollback and lost opportunity overheads, respectively.

In ETA, optimism control is implemented in the form of delay in the execution of the next event of LP_i. The delay is asynchronous among the LPs and its value results as the output of a local decision (although based also on non-local information). In practice this approach is aimed at minimizing the total overhead function for every single event scheduled at LP_i. In other words, at the time the delay in the execution of the next event, namely e, of LP_i is computed,

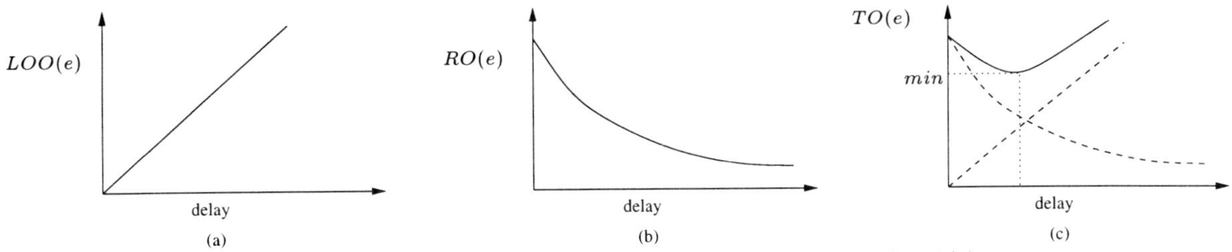

Figure 1. Typical Behaviors of $LOO(e)$, $RO(e)$ and $TO(e)$.

the objective is to minimize the total overhead associated with e, which we denote as $TO(e) = RO(e) + LOO(e)$.

For this type of optimism control, Ferscha and Luthi have proposed a model [3] in which $LOO(e)$ is actually independent of the event e and has the linear behavior shown in Figure 1.a with slope equal to one. Actually, this model holds if the blocking state originated by the delay is not opaque, i.e. if no operation, such as state saving or message probing, is allowed in the blocking state. In this case the blocking time results as pure overhead added to the completion time of the simulation. Correction factors can be introduced for the case of opaque blocking state in order to capture the real fraction of the delay which is translated into overhead. Below, we base our discussion on this model, therefore we assume $LOO(e)$ independent of the event e.

For what concerns $RO(e)$, it changes as a function of the delay in the execution of e according to the characteristic shape shown in Figure 1.b [3, 17]. Note that, differently from $LOO(e)$, $RO(e)$ is not independent of the event e. Specifically, it depends on the probability for e to be eventually rolled back (and on how this probability changes with delay in the execution) and also on the real rollback penalty associated with the undoing of e. The values of these quantities are typically different for different events as they depend on several event specific features, such as, for example, the timestamp and the granularity of the event.

The objective of an adequate delay selection is to get a balance between $RO(e)$ and $LOO(e)$ as close as possible to the best one, identified by the value min in Figure 1.c.

To understand our perspective on the translation of the EP value into delay performed by the function M_2 in (2) associated with ETA, let us consider the case of two distinct events e and e' of LP_i, and let us denote as EP_i^e (resp. $EP_i^{e'}$) the EP value associated with LP_i when e (resp. e') is the next event to be executed.

There is the possibility that:

1. $EP_i^e = EP_i^{e'}$; and

2. The two functions $RO(e)$ and $RO(e')$ follow the behavior shown in Figure 2.

Given equality in point 1, and given that the function M_2 in (2) translates the EP value into delay based on a constant factor, then ETA associates with both e and e' the same delay, namely δ^*.

On the other hand, point 2 indicates that, except for very large values of the delay, the rollback overhead function $RO(e')$ associated with e' is much larger than the rollback overhead function $RO(e)$ associated with e. This distance between the two functions is an indicator of the fact that, even though both those events are associated with the same EP value, the real rollback penalty in case of undoing of e' is larger than the real rollback penalty in case of undoing of e. This may occur, for example, because the granularity of the event e' is much larger than the granularity of the event e (therefore the undoing of e' results in much larger waste of CPU time as compared to the undoing of e) and/or because the communication overhead associated with the undoing of e' is much larger than the one associated with the undoing of e (for example because e' requires much more antimessages to be sent in case of rollback).

As a consequence, given that $LOO(e) = LOO(e')$ (due the fact that the LOO function is independent of the events), the two optimal delays associated with e and e' are α and β, respectively (see Figure 2), with $\alpha < \beta$. Note that, the larger the distance between $RO(e)$ and $RO(e')$, the larger the difference between the two optimal delays.

If the delay δ^* computed by M_2 for e and e' is close to α, then ETA actually keeps low the total overhead $TO(e)$ associated with the event e, but could be less effective in keeping low the total overhead $TO(e')$ due to e'. On the other hand, if the computed delay is close to β, then we get the converse effect.

Overall, if scaling the EP value based on a constant factor produces a delay well tailored to one of the two events, for the other event this delay could be distant from the optimal one. This problem derives from the fact that in ETA the attempt to get the best balance between rollback and lost opportunity overheads is done without taking into account the real rollback penalty associated with the execution of different events (i.e. without taking into account execution costs having an impact on the height of the rollback overhead function). Taking into account this penalty in the translation of the EP value into delay is the objective of the SETA algorithm we present in the next section.

4 Scaled ETA

The approach we have selected for tackling the problem raised in the previous section consists of a light modification of the function M_2 in (2). Specifically, we introduce an additional scaling factor in the translation process of the EP value into delay, which we call Rollback Penalty Factor (RPF). The outcoming synchronization algorithm, namely SETA, is therefore characterized by the following translation function:

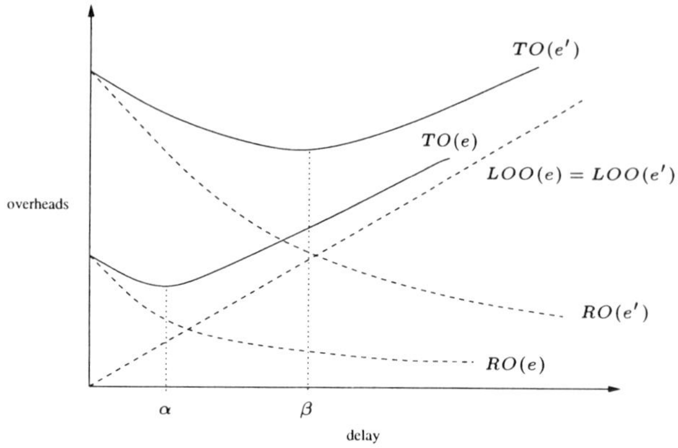

Figure 2. Optimal Delays for e and e'.

$$M_2 : \delta_i = RPF_i \times s \times EP_i \qquad (4)$$

where RPF_i (with value larger than or equal to zero) is the rollback penalty factor associated with LP_i. While EP_i is an indicator of the likelihood for the next event of LP_i to be eventually rolled back if currently executed, RPF_i is an indicator of the real rollback penalty in case of rollback of that event. Both RPF_i and EP_i are indicators of the height of the RO function associated with the next event of LP_i. In particular, the higher RPF_i and EP_i, the higher the RO function.

The presence of RPF_i allows us to associate different delays with events characterized by the same EP_i value, thus coping with previous problem. In other words, RPF_i allows fine tuning of the delay in the way to move its value closer to the optimal one whenever events with the same EP_i value are actually characterized by different rollback penalties in case they are undone.

Specifically, RPF_i should amplify the delay in case the real rollback penalty associated with any future undoing of the next event of LP_i is high. This is because, once fixed the EP_i value, the larger the real rollback penalty, the higher the RO function, thus the longer the optimal delay. On the other hand, RPF_i should shorten the delay in case the rollback penalty is low, otherwise there could be unjustifiable lost opportunity overhead associated with that event. As an extreme, the value $RPF_i = 0$ is an indicator of the fact that the rollback penalty associated with any future undoing of the next event of LP_i is null (obviously this is a non-realistic case), therefore no delay at all should be introduced.

With the help of the example in Figure 3, related to the case of a simulation model with three LPs (LP_k, LP_j and LP_i) characterized by the communication graph in Figure 3.a, we provide an intuitive explanation of the difference between ETA and SETA. In the explanation we use the same analogy used in [17] allowing an easy understanding of the real effect of these synchronization algorithms on the progress of an LP. In this analogy, optimism control is represented as an elastic band tying LP_i to the LPs belonging to $PS(LP_i) = \{LP_k, LP_j\}$. The elastic band slower the progress of LP_i anytime it attempts to run far ahead in simulation time from any of its predecessors.

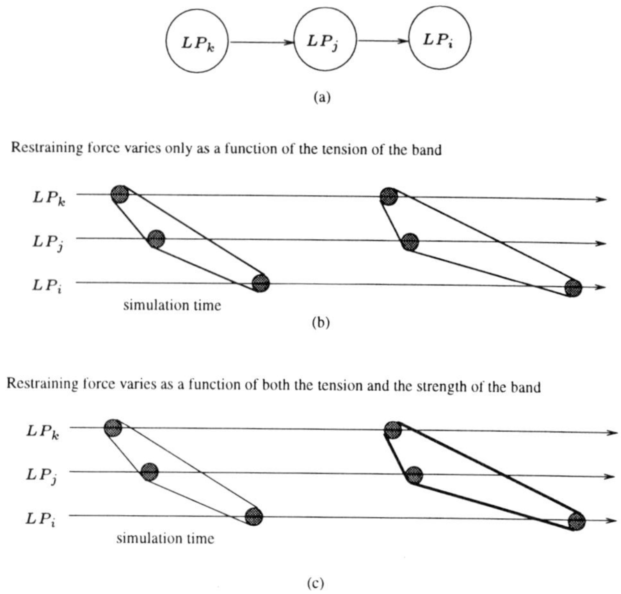

Figure 3. An Intuitive Description of the Effects of ETA and SETA.

For the case of ETA, depicted in Figure 3.b, we can think of the elastic band associated with LP_i as an elastic band whose strength is fixed. Actually the strength is determined by the value of the factor s. This interpretation derives from the fact that the restraining force on LP_i varies only as a function of the tension of the band, which corresponds to the distance in simulation time between LP_i and its predecessors (i.e. the EP_i value). In other words, to any given value of the tension (i.e. to any given value of EP_i) corresponds a specific value of the restraining force since the strength s of the elastic band does not change.

Instead, for the case of SETA, depicted in Figure 3.c, the restraining force on LP_i varies as a function of both the tension and the strength of the band since the strength, determined by the product $RPF_i \times s$, changes dynamically based on the value of RPF_i. Specifically, for any given value of the tension (i.e. of EP_i), the larger RPF_i, the higher the strength of the elastic band, thus a stronger restraining force acts on the progress of LP_i. Such a dynamical determination of the strength should provide optimism control better tailored to the requirements of the overlying application.

4.1 A Definition of RPF

As explained in the previous section, RPF_i should be an indicator of the real rollback penalty associated with any future undoing of the next event of LP_i. This penalty includes: (A) the waste of CPU time due to the event invalidation, (B) the state recovery cost and (C) the communication cost due to both antimessages and the corresponding messages (to be sent as a result of the execution of that event) that will be eventually revoked.

Although the ideal approach to define RPF_i would be to take all these contributions into account, we limit our approach in the definition of RPF_i by including only the contribution in point (A). In other words, we define an RPF_i factor which is an approximation of an ideal one since we approximate the real rollback penalty due to the invalidation of an event with the granularity of that event ([2]).

The advantage of discarding contributions in points (B) and (C) is that the final RPF_i structure results very simple, thus allowing easy calculation of this factor. Nevertheless, taking into account exclusively the event granularity should be effective in practice due to the following main reasons. Typically, parallel simulation technology is used for models with non-minimal event granularity and is usually supported by architectures with very low communication cost (examples are shared memory multiprocessors or clusters of workstations coupled with light communication layers), therefore the contribution in point (A) should be in most cases relevant as compared to the one in point (C) ([3]). Also, there exist several optimized techniques for checkpointing and state recovery [4, 12, 14, 20] allowing the state recovery overhead per event to be kept low. Therefore, discarding the contribution in point (B) while defining RPF_i, should not produce relevant inaccuracy. Furthermore, we underline that a common feature of several real world simulations is that different event types exhibit different granularities, therefore, even though fine tuning of the event execution delay is done only as a function of the event granularity, this should yield real benefits. As a further support to the relevance of "fine decisions" based just on the event granularity, a processor scheduling algorithm for optimistic synchronization, which allows performance improvement by exploiting information on the event granularity, has been recently presented in [13].

Given previous perspective on the contributions in points (A), (B) and (C), and denoting with:

G_i the granularity of the next event of LP_i;

$\bar{G}_i$ the average granularity of the events executed by LP_i;

we define RPF_i as follows:

$$RPF_i = \frac{G_i}{\bar{G}_i} \qquad (5)$$

Proportionality of RPF_i to the event granularity derives from the fact that (i) the event granularity is an indicator of the height of the RO function associated with the next event of LP_i and (ii) the higher the RO curve, the larger the optimal execution delay. The normalization factor $\bar{G}_i$ has been introduced in order to let SETA behave exactly like ETA in case all the events at LP_i have the same granularity. In other words, if there is no granularity difference at all among distinct events at LP_i, then RPF_i is always equal to one, thus fine tuning is deactivated.

[2] We are implicitly assuming that rollback is non-preemptive, therefore, when an event is rolled back, the waste of CPU time due to the event invalidation really corresponds to the event granularity. However, we remark that non-preemptive rollback is the common solution since preemption usually results too expensive to support.

[3] In addition, we recall that the communication overhead per event due to rollback can be further reduced with the help of lazy antimessage sending mechanisms [7].

As a final point, we recall that the granularity of any given event type could be either deterministic or of a stochastic nature. In the second case, a mechanism for tracking the average granularity $\bar{G}_i$ of the events executed by LP_i and for predicting the expected granularity G_i of the next event should be employed.

For what concerns the parameter s in (4), the same solution presented in [16] allowing automatic selection of the "best suited" value (i.e. the value that is likely to maximize performance) can be used.

5 Performance Analysis

This section is devoted to an empirical analysis evaluating SETA vs ETA and classical Time Warp. In the analysis we use as benchmark the PHOLD model [5] organized in a torus topology. PHOLD has been selected since, in practice, it is a standard benchmark for parallel discrete event simulation. The torus topology has been selected since it has been used in [17] to evaluate ETA vs Time Warp. The remainder of this section is organized as follows. First we describe the testing environment and provide hints on the implementation. Then we present details on the benchmark and introduce the metrics we have selected for the comparison. Finally we report the results.

5.1 Testing Environment

The experiments were all performed on a cluster of four PCs Pentium II 300 MHz (128 MB RAM) running LINUX as operating system, interconnected by a high speed Myrinet switch. Any PC is connected to the Myrinet switch through an interface implemented on a card consisting of a LANai processor, a local memory and supports for DMA. The LANai's local memory is mapped into the address space of the host PC, therefore it can be accessed directly or using DMA. The LANai processor runs a *control program* that performs send and receive operations. This program can be designed according to requirements of the specific application. Depending on the structure of the control program and of the associated message passing layer run at the host PC, messages at the receive side can be buffered into host PC memory or into the memory on board of the interface card and then transferred on demand into the host memory. We have developed a high speed layer, namely Minimal Fast Messages (MFM), allowing low delivery latency for small size messages, typical of parallel discrete event simulation, and in which the buffering at the receive side is done into the on board memory of the interface card. Therefore messages are transfered into the host memory only when a receive operation is issued by the application.

In the simulation software, memory space for new entries into the input and output queues of the LPs is allocated dynamically using classical `malloc()` calls. Therefore there is no pool of pre-allocated buffers. The same dynamical approach has been used for entries of the stack of saved state vectors. The cancellation phase is implemented following the aggressive strategy, that is antimessages are sent as soon as the LP rolls back [7].

To support the calculation of EP, we have implemented a reduction model similar to the one presented in [18], which has been specifically designed for Myrinet based clusters. In this solution, each host maintains a table whose slots record state information associated with the LPs and the implementation can be seen as consisting of two main software modules: (i) a module to disseminate state information among the hosts and to update the slots of the table and (ii) a module to calculate the minimum future time $\alpha'_i = min_{LP_k \in PS(LP_i)}(\alpha_k)$ using as input the information maintained in the local table. The main difference, as compared to our implementation, is in that the implementation in [18] relies on the FM communication layer [11] in which buffering of incoming messages is done into the host memory. In this solution the LANai processor is responsible for partitioning the incoming message stream into two distinct streams - the messages carrying state information to be manipulated by the reduction system and the messages/antimessages proper of the simulation - and the update of the slots of the local table is done through DMA. Instead, as already outlined, in MFM buffering is done into the on board memory of the interface card, therefore, in our implementation the responsibility to separate the incoming stream into the two distinct streams and to update the slots of the local table pertains to the message passing layer run at the destination host.

In our implementations of ETA and SETA, the blocking state due to the execution delay is opaque. Specifically, the LP is allowed to receive messages while in that state. Waiting is aborted in case of receipt of a message/antimessage that causes rollback.

5.2 Benchmark and Performance Metrics

The PHOLD model consists of a fixed number of LPs, organized into a given topology, and of a constant number of messages circulating among the LPs. Both the routing of messages among the LPs and the timestamp increments are taken from some stochastic distributions. In our experiments, we have selected a PHOLD model consisting of 4 LPs, each one hosted by a different machine of the cluster, organized in a torus topology. As already outlined, such a model has been used in the experimental study of ETA presented in [17]. Routing is such that any message is equally likely to be forwarded to any of the two neighbor LPs. Timestamp increments are selected from an exponential distribution with mean 5 simulation time units.

There are two distinct event types (i.e. two distinct message types), say *light* and *heavy*. Any light event has granularity of 50 microseconds and the effect of its execution is the production of a new light event. A heavy event has granularity of 200 microseconds and its execution produces a new heavy event. These granularity values have been obtained by using busy loops. We have fixed the message population at 10 messages per LP (a similar message population has been used in some experiments in [17]) and we have varied the percentage of heavy messages from 0% to 100%. In addition, we have performed experiments for both the case of deterministic event granularity and exponentially distributed event granularity. In the second case, 50 and 200 microseconds are expected granularity values and the parameter G_i in the expression of the RPF_i factor corresponds to these expected values.

Checkpointing is performed after the execution of each event. Since this application is actually stateless, checkpointing consists only of copying the simulation clock and the seeds for the random number generation.

We report measures related to the following parameters:

- The *event rate* that is, the number of committed events per second. This parameter indicates how fast is the simulation execution with a given synchronization algorithm, it is therefore representative of the achieved performance;

- The *rollback frequency* and the *average rollback length*. These parameters are indicators of how ETA and SETA modify the rollback pattern of Time Warp. In addition, these parameters indicate whether the possible performance difference between ETA and SETA derives from strong differences in the rollback pattern or not.

For each configuration of the benchmark we report the average values of previous parameters, computed over 5 runs that were all done with different seeds for the random number generation. At least 1×10^6 committed events were simulated in each run. For both ETA and SETA we report the parameter values obtained in correspondence to the "best suited" value of s, i.e. the value yielding the maximal observed event rate, namely the best final performance ([4]).

5.3 Results

The data reported in Figure 5 and in Figure 6 indicate that, regardless of the type of the event granularity (deterministic or exponentially distributed), ETA and SETA modify the rollback pattern of Time Warp (i.e. reduce both the rollback frequency and the average rollback length) practically at the same way. The final effect of this modification is that they outperform Time Warp independently of the percentage of heavy messages circulating in the system. In particular, both ETA and SETA allow higher event rate as compared to Time Warp, with gain between 11% and 18%.

From plots in Figure 4 we get that when the percentage of heavy messages is 0% or 100%, that is when there is no (expected) event granularity difference among distinct events, SETA provides the same performance of ETA. This is an expected behavior when considering that for the case of deterministic event granularity, no granularity difference among distinct events means that the RPF_i factor is always equal to 1, and for the case of exponentially distributed event granularity it means that the value of RPF_i is in narrow proximity to 1. Therefore, the function M_2 in (4) of SETA practically boils down to the function M_2 in (2) of ETA. For any other value of the percentage of heavy messages, the RPF_i factor actually changes dynamically and the two functions in (2) and in (4) perform different translations of the EP_i value into delay. In this case we note that SETA yields improvements of the event rate. On the

[4] In the experiments we have varied manually the value of s between 0 and 300 microseconds per simulation time unit, with step of 10 at each increment. For both ETA and SETA the characteristic peak in performance has been noted for values of s within that interval.

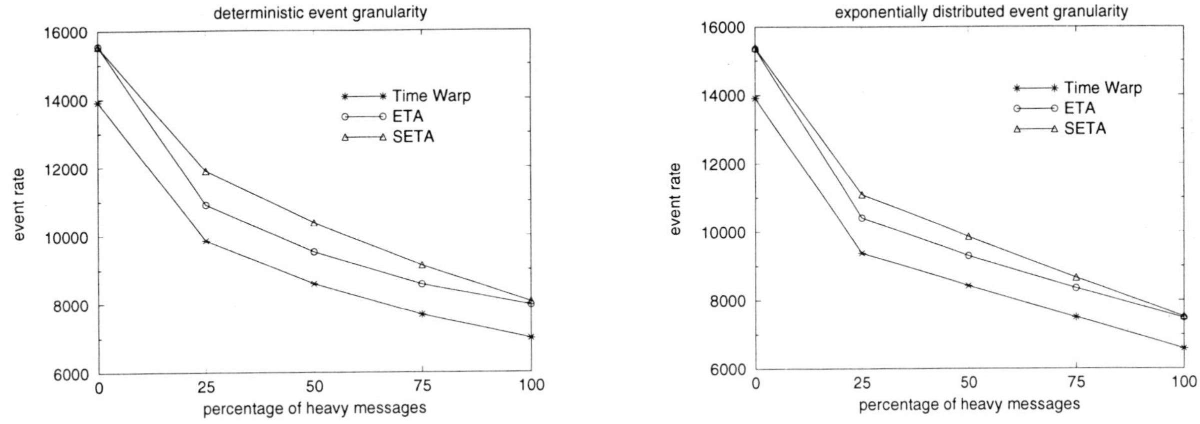

Figure 4. Event Rate vs the Percentage of Heavy Messages.

basis of the previous observation on the similarity of the rollback patterns of ETA and SETA, the improvements are supposed to derive from the fact that, at the point in which performance is maximized, SETA actually provides better balance between rollback and lost opportunity overheads, which derives from the fine tuning provided by RPF_i.

As a final point, it is important to note that the gain provided by SETA is larger in case of deterministic event granularity and tends to get lower in case of exponentially distributed event granularity. That is something we could have expected since, in case of deterministic event granularity, the parameter G_i, that defines the RPF_i factor, is a reliable indicator of the height of the RO function associated with the next event of LP_i, therefore RPF_i should actually provide effective fine tuning. In case of exponentially distributed event granularity, G_i is a reliable indicator only if the real granularity of the next event of LP_i is sufficiently close to the expected one. In the negative case, fine tuning provided by RPF_i could be less effective.

6 Summary

In this paper we have presented a synchronization algorithm with controlled optimism for parallel discrete event simulation, which is a modification of the Elastic Time Algorithm. While in the Elastic Time Algorithm event execution delay (i.e. optimism control) is determined using only temporal information (simulation clocks, non-executed event timestamps etc.), in the version we propose the delay is determined using also information on real execution costs. Specifically, in our solution the translation of temporal information into event execution delay is done by adding a scaling factor in the translation process which is based on the (expected) event granularity, hence Scaled Elastic Time.

We have presented implementations of Elastic Time and Scaled Elastic Time, as well as classical Time Warp, for a cluster of PCs connected by a Myrinet switch. An empirical analysis based on a common benchmark has shown the potential of Scaled Elastic Time to increase the execution speed of the simulation when there is difference in the (expected) granularity of different event types. This points out the practical relevance of Scaled Elastic Time since difference in the (expected) granularity is typical of several real world simulation applications.

References

[1] S. Das and R.M. Fujimoto, "An Adaptive Memory Management Protocol for Time Warp Parallel Simulation", *Proc. ACM SIGMETRICS'94*, pp.201-210, May 1994.

[2] A. Ferscha, "Probabilistic Adaptive Direct Optimism Control in Time Warp", *Proc. 9th Workshop on Parallel and Distributed Simulation (PADS'95)*, pp.120-129, June 1995.

[3] A. Ferscha and J. Luthi, "Estimating Rollback Overhead for Optimism Control in Time Warp", *Proc. 28th Annual Simulation Symposium*, pp.2-12, April 1995.

[4] J. Fleischmann and P.A. Wilsey, "Comparative Analysis of Periodic State Saving Techniques in Time Warp Simulators", *Proc. 9th Workshop on Parallel and Distributed Simulation (PADS'95)*, pp.50-58, June 1995.

[5] R.M. Fujimoto, "Performance of Time Warp Under Synthetic Workloads", *Proc. Multiconf. Distributed Simulation*, Vol.22, No.1, January 1990.

[6] R.M. Fujimoto and M. Hybinette, "Computing Global Virtual Time in Shared-Memory Multiprocessors", *ACM Transactions on Modeling and Computer Simulation*, Vol.7, No.4, 1997.

[7] A. Gafni, "Space Management and Cancellation Mechanisms for Time Warp", *Tech. Rep. TR-85-341*, University of Southern California, Los Angeles (Ca,USA).

[8] D. Jefferson, "Virtual Time", *ACM Transactions on Programming Languages and Systems*, Vol.7, No.3, 1985, pp.404-425.

[9] B. Lubachevsky, A. Weiss and A. Shwartz, "Rollback Sometimes Works ... if Filtered", *Proc. 1989 Winter Simulation Conference*, pp.630-639, December 1989.

[10] V.K. Madisetti, D.A. Hardaker and R.M. Fujimoto, "The MIMDIX environment for Parallel Simulation", *Journal of Parallel and Distributed Computing*, Vol.18, 1993, pp.473-483.

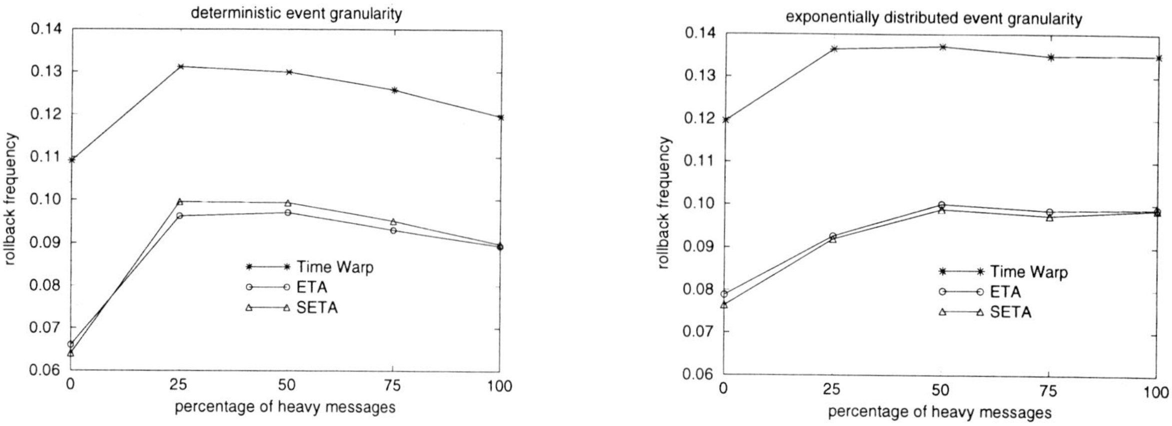

Figure 5. Rollback Frequency vs the Percentage of Heavy Messages.

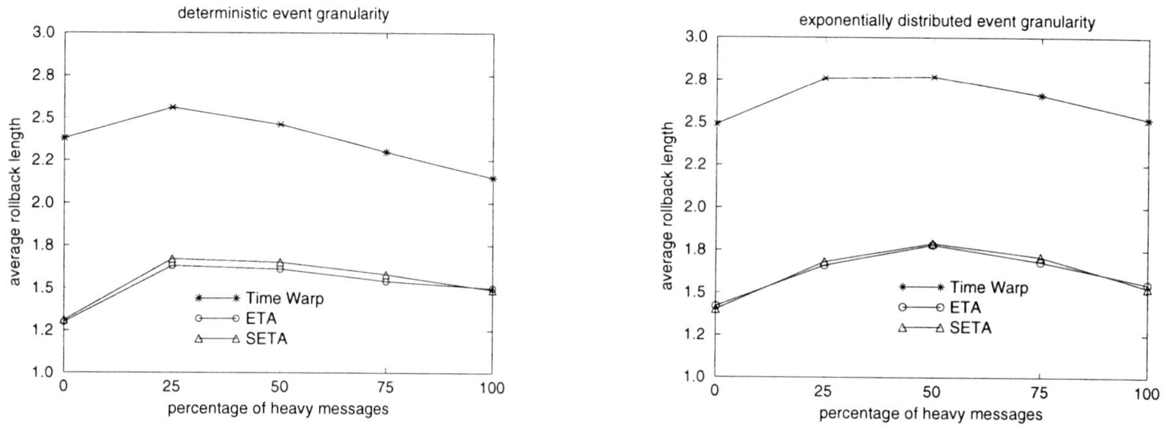

Figure 6. Average Rollback Length vs the Percentage of Heavy Messages.

[11] S. Pakin, M. Lauria and A. Chen, "High Performance Messaging on Workstations: Illinois Fast Messages (FM) for Myrinet", *Proc. Supercomputing'95*, 1995.

[12] F. Quaglia, "Combining Periodic and Probabilistic Checkpointing in Optimistic Simulation", *Proc. 13th Workshop on Parallel and Distributed Simulation (PADS'99)*, pp.109-116, May 1999.

[13] F. Quaglia and V. Cortellessa, "Grain Sensitive Event Scheduling in Time Warp Parallel Discrete Event Simulation", *Proc. 14th Workshop on Parallel and Distributed Simulation (PADS'00)*, pp.173-180, May 2000.

[14] R. Ronngren and R. Ayani, "Adaptive Checkpointing in Time Warp", *Proc. 8th Workshop on Parallel and Distributed Simulation (PADS'94)*, pp.110-117, May 1994.

[15] L.M. Sokol, D.P. Briscoe and P.A. Wieland, "MTW: a Strategy for Scheduling Discrete Events for Concurrent Execution", *Proc. SCS Multiconference on Distributed Simulation*, pp.34-42, July 1988.

[16] S. Srinivasan, "NPSI Adaptive Synchronization Algorithms for PDES", *Ph.D. Thesis*, Department of Computer Science, University of Virginia, August 1995.

[17] S. Srinivasan and P.F. Reynolds Jr., "Elastic Time", *ACM Transactions on Modeling and Computer Simulation*, Vol.8, No.2, 1998, pp.103-139.

[18] S. Srinivasan, M.J. Lyell, P.F. Reynolds Jr. and J. Wehrwein, "Implementation of Reductions in Support of PDES on a Network of Workstations", *Proc. 12th Workshop on Parallel and Distributed Simulation (PADS'98)*, pp.116-123, May 1998.

[19] J. Steinman, "Breathing Time Warp", *Proc. 7th Workshop on Parallel and Distributed Simulation (PADS'93)*, pp.109-118, May 1993.

[20] J. Steinman, "Incremental State Saving in SPEEDES Using C Plus Plus", *Proc. 1993 Winter Simulation Conference*, pp.687-696, December 1993.

[21] S.J. Turner and M.Q. Xu, "Performance Evaluation of the Bounded Time Warp Algorithm", *Proc. 6th Workshop on Parallel and Distributed Simulation (PADS'92)*, pp. 117-126, January 1992.

Causality Representation and Cancellation Mechanism in Time Warp Simulations

Malolan Chetlur and Philip A. Wilsey
Experimental Computing Laboratory
Dept. of ECECS, PO Box 210030, Cincinnati, OH 45221–0030
mal@ececs.uc.edu, philip.wilsey@uc.edu

Abstract

The Time Warp synchronization protocol allows causality errors and then recovers from them with the assistance of a cancellation mechanism. Cancellation can cause the rollback of several other simulation objects that may trigger a cascading rollback situation where the rollback cycles back to the original simulation object. These cycles of rollback can cause the simulation to enter a unstable (or thrashing) state where little real forward simulation progress is achieved. To address this problem, knowledge of causal relations between events can be used during cancellation to avoid cascading rollbacks and to initiate early recovery operations from causality errors. In this paper, we describe a logical time representation for Time Warp simulations that is used to disseminate causality information. The new timestamp representation, called Total Clocks, *has two components: (i) a* virtual time *component, and (ii) a* vector of event counters *similar to Vector clocks. The virtual time component provides a one dimensional global simulation time, and the vector of event counters records event processing rates by the simulation objects. This time representation allows us to disseminate causality information during event execution that can be used to allow early recovery during cancellation. We propose a cancellation mechanism using Total Clocks that avoids cascading rollbacks in Time Warp simulations that have FIFO communication channels.*

Keywords: *Logical Time, Vector Clocks, Virtual Time, Time Warp.*

1 Introduction

Rollback is an inherent operation in the Time Warp mechanism. Rollback restores the state of an LP to a causally consistent state from which normal event processing can continue. During cancellation, rollbacks occurring in one LP can propagate to other LPs to cancel out causally incorrect event computations. Conventionally, rollbacks are informed through anti-messages with the timestamps specifying the rollback time of the LPs. Rollbacks can occur frequently and may be cascaded and inter-related. In contemporary Time Warp simulators, time representations generally maintain only the local simulation time and do not usually carry information about causal relations between rollbacks and the associated events. However, logical time representations can be designed to carry causal information that can be exploited during rollback to accelerate the cancellation process.

Logical time can be used to order events in distributed processes [11]. Ordering events among arbitrary processes is dependent on the size (number of bits) of the logical time representation. Several representations such as scalar clocks, vector clocks, and matrix clocks have been used to represent logical time in distributed systems [16].

In this paper we present *Total Clocks* for the maintenance of time in Time Warp synchronized parallel simulations. Total Clocks can be used to determine causal relationships between events among any arbitrary processes. Two events can be concurrent or causally dependent and precise knowledge of their relation enables optimizations in various Time Warp algorithms. In particular, causal information can be useful while canceling events during rollback. In this paper, we present and prove properties of Total Clocks. We present cancellation mechanisms to avoid cascading rollbacks using the Total Clocks representation.

The remainder of this paper is organized as follows. Section 2 presents the background work in logical time representations and cancellation mechanisms in Time Warp. Section 3 presents scenarios in Time Warp simulations where causal information is useful to perform intelligent decisions. Section 4 presents the Total Clocks representation for Time Warp simulations that captures causality information between events. Section 5 presents a new cancellation mechanism exploiting the causal information disseminated by Total Clocks. Section 6 discusses implementation considerations and concluding remarks.

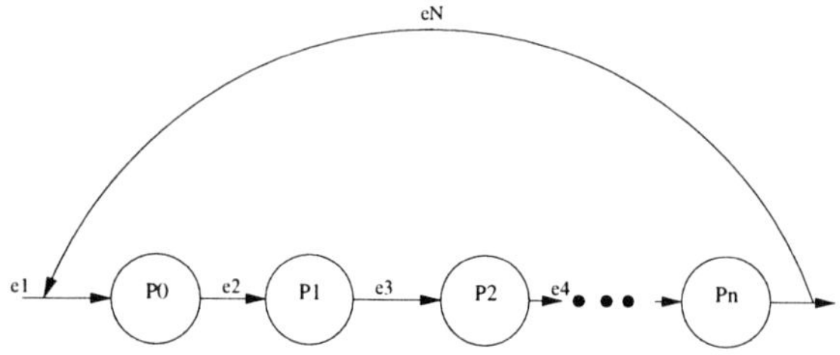

Figure 1. Cascading Event Dependency

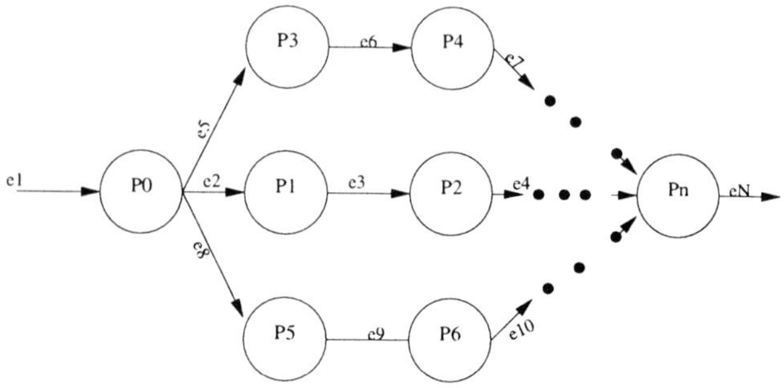

Figure 2. Inter-related Event Dependencies

2 Background and Related Work

Logical Time representation is of critical importance in distributed systems. Several logical time representations such as *Scalar Clocks* [11], *Vector Clocks* [5, 13], and *Matrix Clocks* [16] have been proposed to model time in distributed systems. In the scalar clock representation, a scalar quantity (integer) is used to represent the logical time. Each process increments the value of its local clock before executing an event and then piggybacks this value at the time of sending a message. The vector clock representation has an n-element array of non-negative integers. Each process P_i maintains this n-element array and an element at index i represents the logical time progress at P_i and other indices specify the latest known time value of other processes [1,5,13,16,19]. While vector clocks provide a mechanism to represent causality information, the vector clock representation is not readily usable in optimistic protocols due to the forward and backward motion of time. In matrix clock representation, a process maintains a $n \times n$ matrix of non-negative integers [18,21]. A process maintains this matrix as its clock value. This representation has all the properties of vector clocks. In addition, a process P_i knows the minimum time value of process P_k that is known to every other process P_j. This allows processes to discard obsolete information received from processes [16]. Matrix clocks can also be used to assist in the calculation of GVT [4].

In a Time Warp synchronized discrete event simulation, *Virtual Time* is used to model the passage of the time in the simulation [7]. The simulation is executed via several processes called Logical Processes (LPs). Each LP has an associated event queue and maintains a Local Virtual Time (LVT) clock. A causality error arises if an LP receives a message with a time-stamp earlier than its LVT value (a *straggler* message). Canceling events in the input queue of other LPs is performed by cancellation strategies such as *Aggressive*, *Lazy*, or *Dynamic* Cancellation [8, 15, 17]. However, these cancellation strategies do nothing to prevent cascading rollbacks. Several strategies have been suggested to stop the incorrect computations [3, 12, 20]. Deelman *et al* propose a Breadth First rollback mechanism to stop the propagation of erroneous computations in adjacent simulation objects on the same processor [3]. However, this does not handle the propagation of erroneous computation across processors where conventional cancellation mechanisms are employed. Madisetti [12] proposes the use of "Wolf calls" where cancellation information is sent as a high-priority broadcast or multicast to halt the erroneous computations. However, these are reactive strategies and do not avoid cascading or inter-related rollbacks.

3 Motivation

In Time Warp simulations, rollbacks recover LPs from causality errors. Rollbacks can be cascaded and inter-related. In a simulation, useful computation performed is inversely proportional to the number of events rolled-back and hence frequent rollbacks reduce efficiency and degrade performance. Optimizations in Time Warp concentrate on reducing the number of rollbacks or reducing the effect of rollbacks to improve performance [8, 15, 17].

In Time Warp, the anti-messages sent to other LPs could result in new anti-messages to the LP that sent the initial anti-messages. Such cascaded rollbacks degrade efficiency and run-time performance of the simulation. In addition to cascading rollbacks, a positive straggler event in a causally preceding LP can rollback another LP several times. These rollbacks are due to an LP sending events through several parallel paths of computation to another LP. The cause for such cascading and inter-related rollbacks is due to the fact that the events that are causally dependent on the events rolled-back are not identified at the time of a causality error. Any causal information that can specify this information can save a huge amount of computation and communication time by ignoring events that will be rolled-back eventually.

Figure 1 shows a typical scenario for the occurrence of cascading rollbacks. Event $e1$ causes the generation of event eN. Rolling back event $e1$ could trigger rolling back events $e2, e3, \ldots$ and so on and this will result in rolling back event eN. Figure 2 shows event $e1$ causing several events in parallel paths to LP Pn. Rolling back event $e1$ could

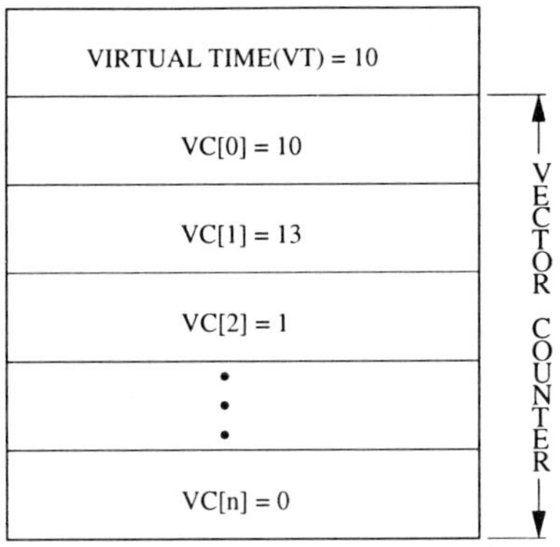

Figure 3. TOTAL CLOCK Representation

result in several rollbacks at LP Pn. In the event of LPs knowing the causal dependency between events can avoid such cascading and inter-related rollbacks. The above explained scenarios are frequent and motivates us to a logical time representation that captures causality information and exploit this information during rollbacks.

4 Total Clocks

We have seen in the previous sections that Time Warp mechanism implementing Virtual Time paradigm allows the forward and backward motion of simulation time. In contrast, a vector clock representation allows tracking causal relationship between events in a distributed system. In Time Warp simulations, a logical time representation that implements virtual time paradigm and tracks the causal relation between events will be useful for the LPs to make intelligent decisions while detecting causality errors. In this paper we present Total Clocks, a logical time representation, for Time Warp simulations which is an attempt towards this goal. Total Clocks have two components namely, virtual time component and a vector counter component. Virtual time component is the global one dimensional temporal coordinate system that ticks virtual time [10]. The virtual time component is a scalar value that denotes the progress in simulation time of the LP. The second component of Total Clocks is a vector of event counters. The number of elements in the vector is equal to the total number of LPs in the simulation. Each LP maintains a counter called *event counter* that is incremented based on specific update rules during simulation. In addition, each LP maintains a local copy of the event counter values of other LPs. This set of event counters is called the *Vector Counter(VC)*. While sending an event, an LP sends the virtual time and the vector counter as the timestamp. This two component representation of timestamp consisting of virtual time and vector counter is called Total Clocks due to the fact that this representation can provide a total ordering of events with ordering rules imposed

```
PROCESS(e) BEGIN
   TC(Pi).VT = TC(e).VT;
   TC(Pi).VC = sup(TC(Pi).VC, TC(e).VC);
   TC(Pi).VC[i]++; (this value is denoted
         by TC((Pi)after e))
   execute_event e; (update, save state;
         send events to other LPs)
END
```

Figure 4. Total Clock value update while processing an Event e in a simulation Object P_i

on the virtual time component and the vector counter component. Figure 3 shows the Total Clock and its components. The Virtual time component of Total Clock is referred as *VT* and the vector counter as *VC* in the logical time representation. $VC[i]$ refers to the ith element in the vector counter containing the event counter value of LP i. $TC(P_i)$ refers to the Total Clock value of LP P_i and $TC(e)$ refers to the Total Clock value of an event e. $TC(P_i).VT$ refers to the virtual time component and $TC(P_i).VC$ refers to the vector counter component of Total Clock.

Each LP maintains a Total Clock. An LP processes events in the order of the virtual time component of the event's Total Clock. While sending an event, the LP assigns the time at which the event has to be processed as the VT component of the timestamp. The vector counter of the LP is assigned as the VC component of the timestamp. Thus elements of the vector in the timestamp denotes last known event counter values of the sending LP. An LP i learns about the latest value of the event counter of another LP j through an event from j or from an object that has learnt about LP j. Therefore, the vector counter of an LP specifies the latest event counter values of other LPs. However, there could exist LPs and events that are causally independent of other LPs and events respectively. The causal relation and causal independence of the states of LPs and its events can be determined easily using Total Clocks. The operators($<, \leq, >, \geq, ||, sup, \longrightarrow, succ$) on the vector counter component of Total Clocks is same as the definition for vector clocks [5, 13].

The LPs executing an event must follow specific rules to update their virtual time component and the event counter values. While processing an event, virtual time component is updated to the virtual time component specified by the event e. The vector counter of clock value is updated using the *sup* operator that performs element wise maximum operation [5, 13]. Figure 4 shows the steps updating the total clock value maintained by an LP during event processing. The primitive $execute\_event$ consists of updating the state, sending events to other LPs and saving the state. The $execute\_event$ process may perform different functions depending on the optimizations and algorithms enabled in the

```
SEND(e) BEGIN
   TC(e).VT = Simulation Time at which the
              event has to be processed;
   TC(e).VC = TC(Pᵢ).VC;
   send_message e;
END
```

Figure 5. Total Clock value propagation while sending an Event e

```
RECEIVE(e) BEGIN
   CHECK_FOR_ROLLBACK(e);
   IF LP has to rollback
      THEN ROLLBACK(e) and CANCEL(e);
      ELSE INSERT(e);
END
```

Figure 6. LP receiving an event e from communication layer

kernel [14]. The value of the clock after the *sup* operation and event counter increment is denoted by $TC((P_i)_{after\ e})$. The value of LP's clock value immediately before processing event e is denoted by $TC((P_i)_{before\ e})$. Figure 5 shows the operations performed while sending an event. The virtual time component of the event is set to the simulation time at which the event has to be processed and the vector counter values is set to that of the LP. The primitive *send_message* sends the event through the physical communication layer.

Figure 6 shows the steps performed while receiving an event from the communication layer. The LP checks for rollback and rolls-back to the time before the simulation time of the event. In addition, the LP cancels the events that are to be undone due to rollback. The cancellation mechanisms such as aggressive cancellation and lazy cancellation are usually performed to cancel out the messages [17]. In the following section, we will present a new cancellation mechanism that takes advantage of the information present in the Total Clocks to cancel out events upon receiving a straggler event.

Having seen the clock update and propagation rules, certain properties could be inferred from Total Clocks. The value of the event counter of an LP increases monotonically irrespective of the progress of the simulation time. This property disambiguates between two simulation times (VT component) of same value before and after a rollback. This feature of Total Clocks can be used in optimizations and algorithms that clearly needs to disambiguate such scenarios. The events that are considered in the following theorems are the events that have been processed by an LP and not rolled-back by any cancellation message. The relations and theorems may not hold good between events that consists of one being processed and the other being rolled-back. In addition, the following theorems may not be applicable when an LP is canceling the events that it has sent before or at the time of state restoration due to a straggler event.

Theorems 4.1-4.3 are stated without proof and can be easily verified from procedure PROCESS (Figure 4).

Theorem 4.1 *Vector Counter component of Total Clock of an LP increases monotonically with event processing.*

Theorem 4.2 *If* $\longrightarrow$ *denotes causally precedes relation then* $e_1 \longrightarrow e_2 \Leftrightarrow TC(e_1).VC < TC(e_2).VC$

Theorem 4.3 *if* e_{i1} *and* e_{i2} *are events scheduled at LP* P_i *and* $e_{i1} \longrightarrow e_{i2}$ *then*

$$TC((P_i)_{after\ e_{i1}}).VC[i] \leq TC(S(e)).VC[i] < TC((P_i)_{after\ e_{i2}})$$

where $S(e) = \{e \mid e \in Succ(e_{i1}) \wedge e \notin Succ(e_{i2})\}$.

Theorem 4.4 *If* e_{i1} *is an event scheduled at LP* P_i*, then an arbitrary LP* j *can determine the states and set of events in its input queue that are causally related to event* e_{i1}.

Proof: From procedure PROCESS (Figure 4), we can see that the Total Clock value of LP P_i gets updated upon processing event e_{i1}. The states of the LP that are saved after a call to PROCESS(e_{i1}) will be at least $TC((P_i)_{after\ e_{i1}})$. From theorem 4.2, we can infer that the set of events that causally succeeds event e_{i1} has a vector counter value greater than or equal to $TC((P_i)_{after\ e_{i1}})$. Using these two properties, a LP can determine the set of states and events in its input queue that are causally related to event e_{i1}. ■

Corollary 4.1 *If* e_{i1} *and* e_{i2} *are two events scheduled in LP* P_i *and* $e_{i1} \longrightarrow e_{i2}$*, then an arbitrary LP* P_j *can determine the states and set of events in its input queue that are causally related to the events that are in the set* $Succ(e_{i1}) - Succ(e_{i2})$.

Proof: Let $S(e^k) = \{e_{ki} \mid e_{ki} \in Succ(e_{i1}) - Succ(e_{i2}) \wedge$ e_{ki} *scheduled at LP* $P_k\}$. Then applying theorem 4.4 to all the elements of $S(e^k)$, it can be seen that an arbitrary LP can determine the states and set of events in its input queue that are causally related to the events that are in the set $Succ(e_{i1}) - Succ(e_{i2})$. ■

Theorem 4.4 and corollary 4.1 forms the basis for the distributed cancellation algorithm explained in the following section.

5 Total Clocks and Event Cancellation

In the previous section we see that Total Clocks representation can capture causal dependencies between events and states. This property can be exploited in cancellation strategies. Total Clocks disseminate causality information and new cancellation mechanism can be designed to exploit this information. Cancellation messages can be designed instead of anti-messages to specify the events to be rolled-back in an LP. In addition, if the events that are causally related to the events to be rolled-back are identified, then those events can be rolled-back along with the events specified by the cancellation message. This is due to the fact that, assuming aggressive cancellation strategy, the events causally dependent on the rolled-back event will eventually be rolled-back. Doing pro-active cancellation can completely prevent cascading rollbacks. In addition, early recovery operations such as restoring state and ignoring events that will be rolled-back can be performed for rollbacks that are inter-related. Thus, knowing the causal relation between rolled-back events and other events and performing cancellation can save huge amount of computational and communication time by not spending resources on events that will be eventually undone.

In conventional Time Warp, anti-messages are used to initiate singleton cancel information. Anti-messages are similar to positive events and the distributed control is through messages and anti-messages. The cancellation mechanism presented here deviates from this paradigm. In particular, the cancellation mechanism introduces a new set of messages in the simulation called CANCEL_MESSAGE to inform LPs of causality errors in the preceding LPs. The virtual time update rules at the time of processing events are similar to that of conventional Time Warp. However, the virtual time update rules with cancellation messages are different and are performed only when the LP has not performed the recovery operations due to the causality error informed by the cancellation message. CANCEL_MESSAGE consists of a VT component and a VC component similar to that of an event. In addition, CANCEL_MESSAGE has a field called SIGNATURE. At the time of creating a new cancellation message, the VC component of the LP along with its id is used as the signature. In addition, CANCEL_MESSAGE contains the minimum and maximum event counter values called the *event counter range*. This range along with the LP id in the signature specifies the events to be removed due to rollbacks.

The new cancellation mechanism uses the event counter ranges to keep track of the events to be rolled-back. Events causally dependent on rolled-back events generated from an LP lie within the same event counter range (Corollary 4.1). The cancellation mechanism propagates the event counter range in the cancellation messages. A virtual time component is specified along with the event counter range in the cancellation message to specify the rollback time of the LP. A cancellation message could rollback an LP and hence can generate new cancellation messages and the same signature field is used to these set of cancellation messages . This

```
ROLLBACK(e) BEGIN
   restore the state of the LP to
      the state before e.TC.VT;
   restore the input queue with events
      moved from processed queue to
      unprocessed queue whose events
      are ≥ e.TC.VT;
END
```

Figure 7. LP rolling back due to an event e from communication layer

helps to identify related cancellation messages and hence inter-related rollbacks and cascading rollbacks.

Figure 7 shows the steps performed during rollback due to event e at LP P_i. Upon rollback, an LP must cancel messages to undo the events that has been sent to other LPs. This is performed in the procedure CANCEL(e) (Figure 8). Each LP maintains a data structure called *CANCEL_RANGE_LIST*. This data structure contains the list of ranges with an LP id as the index. This list is used to ignore messages whose VC component value at index i of the timestamp lies within this specified range of event counter values. The CANCEL_RANGE_LIST is built and maintained by the LP based on specific rules. Procedure *ADD_TO_CANCEL_RANGE_LIST* (Figure 9) performs the necessary rules to add the range information from CANCEL_MESSAGE(cancellation message). If a cancellation message has a signature different from other cancellation messages, then this cancellation message is added to the CANCEL_RANGE_LIST. If a new cancellation message has the same signature as that of any CANCEL_MESSAGE received previously and its VC component is concurrent to the VC component of the new cancellation message, then the new cancellation message range is added to CANCEL_RANGE_LIST. This implies that this cancellation message is due to anti-message generation in a different path of computation when compared to the cancellation messages received with the same signature. When a cancellation message received with the same signature as that of any previously received cancellation messages and its VC component is less than the cancellation messages with the same signature, then the new event counter range is added to CANCEL_RANGE_LIST. In addition, the event counter ranges with greater VC component (with same signature) that were received before are removed. This rule is to avoid rollbacks in an LP due to cascading rollbacks (since the recovery operations for the initial rollback can remove all the causally dependent events).

Procedure *CHECK_FOR_ROLLBACK* (Figure 11) performs the check to see if the LP must rollback for the cancellation message. An LP removes all the causally dependent events upon receiving a positive straggler or cancel-

```
CANCEL(e) BEGIN
   TC(P_i).VC[i]++;
   IF e is a CANCEL_MESSAGE
   THEN ADD_TO_CANCEL_RANGE_LIST(e);
   Cancel(e)={e_r | e_r has to be rolled back};
   S_cancel={i | P_i to be rolled back by e};
   Find Rollback time RollbackTime_i for
        objects in S_cancel;
   eventcounter_min = ∀ e_r, e_r ∈ Cancel(e_r),
        min(TC(e_r).VC[i]);
   eventcounter_max = TC(P_i).VC[i]
   TC(P_i).VC = sup(TC(P_i).VC, TC(e).VC);
   IF e is a CANCEL_MESSAGE
   THEN SIGNATURE = e.SIGNATURE;
   ELSE SIGNATURE = SIGNATURE(i,TC(P_i).VC);
   cancelmessage = CANCEL_MESSAGE(
      SIGNATURE,e_min, e_max, TC(P_i));
   ∀ k, k ∈ S_cancel, send_message(cancelmessage);
   ADD_TO_CANCEL_RANGE_LIST(cancelmessage);
   CANCEL_LOCAL_EVENTS(cancelmessage);
END
```

Figure 8. Canceling events due to event e

```
ADD_TO_CANCEL_RANGE_LIST(e) BEGIN
   IF e is a CANCEL_MESSAGE THEN
     IF ∀ cm, cm ∈ CANCEL_RANGE_LIST
          ((TC(e).VC || TC(cm).VC) ∧
          (SIGNATURE(e) = SIGNATURE(cm)))
       THEN add e to CANCEL_RANGE_LIST;
     IF ∃ cm, cm ∈ CANCEL_RANGE_LIST,
          TC(cm).VC > TC(e) ∧
          (SIGNATURE(e) = SIGNATURE(cm))
       THEN remove all such cm and
          add e to CANCEL_RANGE_LIST;
     IF ∀ cm, cm ∈ CANCEL_RANGE_LIST
          SIGNATURE(e) ≠ SIGNATURE(cm)
       THEN add e to CANCEL_RANGE_LIST;
     END
```

Figure 9. LP P_i checking a Cancel Message to add to Cancel Range List

```
CANCEL_LOCAL_EVENTS(e) BEGIN
   j = e.objectId;
   event_counter_min = e.event_counter_min;
   event_counter_max = e.event_counter_max;
   Remove all events in input queue
       whose timestamp is within the range
       (event_counter_min,event_counter_max)
       at index j of the vector counter;
END
```

Figure 10. LP P_i canceling events in its input queue due to CANCEL_MESSAGE e

```
CHECK_FOR_ROLLBACK(e) BEGIN
    IF e is a CANCEL_MESSAGE THEN
      IF (TC(e).VT < TC(P_i).VT) ∧
          ∀ cm ∈ CANCEL_RANGE_LIST,
          ((TC(e).VC < TC(cm).VC) ∨
          (TC(e).VC || TC(cm).VC) ∨
          (SIGNATURE(e) ≠ SIGNATURE(cm)))
      THEN Rollback is true;
      ELSE IF  (TC(e).VT < TC(P_i).VT)
           THEN Rollback is true;
   END
```

Figure 11. LP P_i checking if it has to rollback due to event e

lation message. Hence an LP checks to see if the cancellation message informs a different causality error from the one learnt by the LP. The rules to check for rollback are similar to rules in ADD_CANCEL_RANGE_LIST and in addition checks if the VT component is less than the current simulation time.

Procedure CANCEL_LOCAL_EVENT (Figure 10) cancels the events causally dependent on the rolled-back events. This is performed by checking if the events in the input queue lie within the event counter range specified by the cancellation information in the CANCEL_RANGE_LIST. Events within the rollback range specified by CANCEL_MESSAGE at the index i of the VC component of timestamp are either to be rolled-back or causally dependent on the events to be rolled-back. CANCEL_LOCAL_EVENT checks all the events in the input queue for this condition and removes them. This procedure performs recovery operation for the current cancellation message and pro-active recovery operations for the cancellation messages that will be received due to this cancellation message and therefore avoids cascading rollbacks.

Procedure CANCEL cancels the events in its local input queue and sends cancellation messages to other LPs to inform them about causality errors. A cancellation message with a new SIGNATURE is created only when an LP is rolled-back due to a positive straggler event. On the other hand, the signature of the received CANCEL_MESSAGE is used when this message sends new cancellation messages to other LPs. This is to identify cancellation messages generated due to inter-related and cascading rollbacks. Seeing the signature, an LP can ignore a cancellation message if recovery operations have been already performed. An LP determines $Cancel(e)$ that contains the set of events to be rolled-back due to event e and the set S_{cancel} that contains the LP ids to send a cancellation message. The minimum event counter value $eventcounter_{min}$ and maximum event counter value $eventcounter_{max}$ are determined from $Cancel(e)$. The rollback time, $RollbackTime_k$,

```
INSERT(e) BEGIN
  IF e is a CANCEL_MESSAGE THEN
    TC(P_i).VC[i]++;
    TC(P_i).VC = sup(TC(P_i).VC, TC(e).VC);
    ADD_TO_CANCEL_RANGE_LIST(e);
    CANCEL_LOCAL_EVENTS(e);
  ELSE IF ∀ cm ∈ CANCEL_RANGE_LIST,
     ((e.VC[cm.objectId] > cm.evencounter_max) ∨
     (e.VC[cm.objectId] < cm.evencounter_max))
  THEN insert into input queue;
END
```

Figure 12. LP P_i inserting event e

to each LP k is determined from $Cancel(e)$. The event counter value($TC(P_i).VC[i]$) of LP i is incremented initially in the procedure and the VC component's value is updated to the $sup(TC(P_i).VC, TC(e).VC)$ before sending the CANCEL_MESSAGE. Procedures ADD_TO_CANCEL_RANGE_LIST and CANCEL_LOCAL_EVENTS are called in procedure CANCEL to update the data structure having the cancellation range information and to cancel out the events in the input queue.

While inserting an event (Figure 12), the event is checked against the ranges specified in the CANCEL_RANGE_LIST and events are ignored if they lie within any one of the ranges. This is to handle events that have been in transit at the time of canceling events in the local input queue.

Theorem 5.1-5.6 prove properties of the new cancellation mechanism. $Canceled(e)$ introduced in the following theorems defines the set of events that are rolled-back due to receiving event e in LP i.

Theorem 5.1 *Given CANCEL_MESSAGE* cm_1, cm_2, $((SIGNATURE(cm_1) = SIGNATURE(cm_2)) \wedge (TC(cm_1).VC < TC(cm_2).VC)) \Rightarrow Canceled(cm_1) \supset Canceled(cm_2)$

Theorem 5.2 *Given CANCEL_MESSAGE* cm_1, cm_2, $((SIGNATURE(cm_1) = SIGNATURE(cm_2)) \wedge (TC(cm_1).VC \parallel TC(cm_2).VC)) \Rightarrow \exists\, e, e \in Canceled(cm_1) \wedge e \notin Canceled(cm_2)$

Theorem 5.3 *Given CANCEL_MESSAGE* cm_1, cm_2, $SIGNATURE(cm_1) \neq SIGNATURE(cm_2) \Rightarrow \exists\, e, e \in Canceled(cm_2) \wedge e \notin Canceled(cm_1)$

Theorem 5.4 *Procedure CANCEL_LOCAL_EVENTS removes the events from input queue of an LP for all CANCEL_MESSAGE and event stragglers that have been received.*

Theorem 5.5 *Procedure INSERT inserts only events that are not causally dependent on events that have been canceled.*

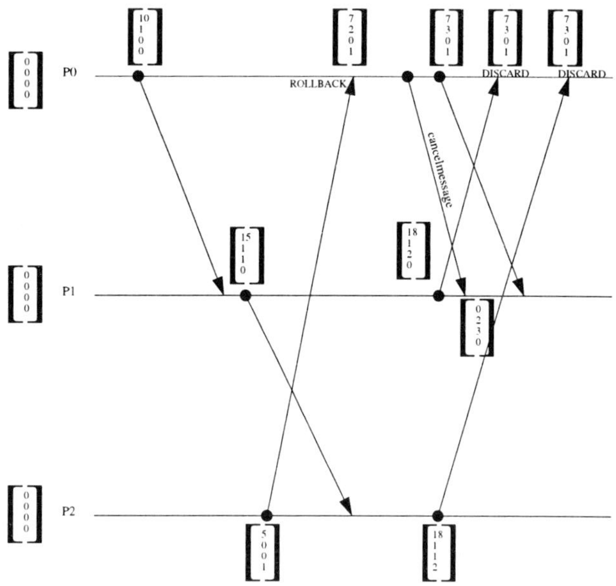

Figure 13. Space Time diagram explaining Total Clock update and Cancellation

Theorem 5.6 *Procedure CANCEL at LP P_i generates cancellation messages that cancel only the events that are causally dependent on the events canceled during the call to CANCEL(e).*

We can see that the cancellation mechanism is efficient in removing all the events in the input queue that are to be undone either directly or indirectly due to a rollback in causally preceding LP. Figure 13 shows the update of the Total Clock value in the processes and the cancellation mechanism through a space time diagram. The timestamp consist of a VT component followed by 3-element vector counter for three object simulation. Upon receiving a straggler from process $P2$, process $P0$ sends a cancellation message to $P1$ and discards the events from other objects that are causally dependent on the rolled-back events. This saves huge amount of computational resources that would have been spent on processing those events. In addition, the constant vigil on the events that are inserted to the input queue removes any extra overhead incurred on the messages that will be rolled-back eventually. LPs in the critical path are frequently rolled-back and they are exposed to cascading rollbacks. The huge amount of time spent in such uncommitted computations can be avoided by employing the cancellation mechanism with Total Clocks.

6 Conclusion

Total Clock representation is suitable for models that spend most of their time in recovering from rollbacks. Total Clocks representation is also useful in taking decisions among LPs in the critical path of the simulation that are exposed to frequent rollbacks. Total Clocks inherit all the pros and cons of vector clocks in addition to the applicability in the field of Time Warp simulation. Several researchers have found efficient and practical implementations of vector clocks [6, 9, 19]. Studies performed by Chetlur *et al* [2], found that the overhead in the communication caused by the size of the message is not that significant compared to the frequency of calls to the communication subsystem. The overhead of communication for messages within a range of message sizes remains the same. With optimizations that propagate only changes to values of the vector counters, the message sizes can be kept within the same range as that of messages without Total Clocks representation.

The Cancel Range list maintained by the LP to ignore/accept the incoming events may grow larger if they are not pruned frequently. A simulation time can be attached to the CANCEL_MESSAGE that specifies the time up to which the event counter range check has to be performed. This time can be the maximum of the VT component of rolled-back events. Cancel range information could be removed from the CANCEL_RANGE_LIST once GVT sweeps past this VT value.

In this paper, we have shown the representation of causal information using Total Clocks and the utility of such a representation in cancellation mechanism. We presented a cancellation mechanism that exploits Total Clocks representation. The cancellation mechanism described reduces to sending a message to all its output channels about the rollback of its predecessors and can cancel events received from its predecessors that could also be rolled back. This cancellation mechanism avoids cascading and inter-related rollbacks. Further exploration is done to exploit the Total Clocks representation in Time Warp algorithms such as State Savings and other synchronization mechanisms.

References

[1] B. Charron-Bost. Concerning the size of logical clocks in distributed systems. *Information Processing Letters*, 39(1):11–16, July 1991.

[2] M. Chetlur, N. Abu-Ghazaleh, R. Radhakrishnan, and P. A. Wilsey. Optimizing communication in Time-Warp simulators. In *12th Workshop on Parallel and Distributed Simulation*, pages 64–71. Society for Computer Simulation, May 1998.

[3] E. Deelman and B. K. Szymanski. Breadth-first rollback in spatially explicit simulations. In *Proc. of the 11th Workshop on Parallel and Distributed Simulation (PADS 97)*, pages 124–131. Society for Computer Simulation, June 1997.

[4] E. Deelman and B. K. Szymanski. System knowledge acquisition in parallel discrete event simulation. In *IEEE International Conference IN SYSTEMS, MAN and CYBERNETICS*, pages 2296–2301. COMPUTATIONAL CYBERNETICS AND SIMULATION, 1997.

[5] C. Fidge. Logical time in distributed systems. *Computer*, 24:28–33, 1991.

[6] J. Fowler and W. Zwaenpoel. Causal distributed breakpoints. In *Proceedings of 10th International Conference on Distributed Computing Systems*, pages 134–141, 1990.

[7] R. Fujimoto. Parallel discrete event simulation. *Communications of the ACM*, 33(10):30–53, Oct. 1990.

[8] A. Gafni. Rollback mechanisms for optimistic distributed simulation systems. In *Distributed Simulation*, pages 46–53. Society for Computer Simulation, Jan. 1988.

[9] C. Jard and G.-C. Jourdan. Dependency tracking and filtering in distributed computations. In *Brief Announcements ACM Symposium on Principles of Distributed Computing*, pages 134–141. ACM Press, New York, 1994.

[10] D. Jefferson. Virtual time. *ACM Transactions on Programming Languages and Systems*, 7(3):405–425, July 1985.

[11] L. Lamport. Time, clocks, and the ordering of events in a distributed system. *Communications of ACM*, 21(7):558–565, July 1978.

[12] V. Madisetti, J. Walrand, and D. Messerschmitt. Wolf: A rollback algorithm for optimistic distributed simulation systems. In *Winter Simulation Conference*, pages 296–305. Society for Computer Simulation, Dec. 1988.

[13] F. Mattern. Virtual time and global states of distributed systems. In *Proceedings of Parallel and Distributed Algorithms Conference*, pages 215–226, 1988.

[14] R. Radhakrishnan, T. J. McBrayer, K. Subramani, M. Chetlur, V. Balakrishnan, and P. A. Wilsey. A comparative analysis of various Time Warp algorithms implemented in the WARPED simulation kernel. In *Proceedings of the 29th Annual Simulation Symposium*, pages 107–116, Mar. 1996.

[15] R. Rajan, R. Radhakrishnan, and P. A. Wilsey. Dynamic cancellation: Selecting Time Warp cancellation strategies at runtime. *VLSI Design*, 9(3):237–251, 1999.

[16] M. Raynal and M. Singhal. Logical time: Capturing causality in distributed systems. *IEEE Computer*, pages 49–56, Feb. 1996.

[17] P. L. Reiher, R. M. Fujimoto, S. Bellenot, and D. Jefferson. Cancellation strategies in optimistic execution systems. In *Proceedings of the SCS Multiconference on Distributed Simulation*, volume 22, pages 112–121. Society for Computer Simulation, Jan. 1990.

[18] S. Sarin and L. Lynch. Discarding obsolete information in a replicated database system. *IEEE Transactions on Software Engg.*, SE(13.1):39–46, Jan. 1987.

[19] M. Singhal and A. Kshemkalyani. An efficient implementation of vector clocks. *Information Processing Letters*, 43(1):47–52, Aug. 1992.

[20] S. Srinivasan and P. F. Reynolds Jr. Elastic time. *ACM Transactions on Modeling and Computer Simulation*, 8(2):103–139, Apr. 1998.

[21] G. Wuu and A.J.Bernstein. Efficient solutions to the replicated log and dictionary problems. In *Proceedings of 3rd ACM Symposium on Principles of Distributed Computing(PODC)*, pages 233–242. ACM Press, 1984.

Optimistic Simulation of Parallel Message-Passing Applications

Thomas Phan and Rajive Bagrodia

The University of California at Los Angeles
Computer Science Department
Los Angeles, CA 90095
{phantom,rajive}@cs.ucla.edu
http://pcl.cs.ucla.edu

Abstract

Optimistic techniques can improve the performance of discrete-event simulations, but one area where optimistic simulators have been unable to show performance improvement is in the simulation of parallel programs. Unfortunately, parallel program simulation using direct execution is difficult: the use of direct execution implies that the memory and computation requirements of the simulator are at least as large as that of the target application, which restricts the target systems and application problem sizes that can be studied. Memory usage is especially important for optimistic simulators due to the need for periodic state-saving and rollback. In our research we addressed this problem and have implemented a simulation library running a Time-Warp-based optimistic engine that uses direct execution to simulate and predict the performance of parallel MPI programs while attaining good simulation speedup. For programs with data sets too large to be directly executed with our optimistic simulator, we reduced the memory and computational needs of these programs by utilizing a static task graph and code-slicing methodology, an approach which also exhibited good performance speedup.

1 Introduction

Optimistic execution is a well-known approach used to improve the performance of many discrete-event simulations. Indeed, simulation engines implementing optimistic techniques such as Time-Warp have been shown to achieve large degrees of speedup over conservative execution. However, one area of investigation where research efforts have failed to demonstrate the utility of optimistic techniques is in the simulation of parallel programs. This inability to attain significant speedup is due to the nature of most nontrivial parallel applications. The programs we studied are from the scientific community, written to take gratuitous advantage of memory capacity and computational horsepower, two traits which fail to aid most optimistic simulators due to the need for periodic state-saving and rollbacks.

Simulation can greatly aid the development and use of a parallel application by using techniques that can evaluate the behaviour of the application under varying architectural, network, and operating system conditions. System simulation can provide insight into the scalability of a parallel program, analyze the effects of variable workloads, assess processor and network hardware requirements, locate bottlenecks in software, and investigate the effectiveness of inter-process communication patterns. When properly used, these techniques can help designers and users evaluate code for architectures and networks that are as yet unavailable.

However, parallel programs are inherently difficult to simulate, especially for optimistically-executing simulators. In the case of direct-execution program simulation, the physical system to be simulated and its representative model are closely related: the physical system is already a program that can be executed on the simulation engine with some modification. Although direct execution of sequential code is typically faster than its simulation, for applications that are designed to execute on large-scale target architectures operating on large data sets, the mismatch between intended system conditions and simulator capability makes parallel program simulation difficult and can be a significant bottleneck. The use of direct execution in the simulator implies that the memory and computation requirements of the simulator are at least as large as that of the target application, which restricts the target systems and application problem sizes that can be studied even using parallel simulators.

Previous work by other researchers [10] [11] have tried to use abstract models of the sequential code fragments that make the model essentially independent of program control flow. An alternative approach is to use a compiler-synthesized static task graph model for sequential code fragments [1]. This model is an abstract representation that clearly identifies the sequential computations (tasks), the parallel structure of the program (task scheduling, precedences, and explicit communication), and the control-flow that determines the parallel structure. In order to ensure that control flow is not ignored, a methodology called program slicing [13] is used which isolates and abstracts away portions of sequential non-message-passing code that affect the parallel structure of the program. The execution times of the abstracted sequential tasks are approximated during the course of the simulation by using symbolic expressions. Incorporation of these techniques in direct execution simulators has been shown to dramatically improve their execution

0-7695-1104-X/01 $10.00 © 2001 IEEE

time while still providing good accuracy.

In this paper we make the following contribution to the field of discrete-event simulation: we have implemented a simulation library running a Time-Warp-like optimistic engine that uses direct execution to simulate and predict the performance of parallel MPI programs while attaining good simulation speedup. For applications whose data sets were too large to be directly executed with our optimistic simulator, we reduced the memory and computational needs of these programs by utilizing the static task graph model methodology, an approach which also exhibited good performance speedup. To the best of our knowledge, this is the first successful use of optimistic techniques in improving the execution time of parallel program simulations.

In our research we simulated two large scientific parallel programs, ASCII Sweep3D and NAS SP. Using a standard direct-execution methodology and our optimistic simulator, the Sweep3D simulation time was reduced by 68% with eight processors running a 25x25x25 problem size but failed to execute at all with a problem size of 100x100x100 due to memory constraints. In a similar vein, the simulation of SP ran 11.0% faster with eight processors while executing the smallest possible dataset but could not run the next largest data configuration. In order to minimise the memory and computational needs of these parallel programs, we used the static task graph model and program-slicing technique to allow the optimistic simulator to achieve speedup. Using this combination allowed us to run simulations of the large datasets that otherwise we would not even have been able to execute at all. As an additional benefit, with this technique we obtained a performance increase over the simple direct-execution technique of up to 28% for Sweep3D and up to 70% for SP for the small configurations.

Our simulation library is called the Component-based Parallel System Simulator (COMPASS). COMPASS is written in the PARSEC programming language [2], executes an optimistic runtime system based on Time Warp, provides a programming interface of core MPI function calls, and is portable across a variety of platforms.

The rest of this paper is organised thusly: In §2 we discuss related work and background information, followed by an overview of COMPASS in §3 and a description of our experimental benchmarks in §4. We offer results in §5 and conclude this paper in §6.

2 Related Work

A number of techniques have been used to improve performance of parallel simulations, particularly with conservative algorithms, such as: (1) improving the lookahead in each process by computing precise bounds on the execution time of sequential program fragments between consecutive communication statements [8] or by recognizing deterministic communication statements in data parallel [20] or task parallel programs [21] and (2) exploiting the communication topology to reduce number of neighbours of each process and hence the number of null messages [15]. Other research in the field of parallel simulation for performance prediction include [7], [22], and [23].

Direct execution was shown in [6] as a means to avoid instruction-level simulation by executing portions of code directly on the architecture being studied. The application is compiled for the instruction set architecture of the machine, but the simulator traps all calls that interact with the simulated component.

Research in optimistic simulation [12] of *shared memory* was performed in [5]. This work looked into a direct-execution simulation implemented using incremental state-saving for both an aggressive Time Warp-like mechanism as well as a combination of a conservative and a Breathing Time Buckets-based optimistic engine. For both cases their experiments ended in negative results: a purely conservative simulation ran faster than either optimistic implementations. In the case of the Time-Warp-like technique, the authors noted that this mechanism reduced the frequency of needed synchronizations between processes. However, the cost was a higher likelihood of incorrectly simulated events once processes moved past the global virtual time. A resulting increase of anti-message traffic would flood the system, up to 66%. Computation-bound applications had less synchronization to perform but had a tendency to re-perform operations upon roll-back, with up to a 300% increase in time spent re-executing in one application. These high overheads resulted in performance up to 2.5 times slower than a conservative approach, making their use of optimistic techniques prohibitively expensive.

In previous work, researchers have shown that identification of deterministic communication statements in simulation models of parallel programs [20] [21] can be effective in improving their execution time. In this work a portable, multithreading simulator called MPI-SIM was developed to provide direct-execution simulation of MPI [17] programs. In recent work [1] researchers have shown that compiler synthesized static task graphs can further improve performance of both sequential and parallel simulation of parallel programs that include deterministic communication statements, by dramatically reducing the time to estimate the execution time of sequential code fragments in a program.

In this paper we demonstrate that optimistic techniques can in fact be used to improve the simulation time of message passing MPI parallel programs. For programs whose large memory requirements adversely affect the performance of the simulator, we can take advantage of the memory-reduction techniques of the preceding compiler synthesized task graph models.

3 COMPASS Overview

Our Component-based Parallel System Simulator, COMPASS v2.0, is written using the PARSEC programming language [2]. The PARSEC runtime system provides the underlying simulation, message-passing, and multithreading facilities, while the COMPASS library publishes an MPI-like interface that can be called by the simulated MPI program.

3.1 The PARSEC Parallel Simulation Language

PARSEC is a parallel simulation language based on C. Adding language constructs and keywords to facilitate the modeling of simulated events, PARSEC provides a message-passing API, built-in message queueing and handling, and multiple threads of execution (termed entities). For discrete-event simulation, it can execute a variety of conservative protocols, including null-message, conditional-event, accelerated null-message, and Ideal Simulation Protocol, as well as a Time Warp-based optimistic protocol that implements state-saving and rollback. PARSEC has been successfully ported to a number of operating systems, including Sun Solaris, SGI IRIX, IBM AIX, and Windows NT, that support multiple processors. Since COMPASS is written using PARSEC, it can be easily ported to the preceding platforms.

3.2 The COMPASS MPI Simulation Package

COMPASS publishes an application programming interface of 24 core MPI 1.1 function calls. The simulator can be precompiled into a library archive and interposed between the standard MPI library and a program using MPI. The confluent operation of direct-execution and discrete-event simulation works as follows. The program being simulated directly executes all code except for MPI calls which are intercepted by our COMPASS library and simulated. The message-passing semantics are retained, but the time to send and to receive the messages are estimated as a function of message size based upon previous measurements of message latencies on the same architecture. Collective communication calls are implemented using point-to-point messages sent in a distribution pattern following vendor-provided specifics. When the simulated MPI function returns, the direct-execution of the program continues again.

Each MPI process is implemented as a PARSEC entity, and hence the application program must be transformed in minor ways to support its simulation by COMPASS. Since PARSEC is a superset of C, the simulated program must itself be written in C. We have found that Fortran-77 code can be translated to C using the f2c conversion program with minor corrections. Indeed, the F77 benchmarks we have used in our experiments were integrated with COMPASS using f2c as an intermediate step. Additionally, since PARSEC implements lightweight user-level threads, variables in the global namespace must be protected from inter-thread interference by instantiating them in the local namespace of each PARSEC simulation entity.

3.3 The Optimistic Runtime System

As optimistic simulation is a key issue in this research work, we now discuss issues related specifically with the optimistic runtime system [16]. Our implementation uses a state-saving and rollback mechanism based on Time Warp [12]. The primary overheads associated with this operation are the need to save the state at periodic intervals and the rolling back to a prior saved state if a straggler message is encountered during the course of the simulation.

As is well-known in the literature, there are two primary tunable parameters that affect the performance of an optimistic runtime system. The first is the frequency of the state-saving. Saving the state less often will certainly reduce the time needed to complete the simulation, but this reduction comes at the cost of having to roll back further in the past to find a consistent state from which to restore. The default state-saving interval is at every simulation event, but as is well-known, increasing the interval by a small amount can improve performance without invoking the offsetting overhead of farther rollbacks. Figure 1 shows the results of this adjustment for an application called Sweep3D that we shall describe in detail in 4. The graph displays the execution of two versions of this program, which is not of importance in the context of the current discussion. However, what is important is that the graph shows that gradually increasing the interval improves performance, but at some point the beneficial returns diminish as the running time increases again for each curve due to the longer rollback and coast forward distances. From the graphs, it appears that intervals past 5 events serve only to decrease performance; the state-saving interval for the experiments was chosen accordingly.

The second performance-improving artifice is adjusting the number of events to process optimistically past the last global virtual time (GVT) value. This parameter is called the event throttle window, and it will stop the simulator from proceeding too far ahead and utilizing memory. The default is an infinite window.

Our Time Warp-based optimistic runtime system has as its primary overhead the state-saving of memory allocated to the simulation entities. This necessary procedure detrimentally affects the execution of the simulator in two ways: (1) the running time of the simulation itself increases since the state-saving occurs periodically during the course of the execution, and more significantly (2) the direct-execution time is increased, thereby giving an inaccurate measurement

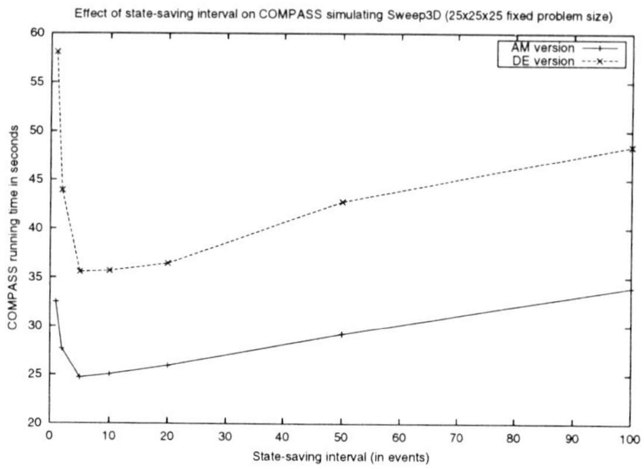

Figure 1: Running time of COMPASS as a function of state-saving interval.

of local code blocks, due to adverse effects on the cache and virtual memory.

We can assuage these problems through three complementary methods: (1) We can tune the frequency of the state-saving through the optimistic runtime system's API so that fewer state-savings are performed, as was shown. (2) Another approach is the use of incremental state-saving [24], which requires the runtime system to maintain a log of only the state changes rather than the whole state. A well-known disadvantage to this is that upon roll-back, the current state must be reconstructed from previous logs entries, a detrimental effect that was experimentally observed in [5]. Furthermore, this approach may not work for scientific programs because the large amounts of memory required by their datasets may already be prohibitively large. A third alternative is that (3) we can use a compiler-assisted optimization wherein large portions of code and memory are excised without affect program semantics; we discuss this approach in the next section.

3.4 Model Optimizations

As we shall show later in our results in section 5, our optimistic runtime system effectively executes our parallel benchmarks using the direct execution technique. For a number of programs, we show the simulation engine provides performance speedup for an increasing number of host processors. However, for some configurations of the benchmarks, the memory requirements became prohibitively large: the optimistic simulation engine failed to execute at all for two scientific programs running particularly large datasets. In these cases, we had to resort to using a memory reduction technique we shall now detail.

Using static task graph analysis [1], a compiler automatically analyzes a parallel program to derive an abstract representation, termed a static task graph, that pinpoints portions of sequential, parallel, and control-flow code. From this information it can be decided which segments of code can be excised so that an equivalent valid program can be produced and made ready to be run by the simulator. These segments to be removed are first instrumented and executed to produce empirical running times. During the simulation, these segments are *not* executed again, but their pre-measured running times contribute to the predicted times produced by the simulator. Specifically, these segments of code are replaced by a COMPASS function call that allows the simulation clock to be incremented by the equivalent amount of time that the directly-executed code would have taken.

As a primary benefit, all data structures associated with these code portions are removed as well. It was shown that these optimizations resulted in a factor of 5 to 2000 less memory, thereby allowing our optimistic engine to execute the benchmarks with problems sizes that otherwise would not have run.

As a secondary benefit, the memory-reduction technique improves the optimistic simulation performance. For the applications we studied, the compiler reduced the amount of memory state that needed to be checkpointed. With this reduction in overhead, we anticipated a faster execution time for our simulations.

Two versions of the simulation models for each of the studied applications were generated: the first version, termed **DE** for Direct Execution, retained all the computational code which was simulated using direct execution, and the second version, termed **AM** for Analytical Model, was processed by our compiler tool to replace some of the computational fragments by the analytical model.

Throughout our experiments we leveraged key characteristics, shown in [1], of the code-slicing technique and its resultant AM version of the code. Code-slicing removes only the sequential portions of the original code, leaving behind the parallel and control-flow segments. This procedure does not affect the semantics of the program logic. Additionally, the simulator has been validated and, even when utilizing the compiler optimizations using the AM version, can predict the running time of both the Sweep3D and SP programs to within 7% accuracy on a varying number of processors and benchmark configurations.

4 Benchmarks

We performed our experiments on our SGI Origin 2000 computer at UCLA. The Origin is a distributed shared memory multiprocessor that provides cache-coherent NUMA behaviour for programs [14]. This Origin contains 10 180 MHz processors with 1280 Mb of main memory, a 32 kb instruction cache, a 32 kb data cache, and a unified 1 Mb secondary cache.

The benchmarks used for the study included two real-world scientific programs. Sweep3D [25] is an application that is part of the Accelerated Strategic Computing Initiative project administered by the Lawrence Livermore, Los Alamos, and Sandia National Labouratories. We can control the problem size and the memory consumed by Sweep by directly adjusting the parameters regulating the three dimensions. Sweep3D was originally written using Fortran and MPI; the Fortran code was converted into C using the f2c translator.

We additionally studied the SP program from the NAS Parallel Benchmark 2.2 suite [4] [18]. The NAS benchmarks are available from the Numerical Aerodynamic Simulation research group at NASA. The SP program in particular computes solutions to system of discretised Navier-Stokes equations and can be configured to a varying number of problem sizes and processors. Like Sweep3D, SP was translated from Fortran to C.

5 Results and Discussion

For our two benchmarks, we simulated the programs initially with small datasets to reveal the effectiveness of the optimistic simulator. Indeed, for Sweep3D and NAS SP, the optimistic direct-execution simulation showed good speedup over an increasing number of processors. However, for large problem sizes, the memory consumption was too much for the simulator, preventing the simulation from running at all. At that point, we utilised the memory-reduction technique using static graph analysis to allow our simulator to run.

5.1 Experiments with Sweep3D

In this section we present the results from our use of Sweep3D, our primary application of study from our benchmark suite. In previous work [20] [21], the authors identified a class of scientific applications whose simulation could benefit from the following strategy: for code fragments that included deterministic receive statements, it was possible to eliminate use of the simulation protocol and thus improve performance of the parallel model. In this paper, we wanted to consider a program where such an optimization may not be applicable either because the communication statements are non-deterministic or because the determinism cannot be recognised by the compiler. To that end, in the Sweep3D benchmark we changed the message receive statements without loss of semantics to be non-deterministic by specifically modifying the MPI_Recv statements. As one of its arguments, this function call typically specifies an integer representing the rank, or identification number, of the sender. By changing this rank value to instead be the constant MPI_ANY_TAG, we induce non-determinism by allowing the process to receive from any rank. We posit that the optimistic approach will be of benefit in this situation.

5.1.1 Analysis Using a 25x25x25 Fixed Problem Size, DE only

We show that for a particular problem size, the optimistic simulation engine shows good performance scalability while directly executing Sweep3D. Consider the graph in Figure 2 which shows the running time of the simulation of the Sweep3D program running a problem size of 25x25x25 with 8 and 32 target processors. The graph shows that the direct execution (DE) of Sweep3D at this problem size benefits greatly from more host processors: the simulation time decreases with an increasing number of hosts.

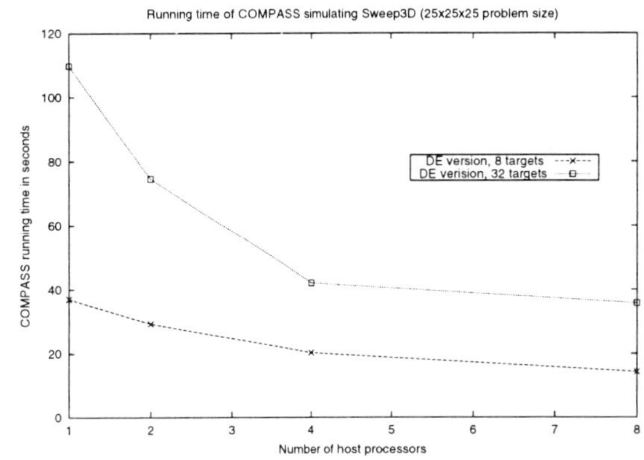

Figure 2: Running time of COMPASS simulating the Sweep3D program with a 25x25x25 problem size.

Comparing the relative performance of the 8 and 32 target processor models, we see a trend. Since the total problem size remains the same, increasing the number of target processors reduces the computation granularity of each thread. For the simulator, this situation also increases the level of multithreading per host processor. These reasons cause the execution time of the simulation model to increase when going from 8 to 32 targets, as seen in the figure. A potential advantage of using 32 threads is that it is possible to exploit additional parallelism in the host architecture by adding more hosts. As seen from the graph, the performance for both the 8 and 32 target processor models improves as we increase the number of hosts from 1 up to 8.

5.1.2 Analysis Using a 100x100x100 Fixed Problem Size

We now consider the case where the problem size of Sweep3D program is increased to a grid size of 100x100x100. At this size the DE version was unable to execute at all on our Origin 2000 with 1280 MB main memory due to memory constraints! To handle this problem, we resort to using the memory reduction approach described earlier. Since the optimizations of the AM version were able to remove the data structures associated with the excised code, the resulting memory requirement of this version was low enough to allow it to be run. The execution time of the AM version at this problem size for 8 and 32 target processors is shown in Figure 3. This graph shows that an increase in host processors from 1 to 8 results in an execution time speedup of 2.45 for the 8 target model and 4.23 for the 32 target model.

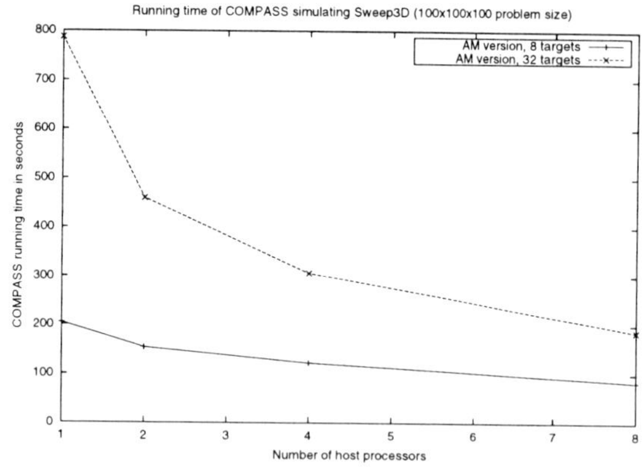

Figure 3: Running time of COMPASS simulating the Sweep3D program with a 100x100x100 problem size and 32 target processors.

5.1.3 Analysis Using a 25x25x25 Fixed Problem Size, AM and DE

For completeness, we now show the *secondary* benefit of using the memory reduction technique. The AM version of the code allows us to not only optimistically execute very large problem sizes (that we could otherwise not have been able to execute) but also to reduce the running time of the simulations themselves. In Figure 4 we show the simulation time of the Sweep3D program for a 25x25x25 problem size with 8 and 32 targets. This graph is similar to Figure 2, but now both the AM and DE versions are displayed.

The graph illustrates that first, the AM version outperforms the DE version for a given number of target processors, which is in accordance with our expectations since the AM version has less computation to execute and less memory to occupy. Second, we observe that the DE model benefits much more from parallelism than the AM model: for the 8 target processor model, execution time of DE version is reduced by a factor of nearly 4 with 8 host nodes; the corresponding improvement in the execution time of AM version is about 2.7. Once again this is due to the larger computation granularity and state size of the DE version. This hypothesis is confirmed by the rollback counts collected for the various configurations. For instance, Table 1 presents the average number of rollbacks/entity for the configuration

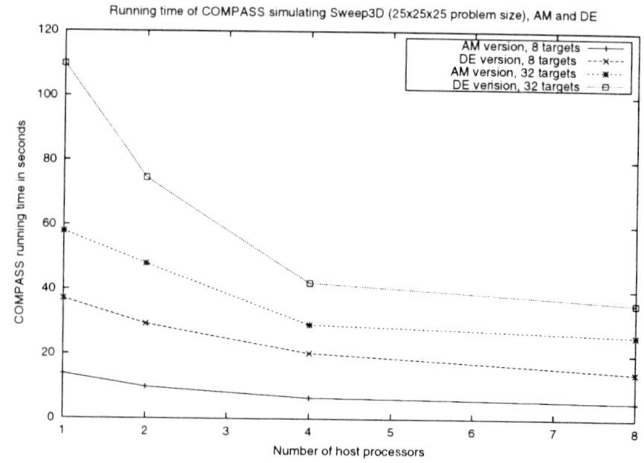

Figure 4: Running time of COMPASS simulating the Sweep3D program with a 25x25x25 problem size and both AM and DE versions.

with 32 target processors for the DE and AM versions. The table shows that first, the total number of rollbacks in both the DE and AM implementations are relatively few; second, the DE version actually has more rollbacks than AM for a given number of hosts, so clearly a reduction in rollbacks does not account for the better relative speedup for DE.

AM Version			DE Version		
Hosts	Rollbacks	Distance	Hosts	Rollbacks	Distance
1	0	0	1	0	0
2	12.60	1.01	2	14.33	1.00
4	14.58	1.44	4	16.04	1.49
8	25.03	2.26	8	41.42	1.58

Table 1: Average number of rollbacks and average rollback distances in a 32-target experiment with a 25x25x25 problem size.

As was similarly noted in section 5.1.1, the simulation times differ between the 8 and the 32 target processor models. Note that for the DE version's 32 target model, we attained a speedup of 3.07 with 8 hosts as opposed to the 8 target model's speedup of 2.58. The relative speedup with the AM version, on the other hand, are much lower. The 32 target model has a speedup of 2.25, while the 8 target model has a speedup of 2.66. In this version, the benefit of increased parallelism that 32 targets should provide is negated due to the fact that the problem size is small and that much computation has already been removed in the AM version.

Interestingly, this insignificant difference in speedup for the two target model sizes runs counter to our findings from our experiments with the 100x100x100 problem size in the previous section. In that trial, we found that the speedup difference was non-negligible between the 8 and 32 target models. With that problem size, even after the optimizations were performed, there was residual computation and memory usage remaining in the code to induce the larger speedup with the 32 target model.

5.1.4 Analysis Using a 4x4x100 Per Processor Problem Size

We next looked at the behaviour of COMPASS while simulating Sweep3D with a fixed problem size per simulated processor. In the experiments discussed so far, the problem size has remained constant even as the number of target processors increased. In the fixed size per processor experiments in this section, the size of the problem scales with the number of processors involved. For these experiments we fix the number of host processors and vary the number of target processors.

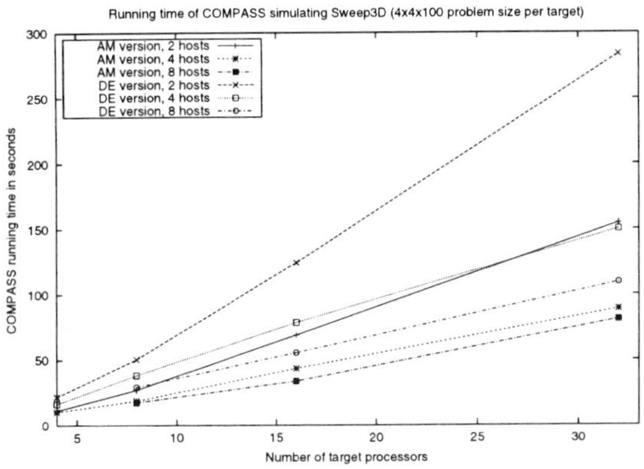

Figure 5: Running time of COMPASS simulating the Sweep3D program with a 4x4x100 per processor problem size.

In Figure 5 the running time of COMPASS is plotted for a varying number of target processors executing a 4x4x100 per processor problem size. There are six curves in this graph, with one curve for the AM and DE versions for each of 2, 4, and 8 host processors, illustrating the effectiveness of the optimistic simulator. Consider the running times from all six curves at 32 target processors. At this point, we can see that the running times of the DE versions increase as the number of hosts decrease from 8 to 2. The 2-host execution is in fact almost 2.5 times slower than the 8-host execution. This expected outcome shows that increasing the number of physical hosts will reduce the running time of the simulation. The running times of the AM version show the same trend as well. Clearly, even as the problem size scales along with the number of target processors, the AM version's performance will scale as well.

5.1.5 Slowdown with Respect to Physical System

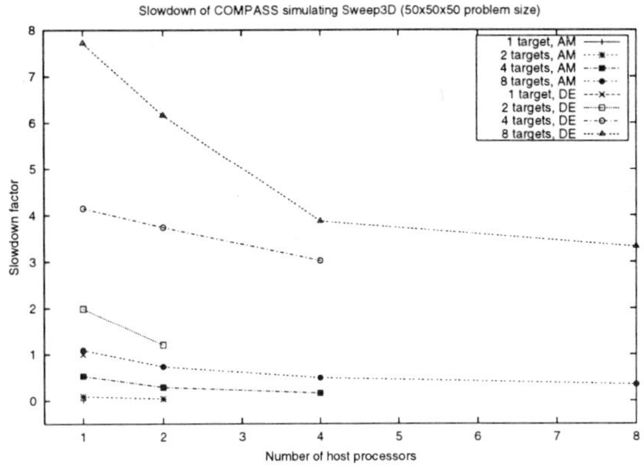

Figure 6: Slowdown factor of COMPASS simulating the Sweep3D program.

Figure 6 presents the data for slowdown, which is defined as:

$$Slowdown(N, P) = \frac{\text{Execution time of the simulator on P host processors for an application running on N target processors}}{\text{Execution time of physical system on N physical processors}}$$

In this experiment we simulated Sweep3D with a 50x50x50 problem size on a varying number of target and host processors. Slowdown is an important metric because the improvements due to parallel execution of the simulation can be measured directly against the execution time of the original non-simulated program. For each configuration, parallel execution of the DE version improved the slowdown metric, showing the effectiveness of the optimistic simulation engine. Furthermore, in every case, given enough processors, the AM model could be executed faster than its non-simulated counterpart! The data in this graph makes a convincing argument for the utility of optimistic techniques for parallel simulation of applications.

5.2 Analysis of NAS SP

Our next set of experiments involved the NAS SP benchmark configured to run with 16 target processors. The SP program can be run with different problem sizes. Figure 7 shows the simulation of SP with size S, the smallest configuration available for the program. Note first that for the DE version, the simulation time actually increases from 1 to 2 hosts. We attribute this behaviour to the large memory footprint of the SP program adding to the simulation overhead; going from a 1-host sequential simulation to a 2-host parallel simulation adds these overheads, and in this case the overhead is so much that adding the second processor does not show a benefit. However, as the curve shows, going to 4 and 8 processors does overcome the simulation overhead, resulting in a performance benefit.

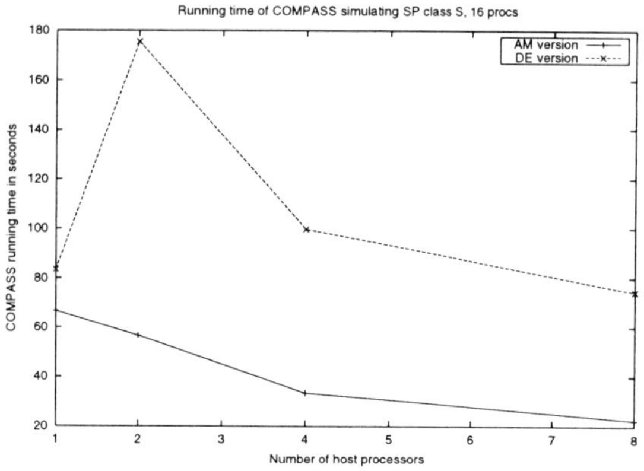

Figure 7: Running time of COMPASS simulating the NAS SP program, size S, with 16 target processors.

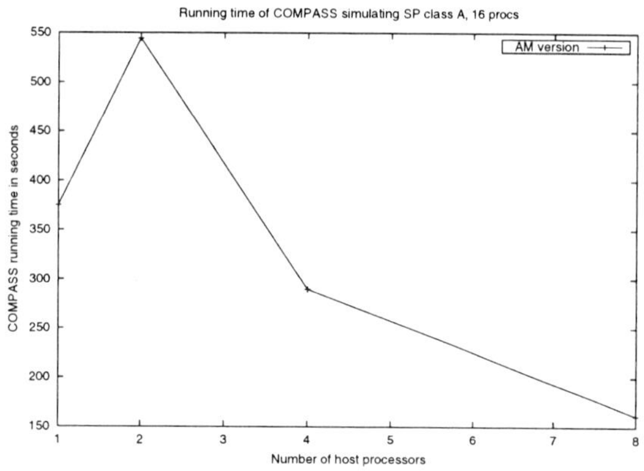

Figure 8: Running time of COMPASS simulating the NAS SP program, size A, with 16 target processors.

We then tried to improve on this small result by executing the AM version of the code. The result from this trial is also shown in Figure 7. Note that the AM version's curve does not have the initial rise as with the DE: the AM version shows a monotonically decreasing effect because SP's memory usage for this small configuration size has been cleaved.

We next consider a problem size configuration that was too large to be executed with the DE version. In Figure 8 we show the simulation time of the AM version of SP running on 16 target processors but with the larger class A problem size requiring over 125 times the amount of memory of class S. In this case we again see an increase in running time from 1 host to 2 hosts and then a decreasing curve with an increasing number of hosts. Again, this pattern can be attributed to the simulation overhead being impacted by the large memory requirements. Although the AM version does remove significant amounts of memory, there is still considerable remaining memory not related to the sequential code segments that were excised. Clearly, this residual memory was large enough to affect the simulation's behaviour.

6 Summary

In this paper we have demonstrated that large parallel programs can be simulated via direct execution using an optimistic Time Warp-based technique. From our results we have shown that our optimistic simulation engine provides good speedup for several benchmarks, including two real-world scientific applications. As was clearly seen, for an increasing number of host processors, the simulator's performance scaled as well, resulting in a decreasing amount of simulation time. However, we found that some problem sizes were too large to allow the simulator to run with simple direct execution (DE) due to the optimistic engine's need for state-saving. At that point, we were forced to utilise the memory-reduction technique that entailed the use of static task graph analysis. With memory and also computation reduced in the resulting abstract model (AM) version of the code, we were able to execute large problem sizes that otherwise would not have been runnable. Our experiments showed that the AM versions also showed good performance speedup. For example, the DE simulation of our primary benchmark, Sweep3D, runs up to 68% faster with 8 host processors for a small application configuration thanks to the optistic implementation. For a larger memory configuration that could not fit into memory, we used the AM version to allow the simulation to run. As an additional benefit, the AM simulation was shown to actually execute faster than the real non-simulated application. From the culmination of our experimental results, we have shown that our optimistic runtime mechanism has been successful in direct execution simulation of parallel programs.

The COMPASS simulator plays an integral role in the collaborative work being done as part of POEMS, a Performance-Oriented End-to-end Modeling System [19]. The work in POEMS involves ongoing investigations into performance prediction of parallel and distributed implementations of large-scale adaptive applications.

7 Acknowledgments

We would like to thank Jay Martin, Ewa Deelman, and the good folks at Los Alamos National Labouratory for their help in this research work.

References

[1] V. Adve, R. Bagrodia, E. Deelman, T. Phan, and R. Sakel-

lariou. "Compiler-Supported Simulation of Highly Scalable Parallel Applications," *Proceedings of Supercomputing '99*, Portland, Oregon, November 1999.

[2] R. Bagrodia, R. Meyer, M. Takai, Y. Chen, X. Zeng, J. Martin, B. Park, and H. Song. "PARSEC: A Parallel Simulation Environment for Complex Systems," *IEEE Computer*, vol. 31(1), October 1998.

[3] R. Bagrodia, E. Deelman, S. Docy, and T. Phan. "Performance Prediction of Large Parallel Applications Using Parallel Simulations," In *Proceedings of ACM SIGPLAN Symposium on Principles and Practice of Parallel Programming*, Atlanta, Georgia, May 4-6, 1999.

[4] D. Bailey, T. Harris, W. Shaphir, R. van der Winjngaart, A. Woo, and M. Yarrow. "The NAS Parallel Benchmarks 2.0," *Report NAS-95-090*, NASA Ames Research Center, 1995.

[5] S. Chandrasekaran and M. Hill. "Optimistic Simulation of Parallel Architectures Using Program Executables," *Workshop on Parallel and Distributed Simulation*, May 1996.

[6] R. Covington, S. Dwarkadas, J. Jump, J. Sinclair, and S. Madala. "The Efficient Simulation of Parallel Computer Systems," *International Journal in Computer Simulation*, vol. 1, 1991.

[7] H. Davis, S. Goldschmidt, and J. Hennessy. "Multiprocessor Simulation and Tracing Using Tango," In *Proceedings of the 1991 International Conference on Parallel Processing*, August 1991.

[8] P. Dickens, P. Heidelberger, and D. Nicol. "Parallelized Network Simulators for Message-Passing Parallel Programs," In *Proceedings of the Third International Workshop on Modeling, Analysis, and Simulation of Computer and Telecommunication Systems (MASCOTS)*, Durham, NC, USA, 18-20 Jan. 1995.

[9] P. Dickens, P. Heidelberger, and D. Nicol. "Parallelized Direct Execution Simulation of Message-Passing Parallel Programs," *IEEE Transactions on Parallel and Distributed Systems*, vol.7, (no.10), Oct. 1996.

[10] M. Dikaiakos, A. Rogers, and K. Steiglitz. "FAST: a Functional Algorithm Simulation Testbed," In *Proceedings of MASCOTS 94*.

[11] M. Dikaiakos, A. Rogers, and K. Steiglitz. "Function Algorithm Simulation of the Fast Multipole Method: Architectural Implications," *Parallel Processing Letters*, 6(1), March 1996.

[12] D. Jefferson. "Virtual Time," *ACM Transactions on Programming Languages and Systems*, vol. 7, 1985.

[13] S. Horwitz, T. Reps, and D. Binkley. "Interprocedural Slicing Using Dependence Graphs," *ACM Transactions on Programming Languages and Systems*, 12(1), January 1990.

[14] J. Laudon and D. Lenoski. "The SGI Origin: A ccNUMA Highly Scalable Server," *The 24th Annual International Symposium on Computer Architecture*, May 1997.

[15] U. Legedza. "Reducing Synchronization Overhead in Parallel Programs," *MIT Technical Report MIT/LCS/TR-655*.

[16] J. Martin and R. Bagrodia. "COMPOSE: An Object-Oriented Environment for Parallel Discrete-Event Simulations," In *Proceedings of the 1995 Winter Simulation Conference*, December 1995.

[17] "Message-Passing Interface - MPI," `www.mcs.anl.gov/mpi/`

[18] "The NAS Parallel Benchmarks," `www.nas.nasa.gov/Software/NPB/`

[19] *The POEMS Homepage*. `www.cs.utexas.edu/users/poems/`

[20] S. Prakash and R. Bagrodia. "Parallel Simulation of Data Parallel Programs," In *Proceedings of the 8th Workshop on Languages and Compilers for Parallel Computing*, Columbus, Ohio, 1995.

[21] S. Prakash and R. Bagrodia. "Using Parallel Simulation to Evaluate MPI Programs," In *Proceedings of the 1998 Winter Simulation Conference*.

[22] S. Reinhardt, M. Hill, J. Larus, A. Lebeck, J. Lewis, and D. Wood. "The Wisconsin Wind Tunnel: Virtual Prototyping of Parallel Computers," In *Proceedings of the 1993 ACM SIGMETRIC Conference*, May 1993.

[23] M. Rosenblum, E. Bugnion, S. Devine, and S. Herrod. "Using the SimOS Machine Simulator to Study Complex Computer Systems," *ACM Transactions on Modeling and Computer Simulation*, 7(1), January 1997.

[24] J. Steinman. "Incremental State Saving in SPEEDES Using C++," In *Proceedings of the 1993 Winter Simulation Conference*, December 1993.

[25] Sweep3D. "The ASCI Sweep3D Benchmark," `www.llnl.gov/asci_benchmarks/asci/limited/sweep3d.html`

Session 10

Optimizing Parallel Simulation

SYNCHRONOUS RELAXATION FOR PARALLEL ISING SPIN SIMULATIONS

Boris Lubachevsky
bdl@bell-labs.com
Alan Weiss
apdoo@bell-labs.com
Bell Labs, 600 Mountain Avenue, Murray Hill, New Jersey, USA

Abstract

A new parallel algorithm for simulating Ising spin systems is presented. The sequential prototype is the n-fold way algorithm [2], which is efficient but is hard to parallelize using conservative methods. Our parallel algorithm is optimistic. Unlike other optimistic algorithms, e.g., Time Warp, our algorithm is synchronous. It also belongs to the class of simulations known as "relaxation" [3]; hence it is named "synchronous relaxation." We derive performance guarantees for this algorithm. If N is the number of PEs, then under weak assumptions we show that the number of correct events processed per unit of time is, on average, at least of order $N/\log N$. All communication delays, processing time, and busy waits are taken into account.

Key words: *conservative simulation, optimistic simulation, computational physics, Metropolis algorithm*

1 Introduction

The Ising model of computational physics was introduced in 1925 [7] for describing magnetization phenomena. It has since been in use both for its original purpose, and as a computational metaphor in areas ranging from economics [10] to wireless communications [1, 4] to material science [16].

In a simple version of the model we have a planar lattice of atoms, each of which may be in one of two spin states, +1 or −1. The atoms flip their spins stochastically in a way that depends only on the states of their nearest neighbors, on an external magnetic field, and on temperature.

Ising spin simulations have always been slow. There have been a number of proposals for speeding them up. The fastest available serial algorithm that does not violate the stochastic properties of the procedure by Metropolis et al. [14] is the *n-fold way* algorithm [2]. A parallel version of the n-fold way was proposed in [11, 12] and implemented in [9]. Its speedup with respect to the serial n-fold way algorithm was not very high in low temperature. This was because at low temperature the algorithm performed many tentative calculations of flips that were rejected at the end. In the procedure atoms along the boundaries of regions hosted by different processing elements were subject to such rejections; only atoms in the interior of regions were not. As the rejection rate asymptotically approaches 100%, even if the fraction of atoms on the boundaries is small, the rejection overhead becomes the dominant bottleneck in simulation. Note that the main advantage of the n-fold way over the procedure in [14] is absence of rejections.

The parallel algorithms in [11, 12] are *conservative.* Herein we describe a new algorithm for Ising spin simulations whose aim is to eliminate the drawbacks associated with rejections. The algorithm is *optimistic;* it belongs to the class of "relaxation" simulations [3]. It is also a synchronous algorithm, and as such, it differs from Time Warp [8]. Our "synchronous relaxation" implements the n-fold way algorithm in parallel by repeatedly generating a time segment of the spin flip trajectory. After each iteration, the PEs exchange information they generated, and correct the errors thus revealed. Unlike conservative schemes in [11, 12], computations are not wasted on rejections. And unlike Time Warp, erroneous events are corrected in a synchronous, iterative fashion rather than asynchronously. However, iterations might introduce extra computations.

Since Time Warp is asynchronous, and our algorithm is not, the behavior and analyses of these algorithms are quite different. In our analysis we estimate the number of iterations needed to correct mistakenly simulated events and the amount of work in each iteration. Under weak assumptions, we show that the former is small and the latter is not excessive. Synchronous relaxation was discussed in [4] in a different context, and without formal proofs.

Note that Metropolis algorithm in [14] simulates a certain Markov Chain. Markov Chain uniformization is put forward in [6, 15] as a tool for parallelizing a sequential Markov Chain simulation. Algorithms in [11, 12] turn out to be a specialization of more general schemes in [6]. It should be noted that the actual development of Ising spin simulations did not follow this logic. Specifically, the rejection scheme [14], was proposed as an inherently serial algorithm, without any reference to parallel processing or uniformization. Then scheme [2] was proposed as a derivative of, and an improvement over [14], since it got rid of event rejections. Note that according to [6, 15] it is the scheme in [14] that would rather be considered a derivative of [2], the derivative which is more amenable to parallelization. Actually, it took a while [11, 12] to break the tradition of thinking the scheme [14] as being inherently serial. Optimistic methods of parallelization of Markov Chain simulations are discussed in [15], but still in connection with uniformization, i.e., with event rejections. Since our present synchronous relaxation method for parallelization of the scheme in [2] eliminates rejections, it apparently does not follow from [15]; its efficiency analysis is certainly new.

2 The Ising model

In the model atoms are located at the vertices of a rectangular subset G of an orthogonal lattice. A configuration is defined by the spin variables $s(v) = \pm 1$ for atoms $v \in G$. In accordance with [14], the time evolution of the configuration is a sequence of single spin updates: given a configuration, define the next configuration by choosing a vertex v uniformly at random and changing $s(v)$ to $-s(v)$ with independent probability p, computed as described in the next paragraph. With probability $1-p$, the $s(v)$ remains unchanged.

Computing the probability $p = p(v)$ involves the 4 nearest neighbors of vertex $v = (i,j)$: $(i+1,j), (i-1,j), (i,j+1), (i,j-1)$. Periodic boundary conditions are assumed in both directions. Computing the $p(v)$ also involves the Hamiltonian

$$E = -J \sum_{v,v' \in G} s(v)s(v') - H \sum_{v} s(v) \qquad (2.1)$$

where $J > 0$ and H are constants, and the pairs (v, v') of indices in the first sum are nearest neighbors. The value of p is given in [14] by

$$p = \min\{1, \theta\}, \quad \theta = \exp(-\Delta E / k_B T_{\text{abs}}) \qquad (2.2)$$

where $\Delta E = \Delta E(v)$ is the energy change that would result from the flip of the spin at site v, k_B is Boltzmann's constant, and T_{abs} is the absolute temperature. In [5] a different expression for p is used:

$$p = \theta/(1+\theta) \qquad (2.3)$$

with the same θ. Note that computing $\Delta E(v)$ for spin v involves only the values of $s(v)$ and $s(v')$ for the nearest neighbors v' of v. According to (2.2), a spin flip which results in lower energy, $\Delta E < 0$, certainly occurs, because in such a case, $p = 1$; but in (2.3) $p < 1$ always and even the flips with $\Delta E < 0$ can sometimes be rejected.

3 The n-fold way algorithm

We suppose that attempts of a flip by each atom constitute an independent Poisson process[1] with fixed rate, say λ. Then the successful attempts is also a Poisson process, but with a smaller rate λp, $p = p(t)$, which, in general, varies in time.

The n-fold way algorithm in [2] splits all atoms into n classes, where a class is defined as those atoms with the same flip probability p, given either by (2.2) or (2.3). In the 2D Ising model there will be no more than $n = 10$ classes: each atom may be either up or down, and its four neighbors have 5 possibilities (none up, one up,..., 4 up), so there are 2×5 possible configurations for each atom For each class k define

$$N_k = \text{number of atoms in class } k \qquad (3.1)$$

$$p_k = \mathbb{P}(\text{atom in class } k \text{ flips when chosen}). \qquad (3.2)$$

Given that the Poisson rate of flips of a single atom of class k is λp_k, the combined rate of flips of all atoms is

$$\Lambda = \lambda \sum_k N_k p_k, \qquad (3.3)$$

[1] In [2, 14] system state changes are just a sequence. For the sake of parallelization we need spin flips to be a Poisson process in continuous time. This assumption is consistent with the models in [2, 14], but is not mentioned there.

and the combined process whose arrivals coincide with spin flips at any atom also enjoys the Poisson property. As spins flip, membership of atoms may change, N_k may vary in time $N_k = N_k(t)$, and so may the Poisson rate of the combined process $\Lambda = \Lambda(t)$.

It follows that given the time τ_{i-1} of the $(i-1)$th flip, the time of the ith flip can be generated as

$$\tau_i = \tau_{i-1} + \frac{-\log U_i}{\Lambda(\tau_{i-1})}, \tag{3.4}$$

where U_i is the ith independent sample of a random (0,1) uniformly distributed variable. The first spin flip time τ_1 can be generated as in (3.4) with $i = 1$ if we formally set $\tau_0 = 0$.

We should then select the atom whose spin is to flip. This is done in three phases. In Phase 1 we generate an independent random (0,1) uniformly distributed variable V_i. In Phase 2 we choose a class k_* to which the atom to be flipped belongs. This is done by linearly scanning the sequence of classes $k = 1, 2, \ldots n$ while summing the weights of their chances to be selected

$$W(k) = \sum_{j=1}^{k} \frac{N_j p_j}{\sum_i N_i p_i}. \tag{3.5}$$

Once the inequality

$$W(k-1) < V_i \le W(k) \tag{3.6}$$

is detected for $k = k_*$, we stop.

In Phase 3 we choose an atom in class k_*. All atoms in each class are maintained in a linear order. To determine the index of an atom in the order we take the normalized residual R_i of the random sample V_i. This is defined as

$$R_i = \frac{V_i - W(k_* - 1)}{\frac{N_{k_*} p_{k_*}}{\sum_j N_j p_j}}, \tag{3.7}$$

where k_* is the class index found in Phase 2. The required index is then

$$\text{access index} = \lfloor R_i N_{k_*} \rfloor + 1. \tag{3.8}$$

Note that each spin flip changes the class membership of several atoms. We omit here the discussion of an elaborate data structure [2] which maintains the classes in the computer memory so that the atoms in the classes are positioned in the required linear order. We note that it only takes $O(1)$ computations to adjust this order at each spin flip. Experiments [2] confirm that at a low temperature, the n-fold way algorithm is much faster than the original Metropolis et al. algorithm with rejections in [14].

4 Synchronous relaxation: a general formulation

Suppose that a simulation of a system is to be performed on a multiprocessor with N processing elements (PEs). Our procedure is to give each PE a subsystem to host, and have the PE produce the history of that subsystem.

Each PE will keep track of the simulated time before which all simulated histories are known; this quantity is called *committed time*. Committed time increases in steps, in synchrony among all PEs; its value is common to all PEs. Each step consists of several iterations. At each iteration, each PE produces a tentative or speculative history of the subsystem it hosts beyond the current committed time. The PE extends its local history until its local time reaches the committed time plus $T_{\max}$, where $T_{\max}$ is the step size of committed time increases. Since subsystems are, in general, connected, in order to produce a correct local history, a PE needs to know the correct local histories of other PEs. But they are not known, because other PEs are in the same quandary. If, by some miracle, a PE knew the correct histories of all others, then it would produce a correct history for itself; when all PEs produce correct histories, then the next committed time will become committed time plus $T_{\max}$. So all we have to explain is how to achieve this miracle.

The mechanism is by iterations. During the first iteration, each PE makes the simplest assumption about the histories of the other PEs; we call this the canonical assumption. For example, it may assume that the states of the other subsystems do not change. This assumption will enable it to produce its own history. After all the PEs generate local history for an additional $T_{\max}$ units of simulated time, they compare their histories. This comparison is done in synchrony, in the sense that the PEs perform the comparison only after they have all completed the previous task of generating their histories. As a rule, there will be inconsistencies between the assumed and actual (generated) histories of other PEs. If so, the PEs need to perform more iterations.

During subsequent iterations, if a PE needs to know the local history of another PE, it uses that history generated in the last iteration. The goal of producing correct histories at a step is achieved if no PE detects any inconsistencies between the assumed and actual history of any other PE. Once this happens, all PEs increase committed time by $T_{\max}$, and continue.

We now give a representation of the synchronous relaxation algorithm. In the outset of the simulation, committed time is set to zero. The subsystems hosted by the PEs are set to their initial states. Then each PE executes the following code. The execution is asynchronous except for the two "synchronize" statements. While executing a "synchronize," each PE waits for the other PEs to reach the same statement.

DO (step)

1. Choose a step size $T_{\max}$ for committed time increase.
2. Make canonical assumption about other PEs' histories.

   DO (iteration)

   (a) Generate local history, starting with committed time until local time $\geq$ committed time $+T_{\max}$.
   (b) Synchronize.
   (c) Compare generated history of other PEs with the corresponding assumptions. If they differ, replace the current assumptions with the corresponding histories.
   (d) Synchronize.

   UNTIL (iteration) all PEs detect no difference in the comparison in step 2c.
3. Increment committed time by $T_{\max}$.

UNTIL (step) committed time exceeds a prespecified value.

There are two issues that need to be addressed. Will there ever come a time when no inconsistencies are detected? Another is the question of correctness. Is the lack of inconsistencies equivalent to correctness of the history? Generally, the iterations will not terminate. However, when applied to discrete event simulations, under mild conditions we can show that the iterations do terminate. Also, under weak conditions, we can show that lack of inconsistency is equivalent to correctness (see [13]).

The preceding algorithm turns out to be applicable not only to deterministic simulations, but to stochastic simulations, too, using the following technique. Sequences of (pseudo)random numbers are employed in stochastic simulations. We should treat these sequences as deterministic. To this end, all we have to do is to *reuse* the (pseudo)random numbers generated at an iteration, during the course of the following iterations. An extreme way of effecting this is to generate all random numbers in a list before the rest of the simulation begins. This is a helpful way to think about simulation, whether or not it turns out to be a practical method in any instance.

The general description above may not give enough details for a specific implementation. Furthermore, it may not be clear how to estimate the efficiency of the algorithm; specifically, how to bound the number of iterations in each step. The next sections will fill in these details for the Ising model.

5 Synchronous relaxation for Ising simulation

In this section we detail the synchronous relaxation algorithm for Ising simulation using the n-fold way algorithm. While simulations can be implemented correctly even if different PEs run different serial algorithms to generate local history, we are interested in high performance, so we will concentrate on a parallelization of the most efficient serial algorithm.

We follow the algorithm outlined in Section 4. The set G is partitioned into subsets G_i, $1 \leq i \leq N$, and each G_i is hosted by a separate processing element, PE_i. Each G_i corresponds to a subsystem in the general description of Section 4. As before, the boundary of G_i is denoted ∂G_i.

Statement 1 of the general relaxation procedure requires a choice of step size $T_{\max}$ for each committed time increase. In the simplest algorithm formulation, we choose the *same* step value to serve for all committed time increase steps,

$$T_{\max} = \frac{\log N}{\lambda\,|\partial G_i|}, \tag{5.1}$$

assuming that all the sizes of boundary regions $|\partial G_i|$ are equal, and where λ, as in Section 3 is the largest rate at which any atom can flip.

Statement 2 of the general relaxation procedure requires each PE to make a canonical assumption concerning its neighbors' histories. We choose the assumption that no spin flip occurs in any neighboring atom during the initial committed time increase step $T_{\max}$.

Statement (a) requires each PE at each iteration to generate a segment of local history. The segment begins at the current committed time value, let us call it t_c, and ends at time $t_c + T_{\max}$. The history can be identified with a sequence $t_c \leq \tau_1 < \tau_2 < \ldots < \tau_m < t_c + T_{\max}$ of spin flip times and the corresponding sequence of atoms $v_1, v_2, \ldots v_m$ that flip their spins at these times. Because the procedure is complex and subtle, our discussion will be lengthy. We split it into several cases.

First iteration, first step. Thanks to the canonical assumption, the procedure executed by each PE in this case is almost a literal repetition of the sequential algorithm described in Section 3. As in that algorithm, a sequence of pairs $(U_1, V_1), (U_2, V_2), \ldots, (U_m, V_m)$, of independent samples of uniform (0,1) distributed random variables U_i and V_i, feeds the generation of the spin flip history. The U_i feeds formula (3.4), which generates τ_i, given τ_{i-1} and given the previous system state. The V_i feeds the procedure that selects the class of the atom v_i to flip and selects the v_i's index according to formulas (3.7) and (3.8). To compute τ_1 using (3.4) for $i = 1$ we formally assume $\tau_0 = 0$. As in the sequential case, this can be done, because the state of the system at time $t_c = 0$ is known. The computations continue for as long as τ_i computed by (3.4) is smaller than $t_c + T_{\max}$. The last τ_i that satisfies this condition becomes τ_m.

Steps (b), (c), and (d), that follow are obvious. Note that while comparing the generated histories with the assumed histories, as required in step (c), the PE pays attention only at the single layer of atoms that border its region. This is due to the specific neighborhood structure that consists of 4 neighbors which we have assumed in our Ising model (see Section 2). If the geometry were different (e.g., more dimensions, leading to more neighbors; or deeper penetration of influence) then we might need to check more atoms.

After exchanging information about their produced histories in step (c), the PEs detect inconsistencies. Any boundary flip generated at the initial iteration causes inconsistencies in neighbors, because of the canonical assumption that there were no flips in boundaries. The communication in step (c) leads the PEs to have new assumptions about the histories of their neighbors, in place of the canonical assumption.

Subsequent iterations, first step. After the PEs synchronize in step (d), they execute step (a) again. The first important distinction of this parallel procedure from its sequential prototype is that the feeding sequence $(U_1, V_1), (U_2, V_2), \ldots$ of random numbers at the subsequent iterations has to be the *same* as at the first iteration. No new random sample U_i or V_i in place of the previously generated one should be produced. This is in keeping with the notion given at the end of Section 4 that these numbers are viewed as presimulated, and need to be used in order.

As in the first iteration, each *old* U_i is employed to generate τ_i and each *old* V_i is employed to select atom v_i for the flip. Because of different boundary conditions, the resulting τ_i and selected v_i will generally differ from those computed at the previous iteration.

Moreover, the second main distinction between parallel and serial algorithms is that computing τ_i, given τ_{i-1} and given the system state at time τ_{i-1}, is not as straightforward as simply applying (3.4). The complication arises because spins in the neighborhood may flip during time interval (τ_{i-1}, τ_i), say at time t_b, which we call a *break point* time, $\tau_{i-1} < t_b < \tau_i$.

The class membership of some atoms hosted by the PE may change at time t_b as a result. This in turn may change some N_i and hence may change the Λ computed by (3.3) and used in (3.4). The presence of a break point t_b inside interval (τ_{i-1}, τ_i), and the change of Λ at t_b, makes formula (3.4) unusable as it is.

A more general method adjusts τ_i so as to satisfy the following equation

$$\int_{\tau_{i-1}}^{\tau_i} \Lambda(t)\, dt = -\log U_i. \tag{5.2}$$

Solving (5.2) for τ_i is easily accomplished since $\Lambda(t)$ changes in time in a piecewise constant fashion. One way of solving (5.2) is, with self-evident notation, to order the break points from $\tau_{b,0} = \tau_{i-1}$ to the maximum $\tau_{b,m} = t_c + T_{\max}$, and to compute for $1 \leq i \leq m$ the sums

$$b_k = \sum_{j=1}^{k} (\tau_{b,j} - \tau_{b,j-1}) \tag{5.3}$$

$$= \int_{\tau_{i-1}}^{\tau_{b,k}} \Lambda(t)\, dt \tag{5.4}$$

If $-\log U_i > b_m$ then $\tau_i > t_c + T_{\max}$, and we are done. If $-\log U_i \leq b_m$, then since the b_k are monotone increasing, we easily find k such that

$$b_{k-1} < -\log U_i \leq b_k. \tag{5.5}$$

Given k, we have (analogously to equation (3.4))

$$\tau_i = \tau_{b,k} + \frac{-\log U_i - b_{k-1}}{\Gamma(\tau_{b,k-1})}. \tag{5.6}$$

Another, more efficient, way to solve (5.2) for τ_i, is to generate the b_k one at a time until equation (5.5) is satisfied.

Another distinction from sequential simulation is a possible need for *additional* random numbers. The need may arise as a result of change of spin flip times τ_i at iterations. A subsequent iteration may fit more spin flips, or fewer spin flips, within the time interval $(t_c, t_c + T_{\max})$. Recall that a presimulated list will have the random numbers drawn in order, and so additional random numbers must be drawn after the original ones are used. In particular, the random number U_{m+1} that caused τ_{m+1} to exceed $T_{\max}$ would be the first one used if more random numbers are needed. If fewer flips are needed, we save unused random numbers for possible use in future iterations or subsequent time steps.

Iterations of the synchronous relaxation steps a, b, c, and d continue until all PEs realize that the assumptions they made at the beginning of an iteration agree with the information they receive at the iteration's end; that is, the times τ_i and flipped atoms v_i are the same as in the previous-iteration assumption and this hold for all $\tau_i < T_{\max}$. This signals that it is time to advance the committed time to $t_c = T_{\max}$ for a new time step, and to continue with a new round of iterations if necessary.

Subsequent steps. The only difference of this situation from those already described is in defining initial conditions. Whereas $\tau_0 = 0$ at the first time advancement step and the initial system state is that at time 0, for the following steps, the initial state of the subsystem hosted by a PE is the state resulting from the last simulated event at the previous time advancement step.

Let m be the index of the last spin flip simulated in the previous step. Using the notation above, the last event if any of the previous step was (τ_m, v_m). If, by chance, there were no events until now, then $m = 0$, $\tau_m = 0$, and v_m is undefined. Redefining notations for the current time step, the old τ_m becomes the τ_0 for this time step. This τ_0 is used in this time step in the same way as the τ_0 of the first time step was used. In particular, the τ_1 can be found using either formula (3.4) or by solving equation (5.2) with respect to τ_i, for $i = 1$.

What we called U_i and V_i at the previous time step we now rename to U_{i-m} and V_{i-m}; so U_{m+1} becomes U_1, etc. Again, from viewing random numbers as coming from a presimulated list, any remaining random samples $V_{m+1}, U_{m+2}, V_{m+2}, \ldots$, must be reused before additional random sampling is done. They are to be renamed in the new time step as $V_1, U_2, V_2, \ldots$ respectively.

An alternate approach to subsequent steps. For Ising simulations, properties of Poisson random variables enable us to wipe clean the slate, empty event lists of all PEs, and start afresh at the time $t_c + T_{\max}$. That is, we need not keep any knowledge of tentative events generated at previous steps. New random numbers may be generated at this time, taken later from a presimulated list than any up until now. This procedure may not be desirable; we simply wanted to point out that for Ising simulations it leads to unbiased simulations.

6 Efficiency

One of the nicest attributes of our algorithm is that it is provably efficient. In this section we outline the assumptions that go into the proof, and give a statement of the result. The detailed proofs can be found in the forthcoming paper [13].

The efficiency result is asymptotic as N, the number of PEs, becomes large. Our method is to bound the probabilistic distribution of the number of iterations needed to simulate one step of the algorithm. In addition, we bound the distribution of the amount of work needed to simulate each iteration. We also bound from below the average number of events simulated in each step. These bounds require a particular choice of $T_{\max}$ as a function of N, and also require some regularity of the model being simulated as N increases. They also require that the load of simulated events remains balanced among the PEs as N grows.

Specifically, suppose that the temperature is bounded away from zero during the entire time interval being simulated, and that λ is bounded and is bounded away from zero, so that the ratio between the largest and smallest Poisson rates in the system remains bounded. The blocks of PEs may change size as N increases; we suppose that the ratio between the number of atoms hosted by the different PEs remains bounded, that the ratio of the number of boundary atoms between any two PEs also remains bounded, and that the number of neighbors of any PE remains bounded, all independent of N. We also suppose that the number of boundary atoms per PE grows no faster than $\log N$. We choose $T_{\max}$ so that for each PE, the number of boundary atoms times $T_{\max}$ is within a constant factor of $\log N$. Clearly, this is possible because of the preceding assumptions. This choice ensures that the maximum and minimum expected number of events occurring among the boundary atoms of any PE during a time interval of length $T_{\max}$ is of order $\log N$.

The preceding assumptions relate to the system being simulated. Our efficiency result also requires some assumptions about the machine doing the simulation. We assume that synchronization can be done in no more than order $\log N$ time. We assume that communicating x events from one PE to a neighboring PE takes no more than a constant times $x+\log N$, and that this can be done in parallel, so that if x is the maximum number of events to be communicated from any PE to its neighbor, then all communication can be done in no more than a constant times $x + \log N$ time. We suppose that the speed of each PE is within a constant factor of the speed of any other PE; speed is the number of operations per unit of time. We suppose that the unit of time is chosen so that the speeds of the PEs is constant as N increases.

Now for a bit of notation. For any iteration, we let f represent the maximum total number of events that occur at the boundary atoms of a PE. That is, f is the maximum number of events that need to be communicated at each iteration. We let g denote the number of iterations to complete one step. Our assumptions show that the amount of time required to complete a simulation cycle is bounded above by a constant times fg. Note that f, g, and hence fg are random variables. We let K denote the maximum size of any set consisting of a PE, its neighbors, and their neighbors. K is bounded by the assumption that the set of neighbors is bounded in size.

We write $x \leq_s y$ for real-valued random variables x and y if

$$\mathbb{P}(x > z) \leq \mathbb{P}(y > z) \tag{6.1}$$

holds for any real number z.

Under the assumptions delineated in the preceding section, we derive the following results.

Theorem 1 *If the average number of events in a PE during an iteration is* $\log N$, *then for each constant* $C > 1$,

$$f \leq_s Ce\log N + Y, \tag{6.2}$$

where Y *is a geometrically distributed random variable with parameter* $1/C$.

In particular, this theorem shows that $E(f) \leq Ce\log N + 1/(C-1)$, and $\sqrt{\mathrm{Var}(f)} \leq Ce\log N + 2/(C-1)^2$.

We also find the following.

Theorem 2 *If the average number of events in a PE during an iteration is* $\log N$, *then for each constant* $C > 1$ *we find*

$$g \leq_s CeK\log N + X, \tag{6.3}$$

where X *is a geometrically distributed random variable with parameter* $1/C$.

In particular, this theorem shows that $E(g) \leq CeK\log N + 1/(C-1)$ and $\sqrt{\mathrm{Var}(g)} \leq CeK\log N + 2/(C-1)^2$.

Combining these two theorems, we can bound the average time for a complete simulation cycle of length $T_{\max}$. We may find a constant c such that, for large enough N, by Schwarz's inequality,

$$E(fg) \leq \sqrt{E(f^2)E(g^2)} \leq (c\log N)^2. \tag{6.4}$$

Since our assumptions show that the amount of time to complete a simulation cycle is no more than proportional to fg, equation (6.4) gives our bound on the mean real time required to simulate time $T_{\max} = \log N$. Furthermore our assumptions show that in time $T_{\max} = \log N$ we expect to have to within a constant factor $NT_{\max}|G_i|\lambda p_i$ events simulated. Therefore, the number of events simulated per unit time is, to within a factor c,

$$\frac{\#\text{ events}}{\text{unit time}} = c\frac{N\log N}{(\log N)^2} = c\frac{N}{\log N}, \tag{6.5}$$

which is the efficiency estimate we promised.

We summarize our efficiency result as a theorem.

Theorem 3 *Under the assumptions, the efficiency of the simulation is at least of order* $1/\log N$ *as* $N \to \infty$. *Specifically, let* $\tau(N,t)$ *be the amount of real time* *it takes to simulate an interval of time $(0,t)$ with N processors. Then there is a constant B such that*

$$\frac{\tau(N,t)}{(t+1)\log N} \leq B. \qquad (6.6)$$

We note that it can be shown that our scaling is optimal, in the sense that by taking a function $T_{\max} = r(N)$ in place of $\log N$, where either $r(N)/\log N \to \infty$ or $r(N)/\log N \to 0$ as $N \to \infty$, gives strictly worse efficiency. The details of all these results are in the full paper [13].

References

[1] S. Borst, S. Grandhi, Kahn, K. Kumaran, B.D. Lubachevsky, D. Sand Wireless Simulation and Self-Organizing Spectrum Management. Bell Labs Tech. J., V.2, No.3, 1997, pp.81-98.

http://www.lucent.com/minds/techjournal /summer_97/pdf/paper06.pdf

[2] A.B. Bortz, M.H. Kalos, J.L. Lebowitz, "A New Algorithm for Monte Carlo Simulation of Ising Spin Systems," J. Comput. Phys. **17**, No. 1, pp. 10–18, 1975.

[3] K.M Chandy and R. Sherman, "Space-Time and Simulation," Proc. SCS Multiconference on Distributed Simulation, March 1989, Tampa, Florida, (SCS Simulation Series, v.21, No.2), pp.53-57.

[4] S. Eick, A.G. Greenberg, B.D. Lubachevsky, and A. Weiss, "Synchronous Relaxation for Parallel Simulation with Applications to Circuit Switched Networks," *ACM Trans. On Modeling And Computer Simulation* **3**, No. 4, pp. 287–314, 1993.

[5] R.J. Glauber, "Time-Dependent Statistics of the Ising Model," *J. Math. Physics* **4**, 2, pp. 294-307, 1963.

[6] P. Heidelberger and D.M. Nicol, "Conservative Parallel Simulation of Continuous Time Markov Chains Using Uniformization," *IEEE Trans. Parallel Distr. Syst.*, **4**, No. 8 (1995), pp. 906-921.

[7] F. Ising, "Beitag zur theorie des ferromagnetismus," *Z. Physik,* **31**, pp. 253-258, 1925.

[8] D. Jefferson, "Virtual Time," *ACM TOPLAS*, **7** , No. 3, 1985, pp.404-425.

[9] G. Korniss, G. Brown, M.A. Novotny, and P.A.Rikvold, Hard simulation problems in the modeling of magnetic materials: Parallelization and Langevin micromagnetics," in *Computer Simulation Studies in Condensed Matter* Physics XI, D..P. Landau and H.-B. Schuttler eds. (Springer-Verlag, New York, 1998)

http://xxx.lanl.gov/abs/cond-mat/9803118

[10] P.B. Linhart, B.D. Lubachevsky, R. Radner, and M.J. Meurer, "'Friends and Family' and Related Pricing Strategies," Proc. 2nd Russian-Swedish Control Conference, Aug. 1995, St.Petersburg State Technical University, Russia, p. 192-196.

[11] B.D. Lubachevsky, "Efficient Parallel Simulations of Asynchronous Cellular Arrays," *Complex Systems* **1** (1987), pp. 1099-1123.

[12] B.D. Lubachevsky, "Efficient Parallel Simulations of Dynamic Ising Spin Systems," *J. Computational Phys.* **75**, No. 1, pp. 103-122, 1988.

[13] B. Lubachevsky and A. Weiss, "Efficiency study of a new parallel Ising spin simulation algorithm," In preparation.

[14] N.C. Metropolis, A.W. Rosenbluth, M.N. Rosenbluth, A.H. Teller, and E. Teller, "Equation of State Calculations by Fast Computing Machines," J. Chemical Physics **21**, No. 6, 1953.

[15] D.M. Nicol and P. Heidelberger, "Optimistic Parallel Simulation of Continuous Time Markov Chains Using Uniformization," *Journ. Parallel and Distr. Comp.*, **18**, no4, pp.395-410, 1993.

[16] P. Nielaba, V. Privman, and J.-S. Wang, "Irreversible Multilayer Adsorption," in *Computer Simulation Studies in Condensed-Matter Physics V*— (D.P. Landau, K..K Mon, and H-B. Schüttler, Eds.), Proceedings in Physics, Vol 76 (Springer-Verlag, Berlin, 1993), p.143.

Speedup of a Sparse System Simulation

James Nutaro
Hessam Sarjoughian

Arizona Center for Integrative Modeling and Simulation
University of Arizona
{nutaro,hessam}@ece.arizona.edu
www.acims.arizona.edu

Abstract

Optimistic and conservative simulation algorithms have been effective for speeding up the execution of many simulation programs. Event stepped techniques have also been shown to be effective for certain types of problems. This paper presents a conjecture that sparse systems are effectively simulated by conservative and optimistic techniques, where sparseness is characterized by the ratio of output generating states to non-output generating states. The speedup results for a representative sparse simulation are shown to support this conjecture.

1. Introduction

Research into distributed discrete event simulation has focused, primarily, on optimistic and conservative techniques. It is intuitively obvious that some degree of parallelism must be present in the simulation if these techniques are to be effective. However, the source of parallelism in discrete event models has yet to be described in concrete terms. By developing a model that describes the parallelism inherent in a discrete event system, we move closer to being able to reason about the types of algorithms, conservative and optimistic or event stepped, that will be effective for a given simulation problem.

This paper presents a conjecture, which is intuitively nice, that sparse systems are effectively simulated by conservative and optimistic techniques, where sparseness is characterized by the ratio of output generating states to non-output generating states. The speedup exhibited by sparse system simulations is related to Amdahl's Law. Finally, a particular sparse system is simulated using DSE, the Distributed Simulation Environment [6], and the speedup results are shown to conform to these expectations.

2. Sparse DEVS

To state the hypothesis precisely, a formal representation for discrete event systems is needed. While the logical process model is most common in distributed discrete event simulation, this model fails to capture key elements of the system under study. In particular it does not capture, in explicit terms, the system state space, transition function, or output function. Representation of the system in these terms is necessary in order to distinguish between output producing and non-output producing states, a distinction that is at the heart of the definition of a sparse system.

We selected DEVS as a formal system representation for its uniqueness property [9]. That is, DEVS can represent the entire class of discrete systems. This includes the traditional event stepped and process oriented views of discrete event simulation. Hence, it captures the logical process model as well as more esoteric instances of discrete event systems (e.g. quantized continuous systems).

DEVS describes systems in terms of atomic and coupled models. Atomic models are of interest for our purposes here. A parallel DEVS atomic model is a structure

$(X, Y, S, T, \delta_{int}, \delta_{ext}, \delta_{conf}, \lambda, ta)$, where

X is the set of system inputs
Y is the set of system outputs
S is the set of system states
T is the system time base
δ_{int}: $S \rightarrow S$ is the internal transition function
δ_{ext}: $S \times T \times X \rightarrow S$ is the external transition function
δ_{conf}: $S \times X \rightarrow S$ is the confluent transition function
λ: $S \rightarrow Y$ is the output function, and
ta: $S \rightarrow T$ is the time advance function

0-7695-1104-X/01 $10.00 © 2001 IEEE

The input set describes the objects (events, values) that are admissible as input to the DEVS. The output set describes the objects (event, values) that are produced by the DEVS. The state set describes the internal representation of the system (i.e. the state space of the system). The time base is the set of values that can be assumed by the system clock (usually the real numbers or integers).

The internal transition function describes the autonomous (input-free) behavior of the system. The external transition function describes the input response of the system. The confluent transition function describes the response of the system when internal event and external event transitions coincide. The output function describes the system output as a function of the state of the system. Finally, the time advance function indicates the time until the next autonomous state change.

When interpreting a DEVS, system outputs may be assumed to coincide with autonomous state changes. That is, a system output is produced just prior to an input free change of state. More generally, system outputs are due to state changes via the internal or external transition functions. To model outputs that are an immediate response to an input event, a transitory state whose time advance is 0 is used.

To define a sparse DEVS, let $S_O \subseteq S$ be the set of output generating states (i.e. $s \in S_O$ if and only if $\lambda(s) \neq \emptyset$, where $\emptyset$ is the non-event). A sparse system has $|S_O| << |S|$ [5]. Given a set of sparse systems, the probability of any two interacting during a given simulation cycle is small. Consequently, it may be possible to process large numbers of events concurrently, without concern for the timestamps of those events[1].

From the point of view of a distributed algorithm, the event timestamps are consequential only if those events could affect the state trajectory of some other system. By definition, such an event is a system output. Since outputs are infrequent, the distributed algorithm rarely needs to intervene in order to correct and/or prevent a causality violation. On the other hand, if output producing states occur frequently, it would behoove us to minimize the cost of detecting and either correcting or preventing causality violations.

In general, algorithms geared towards sparse systems are expected to have a high overhead cost associated with system outputs. An algorithm that assumes every state is likely to produce output can minimize the overhead associated with an output, but will likely do so at the expense of a larger overhead when non-output generating states occur.

[1] The DEVS abstract simulator is responsible for implicitly assigning time stamps to events. Similarly, logical process simulators assign timestamps to events that are produced by their respective models.

3. Predicting speedup for sparse system simulations

Suppose each state in S occurs with equal probability during a simulation. Then $p = |S_O| / |S|$ is the probability that any given state will result in an output. Since outputs can require the simulators to interact, those simulators involved in the interaction must have their execution serialized (i.e. if simulator A sends output to simulator B, the output producing transition for A must be computed before the resulting input can be processed by B). For the sake of simplicity, we will assume that the entire simulator is serialized for that transaction. Under this assumption, sparseness probability p may be used as the measure of the serial workload of the simulation. Similarly, (1 - p) represents the potentially parallel workload. Both the serial and parallel workloads have a direct relation to p. Using Amdahl's Law, we can anticipate the simulator's potential speedup as follows [3]. Given k processors and sparseness probability p, the simulation speedup Sp(k, p) is $Sp(k, p) = 1 / (p + (1-p) / k)$.

Although it is unlikely that Amdahl's Law will allow us to predict actual speedup metrics, increasing speedup should be observable as p decreases. Similarly, as p increases, we expect to see reduced speedup.

4. Approximating p by experimental methods

For systems with a large, or infinite, state set, it will not be feasible to determine p directly from the model description. In these cases, $|S_O|$ can be approximated by looking at the number of outputs produced by the DEVS during a simulation run. To approximate $|S|$, we count the number of internal transitions that occur. This reflects the portion of the state space explored during the simulation run. Only the internal transition count is considered since model outputs only occur in conjunction with internal events.

5. Speedup of a multi-protocol simulation of a sparse system

The objective of this experiment is to rank simulation algorithms in terms of their ability to exploit parallelism inherent in a sparse system. Towards this end, we can make a few observations that should be easily demonstrated by experimentation. In all cases, we are concerned with sparse systems.

Event stepped algorithms[2] extract the smallest amount of the potential parallelism. In this case, only events with identical timestamps can be processed in parallel. As the model becomes increasingly sparse, event stepped algorithms should exhibit decreasing speedup. This will

[2] Event stepped algorithms are described in [6].

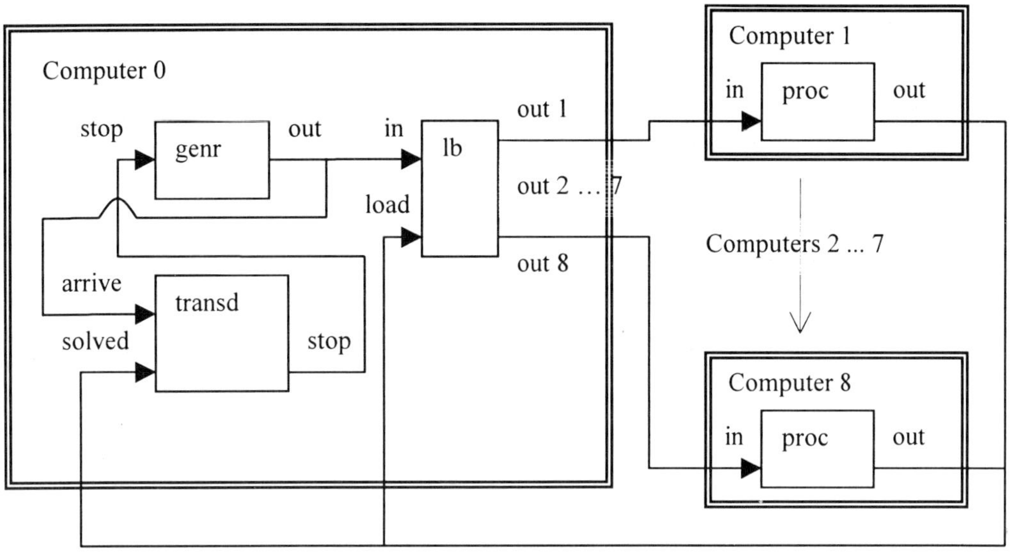

Figure 1: The model partitioned for simulation on 9 computers.

result from the number of concurrent events decreasing relative to the total number of events processed during a simulation run.

Conservative algorithms exploit windows of parallelism that are described by the lookahead of the system. These windows have an upper bound on their size that is independent of the particular output trajectory exhibited by the system during a simulation run. Consequently, a conservative algorithm is likely to miss opportunities for parallelism that are unique to a particular simulation run. As the sparseness of the system increases, these missed opportunities are likely to become more common, thereby degrading the effectiveness of the conservative algorithm.

Optimistic algorithms provide automatic parallelism detection with a potentially large overhead cost. It seems reasonable to expect that optimistic algorithms will scale effectively as the problem size increases. However, if the overhead incurred by check pointing and rollbacks becomes overly large, as would be expected for a non-sparse system, the optimistic algorithm may exhibit severely degraded performance relative to a conservative or event stepped algorithm.

It is much more difficult to make generalized statements concerning mixed mode simulators (e.g. interoperating event stepped and conservative algorithms). It would seem reasonable to assume that, in general, mixed mode simulators can provide some speedup. In cases where some component of a system can not be simulated using, say, an optimistic algorithm, it may be beneficial to simulate those components with an event stepped or conservative protocol. The remainder of the system could then take advantage of a potentially more effective optimistic algorithm. Presumably, the speedup in this case would still exceed the speedup obtained by a purely event stepped or conservative simulation.

5.1. Methods

The model for this experiment consists of a multiple processor server attached to a generator and transducer. The generator produces jobs that need to be processed by the multiprocessor. The transducer collects finished jobs from the multiprocessor and compiles throughput and turnaround time statistics. The multiprocessor consists of eight processors that maintain a job queue and assign time to each job in a round robin fashion. The load balancing process is responsible for equalizing the lengths of the processor queues. Figure 1 shows the partitioning of the model for distributed simulation on 9 computers.

A job is a structure with the following fields:

- processing time – the time required to finish the job. This is a random variable uniformly distributed in [0,40]
- job ID – the job's unique ID number.
- processor ID – the ID of the processor assigned to this job by the load balancer.

The generator (genr) produces a job every **r** units of time, where **r** is a random variable uniformly distributed in [0,10]. When input is received on the *stop* port, the generator stops producing jobs. In the case of optimistic processing, the state of the random number generator is saved along with the generator's state. Consequently, the random number stream is fixed relative to the initial seed.

The load balancer (lb) tries to do load balancing for eight processors. The load balancer maintains a load measurement for each processor. The load measurements are initially set to zero. When the load balancer receives a job on its *in* port, it looks for the least loaded processor, adds one to its load measurement, and then sends that job to the target processor. When a completed job is received on the *load* port, the load measure for the processor that sent the job is decreased by one. The load balancer requires zero units of time to process a job.

The transducer (transd) computes average turnaround time and throughput over an observation interval. At the end of the observation interval, it produces an output on its *stop* port.

A processor (proc) maintains a queue of jobs, and processes the jobs in a round robin fashion, giving 0.01 units of time to each job in turn. When a job is completed, it is removed from the queue and sent to the *out* port. When a job is received on the *in* port, the job is added to the back of the queue. If the queue was empty, the processor immediately starts processing the job. Otherwise, the processor finishes up the time slice for the current job. The processor's lookahead value is the smallest of the processing times of the jobs in the queue.

The model was simulated with six different simulation algorithm configurations, each over four different observation intervals, and the execution time for each configuration was observed. The sparseness of the system as a whole was measured by tallying the number of internal transitions and outputs produced by the component models (i.e. the generator, transducer, load balancer, and processors) and then computing p as described in sections 3 and 4. Each run is begun with the same seed for the random number generator, so the state, input, and output trajectories will be fixed relative to the observation interval.

The configuration and observation intervals for each experiment were as follows. Each configuration was run with four different observation intervals: 500, 3500, 6500, and 9500. The simulation algorithm used on each computer is described in table 1. The optimistic algorithms are risk-free optimistic in all cases.

Table 1: Assignment of simulation algorithms to computers

Computers 0	Odd computers	Even computers
Event stepped	Conservative	Conservative
Event stepped	Optimistic	Optimistic
Event stepped	Optimistic	Conservative
Optimistic	Conservative	Conservative
Optimistic	Optimistic	Optimistic
Optimistic	Optimistic	Conservative

5.2. Results

The experiments were performed using nine Sun SPARC Ultra 5/10 Workstations connected by a 100Mbps local area network. Each workstation has 64MB of memory and is running SunOS 5.7. To generate a baseline for determining speedup and an approximation of p, the model was simulated using a single computer DEVS simulation engine and the execution time and number of internal transitions and outputs observed. The one-sided, 95% confidence interval for the single computer execution was less than 0.8 seconds in all cases, with means of 17, 121.6, 226, and 326.6 seconds for the respective observation intervals.

Table 2 shows the measured experimental values of p^{-1} for the system as a whole. It can be seen that p^{-1} remains reasonably constant, decreasing by about 6.4 percent overall. Using Amdahl's Law, we could expect a change in speedup of about 3.06×10^{-3}.

Table 2: p^{-1} versus the observation interval

Observation interval	p^{-1}
500	1614.07
3500	1532.79
6500	1523.01
9500	1509.38

Figures 2 and 3 show execution times and speedup for each simulation experiment configuration. The execution times shown are mean values, with the one sided 95% confidence interval being less than 15 seconds in all cases. The format for the legend is <even computer type>.<odd computer type>.<computer zero type> (simulation configuration). Conservative, risk-free optimistic and event stepped simulators are denoted by *con*, *rfo*, and *es* respectively.

5.3. Discussion

The purely optimistic case appears to be the most scalable configuration. This matches our intuition, where the optimistic algorithm was expected to discover parallelism automatically. It seems safe to assume that, in the purely optimistic case, the state management overhead was small compared to the cost of doing useful simulation.

The mixed mode simulators exhibit erratic speedup, but are generally faster than the single processor case. The degraded performance of the partially optimistic configurations can likely be attributed to excessive optimism (and, consequently, excessive overhead) on the part of the optimistic simulators. On the other hand, the conservative/event stepped mixed mode configuration appears to exhibit fairly constant performance. Since the overhead in this case is fixed, the consistent performance is not surprising.

Consider the partially optimistic case. As the length of the simulation run increases, the non-optimistic portions of the simulation will tend to fall increasingly further behind the optimistic portions. As a result, the optimistic portions will either run out of memory or require lengthy rollbacks. In the first case, the optimistic simulator is dependent on the increasing global clock to allow it to free up memory needed to do more processing. Consequently, the optimistic simulator can only advance its local clock at the same rate as the global clock. In the second case, every saved state beyond the input timestamp must be deleted before optimistic processing continues. For the implementation used in this experiment, this is an O(N) operation. Hence, the cost of a rollback grows linearly with the distance of the local clock from the global time of next event.

The worst of the four partially optimistic cases involves the generator, transducer, and load balancer models being simulated optimistically, while the processor models are attached to conservative simulators. Given the large amount of memory required to save the state of the three models, it is not surprising that the overhead in this case grows faster than when just the processor models are involved in optimistic processing. To get a sense of the difference in memory requirements, the processor requires a job and a Standard Template Library (STL, see [1]) list to represent the state of the model. The generator, transducer, and load balancer models require, collectively, a 624 byte random number generator, two STL maps, and an STL list.

It is likely that the performance of the partially optimistic cases could be substantially improved by employing a more intelligent state saving strategy. Soliman studies tradeoffs between periodic state saving and incremental state saving techniques [7]. Steinman considers the use of an event horizon to limit the amount of optimistic processing performed between global time calculations [8]. In both cases, the speedup of an optimistic simulator was improved by selecting an appropriate state management strategy.

6. Varying parallelism and the speedup of a sparse system simulation

This experiment seeks to verify the claim concerning the relationship between speedup and p with respect to a risk free optimistic algorithm and sparse system. As p increases, the speedup achieved by the optimistic algorithm should increase. Similarly, as p decreases, the optimistic algorithm should exhibit less speedup. A plot of p versus speedup is expected to show a scaled version of the plot predicted by Amdahl's Law.

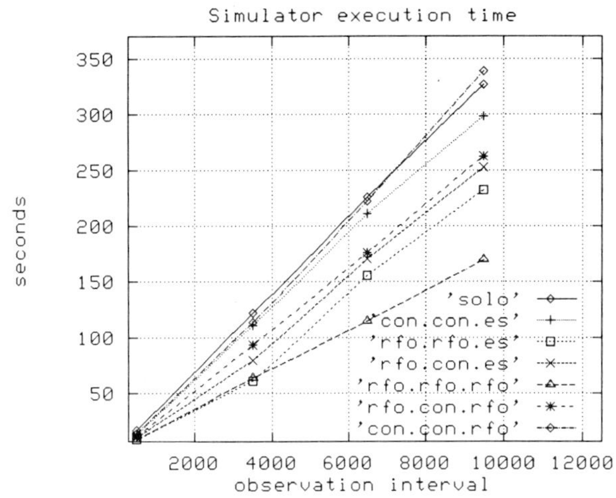

Figure 2: Simulator execution time

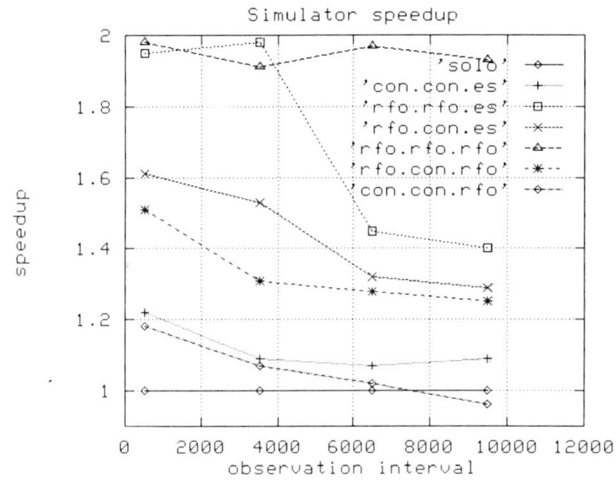

Figure 3: Simulator speedup

6.1. Methods

The multiprocessor model was partitioned as before and simulated using a risk free optimistic algorithm on each computer. The model parameters were set as before, with the exception of the time slice length and observation interval. The observation interval was fixed at 9500 units of time. The time slice was varied from 0.01 to 0.0001. The speedup for each case was observed.

In order to relate speedup to p, the model was executed once on a single computer and the number of internal transitions, number of outputs, and the execution time was recorded. Since the state trajectory is fixed relative to the system's initial state, a single observation for p is sufficient.

6.2. Results

The experiment was performed using eight 400 MHz processors installed in an SGI ORIGIN 2000 running the

IRIX 6.5 operating system. Each processor has 1024 MB of memory. One 400 MHz processor is used for the single computer case.

Table 3 shows the value of p^{-1} for the system as a whole for each time slice. As the time slice decreases, an increasing number of internal transitions are required by the processors to simulate the round robin scheduling of jobs. Consequently, the sparseness of the system is seen to increase as the time slice decreases.

Table 3: Processor time slice vs. p^{-1}

Time slice	p^{-1}
0.01	1509.4
0.001	15074.17
0.0005	30146.14
0.0001	150722.00

Figures 4 and 5 show execution times and speedup for each simulation experiment configuration. The one-sided 95% confidence interval for the simulation execution time is less than 1000 seconds in all cases. The solo line indicates the execution time and speedup of the single computer case. Risk-free optimistic line indicates the execution time and speedup of the risk free optimistic simulation.

6.3. Discussion

The experimentally determined speedup vs. p and the speedup vs. p predicted by Amdahl's Law are shown in figure 6. The observed data was scaled to match the range of values exhibited by Amdahl's Law. The results of the experiment show that as p decreases the observed speedup increases at approximately the predicted rate.

Amdahl's Law does not predict actual speedup figures. This is not surprising, since Amdahl's Law is a very simple speedup model. Examples of effects not accounted for by the law include the cost of communication, overhead imposed by synchronization, and the effects of unbalanced computation. The effect of these overheads can be seen in the speedup data for the experiment. In the large p cases, the unaccounted for overhead is significant enough to actually slow down the simulation (speedup < 1)! However, it is significant that, based solely on properties of the model, it is possible to anticipate a speedup trend. Specifically, it has been demonstrated that the performance of a risk free optimistic algorithm improves as p decreases and worsens as p increases.

7. Conclusions

The speedup figures obtained for the queuing system simulation provide evidence that conservative and optimistic algorithms effectively simulate sparse systems.

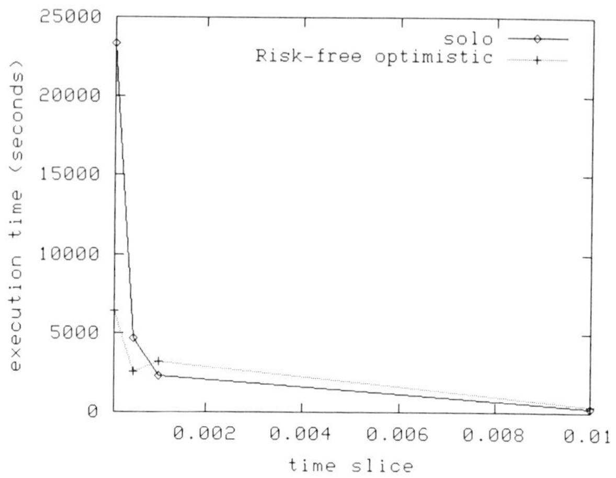

Figure 4: Simulator execution times

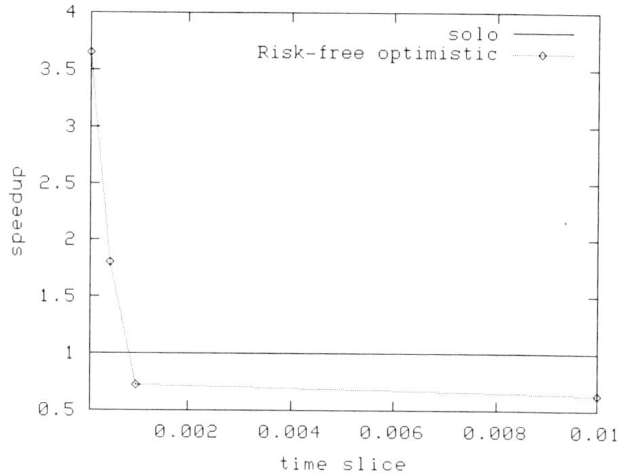

Figure 5: Simulator speedup

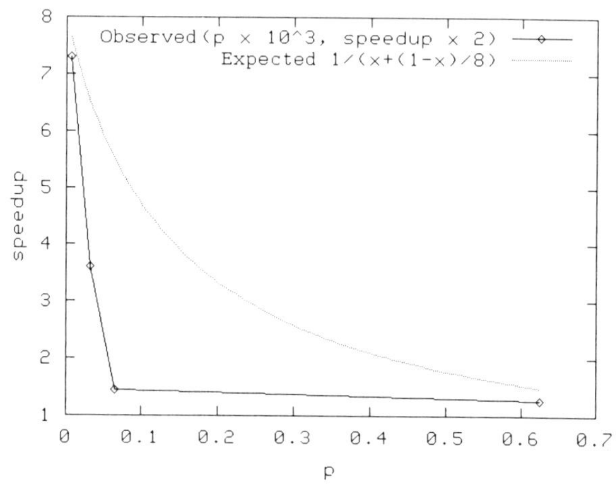

Figure 6: Speedup vs. p

The evidence in not strong enough to draw a general conclusion. However, intuition suggests that the conjecture will hold in the general case.

If Amdahl's Law is a reasonable speedup model for distributed simulations, it suggests that for conservative and optimistic algorithms to be effective, the model needs to be partitioned in such a way that the sub-model residing on each computer is sparse. If this is not the case, then p will begin to approach 1 and speedup will be diminished. It may be reasonable to expect that non-sparse systems would be effectively simulated by event stepped algorithms (replacing p with s, where s = 1 - p). This would match the observations made by Kim and Fujimoto where a time granule was used to increase the concurrency of a non-sparse system [4][2].

8. References

[1] Leen Ammeraal, *STL for C++ Programmers*, John Wiley & Sons, New York, 1997.

[2] R. M. Fujimoto, "Exploiting Temporal Uncertainty in Parallel and Distributed Simulations", 1999 Workshop on Parallel and Distributed Simulations, May 1999.

[3] Kai Hwang, *Advanced Computer Architecture: Parallelism, Scalability, Programmability*, McGraw-Hill Inc., New York, 1993.

[4] Doohwan Kim and Bernard P. Zeigler, "Orders of Magnitude Speed Up with DEVS Representation and High Performance Simulation", Enabling Technology for Simulation Science, SPIE Aerosense 97, Orlando, Florida, 1997.

[5] C. Liao, A. Motaabbed, D. Kim, B.P. Zeigler, "Distributed Simulation of Sparse Output DEVS", in 4th AI, Simulation and Planning in High Autonomy Systems, Conference, pp. 171-177, Gainesville, FL, 1993.

[6] James Nutaro, "Time Management and Interoperability in Distributed Discrete Event Simulation", Master's Thesis, University of Arizona, Department Electrical and Compute Engineering, 2000.

[7] Hussam M. Soliman, "On the Selection of the State Saving Strategy in Time Warp Parallel Simulations", Transactions of the Society for Computer Simulation International, Vol. 16, No. 1, pp. 32-36, 1999.

[8] Jeff S. Steinman, "Breathing Time Warp", Proceedings of the 7th Workshop on Parallel and Distributed Simulation, Vol. 23, No. 1, pp 109-118, 1993.

[9] Bernard P. Zeigler, Herbert Praehofer, Tag Gon Kim, *Theory of Modeling and Simulation, 2nd edition*, Academic Press, New York, 2000.

A Probabilistic Performance Model for Conservative Simulation Protocol

Ha Yoon Song
Dept. of Computer Engineering
Hongik University
Seoul, Korea
library@cs.hongik.ac.kr

Abstract

Extensive research has been conducted on the performance of simulation systems. In this paper, a performance analysis of the conservative parallel simulation protocol is presented. We analyzed several performance factors for the conservative simulation of a model with an arbitrary number of logical processes. The analysis probabilistically identifies the critical path in a conservative model, and also estimates the number of safe messages processed by an logical process during its busy time. This can be used to estimate the busy time of a logical process and hence the duration for which it is blocked. The analytical results are verified using simulation of a real world wireless network simulation model.

1. Introduction

The growing capacity of simulation models has highlighted the use of parallel simulation technology as a viable solution for high-performance simulation. Currently, several simulation systems and protocols are available, based primarily on one of two basic parallel simulation protocols - the optimistic [1] and conservative [2]. The benefit from parallel execution of a model is directly related to the overhead incurred by the protocol to implement the necessary synchronization. The overhead factors are usually divided into two categories: protocol-independent and protocol-dependent factors. In the protocol-independent case, idle time exists in an LP (Logical Process) because the computational load may not be distributed evenly among processes. Additional source of overhead includes factors such as context switching, scheduling within LPs, event queue manipulation, etc. For the protocol-dependent factors, conservative protocols have a unique overhead due to excessive blocking of an LP until an available message is identified as being safe to process. The optimistic system has rollback and state-saving overheads.

In this study, we will discuss protocol-dependent performance factors. Our goal is to estimate the blocking time overhead of a conservative parallel simulation model. To date, there has been a limited amount of research in analytical approach. Felderman and Kleinrock used queuing theory to analyze the performance of optimistic and conservative simulation systems. In the conservative version [3], they developed a Markovian model for the analysis of two processors running a conservative distributed simulation protocol. The models allow for quantitative approaches in speedup, attributed to null messages, as well as for degradation due to the cost of breaking deadlocks. However, these researchers did not generalize their case to that of more than two processors. Another stochastic methodology comes from Nicol [4], who analyzed the performance and cost of synchronous conservative protocols. His model uses the time window as a basis for synchronization; no processor can exceed the window's time boundary. Nicol analyzed the overhead of synchronization, event list manipulation, lookahead calculation, and the processor idle time.

In this paper, we analyzed a variant of the Chandy-Misra null message protocol addressed in [5]. Unlike preceding approaches, our study analyzes an asynchronous conservative parallel protocol for an arbitrary number of LPs. Our analysis is done in the following sequence: We first separate the logical factors from the physical factors in a simulation system. We introduced the concept of critical path of LPs which could vary dynamically. It enables us to estimate the average number of safe events for an LP. With the size of intervals and number of safe messages, we can estimate the busy time as well as the blocking time of an

This work was funded in part by the DARPA under contract AAB07-97-C-D321, as a part of the GloMo program, and N66001-00-1-8937 as a part of the Maya program.

LP. Finally, we validate our analysis with real experiments that include a simple example and a wireless network simulator.

2. Conservative simulation protocol

The simulation progresses on two time axes: physical and logical. While physical time (wall clock time) is continuous, logical time (simulation clock) for the simulation is discrete, manageable, and even revocable. LPs manipulate their logical time to advance the simulation, and the simulation system manages the synchronization between LPs and events. The simulation ends usually when the logical time exceeds the maximum simulation time, and the corresponding physical time determines the total execution time of the simulation. Since there are several variations of the Chandy-Misra-Bryant protocol, we will begin with the description of our protocol. A PDES (parallel/distributed discrete event simulation) model is composed of a set of logical processes that are connected in a (possibly dynamic) topology. For the LP named L, we define the following:

- SS_L: the set of LPs which send messages to L
- DS_L: the set of LPs to which L sends messages
- EOT_L (Earliest Output Time): the earliest time at which L might send a message to any LP in DS_L.
- EIT_L (Earliest Input Time, a.k.a. "*safe time*"): the earliest time at which this LP might receive a message, calculated as $min(EOT_S)$, $LP_S \in SS_L$. Any events with timestamps earlier than EIT_L are safe to process.
- $Lookahead_L$: the difference between EIT and EOT. Lookahead is the degree to which an object can predict its future messages. It is sometimes present in a simpler form, la_L

The EIT of an LP advances in discrete steps, as it receives the EOT information from its predecessors (parent LPs). When the EIT of an LP is updated, the LP executes events as they become safe, and the LP is subsequently blocked until the next EIT update. Whenever an EIT update occurs, the LP updates its EOT as soon as possible, and new EOT must be sent to each LP in its destination set. The sending of EOT is done (transparently to the user) through the use of null messages. Upon receiving a null message, the recipient LP might be able to update its EIT and thus determine safe events.

The above scheme is called as the aggressive null message protocol. In this protocol, it is possible that an incoming null message does not change the receiver's EIT, inasmuch as EIT is the minimum of all EOTs from source LPs. Therefore, we will use the term *EIT update* to denote a situation where a null message actually causes the EIT of the LP to advance. The null message causing the EIT update is termed a *critical null message* for EIT update and the sender of that null message is termed a *critical parent*. After updating the EIT, the LP checks if any safe events exist in the incoming message queue and process the safe events. It then checks to see if there are new null message(s) from parent LPs and tries to update its EIT.

The behavioral abstraction of LPs follows. Like any other simulation model, each LP has its event processing time distribution and event generation time distribution. An event processed by an LP may require some physical time to be processed (which is dependent on hardware factors), and will generate other (child) event(s) with a logical timestamp. Our assumption is that the processing time and child event timestamp have independent distributions defined by an LP. For simplicity, we assume each LP is mapped on a unique physical processor, the simulation topology is static, and each LP processes homogeneous events dedicated to the LP. Each LP has its own non-zero lookahead, which is static, LP-specific, and can be precomputed. The child events are sent to other LPs as messages. We assume that the message transmission time has its own distribution across the whole simulation topology and is dependent on hardware systems. Message delivery is assumed to be FIFO. The number of child events generated by processing an event (birth rate) is also an LP-specific factor, and the ratio of child event being sent to a specific successor is called branching factor of an LP. Every outgoing event has a unique timestamp, and there is no delayed message; i.e., event processing time distribution is the same as event generation time distribution in the logical time domain.

Table 1. Logical factors

LP_i : A logical process named '*i*'
la_i: Lookahead of LP_i
$t(e)$: Local timestamp of an event e
f_i : Generated event time distribution on LP_i
g_i : Birth rate of events after processing an event on LP_i
SS_i: Source set of LP_i.
DS_i : Destination set of LP_i.
$\gamma_{(i,dest)}$: Branching factor of LP_i to $LP_{dest} \in DS_i$

Table 2. Physical factors

T_m : Point to point message transmission delay
$\bar{T_i}$: Average physical time to process an event on LP_i

Table 1 and Table 2 show the notations used in this research. The notations can be categorized into two domains. The model related factors are defined in the logical domain, and the hardware-dependent factors are defined in the physical domain. We assume each LP process homogeneous events and measured physical granularity on a given hardware as well as the message transmission time.

3. Probabilistic performance model

3.1. EIT update interval

The time to compute EIT is the sum of the message transmission time (time to receive null messages from the parent LPs) and CPU time (time to compute the minimum from the definition of EIT). As the computation cost is typically much less than the message transmission time, CPU time will be ignored. Let the EIT of an (arbitrary) LP_i at the EIT update be eit_i. Let the updated EOT values of an LP_i at the EIT update be eot_i. At the time of EOT update, there must be an $LP_{critical} \in SS_i$ which send a null message to LP_i so that $eot_{critical} = eit_i$. The $LP_{critical}$ is referred to as the critical parent of LP_i for this EIT update, i.e. the EIT_i can be determined when LP_i receives the value $eot_{critical}$ from critical parent $LP_{critical}$. The message transmission time to send $eot_{critical}$ to LP_i is represented as T_m. Let $T(x)$ be the function that maps from a logical time x to the physical time at which logical time is updated to x. Thus, $T(eit_i)$ stand for the physical time at which the EIT update of LP_i was updated to eit_i, and $T(eot_{critical})$ for the physical time at which the EOT of $LP_{critical}$ is advanced to $eot_{critical}$.

For an LP_i and its critical parent $LP_{critical}$, the physical time of EIT update expressed as following:

$T(eit_i)= T(eot_{critical})+ T_m = T(eit_{critical})+ T_m$

The above expression is recurrent since $T(eit_{critical})$ can be expressed in the same manner, unless $LP_{critical}$ is the source of the simulation topology. Sources do not have any predecessors and autonomously generate events. This expression holds for every $LP_{critical} \in SS_i$. We next define the concept of the precedence closure (PC) and the precedence critical path (PCP) of an LP. The PC_i of LP_i is the set of all LPs that lie on any path from a source LP to LP_i. In other words, PC_i contains every possible path from source LP to LP_i. Every LP in PCP_i must be critical parent of its successor or have no successor (LP_i itself). Thus, PCP_i is a set of LPs in the critical path and in PC_i, meaning the *critical path of LPs* leading to the LP_i from the source LP. If LP_i is in the cycle and the cycle is the critical path, there must be at least one source which autonomously generate event(s) without processing one. Let $|PCP_i|$ be the number of LPs in PCP_i at the EIT update to eit_i. Expanding the above expression using PCP_i, $T(eit_i)$ is expressed as $T(eit_i) = T(eot_{source})+ T_m*|PCP_i|$. Note that $T(eot_{source})$ is specific to the simulation model. It is the physical time of event generation at simulation source.

In general, however, the critical parent varies. Whenever an LP has a new critical parent, the LP starts a new EIT update. Therefore, we must differentiate each EIT update. Let eit_i^r be the value of EIT at r-th EIT update for LP_i, and $T(eit_i^r)$ be the corresponding physical time of r-th EIT update. Also, PCP_i^r be the corresponding precedence critical path for eit_i^r. We define $\Psi_i^r=[T(eit_i^{r-1}), T(eit_i^r)]$ as a physical EIT update interval, as well as $\psi_i^r=[eit_i^{r-1}, eit_i^r]$ as a logical correspondence of r-th EIT update interval. Note that $T(eit_i^0)= eit_i^0=0$ for any LP_i. Let $|\Psi_i^r|$ represent the duration (size) of the physical interval and $|\psi_i^r|$ be the logical size of the interval.

The size of an interval Ψ_i^n can be expressed as:

$$
\begin{aligned}
&|\Psi_i^n| \\
&= T(eit_i^n) - T(eit_i^{n-1}) \\
&= T(eot_{source}^n) + T_m \times |PCP_i^n| - (T(eot_{source}^{n-1}) + T_m \times |PCP_i^{n-1}|) \\
&= T(eot_{source}^n) - T(eot_{source}^{n-1}) + T_m \times (|PCP_i^n| - |PCP_i^{n-1}|)
\end{aligned}
$$

Equation 1

The above expression is meaningful only when $|PCP_i^n|$ can be found. It is possible to construct the average value, $E[|PCP_i^n|]$, and the average difference of two consecutive $|PCP_i^n|$, $E[|PCP_i^n|-|PCP_i^{n-1}|]$. $T(eot_{source}^n)-T(eot_{source}^{n-1})$ denotes the physical processing time (granularity) of the source LP when sending the initial simulation events consequently. Of course the two consecutive sources cannot be always unique with multiple sources on the simulation topology, on the contrary, the average of difference can always be calculated from the properties of sources since each source emits events antonomously and independently. It is possible to calculate them manually as shown in section 4. The probability for each predecessor of an LP be a critical parent can be found in appendix A in a process of estimating logical size of EIT update interval.

3.2. Minimum number of events in an interval

Not all the events generated are sent to a single LP. Let $\gamma_{(i,j)}$ be the branching factor from LP_i to LP_j, which is the fraction of total outgoing message from LP_i that are sent to LP_j and it covers dynamic flow of messages over static simulation topology assumption. To estimate the number of safe message, we tentatively assume that the EOT increment caused by each event processed by LP_i is fixed by la_i. Under the assumption, we can have the following theorem as shown in the Appendix B.

When an LP processes an event, it generates other events; these events are referred to as *child events*. Let $g_i(x)$ be the birth-rate function mapping the number of processed events x to the number of generated (child) events for LP_i, and g_i be for an LP_i since we assume each LP processes homogeneous events.

Theorem Every event from the critical parent is safe to process with a fixed delay of la_i.

Figure 1 further illustrates the above theorem. The critical parent $LP_{critical}$ starts a new interval $\Psi_{critical}^r$. Since it has new EIT to start a new interval, it can calculate its new EOT and send the EOT, say, $eot_{critical}^{r}$ to the descendents as soon as possible. Then, after T_m, LP_i receive the $eot_{critical}^{r}$, and since the EOT is from critical parent $LP_{critical}$, it then calculates its eot_i and starts a new interval Ψ_i^n. The events processed on $LP_{critical}$ can generate and send out events.

From the fact that $eot_{critical}^{r}=eit_i^n$, we can establish the (probabilistic) relationship between r and n. At a given EOT $eot_{critical}^{r}$ and average of $|\psi_i|$, from Appendix A, $r=\frac{eot_{critical}^{r}}{|\psi_{critical}|}$ and $n=\frac{eit_i^n}{|\psi_i|}=\frac{eot_{critical}^{r}}{|\psi_i|}$. Thus, $n=\frac{r\times|\psi_{critical}|}{|\psi_i|}$. This expression shows the logical relationship in speed of the number of EIT updates among the parents and child LPs.

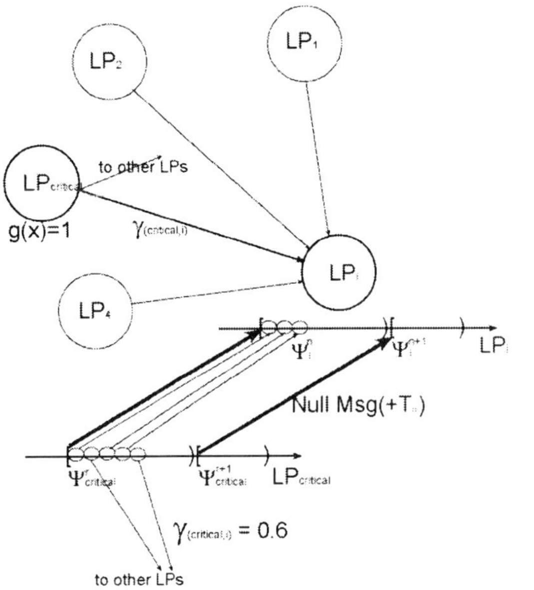

Figure 1. The Critical parent and its child

The estimation of the number of safe events is required. It is certain that n_i, the number of events for LP_i, contains events from critical parent. Let $n_{critical}(\Psi_i^n)$ be the number of messages from the critical parent in the view of LP_i. Also, let $n_i(\Psi_i^n)$ be the total number of messages for an interval Ψ_i^n meaning the total number of messages for an n-th EIT update interval of LP_i.

From theorem above, $n_{critical}(\Psi_i^n)$ events can be processed safely in an interval Ψ_i. Then we can conclude that $n_{critical}(\Psi_i^n) = g_{critical} * n_{critical}(\Psi_{critical}^r) * \gamma_{critical,i}$ for some interval $\Psi_{critical}^r$. Other LPs in the source set, which are faster than the critical LP, can send safe or unsafe events. Clearly, the minimum number of safe events for LP_i is $n_{critical}(\Psi_i^n)$, and it is a base for number of safe message estimation.

3.3. Estimation of number of safe events

The results in the previous section hold only for a fixed increment of the EOT by LP_i. In general, an incoming event of an LP becomes safe in a subsequent EIT update interval. With the average logical time increase of an EIT update interval, we can estimate how many intervals will be required for a given event to be safe. We estimate the blocking time for an event from the distribution of the event processing and intergeneration time, and estimate how many events become safe in a given EIT update interval.

Let $f_L(x)$ be the probability density function of the (logical) timestamp of a child event generated by a processing event in LP_L with the logical time variable x, and $t(child(e))$ be the timestamp of a generated event. It is clear that $t(e)+la_L \le t(child(e)) < \infty$. Let $e \in \psi_i^n$ denote that an event e is generated at ψ_i^n or arrived at ψ_i^n. Suppose that the event was generated at $\psi_{critical}^r$, $e \in \psi_{critical}^r$, in critical parent, $LP_{critical}$ and sent to LP_i. In LP_i, the event is received in ψ_i^n, $e \in \psi_i^n$, $t(e) \ge eit_i^n$, and becomes safe when $t(e) \le eit_i^m$ for some interval of ψ_i^m. The probability that this child event will become safe for a given interval ψ_i^m is $\int_{eit_i^{m-1}}^{eit_i^m} f_{critical}(x)dx$.

With the probability of a single event being safe for a specific interval, we need to expand the probability for every event to be safe in an interval. Finally, the results must be generalized for every possible critical parent by unconditioning the critical parent.

Every event from the critical parent can be safe later than its arrival interval. Let $n^{safe}{}_i(\Psi_i^m | LP_{critical})$ be the number of safe events for an interval Ψ_i^m with a given condition of critical parent $LP_{critical}$. Using the results of the previous subsection,

$$n^{safe}{}_i(\Psi_i^m | LP_{critical}) = \sum_{k \le m \text{ and } r \le \frac{m \times |\psi_i|}{|\psi_{critical}|}} \sum_{e \in \psi_i^k} \int_{eit_i^{m-1}}^{eit_i^m} f_{critical}(x)dx \times n_{critical}(\Psi_{critical}^r) \times g_{critical}$$

Using the probability of a parent to be a critical one from Appendix A, we obtain the estimated number of safe events for a given interval ψ_i^m. Unconditioning the above expression, we can estimate the number of safe events for the interval,

$$n^{safe}{}_i(\Psi_i^m). = \sum_{LP_s \in SS_i} n_i^{safe}(\Psi_i^m | LP_s) \times \Pr(LP_s \text{ is a critical parent})$$

$$= \sum_{LP_s \in SS_i} \{ \Pr(LP_s \equiv critical(LP_i)) \times \sum_{k \le m \,\&\, r \le m \frac{|\psi_i|}{|\psi_{critical}|}} \sum_{e \in \psi_i^k} \int_{eit_i^{m-1}}^{eit_i^m} f_s(x)dx \times n_s(\Psi_s^r) \times g_s \}$$

Equation 2

3.4. Blocking time of an LP

The results of the previous subsections enable us to estimate the busy time and the blocking time of a conservative LP. Since we have the length of the EIT update interval and the estimated number of safe events for the interval, we can estimate the LP busy time for the interval.

The busy time to process safe events for an EIT update interval ψ_i^n is the product of the number of safe messages for this interval and the average event processing time: $\overline{T}_i \times n_i^{safe}(\Psi_i^n)$. Therefore, the sum of idle time and blocking time for this interval is: $|\Psi_i^n| - \overline{T}_i \times n_i^{safe}(\Psi_i^n)$. Note that this sum cannot be below zero. In the case when the sum is zero, it means that there are enough safe events to keep the processor always busy. Summarizing the above busy time for each interval, and subtracting from the total length of EIT update interval, we can obtain the total LP non-busy time already defined as a conservative overhead.

$$oh_{cons} = \sum_{\Psi_i^n \in \Psi_i} |\Psi_i^n| - \sum_{\Psi_i^n \in \Psi_i} \overline{T}_i \times n_i^{safe}(\Psi_i^n)$$

Equation 3

Of course, the sum of oh_{cons} for all LP in the conservative simulation system is the total conservative overhead.

4. Verification of conservative performance

The analysis presented in Section 3 estimates the overhead of conservative LPs expressed as the total time during which the LP is blocked (does not have a safe message) or idle (does not have any message in the input queue). A set of real experiments is conducted to verify this analysis. First, we consider a simple example. We control factors of this model and check the validity of the analysis. Second, we introduce the analysis of a real simulator. The real simulator is a wireless network simulator, called GloMoSim (global mobile network simulator), described in [6].

4.1. Case 1: Closed queuing network simulator

CQNF (closed queuing network with FIFO servers) models are used for the first verification. Figure 2 shows the CQNF model. Virtually, every logical factor of CQNF is artificially controllable. The size of the EIT update intervals and the initial number of events are chosen for validation. Initially, the routers (Router0 and Router1) have n events to process. The two routers then distribute incoming messages to two rows of queues uniformly.

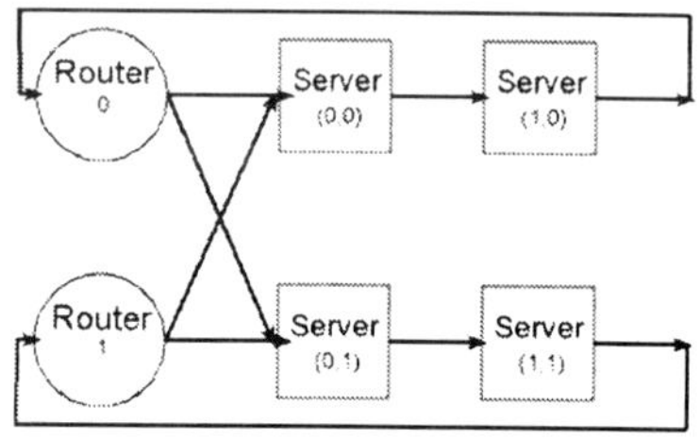

Figure 2. CQNF Topology

For the nontrivial case, the blocking time of Router1 is noticed. Every critical path is in a form of a cycle, and there are different critical paths. The typical one is composed of {Router1, Server(0,1), Server(1,1)} and the general one is composed of {Router1, [Server(0,0), Server(1,0), Router0]*, Server(0,1), Server(1,1)}[1]. Since the longer path includes all the elements in the shorter path, the $|PCP_{router1}^n| - |PCP_{router1}^{n-1}|$ is dominated by a shortest critical path with very high probability. Thus, from Equation 1, we estimate the physical EIT update interval length with a controllable factor of T_{gen}, the (physical) birth time of events from Router1 as a source of simulation.

For Router1, the interval size can be remain invariant $|\Psi_{router1}^n| = T_{gen}/n$ when n is the number of initial events. The average (physical) processing time, called granularity, for an event is one millisecond. Every queue generates one child event by processing an event ($g_{queue}=1$), and the generated timestamp of child events is expressed as $f_{queue} = T_{gen} + exp(T_{gen})$. Figure 3 shows the experimental results in terms of T_{gen} and n on a eight processor Sparc 1000 shared memory multiprocessor.

The actual values are from the runtime statistics of Router1. In Figure 3 and Figure 4, results are for one EIT update interval, and the blocking time axis shows the actual blocking time for a router in microseconds. Figure 4 shows the analyzed blocking time for an LP in these experiments. Figure 5 shows the combined results of the above two figures for the specific average of EIT update interval of 100 and 10, not only the blocking time but also the busy time of Router1. The actual and analyzed values plotted are that of a logarithmic function since $f_{queue} = T_{gen} + exp(T_{gen})$.

Although we eliminate other runtime overheads, such as entity creation, message queue checking, and so on, the results in Figure 3 show some fluctuations. The real blocking time decreases as the number of initial events is increased, it is not zero as indicated by analysis. This is due to the practical issues involved in implementing conservative runtime systems. Even with enough safe messages to process in the implemented system, the runtime system must compare the timestamp of messages with EIT to determine if the messages are safe to process. The runtime system cannot be free from this overhead.

[1] x* stands for zero or more repeat of x.

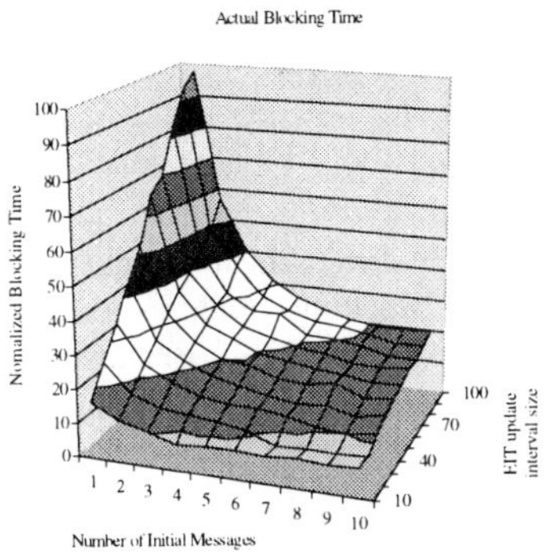

Figure 3. Actual blocking time

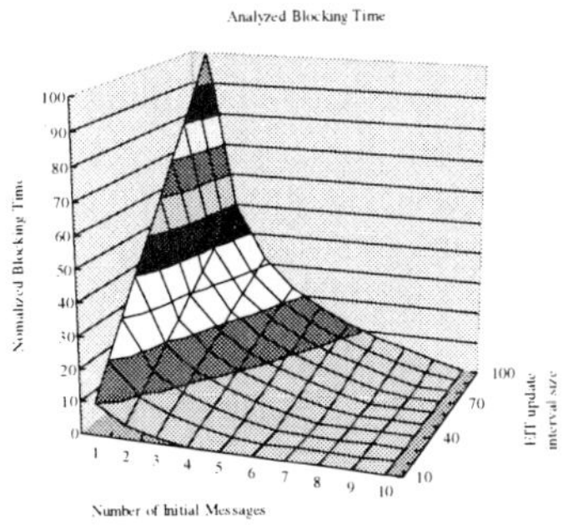

Figure 4. Estimated blocking time

This basic runtime overhead increases as T_{gen} increases. A larger number of unsafe messages also makes the message queue longer and causes a greater runtime overhead. When the analysis predicts zero overhead as $n \rightarrow 10$, the difference between analysis and experience becomes larger because of the increasing message queue size. Therefore, we can conclude that the experienced blocking time from $T_{gen} = 10$ shows the actual minimum of event queue manipulation overhead for the runtime system. This experiment with simple, controllable CQNF model appears to validate our analysis model.

4.2. Case 2: GloMoSim

In addition to the simple model, we adapt our analysis to the existing network simulator, GloMoSim [6]. The model is divided into contiguous geographical regions, each containing a stack of simulation objects that handle the processing for all of the mobiles within that region, as shown in Figure 6. Hence, if we choose to model the bottom four layers of the stack model over a 4x4 grid, there will be 64 simulation objects (16 partitions, each with four objects) regardless of the actual number of mobile nodes being modeled. The different time scales employed at each layer and the feedback loops between layers forces the logical EIT update interval to be very small. The traffic generator at the network layer typically generates packets with an inter-arrival time of 50 to 100 milliseconds for each mobile node, but operations at the lower layers function on a much smaller scale, on the order of microseconds. Typical lookahead values are shown in Figure 6.

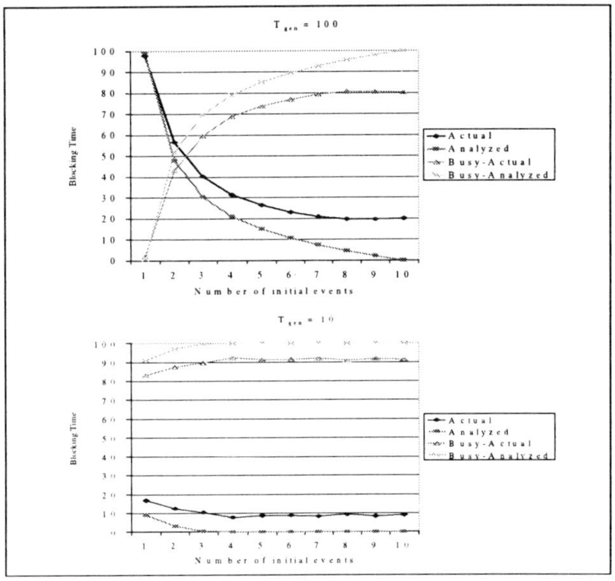

Figure 5. Experimental result of T_{gen} = {10, 100}

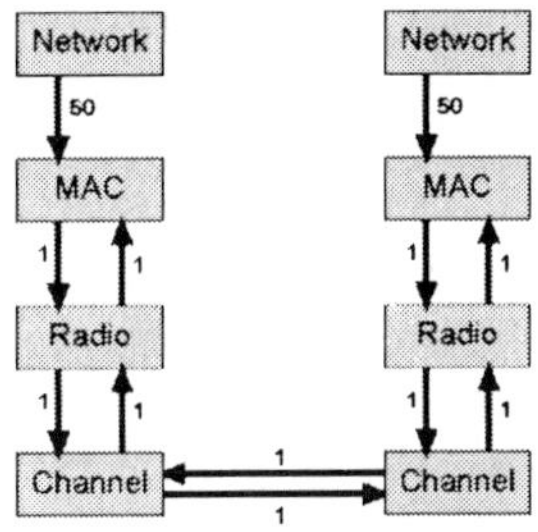

Figure 6. Lookahead for each object in the GloMoSim LP

The verification experiments were run on a 16-processor Sun Enterprise server. The parameters for the network simulator model were chosen to be characteristic values commonly related for analysis of simulator performance: free-space channel model, non-capture spread-spectrum radio model, 800 x 800 meter region of 1000 mobile nodes deployment, 50 meters radio range of mobile nodes, a 4 x 4 geographical partition, and MACA (multiple access collision avoidance) protocol for MAC layer [7].

Among four LP types, the most nontrivial LP is the channel, especially the one of the four inside partitions. It has nine neighbors, both in source set and destination set, and will be termed as $LP_{channel}$. We will name the neighboring channels "channel-LD" (left-down neighborhood), "channel-U" (upper neighborhood), and so on. In order to analysis the actual LP busy time of $LP_{channel}$, we must have the factors of $LP_{channel}$ and possible PCP of $LP_{channel}$. Table 3 lists the factors required for the analysis shown in section 3. The complexity of MACA protocol and the sequence of random number generations of network layer lead to the coarse granularity of computation. Table 4 shows the factors of other LPs such as the traffic generator (network), MAC (MACA), and radio layers. The MAC and radio LPs have mostly similar factors because of similar locations in the simulation topology.

There are 16 homogeneous $LP_{Network}$ which generates the network packet (event) in every 423.0013us of physical time. The number of events for the MAC layer comes from the network traffic generator and from the radio. The number of messages from the radio is the sum of that from the MAC layer (downflow from the network) and that from the channel. The channel receives messages from the radio and other neighboring channels. Simply, the number of messages for radio is equal to that of MAC, since only the downstream can reach the channel. Events from network to MAC occur for several hundreds of simulation clock (depending on the traffic generation rate), while the average logical length of the EIT update interval of MAC, radio, and channel is one. The poor lookahead of the MAC layer makes most of the events from the traffic generator unsafe, thus, there are very few safe events for the MAC and radio. The channel can receive events from eight channel neighborhood, also with the events from the upper layer. Based on these model characteristics, Table 5 shows the average number of safe messages for an interval of channel LP calculated from Equation 2 and factors from the above tables. For example, the lookahead of TG becomes 100 using 10us as one simulation clock with a traffic generation of 0.001 sec/packet.

With the values from Table 4 and 5, we calculate the actual busy time of the LPs, the size of physical EIT update interval $|\Psi_{channel}|=430.2766\mu s$, and logical size of $|\psi_{channel}|=1$. Table 6 shows the blocking time of $LP_{channel}$ with the analyzed blocking time, experimental blocking time, and the execution time. Because of the coarse granularity of channel LP and the minute number of safe messages, the blocking time does not vary too much, although the traffic generator has differences of generation rate in the order of tens. The coarse granularity comes from the design feature of GloMoSim wherein each layer has its own queue for network node management. In this experiment, analyzed and measured values are not as different as those in the CQNF case. The other three LPs on the same processor run one by one, filling out the blocking time of the channel LP.

The possible reason is the difference of simulation model properties in this experiment from our basic assumptions. There are four LPs (network, MAC, radio, and channel) on one processor, while our assumption requires one LP on each processor. The extra overhead with four LPs on one processor contains context switching, LP queue management, higher memory requirement, etc., those are not counted as blocking times in our runtime system. In addition, the small message transmission time of the Enterprise server barely affects the length of the EIT update interval. Only when there is a very small event population in the case of a 0.00001 traffic generation rate, will the other three LPs on the same processor fail to make up the blocking time of the channel LP.

Table 3. Factors for $LP_{channel}$ busy time analysis

FACTOR	NOTATION	VALUE
Message transmission time (physical)	T_m	11.939us
Average PCP difference	$\overline{\lvert PCP^{n+1}_{Channel}\rvert - \lvert PCP^{n}_{Channel}\rvert}$	0.609375
Source Set (same to destination set)	$SS_{channel}$	{Radio, Channel, Channel-L, Channel-LU, Channel-U, Channel-RU, Channel-R, Channel-RD, Channel-D, Channel-LD}
Incoming branch factor	$\gamma_{(Critical,Channel)}, LP_{critical} \in SS_{Channel}$	{0.0625, 0.426845, 0.106711, 0.020953, 0.106711, 0.020953, 0.106711, 0.020953, 0.106711, 0.020953}
Average granularity (physical)	$T_{channel}$	414.664us
Average event generation rate	$g_{channel}$	6
Child event timestamp of parent LP	$f_{channel}, f_{radio}$	1

Table 4. Factors for other LPs

Factors	NETWORK	MAC	RADIO
Granularity	423.0013us	92.34807us	46.74833us
Physical EIT update interval size	423.0013us	430.2766	430.2766
Logical EIT update interval size	1	1	1
Source Set	MAC	Radio	MAC, Channel
Incoming branch factor	N/A	$\gamma_{(TG,MAC)}=0.941$ $\gamma_{(Radio,MAC)}=0.059$	$\gamma_{(MAC,Radio)}=0.941$, $\gamma_{(Channel,Radio)}=0.059$
Lookahead	50	1	1
Generation rate	1	1	1
Child event timestamp function	1	1	1

Table 5. Number of safe messages for Channel

Traffic generator rate	*0.001*	*0.0001*	*0.00001*
Lookahead of generator	100	1000	10000
# safe messages for an interval	0.19909153	0.019909	0.001991

Table 6. Blocking time

Traffic generate rate	*0.001*	*0.0001*	*0.00001*
Analyzed blocking time	42.2021	42.61488	42.94511
Actual blocking time	42.16599	44.09431	46.8119
Execution Time	68.26231	70.2582	70.60015

5.Conclusion

In this paper, we analyzed the performance factors of the conservative parallel simulation protocol. For the analysis, we divided the simulation progression into two time domains: physical time and logical time. Simulation is usually progressed on the logical domain while logical time progression is dependent on the physical time and must be expressed in terms of physical time. As a prerequisite of the analysis, detailed protocol definition was reviewed and the abstraction of simulation models was introduced to identify model factors. In addition to the logical simulation factors, two core factors from the physical domain were also required. Those are point-to-point message transmission time and the speed of the processor expressed as the granularity of LP.

We then analyzed the actual performance of the conservative parallel simulation. We defined EIT update, and the time axes of an LP were divided into a set of (physical) EIT update intervals. The length of the interval is generally dependent on the physical birth rate of the simulation source and the critical path of LPs. We introduced the notion of a critical parent of LPs (PCP) that governs the length of EIT update intervals and the number of safe messages for an LP. By estimating the number of events in an EIT update interval, we derived the busy time and the blocking time of an LP. The overhead of the conservative simulation system is the sum of the blocking time on every EIT update interval across all the LPs in the system.

As our analysis showed, we derived several interesting results. First, we showed that the length of the EIT update interval is dependent on the birth rate of a source LP of simulation and the difference in consecutive PCP length. Second, the concept of a precedence critical path gives us an idea of the factors on which the EIT update interval depends. The result also proves that the message transmission time is one of the critical factors in conservative simulation performance. Third, we derived a theorem that states that every event from the critical parent is safe to process under some restrictive condition. This theorem worked as an induction base for the number of safe events of an EIT update interval. Fourth, based on this theorem, we can calculate the average number of safe events from the critical parent with the general distribution of event generation time. The result shows that the number of safe events for an LP is dependent on its critical parent.

We used a CQNF simulation model and the GloMoSim system to verify results of our analyses. The results show that our theory works in general, although there is still some fluctuation in the experimental result because of real-world factors and simulation runtime implementation issues. The tentative assumption of the homogeneous event processing granularity for an LP can be revised by another methodology such as the queueing theory. Verification of the GloMoSim analysis shows how can we expand our result to the case of much more generalized, less restrictive, real-world simulators.

Our analysis suggests several applications of simulation protocol performance. The first concerns scheduling criteria for conservative LPs. Based on the idea of the critical parent, a set of experiments were done to validate the idea [8] and the scheduling was proven to be a safe one in [9]. The second suggestion concerns load balancing. Since we can estimate the LP busy time and blocking time, we can partition a simulation topology in such a manner that the blocking time for a LP is filled by the processing time of other LPs on the same processor. With static partitioning, we can balance the load of each physical processor from the very starting point of simulation. Other applications of analysis are still open for further research.

References

1. Jefferson, D., Virtual time. ACM Transactions on Programming Languages on Systems, 1985. 7(3): p. 404-425.

2. Chandy, K. and J. Misra, Asynchronous Distributed Simulation via a Sequence of Parallel Computations. Communications of the ACM, 1981. 24(4): p. 198-206.

3. Felderman, R. and L. Kleinrock. Two Processor Conservative Simulation Analysis. in 6th workshop on Parallel and Distributed Simulation. 1992.

4. Nicol, D.M., The cost of conservative synchronization in parallel discrete event simulation. Journal of ACM, 1993. 40(2): p. 304-33.

5. Bagrodia, R., et al., Parsec: a parallel simulation environment for complex systems. Computer, 1998. 31(10): p. 77-85.

6. Zeng, X., R. Bagrodia, and M. Gerla. GloMoSim: a library for parallel simulation of large-scale wireless networks. in Proceedings of the 12th Workshop on Parallel and Distributed Simulation. 1998. Banff, Alberta, Canada: IEEE Computer Society Press.

7. Karn, P. MACA - a New Channel Access Method for Packet Radio. in ARRL/CRRL Amateur Radio 9th Computer Networking Conference. 1990.

8. Song, H.Y., R.A. Meyer, and R.L. Bagrodia. An Empirical Study of Conservative Scheduling. in Proceedings of the 14th Workshop on Parallel and Distributed Simulation (PADS 2000). 2000. Bologna, Italy.

9. Naroska, E. and U. Schwiegelshohn. A new scheduling method for parallel discrete-event simulation. in Euro-Par '96 Parallel Processing. Second International Euro-Par Conference. 1996. Lyon, France.

Author Index

Steering Committee
R. L. Bagrodia
UCLA, USA
D. I. Bruce
DERA, UK
A. S. Elmaghraby
Univ of Louisville, USA
R. M. Fujimoto (Honorary)
Georgia Inst. of Tech, USA
B. W. Unger
Univ of Calgary, Canada
F. P. Wieland
The MITRE Corp, USA
P. A. Wilsey
Univ of Cincinnati, USA
General Co-Chairs
F. P. Wieland
The MITRE Corp, USA
P. A. Wilsey
Univ of Cincinnati, USA
Program Co-Chairs
L. Donatiello
Univ of Bologna, Italy
F. Quaglia
Univ of Rome, Italy
Program Committee Members†
R. L. Bagrodia
UCLA, USA
A. Boukerche
Univ of North Texas, USA
D. I. Bruce
DERA, UK
W. Cai
Nanyang Tech Univ, Singapore
C. D. Carothers
Rensselaer Polytechnic, USA
J. G. Cleary
U. of Waikato, New Zealand
S. R. Das
Univ of Cincinnati, USA
A. Ferscha
Univ of Linz, Austria
P. A. Fishwick
Univ of Florida, USA
R. M. Fujimoto
Georgia Inst. of Tech, USA
D. M. Nicol
Dartmouth College, USA
E. H. Page
The MITRE Corp, USA
C. D. Pham
Univ of Lyons, France
B. R. Ronngren
Royal Inst. of Tech., Sweden
M. Takai
UCLA, USA
C. Tropper
McGill Univ, Canada
S. J. Turner
Nanyang Tech Univ, Singapore
B. W. Unger
Univ of Calgary, Canada

CALL FOR PAPERS

16th Workshop on Parallel and Distributed Simulation
PADS 2002

May 12-15, 2002, Washington, D.C., USA

Sponsors: ACM Special Interest Group on Simulation (SIGSIM)†, IEEE Computer Society Technical Committee on Simulation (IEEE-TCSIM)†, and Society for Computer Simulation (SCS)†.

Topics: PADS provides a forum for presenting recent results in parallel and distributed simulation. The scope of the conference includes, but is not limited to:

- Algorithms and methods for parallel simulation (e.g. synchronization, scheduling, memory management, load balancing, partitioning and allocation.)
- Models of parallel simulation (e.g. stochastic, Markovian, process algebraic, temporal logic.)
- Methodology for parallel simulation. (e.g. system modeling for parallel simulation, specification, adapting sequential methodologies, parallelizing existing simulations.)
- Parallel simulation languages and models (e.g. language and implementation issues, models of parallel simulation, execution environments, libraries.)
- Performance of parallel simulation (e.g. theoretical and empirical studies, prediction and analysis, cost models, benchmarks, comparative studies.)
- Application of parallel simulation (e.g. computer architecture, VLSI, telecommunication networks, manufacturing, dynamic systems, biological/social systems, parallel and distributed computing.)
- Web based distributed simulation (e.g. multimedia and real time applications, fault tolerance, implementation issues, use of Java, CORBA.)
- Distributed interactive simulation (e.g. synchronization in multi-user distributed simulation, virtual reality environments, HLA, interoperability.)

Schedule: Send submissions to the program co-chairs by **September 28, 2001** for hardcopy or by **October 5, 2001** for electronic submission. Notification of acceptance will be made by **December 20, 2001**. Camera ready copy is due **February 28, 2002**.

Submissions: Papers must be written in English and should not exceed 5000 words. Papers must be unpublished and must not be submitted for publication elsewhere. Authors are encouraged to submit their papers in electronic form (Postscript only.) Guidelines for electronic submission are available on the World-Wide Web at the URL given below. Papers may also be submitted in hardcopy form in which case **six** copies are required. Each submission must be accompanied by the following information: a short abstract, a complete list of authors and their affiliations, a contact person for correspondence, post and email addresses. All submissions will be reviewed using a double-blind review process, i.e., the identity of authors, and referees will not be revealed to each other. To ensure blind reviewing, authors' names and affiliations should not appear in the paper, bibliographic references should be modified so as not to reveal the identities of the authors.

General Co-Chairs:

Frederick P. Wieland
Center for Advanced Aviation Syst. Develop.
The MITRE Corporation
1820 Dolley Madison Blvd.
McLean, VA 22102
Voice: +1 703 883-5385
Fax: +1 703 883-1917
Email: fwieland@mitre.org

Philip A. Wilsey
Experimental Computing Lab
ECECS Dept, PO Box 210030
Cincinnati, OH 45221-0030
Voice: +1 513 556-4779
Fax: +1 513 556-7326
Email: philip.wilsey@ieee.org

Program Co-Chairs:

Lorenzo Donatiello
Dipartimento di Scienze dell'Informazione
University of Bologna
Via di Mura Anteo Zamboni 7
40127 Bologna, Italy
Voice: +39 051 2094512
Fax: +39 051 2094510
Email: donat@cs.unibo.it

Francesco Quaglia
Dipartimento di Informatica e Sistemistica
University of Roma "La Sapienza"
Via Salaria 113
00198 Roma, Italy
Voice: +39 06 49918485
Fax: +39 06 85300849
Email: quaglia@dis.uniroma1.it

Online Information: Up-to-date information about PADS 2002 can be obtained from: **http://www.dis.uniroma1.it/~quaglia/pads2002**. Please send email to **pads@ani.univie.ac.at** with subject: **subscribe** for inclusion in the PADS electronic mailing list.

†approval pending